W9-CDB-888

# THE HOWELL BOOK OF DOGS

## The Definitive Reference to 300 Breeds and Varieties

### LIZ PALIKA

BICENTENNIAL
1807
WILEY
2007
BICENTENNIAL

Wiley Publishing, Inc.

Copyright © 2007 by Wiley Publishing, Inc., Hoboken, New Jersey. All rights reserved.

Howell Book House

Published by Wiley Publishing, Inc., Hoboken, New Jersey

The publisher and the author make no representations or warranties with respect to the accuracy or completeness of the contents of this work and specifically disclaim all warranties, including without limitation warranties of fitness for a particular purpose. No warranty may be created or extended by sales or promotional materials. The advice and strategies contained herein may not be suitable for every situation. This work is sold with the understanding that the publisher is not engaged in rendering legal, accounting, or other professional services. If professional assistance is required, the services of a competent professional person should be sought. Neither the publisher nor the author shall be liable for damages arising here from. The fact that an organization or Website is referred to in this work as a citation and/or a potential source of further information does not mean that the author or the publisher endorses the information the organization or Website may provide or recommendations it may make. Further, readers should be aware that Internet Websites listed in this work may have changed or disappeared between when this work was written and when it is read.

For general information on our other products and services or to obtain technical support please contact our Customer Care Department within the U.S. at (800) 762-2974, outside the U.S. at (317) 572-3993 or fax (317) 572-4002.

Wiley also publishes its books in a variety of electronic formats. Some content that appears in print may not be available in electronic books. For more information about Wiley products, please visit our web site at www.wiley.com.

Library of Congress Cataloging-in-Publication Data:
Palika, Liz, 1954–
  Howell book of dogs / Liz Palika.
    p. cm.
  Includes bibliographical references and index.
  ISBN-13: 978-0-470-00921-5 (cloth : alk. paper)
  ISBN-10: 0-470-00921-7 (alk. paper)
  1. Dogs. 2. Dog breeds. I. Title.
  SF426.P324 2007
  636.7—dc22

                                                  2007008051

Printed in the United States of America

10  9  8  7  6  5  4  3  2  1

Book design by Melissa Auciello-Brogan
Book production by Wiley Publishing, Inc. Composition Services

# Table of Contents

# W

# X

# Y

# Acknowledgments

A book such is this is never the work of only one person; that's almost impossible. Many people shared the vision and enthusiasm for this project and all of them deserve credit. Therefore, I would like to thank many of the people who contributed to this book.

First and foremost, my good friends Sheri and Buddy Wachtstetter deserve a huge round of applause. Both are wonderful photographers and contributed photos to the book. But most of all, as photo editors for the book, they organized the photos as they came in, screened them as to quality, cropped when necessary, and did all those other things that photo editors do. I could not have done this book without both Sheri and Buddy. Thank you!

We received photos from all over the United States, Canada, England, Ireland, Poland, and other European countries. We got photos from South Africa, Mexico, and places in between. People were incredibly generous with photos of their favorite breed, and all of those contributors deserve thanks. Unfortunately, we could not use all of the photos we were sent; even a book as large as this one has its limits. But I thank everyone who helped; I do appreciate your efforts.

Several professional photographers helped us, too. They went to dog shows, agility trials, and other dog events to get us just the right photos. When one photo wasn't quite perfect, they would go out and get another one. Mary Fish Arango, Melinda Peters, and Terry Albert—Sheri, Buddy, and I all thank you from the bottom of our hearts.

I also want to thank the trainers and students at Kindred Spirits Canine Education Center in Vista, California. The trainers (Petra Burke, Kate Abbott, Cayla Horn, Mary Moore, and Maggie Moore) not only organized photo shoots for us, but also posed their own dogs for photos illustrating the text in Part I. Many of Kindred Spirits' students assisted, too, and brought their dogs to photo shoots. Thanks, everyone!

There are many other people I would love to thank, but I don't have the room to do so. I talked via phone, e-mail, and letter with hundreds of people about their breed of choice so that I would have accurate, up-to-date information. To all of you, thanks!

Finally, to my agent, Marilyn Allen: You are wonderful, but I've told you that before. To my editor, Pam Mourouzis: Thanks for trusting me. To my editor, Jennifer Connolly: Thanks for making me better! And last but certainly not least, to my husband, Paul: Thanks for your support, your faith in me, and your patience!

# About the Author

**L**iz Palika has been writing professionally since 1985, when she was first published in *Dog Fancy* magazine. Since then she has written more than 50 books, more than 1,000 magazine articles and columns, and has been called as an expert resource many times, including for *Good Morning, America.* She has been published in *Dog Fancy, Dog World, Cats, Cat Fancy, AKC Gazette,* and other pet publications, as well as *Newsweek, The Saturday Evening Post,* and *Women First.*

Her books include *KISS Guide to Raising a Puppy,* which is becoming a favorite with new puppy owners. Breeders, including Joel Towart of Bellington German Shepherds in Fallbrook, California, are sending the book home with new puppy buyers. *The Ultimate Dog Treat Cookbook* received rave reviews in magazines and newspapers all over the country, including *USA Today. All Dogs Need Some Training* was listed by *Pet Life Magazine* as one of the ten best training books available to dog owners.

Liz's books have been awarded many honors. *Australian Shepherd: Champion of Versatility* won Best Breed Book from Dog Writers Association of America and Best Nonfiction Book from San Diego Book Writers. *Save That Dog* won best General Reference Book from Dog Writers and the first ASPCA Pet Overpopulation Answers Award from the ASPCA. Liz's work has also won awards from Cat Writers and Purina. Liz was honored with the San Diego Leadership Award, was a North County Woman of Merit, and in 2005 was awarded Dog Writers Distinguished Service Award. For a complete list of Liz's work, please go to www.lizpalika.com.

Liz has also been teaching dog obedience classes for more than twenty-five years. Although she has trained at all levels, from puppy through advanced obedience, her primary focus is pet dogs. Her goal is to help pet owners have a well-behaved family companion that will spend his life with his family. She also teaches agility, trick training, carting, and therapy dog classes. For more about Liz's training, go to www.kindredspiritsk9.com.

# Introduction

*I* have been teaching dog obedience classes for dog owners and their dogs for more than twenty-five years and have been involved in purebred dog rescue efforts for almost as long. I have been writing about dogs professionally since 1985. Unfortunately, far too often I see owners and dogs who are horribly mismatched. Some owners are too soft and passive for a very pushy, dominant breed. Some cannot provide enough exercise for a high-activity breed, while others expect something the dog simply cannot give. These relationships rarely succeed, which is very sad. When questioned, many owners say, "No one told me that about the breed!" or, worse yet, the dog was acquired with no research having been done at all.

In the ideal world, I envision a dog and owner well-suited to each other, forming a partnership unlike any other. The dog would be in a home where he is loved for life and treasured for what he is. This book is, I hope, a huge step in that direction.

# The Chapters in Part I

The chapters in Part I take you through the process of choosing the right dog and what to expect afterwards. These chapters should serve as a resource for you in the weeks, months, and years after your dog joins your family.

# The Breed Profiles in Part II

The breed profiles provide a bit of history on each breed; a brief description of the breed's physical conformation; information about grooming requirements, exercise needs, and activity level; suggested training and socialization requirements, and any potential jobs or sports that the dog might enjoy. There are also suggestions for the type of owner best suited for this breed; whether the breed is good with children, cats, and other small pets; and the most common health concerns in the breed. This information is fascinating, or at least I found it so! In addition to providing a lot of information about these breeds, my goal is to help you choose the right dog and breed for your family.

The information in these breed profiles was acquired from a variety of sources. I talked to dog trainers and veterinarians who see these breeds all the time—often at their worst. I also questioned people who have been involved in the breeds in a variety of ways: breeders, owners, exhibitors, and even quite a few who use a particular breed as working dogs. I corresponded with national breed clubs and performance sports clubs. I queried everyone about many breed traits, but I specifically

1

asked everyone, "What should people know about this breed before they acquire one?" I found that most people I talked to were very honest, sharing the good and less than good (or the more difficult) points of their breed. I appreciated their honesty and I think you will, too. My hope is that with better knowledge and awareness of breed characteristics, we can prevent problems in many human-canine relationships in the future.

## BREED IN BRIEF BOXES

The Breed in Brief boxes give you quick, basic information—a very brief summary of the information given in the text. This is particularly helpful if you are looking for a breed within a certain size range or want to compare activity levels between breeds, for example. Because the information in the breed boxes is very limited, I have used some abbreviations. Here is a breakdown of the material in these boxes.

The first line contains the abbreviations of the larger registries that recognize that particular breed. I have focused on the American Kennel Club (AKC), United Kennel Club (UKC), and Canadian Kennel Club (CKC). If a breed is a part of the AKC's Foundation Stock Service, it is listed as AKC FSS. Breeds not recognized by these larger registries may be recognized by the American Rare Breed Association (ARBA). Some breeds are governed by their own registries, and in those instances, the club is listed.

The second line lists the breed's primary occupation. The third shows the breed's height at the shoulders and weight. These are often the sizes listed in the breed standard—the written description of the perfect dog of that breed. Individual dogs may be smaller or larger. The fourth line shows the average number of years this breed lives.

The last three lines detail exercise, training, and grooming needs. Generally, I used the language detailed below. When there was something specific about a breed that should be pointed out, I deviated from the following descriptions. The fifth line gives a brief description of the breed's activity level and exercise needs. This does require some explanation.

+ **Low activity level** means the dog is a couch potato most of the time. A daily stroll and a game or two will keep him happy.
+ **Moderate** exercise means the dog will enjoy a walk or two followed by some playtime, but then will be happy to take a nap.
+ Needs **vigorous daily exercise** means exactly that; this is a high-energy dog who wants to stay active.

The sixth line gives information about training.

+ **Easy** to train means exactly that.
+ **Moderate** training means the dogs will accept training but may be easily distracted, or like to think for themselves, or may be slow to mature.
+ **Difficult** or **challenge** to train refers to dogs bred to think for themselves rather than take direction from people, or dogs that are not particularly compliant. It does not mean the dogs are not smart!

- ✦ **Hard to keep challenged** refers to breeds that may be easy to train initially, but the training must continue, as this breed will absorb it quickly and be ready to move on to something new. Comments about housetraining mean a number of owners, trainers, or breed experts have reported some type of difficulty with housetraining this breed.

The last line refers to the efforts needed to keep this dog clean and neat. These efforts do not refer to conformation dog show grooming, but rather to those dogs living in a pet, performance, or working home.

- ✦ **Easy** to groom refers to those breeds that can be combed or brushed two to three times a week quickly and easily with a minimum of fuss.
- ✦ **Moderate** grooming means the breed may need more than minimal grooming, may develop tangles or mats, and may need additional care such as wrinkle cleaning or ear cleaning.
- ✦ **Difficult** grooming generally pertains to long-coated breeds, breeds that shed a considerable amount of coat, or those that need some very specific grooming skills, such as terriers needing to be hand-stripped.

## ONLINE RESOURCES

There are many resources available to dog owners today via the Internet. Most of the breed clubs and many rescue clubs have very informative websites that detail breed histories, provide grooming advice, and give up-to-date health information as well as contact information. Many of these sites were quite helpful in providing expert breed information for the breed profiles in this book.

I've compiled an appendix of online resource information for the breeds profiled in this book. You can find this appendix at www.wiley.com/go/howellbookofdogs. Unfortunately, at this writing, not all breeds covered in this book have an informational website (or, at least, not one in English). However, since websites come and go, if a breed is not listed in the online appendix, try doing a search for it anyway.

# Read On!

As you read on, keep in mind that the information on these pages was provided by many different people who see dogs in a variety of situations: trainers, breeders, groomers, working dog handlers, performance sport participants, and pet owners. Even though only a few people could be quoted directly—primarily due to space restraints—their information is included. So as you think about the next breed you would like to own, take the wisdom of others to heart. This book is here to help you make the right decision and enjoy a happy, successful relationship with your dog.

Enjoy!

# Part I

# Living
## *with* Dogs

# A Dog for You and Your Family

Dogs are wonderful companions. You can share secrets with your dog, and she will never tell a soul. You can be happy, sad, tired, or even cranky with your dog, and she will still love you just as much. Dogs don't care what we look like, how much money we make, or what kind of car we drive. They love us just the way we are. A dog can be the best friend you've ever had, but that only happens when you choose the right dog for you—the right breed (or mixture of breeds), as well as the right sex, age, and temperament. Owning a dog requires a commitment to support and care for the dog throughout her lifetime, usually fourteen to sixteen years.

Caring for a dog requires your time and, certainly, some of your money. In addition, adding a dog to your family may require you to make some changes to your lifestyle. So, before you go get a dog, let's take a look at both dog ownership and dogs in general so you can make the best choice possible, both for you and your future dog.

## The Realities of Dog Ownership

Before you go looking for a dog, make sure you understand the realities of dog ownership. It can require a major change to your family, your schedule, your household routine, and, perhaps most importantly, your budget. On the positive side of dog ownership, a dog will make you laugh and will provide companionship. A dog will help you get more exercise and will increase your social opportunities. After all, it's impossible to go for a walk with a dog without at least one person commenting

6

on what a wonderful dog you have! However, a dog is also a responsibility that you will need to take seriously because this dog is dependent on you for everything.

## WHO WILL BE LIVING WITH THE DOG?

Do you live alone? If so, then the decision whether to add a dog to your household is entirely up to you. No one can argue with you about your choice, but at the same time, you will be solely responsible for caring for the dog. Can you do it by yourself? It's a big commitment.

If you live with other people—roommates or your family—you all need to talk about getting a dog. Everyone needs to be happy with the idea of adding a dog to the household. If someone is unhappy about this decision, he could take out that displeasure on the dog. Even if he isn't blatantly mean to the dog, the dog will know that this person dislikes her, which could result in behavior problems from the dog.

If you have children, you will need to choose the right breed of dog (and the correct individual dog), as not all dogs are patient and tolerant enough for kids. You also will have to be able to spend time with both the kids and the dog so that the dog learns proper, respectful behavior around children. Without guidance, the dog (especially a young puppy) will think of the kids as fellow playmates (littermates) and will jump on them, bite, nip, and steal their food and toys, and could easily become a tyrant rather than a good friend.

If the dog will be living with senior citizens, it is important to choose a breed and an individual dog that is calmer, less apt to paw and scratch fragile skin, and less likely to jump up and potentially knock someone down. Young puppies can be a lot of work, so for many seniors, adopting an older puppy or an adult dog is often the better choice.

If you have other pets, be aware that not all dogs are friendly with other dogs, and some are not trustworthy with other animals, including horses, cats, rabbits, and ferrets. You'll need to take this into consideration when you choose your new dog.

Photo by Sheri Wachstetter

Adding a dog to your family is a big commitment. Make sure you think through your decision and have agreement from everyone in the family. Bella, a Labrador Retriever, pictured with owners Kyle and Amy Gallagher.

## DO YOU HAVE TIME FOR A DOG?

If you have never owned a dog, at least as an adult, you may not understand how much time a dog requires. Dogs are companion animals; that means they are happiest while spending time with their people. When isolated for hours at a time, day after day, many dogs develop bad behaviors (barking, digging, destructive chewing) out of loneliness and boredom. If you live alone and work long hours every day, don't get a dog, unless you have a neighbor who will help you. If he or she will take your dog out a couple of times each day for a potty break, a walk, and a play session, then dog ownership might work. If a neighbor is not available, you might want to check into hiring a professional dog walker or taking the dog to doggy daycare. But look into these services before you get a dog, as they can be expensive. Otherwise, you might be better off with a pet who doesn't require your companionship.

Puppies and newly adopted adult dogs need time to bond with their new owners. Bonding is the deep commitment felt between a dog and her owner. It's a sense of responsibility toward each other, and it doesn't happen automatically; a bond takes time to form. During the first few weeks and even months that your dog lives with you, it's important to spend several hours each day with her so that this bond can develop.

Your new dog also will need some training, and that, too, takes time. Your new dog will need to learn all about housetraining and household rules, as well as proper social behavior. You also will need to schedule time to exercise and play with your dog and to groom her. As your dog grows up, you may want to participate in dog activities and sports. Those, too, take time.

## WILL YOU ENJOY LIFE WITH A DOG?

Adding a dog to your life will change your life. For some people, it changes drastically. You will need to dog-proof your home because a dog's tail can clear a coffee table of knickknacks in one wag. Puppies and young dogs like to chew and do not discriminate between leather chew toys and leather shoes. You will have to learn to put things away, close closet doors, and put up baby gates to head off trouble. Teaching a dog what is allowed to be touched and what isn't takes time, and during that time you'll need to prevent problems.

You'll have to dog-proof the backyard, too, by putting away tools and making sure that the kids keep their toys cleaned up, because those could easily become attractive chew toys. Also, keep in mind that dogs dig, so if you have a favorite garden, you'll want to put a fence around it.

A dog, and especially a puppy, may try your patience time and again. You can't lose your temper; that is never effective, and it won't help your dog learn. Instead, you'll have to learn to control your emotions when problems happen and learn how to train your dog effectively.

Life with a dog isn't all problems, though. Dogs are great social icebreakers. It's almost impossible to go for a walk without stopping to talk about your dog with at least one person. If you have a puppy, you'll be stopped even more because puppies are cute. Floppy ears, big eyes, and a wagging tail are irresistible.

It has been medically proven time and again that laughter is good for us. It helps us mentally and physically, releasing endorphins that make us feel better and lift our spirits. Dogs are great for making us laugh. Clumsy puppies are always doing something funny, from tripping over their own paws to discovering the fun of new toys. Dogs can make us laugh and often will do so on purpose.

Researchers have found that owning a dog is good for us. Petting a dog elevates our mental outlook (brightens our mood) and lowers our blood pressure. Several studies have shown that heart-attack victims who owned dogs had a much longer survival rate than those who didn't own dogs.

Dog owners may be more active, going for walks with their dogs; or perhaps these positive results are simply due to dog owners laughing more often. Dog owners may have more social interaction with other people, which is healthier than social isolation. Personally, I think dogs help us feel needed, wanted, and loved, and that's enough motivation for most people to fight illness or injury.

## WHERE DO YOU LIVE?

You can share your life with a dog just about anywhere; dogs are very adaptable. They can live in mansions or bungalows, in condos or high-rises. Dogs love big yards with room to run but can learn to live with several daily walks and no yard. If you want to share your life with a dog, you can make it work. Some situations just require a little more commitment from you to make them work well.

When you add a dog to your life, your living space becomes your dog's living space, too. It doesn't matter whether you live in a 4,000-square-foot house or a 550-square-foot apartment; your dog will be with you, underfoot, simply because that's where she wants to be. Although most giant-breed dogs are not as active as smaller breeds, they still take up space. If you have a large house, a Great Dane sprawled across the living room floor is not going to seem nearly as large as one sharing a tiny apartment.

Your dog is going to track dirt and dead leaves into your home, and she will probably bring in muddy toys and half-chewed sticks. If you're lucky, she may even bring in the gopher she caught in the backyard. Most dogs shed, especially in the spring and fall, and will be more than willing to share their lovely coats with you, all over the house. Your dog may leave puddles of drool on the floor and may splash her drinking water from wall to wall.

A yard can definitely make keeping a dog easier. Without a yard, you will need to walk your dog several times each day so that she can relieve herself, including first thing in the morning and last thing at night. Bad weather is no excuse; dogs need to go outside, rain, snow, sleet, or shine! A yard also makes playing with your dog easier, especially if you don't want her roughhousing. Daily play sessions are great for bonding with your dog and can be great exercise. If you don't have a yard, you will need to walk your dog, jog with her, or find a safe place where she can run and play.

No matter where you live, you probably have neighbors. They may live very close or farther away, but they are there. What will your neighbors think about your new dog? Although you may think that your dog is none of their business, she certainly will be if she is annoying or poorly trained. To be a good neighbor, let neighbors know that you're bringing home a new dog and ask them to let you know if your dog is being annoying before a problem develops and before they get angry.

## CAN YOU AFFORD A DOG?

It's not polite to discuss finances—especially a personal budget—but this is something you need to talk about before you add a dog to your family. Dogs can be expensive. For the first year of your dog's life, it may seem like money is disappearing from your wallet faster than you can replace it.

## Can You Legally Keep a Dog?

You may think that owning a dog is one of your inalienable rights—one of those rights no one can take away. But that's not necessarily so. If you own your home, do you belong to a homeowners' association? What are its regulations concerning dogs? Many associations limit how many dogs may live in each home or have rules concerning the size of dogs allowed.

If you rent, does your rental contract allow dog ownership? In most states, landlords can legally forbid dog ownership. If they do allow pets, they can limit how many pets may be in the home, the sizes, and even which types (such as forbidding dogs or reptiles). Some cities, counties, states, and even countries have outlawed certain breeds of dogs, and some insurance companies will not insure you if you own particular breeds.

Before you get a dog, do some research and find out if you can legally keep one.

The most common expenses incurred in a puppy's first year include:

- ✦ Cost of puppy from a breeder: $500–$2,000
- ✦ Cost of dog from a shelter: $50–$200
- ✦ Initial supplies: $100–$200
- ✦ First vet exam, including vaccinations and worming: $100
- ✦ Second and third vaccinations and exam during each visit: $100–$150
- ✦ Spaying and neutering, depending on the dog's size: $125–$200
- ✦ Microchipping, heartworm preventative, and miscellaneous vet costs: $100–$200
- ✦ Local licensing: $20–$30
- ✦ A year's worth of high-quality food and treats: $500–$1,000
- ✦ Grooming supplies, including flea and tick prevention: $100
- ✦ Kindergarten training class: $75–$100
- ✦ Cleaning supplies: $20–$40

This list covers only the basics. If you need to build a new fence, shore up an existing one, or build a dog run, your expenses will increase. This doesn't include an emergency room visit, either, should your puppy hurt herself or eat something she shouldn't have eaten. So, before you get a new dog, make sure your budget can handle it.

## WHAT DOES YOUR FUTURE HOLD?

None of us has mastered the ability to see into the future, but most of us have plans or goals of what we would like to accomplish. What are yours? Will a dog fit into those plans ten, twelve, and even fourteen years into the future?

Dogs come in all sizes, from very tiny to very large, from lap dogs to guard dogs, and everything in between. Margaret, an English Mastiff, owned by Arnie Peller; and Gordan, a Pug, owned by Sheri Wachtstetter.

People who do purebred dog rescue and those who work in shelters hear the same stories day after day: "My kids wanted the dog but have now left for college, and we don't have the time (or the desire) to care for the dog anymore." Or, "I got the dog while I was going to school, and now I have a job and can't care for her anymore."

Before you add a dog to your family, try to take a look forward in time. What do you plan to be doing in ten years? Where? Will a dog fit into those plans?

# Dogs Come in All Sizes, Shapes, and Temperaments

No other single species on the planet has more variety in size and shape than the species of domesticated dogs, *Canis familiaris*. You'll find everything from tiny 2-pound lap dogs to 200-pound livestock protection dogs, from dogs with extremely short muzzles to those with elegant long noses, and from those with squat, sturdy bodies and short legs made for power to those with long legs and bodies made for running. There are dogs with no hair and dogs with lots of coat. Some dogs are friendly and social, while others are wary, cautious, and protective. The variables are tremendous.

Choosing the right dog for you and your family should be a carefully thought out decision, not an impulse buy based on little or no research. That puppy in the pet store window may be cute, but do you know anything about her? The Neapolitan Mastiff in the *Harry Potter* movies has a unique look, but would that breed really fit into your lifestyle? Unfortunately, many people do far more research when they buy a new refrigerator than they do when adding a dog to the family!

Part II of this book profiles more than 325 breeds, breed varieties, and mixes. I give a brief history of each breed and the breed's occupation. I also provide information about the breed's personality and temperament, including certain traits, such as playfulness, trainability, protectiveness, and affection toward the owner. The breed's activity level is also discussed, as well as its ability to get along with other dogs, cats, livestock, and children. I queried the experts, especially longtime breeders and owners, as well as trainers, to gain this information. Before you decide on a breed, make sure that the breed's characteristics match what you're looking for and will meld smoothly into your family's lifestyle.

# WHAT IS A BREED? OR A MIXED BREED?

Dogs have aided mankind throughout their shared history, but as dogs became more valuable as workers, and more jobs were found for our canine partners, people began breeding their dogs with the goal of producing better workers. Perhaps one farmer had a female dog who was gentle with sheep yet tough enough to handle cattle. He wanted to perpetuate her abilities, so he found a neighboring farmer who had a male with the same abilities. They bred their dogs in the hopes of passing on those valuable traits.

The same happened within most of the occupations dogs filled: big game hunters, vermin hunters, livestock guardians, and more. The dog's ability was much more important than any other traits at the time. But at various times during our shared history—from early Egyptian, Greek, and Roman civilizations through today—the dog's appearance was also important. People bred to accentuate certain characteristics, such as size, body type or shape, head and muzzle shape, coat color, type, and length, and more. In this way, breeds were developed.

The definition of a dog breed varies, depending on the expert being questioned. However, a breed has several unique characteristics:

✦ The dogs in any given breed must share common ancestors. The gene pool might be smaller (with fewer individual dogs) or larger, but it must be shared.

- The dogs must have similar physical characteristics that make the breed unique from other dog breeds.
- The dogs must share temperament characteristics and, when appropriate, working abilities.
- The dogs must breed true (producing offspring like themselves) and must have bred true for a minimum of six or seven generations.

Modern breeds have a breed standard. This is a written description of the breed that details what dogs within the breed should look like and contains information on size, height, weight, shape of the body, length of the legs, shape of the head, and details of the coat. The breed standard is implemented by the national or international breed club that supervises the breed. At conformation shows, judges must be familiar with the breed standard and should judge those dogs accordingly. Wise breeders use the standard as a guideline to choose those dogs who compare most favorably with it.

Dog owners today, who are often unconcerned with the dog's original occupation, often get purebred dogs because a purebred dog is more of a known entity than a mixed-breed dog. A mixed breed, simply because it is a mix of two or more breeds, is very much an unknown. You cannot know exactly how big the dog will be, how much and what type of coat the dog will have as an adult, and which temperament traits the dog will have. With a purebred, you know what the dog was bred to do (such as hunt or herd), and certain behaviors can be predicted because of this. With a purebred, you even have a good idea as to the breed's lifespan.

But mixed breeds have their fans, too. Many people feel that mixed breeds have fewer health problems than purebreds—that they have hybrid vigor. Others enjoy the surprise of the unknown and love the randomness and creativity that mixed breeds sometimes display. Many dog owners love the uniqueness of a mixed breed. While many purebreds look very much alike, most mixed breeds are one of a kind.

# BIG OR SMALL? LONG BODIED OR SHORT?

Most of the size variation of dogs is due to the breed's original occupation. Dogs required to protect flocks of sheep had to be formidable enough to scare off predators, have the protective temperament and drive to battle predators, and be tough enough to survive the fight. Herding dogs needed to be agile enough to work the stock and small enough to have the stamina to work all day. Property guardian dogs had to be large enough to be intimidating to trespassers and formidable enough to ensure the trespassers left the property. Dogs bred to hunt vermin had to be small enough to fit into tight places or burrows after the vermin, yet tough enough to make the kill.

Body shape was also originally related to the dog's job. The Dachshund's long, low body shape allowed the dog to go down burrows after her prey. The Greyhound's sleek body shape made the breed able to run fast, while the deep chest provided room for a large heart and lungs—all so the dog could run more efficiently.

For you, as a dog owner, size and body shape are usually a personal preference. Many people love the look of the giant breeds and the reaction these dogs instill in other people. Other people like much smaller dogs, especially the toys, because they can snuggle on the lap, fit into smaller places (such as a carrier under the seat of an airplane), or simply because they are so cute.

# LONG HAIR OR SHORT? SLICK OR FUZZY?

Coat types originally developed as a means of protecting the dog. Terriers, with their tough, wiry coats, were better able to fit through tight places and withstand battles with rats and other vermin.

Photo by Sheri Wachstetter

Many people mistakenly believe short-haired dogs don't shed, but they do, and those little hairs can be bristly. Winslow, a Staffordshire Bull Terrier, owned by Steph La Flamme.

Herding dogs with medium-length coats would be protected from briars and brambles, as well as bad weather, yet would not be burdened by too heavy a coat. Sled dogs with a thick double coat could withstand the coldest of temperatures and continue to work hard, pulling sleds in the snow.

Although a coat that enables the dog to work is still important, personal preferences and style trends also play a big part in the coat a breed may have. For example, Border Collies competing in conformation dog shows have a much more elegant coat than the Border Collies usually seen herding sheep.

Short slick coats do not mat or tangle and so are easy to care for in that respect. Nevertheless, these coats still need regular combing and brushing to keep the hair and skin healthy. Short coats shed, usually in the spring and fall, and the short hairs can be bristly. Breeds with short coats include Boxers, Doberman Pinschers, Labrador Retrievers, Rat Terriers, Smooth Fox Terriers, and Weimaraners.

Medium-length coats are not short and slick, but are not long and dragging on the floor either. Australian Shepherds, German Shepherds, Papillons, Japanese Chins, and Silky Terriers have a medium-length coat. These coats, if not combed and brushed regularly, can tangle, especially behind the ears, under the collar, and on the back legs. When these coats shed, the soft hairs usually form hairballs, like dust bunnies, that will float throughout the house.

Long coats require more care than other coat types because the tangles form so easily. These coats are gorgeous, though, and well worth the care. Irish, English, and Gordon setters have wonderful long, flowing coats, as do Afghan Hounds, Cocker Spaniels, Maltese, and Yorkshire Terriers.

Many breeds have coat types that don't fit into these categories; some have coats that are unique. There is nothing quite like the amazing coat of an Old English Sheepdog that has been freshly brushed. A Bichon Frise has a unique coat that needs regular trimming. Some terriers have a tougher, coarser coat, while others, such as the Soft Coated Wheaten Terrier, have a very soft coat. Poodles can have a soft, almost fluffy coat or a curly coat. In all types, the hair grows all the time and needs regular grooming. Puli, Kuvasz, and Komondors have hair that *cords,* or mats, in long, vertical cords all over the dog's body. And then there are the hairless breeds, some of which have a few scattered hairs, while others have tufts on the head and feet. The variety of coat types is really amazing, with something to suit everyone's taste.

Photo by Melinda Peters, owner

The Puli's coat is made up of long, vertical cords or tangles. Once the cords are formed, the coat is relatively easy to care for. Ch. Immerzu Galuska CDX, OA, OAP, OAJ, OAJ, OJP, and TDIA.

## PERSONALITIES AND ACTIVITY LEVELS

One of the keys to a successful relationship with a dog is to try to match your personality and activity level with that of a dog breed. If you are a calm, quiet person, nothing is more annoying than a dog bouncing up and down, barking, and begging you to do something all the time. Although some differences in personality and activity levels can be good—a dog slightly more active and extroverted than you may get you outside more—too many differences are frustrating and aggravating.

# Excited and Extroverted

These breeds are normally easily excited; they react to doorbells with vigor. They are also extroverts in the full sense of the word. As far as these breeds are concerned, the world is theirs!

+ Chihuahua
+ Dachshund
+ Fox Terrier
+ Parson Russell and Jack Russell Terriers
+ Pomeranian
+ Scottish Terrier
+ Shih Tzu
+ Silky Terrier
+ West Highland White Terrier
+ Yorkshire Terrier

# Here, There, and Everywhere!

These are active, curious breeds who want to explore the world. They will relax but don't really want to make relaxing a habit.

+ Cocker Spaniel
+ Smooth and Wire Fox Terriers
+ Miniature Pinscher
+ Miniature Schnauzer
+ Shetland Sheepdog
+ Shih Tzu
+ Silky Terrier

Photo by Sheri Wachstetter

Every dog needs a job to do, although it's more important for some breeds than others. Riker, an Australian Shepherd (with a haircut), owned by Liz Palika, bred by Kathy Usher.

# Give a Dog a Job

These dogs have a strong hunting, herding, or working heritage and are happiest with a job to do. That might be as simple as obedience training or structured play, or may even be a easy as bringing in the newspaper each morning. These dogs need to feel needed.

+ Australian Shepherd
+ Border Collie
+ Doberman Pinscher
+ English Springer Spaniel

- ✦ German Shepherd Dog
- ✦ Golden Retriever
- ✦ Poodle (all sizes)
- ✦ Puli
- ✦ Rottweiler
- ✦ Shetland Sheepdog

## Calmer, More Laid-Back Breeds

Although these breeds are happy to play and more than willing to get into trouble should it head their way, these breeds can also tend toward the couch potato lifestyle.

- ✦ Akita
- ✦ Alaskan Malamute
- ✦ Basset Hound
- ✦ Bloodhound
- ✦ Bulldog
- ✦ Chow Chow
- ✦ Great Dane
- ✦ Greyhound
- ✦ Newfoundland
- ✦ Pug
- ✦ Rottweiler
- ✦ Saint Bernard

## Affectionate Shadows

Although most dogs prefer to be close to their owners, some breeds are more demanding about it than others. These dogs, if isolated too much, will usually develop behavior problems.

- ✦ Australian Shepherd
- ✦ Bichon Frise
- ✦ Border Collie
- ✦ Cocker Spaniel
- ✦ Doberman Pinscher
- ✦ German Shepherd Dog
- ✦ Golden Retriever
- ✦ Maltese
- ✦ Poodle (all sizes)
- ✦ Shetland Sheepdog

## MORE TO THINK ABOUT

After all you've been asked to think about—size, long hair or short, purebred or mixed, temperament, and more—there are actually a couple more things you should mull over before you go looking for a dog.

## Puppy or Dog?

Do you want a puppy or would the best dog for you be an adult? Puppies are cute, there's no doubt about that, and everyone loves a puppy. But puppies are babies and need a lot of care, require very careful supervision, and need to spend a lot of time with you. On the other hand, puppies are like lumps of clay, ready for you to shape and mold. When you raise a puppy, it's your responsibility, yes, but you can also raise the puppy the way you wish her to grow up.

If you don't have the time or the patience for a puppy, or if you have very young children or senior citizens in the house who might be too fragile for a puppy, you may want an older puppy or an adult dog. This dog is past the worst of puppyhood (the housetraining, mouthing and biting, and, I hope, the chewing) and, depending on the dog's age, is usually a little calmer. The downfall of adopting an older puppy or an adult is that doing so is much like buying a used car. You have no idea how she has been treated, whether the dog has had any training, or how she has been socialized to people and other dogs. Like a used car, she may be a gem or a lemon.

## Male or Female?

You also need to decide whether you want a male or female dog. Depending on the individual breed and its characteristics, males are often a little more protective of their property than females and, as puppies, tend to be more destructive. Females are usually a little easier to housetrain, although males often take to obedience training better. Although some breeds may have a little bit of difference, as a general rule there is no difference in levels of excitability, behavior problems, or affection between males and females.

# Finding a Puppy (or Dog)

The ideal place to find a purebred puppy or dog is with a reputable breeder. A reputable breeder knows his breed well, knows the breed standard, and can explain the breed to you in layman's terms. He may even use one of his dogs as an example. He will breed only the best of his dogs and will have any needed health tests done prior to breeding. You will be able to see the puppies' parents and maybe even the grandparents. A reputable breeder will also screen potential puppy buyers and will sell only to those who will provide the best for his puppies; he will turn away people obviously not suited to his breed. A reputable breeder will be available to the new owners and will answer questions when problems arise. If a puppy of his loses her home for any reason, the breeder will take that dog back into his home. You can find a reputable breeder through personal referrals or by asking questions at a local dog show.

Many people breed dogs, but not all fit the definition of reputable breeder; some simply wish to breed a litter from their male or female. Perhaps this breeder bought a dog for what she considers a great deal of money and wishes to recoup that expense by having a litter of puppies. Some may have simply neglected to spay or neuter their dogs and an accidental litter resulted. Others purposefully bred their dogs but have not done what is necessary (health tests or breeder education) to produce the best puppies possible. These breeders, often called *backyard breeders,* do sometimes turn out very nice dogs. More often, though, their dogs are of a lesser quality. The dogs may not measure up to the breed standard or may have health problems, including inherited health defects. Someone who wishes to become involved in breeding should contact a reputable breeder or the national breed club and ask if anyone is interested in mentoring him, guiding him through this confusing and difficult science.

A *puppy mill* is a breeder who produces puppies strictly for profit—often many, many puppies—and is not at all concerned with the breed standard. A puppy mill is usually a farm, and the dogs are housed in cages, often in layers of two or three, with feces and urine raining down on the dogs below. A puppy mill can be a family home, too, though, with simply far too many dogs being bred. The dogs used for breeding at a puppy mill are rarely, if ever, tested for health defects, and to maximize profits, the female dogs are usually bred the very first time they come into season.

You can also adopt a puppy or dog from a shelter. Many wonderful dogs, purebreds and mixed breeds, can be found in local shelters. Though some may have been given up by their owners because of behavioral or training difficulties, many more are at the shelter due to no fault of their own. Perhaps the puppy's owner didn't realize how much work puppies were and gave the puppy up. Or, maybe an elderly owner passed away and the family didn't want the dog. The downfall to a shelter dog is that the dog is an unknown. There will be no information about the dog's parents or genetics, or how the dog was treated previously. The good side to shelter adoption is that by adopting one of these dogs, you're saving a dog's life.

The most common reasons dogs are given up to shelters include:

+ Landlord or homeowners' association issues
+ Moving
+ Dog is ill or injured and owner has no money for the dog's care
+ No time for the dog
+ Too many dogs or pets in the home
+ Divorce
+ Bitch was not spayed and had a litter
+ Behavior problems, including biting

Another source of dog adoptions is a rescue organization. These nonprofit organizations help find homes for dogs who can no longer remain in their homes. Some groups will take in any adoptable dog, while others deal only with specific breeds. Many breed clubs, such as clubs for Labrador Retrievers or Rottweilers, help support or sponsor rescue groups. Other groups operate independently and survive on donations and fundraisers. Many of the dogs given up to rescue groups come

Many wonderful dogs, both purebreds and mixed breeds, can be found at your local shelter. A training class of dogs of various breeds, mixes, sizes, and sexes—many of whom were adopted—at Kindred Spirits Canine Education Center.

with a history, both medical and behavioral, that makes it easier for potential adopters. To find a rescue group in your area, do a Web search. In a search engine, type the name of the breed you're looking for, add a plus sign, and then your local area (Labrador Retriever rescue groups + San Diego County).

## The Interview

When you find someone with a puppy or dog you might be interested in, either with a reputable breeder, a rescue group, or a shelter, the first thing to do is make contact with them. Make an appointment and ask if they have an application you can fill out ahead of time. Bring the family with you for the appointment and have the application filled out so you won't be distracted by that task during the interview.

Find out as much as you can about the puppy or dog. A breeder will be able to tell you everything about the puppy. A shelter or rescue group will not have as much information, but find out as much as you can. How old is the puppy or dog? Has she been vaccinated? How often and for what? Has she been wormed? Has she had any health problems? Has the veterinarian examined her? What is her personality or temperament? Does she get along with other dogs? Cats? Other pets? Does she like children?

Here are five questions to ask any breeder you visit:

+ How long have you been active with this breed? Some experience is good, as it takes time to educate oneself as to the intricacies of both the breed and breeding itself.
+ Are the parents of this litter available to meet? Seeing the parents will give you a good idea of what the puppies will grow up to be.
+ What health checks have the parents (and grandparents) had? Some breeds have problems with certain health threats, including eye problems or hip dysplasia, so the breeder should be able to show you test results.
+ What health problems have been seen in this breed? Every breed has problems, and the breeder should be able to discuss these with you.
+ Ask to see the sales contract and ask the breeder to go over it with you. What is the policy about returning the puppy should there be a problem?

Here are some questions to ask a shelter or rescue group:

+ Why was the dog given up?
+ What background information, if any, do you have on the dog?
+ Is he/she spayed or neutered? Is she up to date on all vaccinations? Does she appear to have any health problems?
+ Has the dog had any training? Does she appear to have any training or behavioral issues? Is she housetrained?
+ Has she shown any signs of aggression toward other dogs? Other pets? Or people?

Be prepared to answer questions, too, as breeders, rescue groups, and shelters will all want to make sure you are an appropriate owner for this puppy or dog. When they place a puppy or dog, they want this to be the dog's "forever home" and not a temporary home. You will be asked if you've had a dog before and what happened to that dog. You will be asked if you've researched this breed (or even mixture of breeds) and what you know about it. Other family members will be asked if they are in agreement that this could be the right dog for you. Other questions may concern your yard, whether it's fenced or not, and how the dog will be cared for during the day and at night.

## CHOOSING THE ONE

Choosing just one puppy or dog can be very difficult. At a shelter or rescue group, you may find yourself wanting to save them all. At the breeder's, it may seem like all the puppies are the right one. Although a purely emotional decision is rarely the right one, emotion should be a part of the decision. You do need to have an emotional attachment to this dog, yet you also need to make an informed and logical decision. So keep your emotions in check while you ask the questions you need to ask. If red flags go up, however, and you feel something is not quite right, walk away before your heart gets involved. But, when your brain tells you everything is all right, well, that's the time to let your heart guide you.

# Bringing Your New Friend Home

ringing home your new canine friend is both exciting and worrisome. This dog will be with you for the next fourteen to sixteen years as a walking partner, a friend to play with, and a confidant. You may decide to participate in dog sports or volunteer work together. There is so much to look forward to, but there are worries, too. Are you really ready? How much is this dog going to change or (gulp!) disrupt your life? Your life is going to change, no doubt about it, but the more prepared you are, the easier things will be.

Keep in mind that this is a big change for your new canine friend, too. If you're bringing home a puppy, it will be his first time away from his mom and littermates. If you're adding an older puppy or an adult dog to the family, this may be his first time away from the kennel or shelter (at least in a while), so it will be a change for him, too. In any event, it will be a time of worry and confusion for everyone. So, before you bring him home, make sure that you are prepared.

## Before Your New Dog Comes Home

Before you bring your new dog (or puppy) home, you and other family members will need to do some necessary chores. These chores will help keep your puppy comfortable and safe and will enable you to care for him without making last-minute runs to the grocery or pet store.

The first thing you need to do is go shopping.

- **Puppy or dog food:** Make sure that you have some of the same type of food the dog has been eating. If you want to change to a different food, do so later. If you change now, abruptly, your dog could suffer gastrointestinal upset, including diarrhea. Not a good way to start out in a new home! Call the breeder, rescue group, or shelter and find out what your new dog is used to eating.

- **Food and water bowls:** Have a couple of unspillable water bowls and decide where you want them. Choose a place where you won't be upset if he splashes and dribbles water. The bathroom is often a good spot, or a corner of the kitchen where you won't trip over it. You also want to have a big water container outside. Metal bowls work well, are unbreakable, and are easy to clean.

- **Identification:** Pick up a temporary collar tag for your new dog. There are tags on which you can handwrite your name and phone number. This will serve until you decide on your new dog's name and can get an engraved tag. Your dog also needs a microchip (a permanent identification chip that is injected under the skin), but you can talk to the veterinarian about that on your dog's first visit.

- **Collar and leash:** Pick up a nice, soft collar that buckles for your dog's everyday wear. His identification tag should be attached to this collar. A 4- or 6-foot leash is fine for walking the dog and for beginning his training.

- **Crate:** A crate will serve as your dog's bed for the first two to three years of his life. It also will keep him safe when you travel and will provide him with a place that's all his. The crate should be big enough for him to stand up, turn around, and lie down, but not so big that he can relieve himself in it and get away from the mess. You may need to buy a couple of crates as your puppy gets bigger. You can place an old towel in the bottom of the crate; don't buy a cushion or bed, as those will get chewed up during puppyhood.

- **Baby gates and X-pens:** Baby gates and X-pens (foldable, portable exercise pens found at pet stores) are wonderful ways to limit a puppy's ability to wander around the house. Baby gates can block off hallways, and X-pens can fence off portions of rooms.

- **Toys:** Your dog will need a few toys to help keep him busy. A few chew toys, such as good-quality rawhides and bones, will give him something to chew on. A couple of interactive toys, like a Kong or a food-dispensing toy, will keep him occupied when you have to leave him alone.

- **Grooming tools:** Your puppy needs some basic grooming tools, including nail trimmer, shampoo, toothbrush and baking soda, soft pin brush, and comb. Depending on your dog's breed, he may need more tools; see chapter 5.

- **Cleaning supplies:** Your new puppy or dog will make messes. He may have housetraining accidents until he learns where to go to relieve himself. He may get overexcited and throw up or might spill his water. He will definitely track in mud from outside, and, at some point, he will chew up something he shouldn't. So, be prepared to clean up anything.

- **Pooper scooper:** You will need a pooper scooper (available at pet stores) or a shovel and rake to clean up after your dog in the backyard. You can use plastic bags to pick up after him on walks—either the commercially available bags made for this purpose or plastic grocery or newspaper bags.

Make sure you have everything you need before bringing your new dog home. You shouldn't have to leave your dog alone right away to run to the store. Hatcreek's Doctor Bashir, an Australian Shepherd, owned by Liz Palika, bred by Karen Russell.

That's it! If you have these supplies on hand, your shopping is done. Now, let's take a look at what you need to do to make your house and yard safe for your new dog.

## PUPPY-PROOFING YOUR HOUSE

Your house is going to be a source of amazing things to your puppy. Puppies explore the world with their noses, followed shortly thereafter by their mouths. Things get sniffed over really well and then, if they smell appealing, are tasted. Unfortunately, your puppy is not going to have any idea what is good for him and what isn't, nor will he know what is valuable to you, so it's up to you to make your house as safe as possible for him and to prevent these kinds of accidents from occurring.

To puppy-proof your house:

- ✦ Put childproof latches on all lower cupboards in the kitchen, bathroom, garage, and anywhere else you have storage cupboards. Don't forget the laundry room.
- ✦ Pick up all knickknacks, magazines, books, and other things that can be chewed in the living room, family room, and other places where the puppy may spend time.
- ✦ Tuck or tape all electrical cords and cables away, out of the puppy's sight.

- Pick up all trash cans or put them inside cupboards. Or, use heavy, covered trash cans.
- In the kitchen, put away all cleaners, waxes, bug sprays, and insect traps behind latched doors.
- In the bathroom, put away all medicines, vitamins, makeup, hair products, and cleaning products.
- In the rest of the house, pick up or put away pens and pencils, computer parts, ink cartridges, felt-tip markers, craft supplies, sewing supplies, and cigarettes. Don't forget electronic devices such as MP3 players, remote controls, and cellphones.
- Check the doors, door latches, and screens to all outside doors. Make sure the dog can't push his way outside.

Chapter 3 discusses how to establish household rules for your new dog, including where he will be allowed to roam, investigate the world, and play, but right now, especially when your new puppy first comes home, his access to the house should be severely restricted. He should be in the room with you where you can supervise him; when you can't watch him, he goes in his crate or to a safe place outside. You can close off his access to the rest of the house by closing doors, putting up baby gates across hallways, or using X-pens to restrict access to specific areas of rooms. By supervising him closely, you can stop problem behaviors before they happen and teach him what you want him to do. Teaching him what to do is much easier than trying to correct bad habits later. This restricted access will help your housetraining efforts significantly, too.

## PUPPY-PROOFING THE YARD

Your yard can be a source of danger for your new puppy. Identify first where your puppy will be allowed to go. If your backyard is fenced and he is allowed to go outside alone, you will need to make sure that the entire yard is safe. If you have a dog run, then only that area needs to be secure right now, although eventually you will need to puppy-proof the entire backyard. If your front yard is not fenced in, he will only be allowed out there on leash with you, so puppy-proofing is not as critical.

To puppy-proof your yard:

- Make sure that the children pick up their toys when they are through playing. Many kids' toys are easily chewed.
- Put away any lawn furniture after use, especially those items that are easily destroyed, such as those with webbing or cushions.
- Make sure that wires or cables (television cables, ground or border lighting wires, or wires to sprinkler system controls) are protected from puppy teeth.
- Gardening tools and supplies should be in a latched cupboard or out of reach.
- Fence off special gardens or favorite areas. A temporary fence can protect these areas from puppy teeth and paws.
- Check your yard for poisonous plants and remove them. (See the lists on the next page.)
- Remove, and do not use again, any snail, slug, or rodent poisons.

You also want to make sure that your fence is very secure. Puppies can fit through amazingly small spaces—between boards or between the ground and the bottom of a fence. Newly adopted

# Poisonous Plants

Many poisonous plants are commonly found in our yards, either naturally or used in landscaping. Here are some of the most common. If you're concerned about a specific plant that is not on this list, take a piece of it to your local garden center and speak to a horticulturist.

## Trees and bushes

- Avocado (leaves)
- Bottlebrush
- Boxwood
- Cherry (seeds)
- Common privet
- Croton
- Dogwood
- English ivy
- Hemlock
- Holly
- Horse chestnut
- Mistletoe
- Oleander
- Peach (seeds)
- Poison ivy
- Poison oak
- Poison sumac
- Privet
- Rhododendron
- Wisteria
- Yew

## Flowering plants

- Amaryllis
- Anemone
- Azalea
- Bird of paradise
- Buttercup
- Christmas cactus
- Crocus
- Cyclamen
- Foxglove
- Impatiens
- Jasmine
- Morning glory
- Larkspur
- Lily of the valley
- Poinsettia
- Snapdragon
- Sweet pea
- Verbena

## Bulbs, tubers, and fungi

- Calla lily
- Daffodil
- Dieffenbachia
- Hyacinth
- Iris
- Many mushrooms
- Tulip

## Vegetables

- Eggplant
- Potato (foliage)
- Rhubarb
- Tomato (foliage)

## Weeds and herbs

- Jimson weed
- Locoweed
- Milkweed
- Pennyroyal
- Pokeweed
- Sage

older puppies or young adults who have no idea where they are can be escape artists, too, especially when worried. These dogs can go through a fence (breaking weak or broken boards), dig under a fence, or go over a fence. If you're bringing home a small dog (say, under 20 pounds), the fence

When you check your fence for security, don't forget to examine the gate, too. It should latch well and have minimal gaps between the bottom of the gate and the ground. Tanakajd Szepe Urbana, a Dogue de Bordeaux puppy, owned by Breaux Bordeaux.

should be at least 4 feet tall. If you bring home a dog between 20 and 30 pounds, the fence should be at least 5 feet tall. For larger dogs, the fence ideally should be 6 feet tall.

So take a look at your fence, checking a wooden fence board by board and a chain-link fence section by section. Replace or repair weakened boards or sections. Fill in holes under the fence, making sure that digging out won't be easy. Move trash cans or other stored items away from the fence so that a determined dog can't use them to climb up and over.

Underground pet fencing has become more popular, especially in communities that restrict fencing or in rural areas where regular fencing may be financially restrictive. This fencing consists of a buried wire that produces a radio signal. The dog wears a collar that senses the radio signal and the dog receives a stimulus from the collar when he ventures too close to the wire. If you would like to use this type of fencing, make sure you and your dog both receive professional training as to its correct use. When misused, the dog can become very confused.

## MAKE THE GARAGE SAFE

Many dog owners also allow their dogs access to the garage from the backyard. This can give the dog shelter in bad weather, especially if no one is at home. If you plan on doing this, you will need to make sure that the garage is safe.

Since you are not going to want your dog dashing in and out when the garage door opens, especially when a car is going in or out, you will want to section off a portion of the garage. You can use an X-pen, fence sections, or even pieces of lattice. Simply divide the areas where you want the puppy to be able to access and those that will be off-limits.

In the area where the dog will be allowed, put away anything that can be chewed—cardboard storage boxes, shelves with food (such as in a pantry), cleaners, insect sprays, rodent traps, laundry soaps, tools, automotive parts (especially antifreeze)—behind latched doors or up out of reach. Don't assume that something will not be chewed because it doesn't appear to be attractive to a dog; dogs have chewed on some amazing things!

# Get Everything Ready

Where is your new dog going to sleep? Ideally, you want to place his crate in your bedroom right next to your bed. There, he can hear and smell you and won't feel so lonely. You'll be able to hear him, too, when he needs to go outside during the night. Do not isolate the puppy by placing his crate in the garage or laundry room; he will be scared and lonely and will cry all night long. Instead, let him be close to you.

Decide where your puppy will eat. If you have a very busy household, you might want to feed him in his crate, or in a quiet corner of the kitchen. Do you want him to have a water bowl in the same place? You also can put a water bowl in the bathroom if the puppy will have access to the bathroom. He will need a larger, unspillable water bowl outside, too.

Where does your family spend a lot of time in the mornings or evenings—the dining room, living room, or family room? Put a basket of the puppy's toys on the floor in that room so that he can find them easily. Close doors and set up baby gates so that the puppy won't be able to sneak off into other rooms and get into trouble. Double-check your puppy-proofing. Okay, you're ready!

## The United Kennel Club's Ten Most Popular Breeds

The United Kennel Club (UKC) has a long history of registering hunting and performance breeds. The most popular breeds in 2005, according to registration numbers, are:

1. Tree Walker
2. American Pit Bull Terrier
3. Bluetick Coonhound
4. English Coonhound
5. Black and Tan Coonhound
6. Redbone Coonhound
7. Beagle
8. Plott
9. Labrador Retriever
10. American Eskimo

# Bring Him Home!

If you're getting your puppy from a breeder, the breeder will tell you when your puppy is ready to come home. Most big-breed puppies are ready between 8 and 10 weeks of age. Many toy breeds are older, even 12 to 14 weeks old. Don't take home a puppy younger than 7 weeks; he needs time to spend with his mom and littermates. Their interactions are important for his mental health later.

If you're adopting a dog from a rescue group or a shelter, you probably will be able to coordinate times and days that will work best for both of you. Ideally, schedule his homecoming for a day when you will have a couple of days off to spend with him. This way, he can get to know you and the rest of the family, and he can learn his way around the house and yard.

Don't bring a young puppy home and then leave again immediately. A very young puppy left alone suddenly will cry and scream, and could make himself sick. An older puppy or dog who feels abandoned in a strange place might try to escape from the crate or yard, even to the point of harming himself. However, if you can spend the next couple of days with him, he should then have enough confidence and security to spend some time alone.

## WHAT WILL YOU CALL HIM?

Have you decided on a name for your new best friend? Obviously, if you have just brought home a baby puppy, you can name him. But you can rename a rescue or shelter dog, too. In fact, it's often a good idea to give even an adult dog a new name; it symbolizes a new era in the dog's life. It's even more important if the dog has bad feelings about his old name; perhaps it was used in conjunction with punishments or mistreatment. Then, too, some dogs come into a shelter with no known background, including their name.

You don't have to have a name ready to tack on to your dog as soon as he comes through the door; in fact, it's usually a good idea to get to know your dog first. He can go for a few days just being called Puppy or Sweetie-pie. Within a few days, you'll start to see more of his personality, and then it will be easier to name him.

Think carefully about your new dog's name, as this will be associated with him for the next fourteen to sixteen years. A name such as Baby is fine right now but won't suit him at all when he's grown up. A name like Lover Boy conveys way too much power and in public may be repeated with scorn. Dogs named Killer often act up because the name implies that they are tough. Choose a name that you will be able to say in public with affection, that will suit your dog for many years, and that doesn't convey a negative emotion.

Teach your dog his name by saying it in a happy tone of voice. When he looks at you, praise him, and if he comes to you, say his name again and pop a treat in his mouth. If you say his name and he doesn't look at you,

Photo by Liz Palika

Riker is named after a character on *Star Trek: The Next Generation*. That character is bright, bold, and a charmer—a perfect fit for this canine! Riker, an Australian Shepherd, owned by Liz Palika, bred by Kathy Usher.

make another noise, like dropping a shoe to the floor, and when he looks, praise him. When he comes to you on his own, take advantage of it and praise: "Yeah! Good boy, Randy!"

If you have purchased a purebred dog, the breeder will have given you a form that you will fill out and send to the appropriate registry to register your new dog. One of the things you will have to decide is your new dog's registered name. This is not the name you use every day—that's his call name. Instead, this is his official name with the registry. Your new dog's breeder may ask that part of his name be the kennel name, such as Ocean Blue for Ocean Blue Kennels or Ocean Blue Australian Shepherds. The registered name must be unique. If you send in a name that has been used before, it may come back with a Roman numeral tacked on (Ocean Blue Big Boy IV), or it may be sent back to you for revision.

## THE FIRST FEW DAYS

The first few days after you bring home your puppy are going to be tough, no doubt about it. Your puppy or dog is going to have no idea where he is and who you are. A puppy is going to miss his mom and littermates, and an older puppy or dog is going to feel alone and scared. Therefore, it's important to keep things calm and quiet. This is not the time to invite the neighbors in to see your new friend; that can wait. Right now Fido (to use a generic name) needs to get to know you and your family.

Show Fido where his toys are and play a little, but don't get him so excited that he's growling and biting. Calm is the key right now. Petting and cuddling should be calm and gentle, and playtime fun but not too rough. He needs to learn to trust you and your family members; if things are too rough, he could become scared and fearful, or he may feel that he has to fight back. You want to build trust, cooperation, and compliance with your new dog, not a sense of having to fight you.

Fido also needs to learn his way around, especially where to go to relieve himself. For the first few days, you can pick up your puppy to take him outside, especially if he's tiny, but as soon as possible, encourage him to walk to the door to go outside. He needs to learn where to go and will not learn it by being carried. Outside, take him to the area where you would like him to relieve himself. Don't play with him right now; just be quiet. When he relieves himself, praise him— "Good boy to go potty!"—using, of course, the phrase you wish to use. Some people say "Get busy!" or "Find a spot," both of which are fine. When he's awake, he will need to go outside hourly at first and after waking up from a nap, after eating, and after playtimes. Newly adopted older puppies and dogs will be able to control themselves longer much more rapidly than a baby puppy, but in the beginning, get him outside often, too, to prevent potential problems.

After your puppy has relieved himself, let him wander around for a little while. He's going to want to explore, and as he does, you can see if you've missed anything in your puppy-proofing of the backyard. After he's explored a little, get him to exercise: encourage him to follow you, praising him when he does, or gently toss a ball or dog toy for him to chase. See chapter 7 for more housetraining information, including housetraining problems.

When he's ready for a nap, put Fido back in his crate. Toss a biscuit in ahead of him and then when he's in, close the door and walk away. Don't let him out if he's barking or crying. Teach him

## Using (and Abusing) a Crate

A crate is a wonderful training tool when used correctly. It gives the dog a place he can call his own; he can take a nap in the crate, retreat to the crate when the household is too noisy or busy, and hide his favorite toys in the crate. With the crate, he uses his instincts to keep his bed clean and therefore develops bowel and bladder control. When the puppy is confined when not supervised, he is prevented from getting into other trouble, such as chewing on the furniture or raiding the trash cans.

He can (and should) spend all night in the crate. He can also spend a couple of hours in the crate twice a day, perhaps two hours in the morning and two hours in the afternoon. He should NOT spend all night in the crate and then all day, too. He needs to be able to run and play, roll around, stretch his legs, and interact with the world. If he's in the crate for so many hours, he can't do that.

If you work during the day and the puppy must be alone, you will need to make plans other than locking the puppy in the crate. Perhaps set up a safe, sheltered dog run in the backyard, or have a neighbor come over a couple of times a day to take Fido outside for a potty break, playtime, and a walk.

that he comes out when he's calm and quiet, when you are ready to let him out. He can spend a couple of hours in the crate a couple times during the day and all night. At night, he may cry and howl; don't give in and bring him up into your bed! That's setting a bad precedent. Instead, give him a warm towel, a stuffed toy, or a ticking clock to make him feel less alone.

# INTRODUCING YOUR OTHER DOG

If you already have a dog at home, introduce the resident dog to the new dog or puppy in a neutral place. Have someone bring the new dog to a park or yard where your resident dog has never been and introduce the dogs to each other on leash. Don't expect them to be immediate fast friends; just be calm and quiet and let them both move around, sniffing and getting to know each other. Plan on spending at least an hour at the park so that they can get to know each other. If all is well, then take them both home.

Once at home, keep both on leash, even in the house, for an hour or so as you determine whether the resident dog is going to accept the newcomer. Even if all seems okay, don't leave both dogs home alone without separating them. Put the newcomer in the crate, if you can, or leave one inside and one outside for a while.

If you have an older resident dog and are bringing home a puppy, all should be okay. Most older dogs will accept a young, nonthreatening puppy. If you're bringing home an adult dog, acceptance could take a little time and patience.

## BOND WITH HIM

One of the things that makes a relationship with a dog so unique is the bond that develops. A dog and owner who are bonded with each other have a genuine concern for each other's well being and happiness. Although people can bond with other animals, particularly horses and cats, those bonds are not usually as strong as the bonds we develop with dogs. That bond is what causes a police dog to give his life for his partner, or what causes a family dog to stay inside a smoke-filled house barking wildly to wake his owners when he easily could have run outside. Although some people do own dogs without developing a bond with the dog, that relationship is never what it could have been.

The ideal age for bonding is between 8 and 12 weeks of age, and this bonding takes time. As you handle your new dog, petting, brushing, and playing gently with him, he learns to trust you. You also get to know him; you learn what he likes and doesn't like, and you learn what his reactions are to new situations.

If you have adopted an older puppy or adult dog, he can still bond with you even if he had bonded with his previous owners. Once a dog has bonded with someone, he can bond again. The difficulty arises when a dog who has never made a connection with people is adopted. Whether or not he can ever bond depends on many things, including his history with people and how he's been treated, his breed and its tendency to bond (or not), and his individual personality. Be patient, consistent, and kind in your handling of this dog, and give him time.

The ability to bond with people is shared by all dog breeds, but the bond's strength can vary. Some breeds tend to bond more strongly to just one person, while other breeds will bond with the entire family. Still other breeds, when well socialized, will bond with everyone they spend time with. As a general rule, the breeds developed to work with people, taking directions on a daily basis, bond more strongly than those breeds developed to work alone, making their own decisions.

# Socialization

*Socialization* is the process of introducing your puppy to the world around him. With the ideal age of socialization occurring between 10 and 16 weeks of age, that means you must make the time to do this during this period. Socialization should continue through puppyhood and into adulthood. If you adopt an older puppy or dog, that dog should be introduced to the sights and sounds of your home and neighborhood. After all, it's his home and neighborhood now, too.

It's very important to keep the socialization process fun and upbeat. Even if the puppy is startled by something, he shouldn't be consoled; the puppy could mistake that consoling as praise for being worried. Instead, jolly him! For example, if he's worried about a flapping trash bag, tell him in a happy tone of voice, "Oh, don't be silly! Come on, brave boy!" as you reach out and touch the trash bag. After he sees you can touch it and no harm befalls you, let him walk up to it.

Your puppy should meet people of all ages, sizes, shapes, colors, and ethnic backgrounds. He needs to find out that people come in wide variety. As you introduce your puppy to people, you must also protect him. Do not let people treat him roughly, even if they are only doing so in play.

Some breeds bond more closely, while others will bond with the entire family. Schapendoes bond strongly to the entire family. Little Beauty Kibo du Bouleau, a Schapendoe, owned by Colette Peiffer.

You must set the rules as to how he is handled, even if it means that you have to step in and tell someone, "Sorry, we don't play those games. Please be gentle."

Don't let crowds of people swarm your puppy, either. When you introduce him to your neighbors, have one or two at a time pet him. If a crowd develops, pick up your puppy and move away. You can explain that a crowd is frightening and ask them to approach the puppy one at a time. Keep in mind that although your dog may be your protector when he's grown up, right now you are *his* protector.

During socialization, introduce your puppy to normal sounds.

Normal household sights and sounds:

- ✦ A trash bag being shaken out and placed in a trash can
- ✦ A vacuum cleaner turned on and moving around the house
- ✦ A broom and mop being used
- ✦ A garbage disposal turned on
- ✦ A trash compactor turned on
- ✦ A metal pan lid dropped to the floor
- ✦ The washing machine and dryer

Normal outdoor sounds:

+ A car engine nearby
+ A motorcycle driving by
+ The lawnmower
+ A weed whacker and leaf blower being used
+ The garbage truck coming down the street
+ A bicycle and a tricycle, as well as other kids' toys

Your puppy should also meet other animals. He can meet healthy, well-vaccinated, friendly adult dogs, and he should meet a dog-friendly cat. Rabbits, ferrets, goats, cows, sheep, horses, and tortoises can also be a part of his socialization.

Your veterinarian may tell you to keep your puppy at home until he has had all his vaccinations. She's telling you this out of fear that your puppy may catch a contagious disease. Yet, this book is telling you to socialize your dog; obviously, there is a conflict. Most puppies have good immunities after two full sets of vaccinations, and most of the threat of disease comes from unvaccinated dogs. So, as you take your dog out in public to introduce him to the world, avoid unknown dogs. Let him be friendly only with those dogs you know are well vaccinated and appear healthy. When you're out in public, do not let your puppy sniff other dogs' feces or urine. Be careful and protect your puppy, yet let him see the world, too.

# Living with Your Dog

*I*f you haven't lived with a dog before, especially as an adult, you will find that a dog changes your life. If you had a dog as a child, you probably remember your dog's companionship, but not the chores and training. The dog you have today, though, is very much your responsibility. She depends on you for everything and, in return, will give you unconditional love.

## Living with a Dog

In chapter 2, we discussed where your puppy or new dog should sleep—ideally, in her crate in your bedroom. Not only can you hear her should she need to go outside, you will also be giving her eight hours of closeness to you. It's a great time for bonding even if you are not consciously doing anything. We also talked about where the puppy should eat: either in her crate or in a quiet corner of the kitchen. She needs peace and quiet to eat; she shouldn't be worried about anyone messing with her food or potentially stealing it. She needs water both in the house and outside.

The puppy-proofing you did inside the house and out has created some safe places where your dog can live and play without many dangers. You may find, though, that things you thought were not of interest to a puppy actually are. Puppies can chew on the strangest things! So puppy-proofing will be ongoing as you watch your puppy over the first few weeks.

We also talked about limiting your puppy's freedom in the house, the garage, and the yard. These restrictions should continue for many months as your puppy learns what you expect of her and as she grows up, both mentally and physically. One of the most common mistakes puppy owners make is allowing the puppy too much freedom too soon. The puppy may have been doing well,

Photo by Sheri Wachtstetter

Dog ownership is all about companionship. Hillary, a Golden Retriever/Labrador Retriever mix, pictured with owner Buddy Wachtstetter.

listening, and not getting into trouble, and the owner thinks he's got a great dog—a prodigy!—so he allows the puppy to have free access to the house, unsupervised. He comes home one day to find the sofa cushion chewed, the trash cans dumped over, and trash spread throughout the house. Puppies need restrictions and limited freedom until they are mentally mature enough to handle the responsibility of unsupervised freedom in the house. And as they are maturing, you will be training them to know what is acceptable behavior and what is not.

But, there is more to living with a dog. A dog is a companion animal. That means she is supposed to spend time with you. She's going to want to be with you, follow you from room to room, and lie at your feet while you read the paper or work at the computer. When you leave the house, your dog is going to want to go with you. Living with a dog means compromises. Let the dog be with you as much as possible to satisfy her needs, yet make enough time for yourself so you don't feel smothered, especially at first. As you get used to dog ownership, though, you may find yourself feeling alone and lonely when your dog isn't with you!

Your daily routine will certainly change once your new dog is home. Young puppies have to go outside often during the day and once or twice each night. Then you'll have to spend time playing with the puppy, grooming and training her, and, of course, feeding her. But even something as simple as going out after work may take more thought. If you go shopping after work, will someone else be able to go straight home to take the puppy outside?

# Establishing Household Rules

Household rules are the guidelines you teach your dog about living with you and your family in your house and yard. When you decide on the household rules you wish to teach your dog, think about the future. How do you want this dog to behave three or four years from now? You may be willing to put up with some things now while she's a puppy because she's very cute, but are those things still going to be okay in the future, or will they bug you to no end later? So, in your mind, picture your dog as an adult. What would you like her to do (or not do) in the house?

✦ Housetraining is, of course, the first household rule Lady (to use a generic name) must learn. She is to relieve herself outside in a specified area, or on leash when you ask her to go, and she must never relieve herself in the house. Chapters 2 and 7 discuss housetraining in more detail.

✦ Lady should never dash out doors, either to the front yard, the garage, or even the backyard. Instead, she should wait for your permission to go through doors. Dashing out front

Do you want your dog on the furniture? It's not a problem with some dog owners, while others would prefer to cut down on the dirt and hair. Pointers.

is particularly dangerous, as she could continue running into the street where she could get hit by a car. Or, if Lady is a protective breed by nature, she could frighten or potentially even bite someone coming to the front door. Chapter 6 discusses basic obedience training that will teach Lady to sit and stay at doors rather than dash out.

✦ Is she allowed on the furniture? Some people don't mind if their dog is up on the sofa, and they use throws or blankets to protect the furniture. Others prefer to keep the dog and the resulting hair and dirt off the furniture. It's totally up to you, but you need to make that decision now. You can't let her up on the furniture now and change your mind later. If Lady jumps up on the furniture, pull her off as you tell her, "Lady, off!"

✦ Is Lady allowed in the kitchen? Some dog owners use the kitchen as an exercise pen and have the dog spend time there, primarily because the floor is easy to clean. Others prefer to keep the dog out of the kitchen so she's not underfoot when cooking is going on. It's harder for her to get into cupboards or raid the kitchen trash can if she's not allowed in the kitchen at all.

✦ Which rooms will be off-limits? Do you want to keep Lady out of the dining room or formal living room? Would you prefer that she not go into the kids' bedrooms? Her freedom in the house should be restricted anyway, so making a few rooms off-limits is absolutely fine. Close doors or put up baby gates.

+ The dog should not be allowed on your bed. She has her own bed and should sleep there. There are too many problems associated with sleeping with the owner to allow this. After all, your bed is where the important people sleep, and if she sleeps with you, that elevates herself in her own mind. Not good!

What else is important to you? Look at your house, walk through it, and look at your new dog. Is there anything that would bother you significantly if your dog did it over and over again? It is so much easier to teach the dog now, when she is new to your household, than to change habits later.

Once you have established some household rules, the entire family must agree on the rules. Then everyone needs to enforce them consistently. If one person doesn't agree and refuses to enforce the rules or, worse yet, encourages the dog to do the wrong thing, the dog will be confused and inconsistent in her behavior. After you decide on the rules, have a family meeting and explain the importance of both the rules and enforcing them. Encourage family members to help Lady by working together to teach her.

# You Are Your Dog's Leader

When your dog was with her mother and littermates, her mom was her leader. Mom fed and cared for her, and if she was too rough with her sharp baby teeth, Mom would growl at her or stop her play. This leadership was important for the puppy's future, as it taught her to accept guidance, rules, and discipline.

When people add a dog to their life, they usually say that they want a companion, a new best friend. Unfortunately, that can't happen right away. You need to be your dog's leader first, especially throughout her puppyhood (up to about 1 year of age) and adolescence (generally from 1 to 2 years of age). When she is grown up, knows your rules, and accepts them, she can be your best friend. Until then, you need to be her leader, her surrogate parent.

If you are not your dog's leader, you will not be respected. A dog who doesn't respect her owner can show the attitude in many different ways; she might growl when you go to move her off the sofa or bed or when she has a toy or bone. She might snap at you when you try to groom her, or she may even try to mount you. Disrespect may also show up in a refusal to do obedience training or even a refusal to play with you.

You can demonstrate your leadership in several ways:

+ Train your dog. Enroll in a dog training class, either a kindergarten class for puppies or a basic obedience class for older puppies and young adult dogs.
+ Enforce your household rules.
+ Give your dog permission to do things. If she's reaching to pick up her toy, tell her as she picks it up, "Good girl to get your toy!" She was going to do it anyway, so give her permission to do it and praise her for it. Think of it as free dog training!
+ Go through doorways first. Just as you don't want your dog dashing through doors to the outside, don't let her shove through doors ahead of you. Block her with your knee or foot and tell her, "Wait!" If she dashes through anyway, turn around and go back the way you

Adding a dog to your life will cause disruptions and changes in your life, but it's all worth it. Huckleberry, a German Wirehaired Pointer, owned by Karen Boman; and Hope, a Labrador Retriever, owned by Tracy Weldon.

came. You can also put a leash on her and make her wait while you walk ahead of her through the doorway.

✦ She should follow you up and down stairs. Just as she shouldn't dash ahead of you through doorways, she shouldn't rush on the stairs, either. This is a safety concern as well as a leadership one; if she dashes ahead of you, you could trip and fall down the stairs. Use her leash to make her wait and follow you up and down the stairs.

✦ At least once each day, sit on the floor and ask your dog to lie in front of you for a tummy rub. This is an enjoyable exercise for both of you, but at the same time your dog is assuming a submissive position for you.

✦ Don't pet your dog too much. When you pet too much and too often, you appear submissive in your dog's eyes. When you pet every time she begs for petting, or if you pet her whenever she's within reach, she will think she's the center of the universe. If you want to pet her, have her do some of her obedience exercises first, and then pet her as a reward for that.

Although many people are leaders at work and can be good at it without thinking about it, being a leader to your dog doesn't always come as naturally. So think about it, put up some notes to remind yourself, and remember: Your dog needs a leader, and it must be you.

# Your New Dog and Your Kids

Although television shows such as *Lassie* and the numerous commercials that feature both children and dogs may lead us to believe that dogs and kids are made for each other, in reality, it rarely happens that smoothly. Dogs tend to think that children are the equivalent of littermates, and that's not good. Dogs don't necessarily respect their littermates; they jump on them, bite them, wrestle roughly, and play chase games. If a dog plays like this with a child, that child is going to get hurt, potentially quite badly.

Instead, you must show the dog that the children must be respected just as you should be. Have the kids do all the leadership exercises we just discussed with a parent right there, ready to step in. If the dog rebels, you should immediately have the dog comply. Never ask a child to do any of these exercises and then walk away; the dog could easily take advantage of your absence.

Let the children help with dog-related chores, too, such as feeding. Most dog trainers will allow kids to come to training classes as long as they aren't disruptive. Your kids can then participate in the dog's training, again with parental supervision. Do not, however, make the child ultimately responsible for the dog's care. Very few children are that single-minded, and it's not fair for the dog to go hungry because a child has a baseball game or a scout meeting.

Even if your dog lives with kids, make sure that she's socialized to other children. Walk your dog to the bus stop or to school so she can meet many other kids. Take her to children's sporting events. This way, when your kids' friends come over to play, your dog will already be well socialized to a variety of children. Be sure to keep your dog on a leash during play sessions so that you can control her actions. If you have to go inside or go to another room away from the kids, bring the dog with you.

Keep playtimes with the dog under control. Children should never wrestle with the dog, as this teaches the dog to be rough with them, to fight them. Never allow a dog to stand over the kids or, of course, to mount the kids. The best games are retrieving games and hide-and-seek games. If you find that after a certain amount of playtime, the dog gets overstimulated and can't control herself, stop the playtimes before they reach that point.

Always supervise the interactions between your dog and children. Never leave your dog and kids alone together, even for a moment, especially babies. It only takes an instant for a dog to hurt a child.

# Your New Dog and Other Pets

Although the adage might be "fighting like cats and dogs," it doesn't have to be true. Dogs and cats (and other pets) can live together quite well and often live very happily together. Introduce your new dog and your other pets carefully, with the dog on leash and the other pet(s) held securely. Let them sniff each other. If the dog lunges, nips, or tries to bite, let her know that's not acceptable: "Ack! No! Not allowed!" If she tries to lick, that's fine.

Keep the dog on leash whenever the other pets are out and about. Never, ever allow the dog to chase the other pets. Chasing kicks in the prey drive, and if she were to catch the other pet, it might be very difficult for her to resist the temptation to kill it. If she wants to chase, use the leash to physically stop her as you tell her, "Ack! No chase!" Then have her sit or lie down and stay.

Supervise the interactions of the dog and other pets very carefully for several months. Make sure that the dog is going to be able to control herself should one of the other pets incite play. Ferrets, for example, will hop sideways and chitter when they want to play; can your dog resist that invitation?

Keep in mind, too, that many dog breeds were bred to chase, hunt, and kill vermin, which include rabbits, mice, rats, voles, moles, and other small creatures. Your dog is not going to understand that your pet rat is different from a wild rat. In these situations, protect the smaller pets from your dog, and never leave them alone together unsupervised.

Dogs and cats do not have to be enemies; in fact, they can be good friends. Just don't allow the dog to chase the cat whatsoever, and supervise their interactions until you're sure the dog is trustworthy. Dax, an Australian Shepherd; and Squash, a domestic medium-haired kitten, both owned by Paul and Liz Palika.

# Making Time for Play

People rarely take the time to play—real play—when acting silly and laughing are perfectly acceptable. We exercise, we make time for sports, but we don't play enough. This is too bad, because both play and laughter are good for our mental health and physical well-being. But dogs, and especially puppies, need time for play, so you, as the dog's owner, are going to have to play with your dog. But don't worry; just because it's good for you doesn't mean you're going to hate it!

Throwing a ball or flying disc for your puppy to retrieve is fun and great exercise, but you can do so much more. First, as a part of your puppy's ongoing socialization, you can take walks in different places. Walk in the city park, in a rural park, and, if dogs are allowed, on the beach. Go for a walk at the local campground. Encourage your pup to walk on different surfaces and to greet other people and friendly dogs.

In the backyard, put together a small obstacle course. Place a wide shelf board over two concrete blocks and then encourage your puppy to walk across it. At a garage sale, find some plastic kids' toys, like a small slide, and have your dog climb up it and slide down the other side. Pick up a small kiddy pool, put an inch of water in the bottom, and encourage your puppy to jump in. When she does, tell her how brave she is! Then drop some ice cubes (or apple slices) in the water, urging her to catch them.

Photo by Sheri Wachtstetter

Don't be afraid to be silly with your dog. Playing and having fun are important parts of your relationship. Puppy, a Chinese Crested, pictured with owner Margaret George.

Teach your puppy to use her nose. Hold a treat in one hand, close your hand into a fist, and let your puppy find it. Then close both fists and have her find which one has the treat. As she sniffs, tell her, "Find it!" When she can find it in your hands, use several small plastic bowls, inverted, with a treat under one of them. Move the bowls around and encourage her to find the treat. Make a big fuss over her when she does.

You can also teach her find-it games around the house. Give a dog treat to one of your kids, have him show the treat to the puppy, and then while you hold the puppy's collar, have the child run away. When he has hidden himself in a fairly open spot, let go of the puppy's collar and have the puppy chase after him. When the puppy finds him, she gets the treat. As she gets better at the game, the kids can make it tougher, hiding in more difficult spots.

As you and your dog get to know each other, other silly games may invent themselves. You may find that your dog likes to "sing," and you can make noises with her. Or she may like to be acrobatic, rolling over and doing headstands or back flips. You might discover that you both enjoy trick training. The important thing is that you both are having fun!

# Keeping Your Dog Healthy

Your new dog's health actually began before he was conceived. Hopefully, his ancestors were healthy and long-lived, and his mother was healthy, parasite free, vaccinated, and well nourished prior to Fido's conception. Reputable breeders only breed healthy dogs because those dogs are then more likely to produce healthy puppies (yet another reason why you should buy your puppy from a reputable breeder). However, accidents do happen sometimes—a male dog jumps the fence to visit a female—or an owner without enough knowledge may allow dogs to breed that should not have been used for breeding. This can affect the health of the future puppies. If the mother was healthy during her pregnancy and the puppies were born without difficulty, her milk came in well, and the puppies nursed vigorously, then those puppies had a great start on life. If the mother was not well vaccinated, was underfed, or had an underlying health condition, the puppies may not thrive as well as they could have. Although it's now up to you, as your dog's owner, to continue his health care so that he can live a long, healthy life, make sure your veterinarian is also a part of your dog's normal health regime.

## Choosing a Veterinarian

A veterinarian will be of tremendous help to you during Fido's puppyhood and will be able to guide you through the vaccination process, spaying and neutering, and any accidents or injuries Fido might have. After all, puppies are clumsy and invariably hurt themselves at some point during puppyhood.

Worse yet, puppies eat anything they can get into their mouths, and your vet can help soothe that upset tummy.

There might be several veterinarians doing business in your neighborhood or city. All probably have nice clinics and informative advertisements in the local phone book. So, how do you find the right vet for you and your dog? Most pet owners find the professionals they work with through word-of-mouth referrals. Ask dog-owning friends and neighbors which veterinarian they do business with and why. Are they happy with her services? What do they like and dislike? How are her prices?

When you have a couple of different names that seem to come up again and again, call each of these vets and make an appointment—not for Fido, but just to go in and talk with the vet. By leaving your dog at home, you can concentrate on getting to know this veterinarian without the distractions of a puppy. Be prepared to pay for this office visit, as you are taking some of the vet's time, but that's okay; this is, after all, an investment in your dog's health. Ask the vet if she prefers working with dogs or cats? Big dogs or little dogs? Does she have any problems with Fido's breed? Ask her, too, about her office hours and how she prefers to handle emergencies. Does she offer payment plans? Which credit cards does she accept? Once you've visited two or three vets, make a decision as to which one you prefer. Then make an appointment for Fido's first visit.

Try to get Fido in to see the vet sometime during the first week he's with you. Not only can this visit get him started on a vaccination schedule, it can also pinpoint any possible health problems. If your vet discovers a congenital health defect (one your puppy was born with), you will need to decide whether you can deal with this problem, and you will need to let the breeder know that a problem exists.

If you adopted a dog from a rescue group or shelter, you still need to get the dog to a vet within the first week. He may or may not have had any vaccinations and may need to be wormed, and, of course, you need to make sure that he's healthy.

# Canine Diseases and Vaccinations

Canine diseases are among the biggest threats to your dog's health. Many of these diseases are fatal to the dog who comes down with them, and prior to the introduction of effective vaccinations, thousands of dogs died each year because of these diseases. Other diseases are not usually fatal but can cause serious health problems.

- **Adenovirus:** This virus affects the respiratory system and shows up primarily as coughing. It is passed through the air by an infected dog coughing out droplets carrying the virus. It can be serious, especially in puppies, but usually is not fatal. There are effective vaccines.
- **Bordetella bronchiseptica:** This bacterial infection affects the respiratory system. An infected dog may experience coughing, sneezing, and a running nose. Secondary infections and pneumonia can be dangerous. It is passed through contact with an infected dog. There are effective vaccines.
- **Canine distemper:** This virus affects a dog's skin, eyes, and nerves. The first symptoms are typically a running nose and eyes, and might even appear to be pneumonia. Canine distemper can be passed through an infected dog's feces or through the air if an infected dog sneezes or coughs. It is usually fatal, and those dogs who do survive often have neurological problems, including seizures. There is an effective vaccine.
- **Canine hepatitis:** This virus usually begins with a sore throat and quickly spreads to other organs, especially the liver. It is extremely contagious and is usually picked up when a healthy dog sniffs the urine or nasal discharge of an infected dog. It is fatal, and dogs can go downhill and die within hours of showing symptoms. There is an effective vaccine.
- **Canine influenza:** This highly contagious virus hits the respiratory system, causing a nasal discharge and coughing in milder cases. More serious cases progress to a high fever and pneumonia. It is passed by contact with a sick dog, especially the respiratory discharges. Most dogs recover with supportive veterinary care, but canine influenza can be fatal to those with the more severe form. There is no vaccination yet.
- **Coronavirus:** This virus most often hits puppies and can cause severe dehydration. The primary symptom is mild to severe diarrhea. There may be blood in the stools in severe cases. It is transmitted through contact with an infected dog's feces. With supportive veterinary care, most puppies survive. There is an effective vaccine.
- **Leptospirosis:** This bacterial infection is often fatal. It is usually picked up from contact with an infected dog's urine or water polluted with urine. Symptoms include fever, vomiting, and dehydration. The organs primarily affected are the liver and kidneys. There is an effective vaccine.
- **Lyme disease:** This bacterial infection affects the nerves and joints, often causing permanent damage. It shows up as a fever, muscle soreness, weakness, and joint pain. It is passed by infected ticks, fleas, and flies. There is a vaccine.
- **Parainfluenza:** This is another virus that affects the respiratory system. It, too, is passed by an infected dog coughing out droplets containing the virus. It can be serious, especially in puppies. There are effective vaccines.
- **Parvovirus:** This virus is continuing to mutate. It primarily affects puppies, although dogs with compromised immune systems and older dogs may also be infected. It causes vomiting, diarrhea, and dehydration and is passed through contact with an infected dog's feces and vomit. It is often fatal, and because it is continuing to mutate, it has been called the most dangerous canine virus. There are vaccines, and the makers are trying to keep up with the mutations.
- **Rabies:** This virus affects the brain, causing staggering, drooling, seizures, and changes in behavior. It is caught by contact with another sick animal, often bats, skunks, squirrels, and raccoons. It is fatal, but there is an effective vaccination.

Photo by Sheri Wachtstetter

Your veterinarian will set up a vaccination schedule for your puppy. The first shots are generally given during your puppy's first visit to the vet, usually at 8 to 10 weeks of age. If the breeder gave the puppy a vaccination before you brought him home, make sure you bring the record with you to the vet's office. He will need to take that into account when setting up the schedule.

If you have adopted an older puppy or an adult dog, bring his shot record with you on the first visit. After your vet sees what has been given (or not given), she can discuss a vaccination schedule with you. Although many vaccines have been given annually for many years, now many vets prefer to space them out, sometimes to every three years. The timing can depend on your dog's immune system and whether a particular disease is an active threat in your area.

Puppies need vaccinations; the key is to work out a reasonable schedule that you and your vet will both be happy with. Chloe, a Labrador Retriever, owned by Danny and Carol Norman.

# Internal Parasites

Most dog owners would prefer to ignore the idea that their dogs might have internal parasites, but parasites are, unfortunately, a fact of life. In fact, they can't be ignored because they can harm your dog, and many can be transmitted to people, especially children who play out in the yard, putting toys or their fingers in their mouth. Gardeners, too, are at risk.

Do not give over-the-counter wormers just because you suspect that your dog may have worms; these can be very damaging to a dog's system. In addition, determining which parasites your dog may have usually requires a fecal analysis. Most over-the-counter (and even prescription) medications are for one or two specific parasites, not all of them.

+ **Coccidiosis:** This protozoa parasite is often carried by birds. If you keep a birdfeeder outside for wild birds, make sure your dog can't get to the leftover seeds underneath. He could eat the seeds as well as bird droppings and could become infected. The first symptoms include coughing, runny nose, eye discharge, and diarrhea.
+ **Giardia:** The protozoa *Giardia* is common in wild animals and is most often picked up in water frequented by wild animals. If you and your dog went camping or hiking and your dog drank out of a pool, pond, or stream, watch for diarrhea, the first symptom of this parasite.
+ **Heartworm:** Heartworms live, as their name implies, in a dog's heart. They damage the heart walls, and poor circulation and poor heart function follow. In severe cases, the heart fails and the dog dies. Mosquitoes are the intermediate hosts and can pass young heartworms

*(microfilaria)* from an infected dog to an uninfected dog. Treatment can be very hard on a dog, especially one with a heavy infestation. Preventives are available.

+ **Hookworms:** Hookworms live in the small intestine, where they attach themselves to the intestinal wall and suck blood. The wounds often leak blood for a while, so bloody diarrhea is one symptom of hookworms. Hookworm eggs are passed in the feces. The eggs can hatch in the soil, where they may attach themselves to the feet of their new host. A fecal analysis will verify a hookworm infestation.

+ **Roundworms:** These long, white worms are very common, and most puppies should be treated for them. Roundworms also are found in adult dogs, people, and many other animals. A young puppy with roundworms will have an unkempt (vets will call it "unthrifty"), potbellied look. His coat may be dull instead of

Photo by Liz Palika

If you go hiking or camping, bring your own water. Drinking from wild water sources could lead to Giardia. Hatcreek's Logan (owned by Petra Burke) and Hatcreek's Doctor Bashir (owned by Liz Palika), Australian Shepherds, pictured with Petra Burke, both bred by Karen Russell.

shiny. A fecal analysis will determine whether worms are present. Good backyard sanitation (picking up feces daily and disposing of them) can help control infestations.

+ **Tapeworms:** These parasites live in the intestinal tract, where they attach to the wall to absorb nutrients. They grow by creating new segments. The first sign of an infestation is often a small, ricelike segment found on or around the dog's rectum. Tapeworms are acquired when the dog eats an infected flea, the intermediate host, or a small animal (such as a mouse) that is also carrying fleas and/or tapeworms. The general rule is that if you control the fleas, you can prevent future tapeworm infestations. A fecal analysis will verify a tapeworm infestation, although if the vet sees tape segments, a fecal analysis is not needed.

+ **Whipworms:** These worms live in the large intestine, where they feed on blood. The eggs are passed in the feces. The eggs can live in the soil for a long time. A dog who buries his bone or eats grass can pick up the eggs. People can pick up eggs under their fingernails, too. A fecal analysis will determine whether whipworms are present.

# Spaying, Neutering, and Breeding

The majority of dogs should be spayed (if female) or neutered (if male). The reasons are many. First of all, the number of dogs being destroyed each year in shelters (and on the streets) all over the

## Is More Always Better?

There has been a movement recently questioning the vaccination schedules that have been used for the past couple of decades. The movement asks, "Are more vaccinations better?" Traditionally, dogs have been given the vaccines available, even when a disease may not be a problem in the region in which the dog lives. Dogs were also given booster vaccines annually. Now experts feel that annual vaccinations may be too much of a good thing and that a booster every three years may be better for the dog.

This questioning has come about because dogs do not seem to be living longer, even with increased veterinary care. More dogs seem to be suffering from allergies (including allergic reactions to the vaccinations themselves) and immune system disorders, and many more are dying of cancers at younger ages. Although these disorders have not been linked directly to over-vaccination, dog owners, breeders, and veterinarians are concerned.

Talk to your veterinarian about the vaccination schedule she follows. Ask about potential problems and discuss your concerns. Find a balance you both will be happy with.

---

world is in the millions. There are so many dogs needing homes that it simply makes no sense for indiscriminate breeding to take place.

Spaying and neutering also have a direct relationship with your dog's ongoing good health and longevity. A female dog (also called a *bitch*) who has been spayed has a lowered risk of breast cancers and is protected against cancers of the reproductive system. In most females, spaying also decreases the incidence of female aggression. A male dog (also called a *dog*) who has been neutered is protected against testicular cancer and will have fewer hormone-related bad behaviors, including leg lifting and marking, humping or mounting, roaming, and fighting. Neutering decreases a male's desire to escape from the yard and decreases the incidences of fighting.

Spaying or neutering your dog does not change her or his personality and temperament. It simply reduces the sexual hormones. Nor do these surgeries cause your dog to get fat; too much food and too little exercise cause a dog to get fat. Nor will your dog pine away, missing sex. Dogs do not copulate as part of a complex relationship; dogs copulate because their hormones tell them to do so. When the hormones are reduced, the behavior stops.

As mentioned in chapter 1, breeding should be left to the experts. Knowing a breed well enough to produce sound, healthy dogs takes a lot of knowledge. However, if you decide that this is something you would like to do, find someone involved in the breed who has an excellent reputation and ask for help. Ask if he or she will mentor you. With help, someday you, too, could be considered a reputable breeder.

# Basic Home Health Care

You are your dog's health care provider; it's up to you to do what is necessary to keep him happy and healthy. Luckily, for the most part, it's not a hard job at all, and parts of it are just downright fun!

## EXERCISE

Every healthy puppy and dog needs daily exercise. It strengthens the muscles, gets blood circulating, releases endorphins that make a dog feel good, and uses up excess energy. Exercise will also help your puppy learn how to control and coordinate his growing body.

A young puppy (2 to 3 months of age) can go for walks around the neighborhood, chase a tennis ball in the backyard, and play with toys in the house. Three- to six-month-old puppies can do things that are a little more vigorous. They can go for short jogs along with their walks. The puppy can also be introduced to swimming. Seven- to twelve-month-old puppies can walk longer distances and do some short jogs on various surfaces (grass, dirt, asphalt), but avoid long runs on concrete, as they can be damaging to growing bones. The puppy can do a little bit of climbing, such as on a small agility course or on playground equipment. After about 14 to 18 months of age, a dog can run farther and faster and can jump more. A dog that age can also begin pulling weight (such as a wagon).

## PLAYTIME

Exercise should also be considered play; that's a sure way to make sure you keep on doing it! But play can be very different from exercise. A favorite playtime might be sitting on the floor with your dog, laughing at (or with!) him as you rub his tummy. You can toss his toys across the living room floor as you encourage him to bring them back. Hide a treat in one hand and tell your dog to find which hand has the treat.

Don't worry if playtime becomes silly; that's fine. You may one day find yourself saying silly rhymes as you play with his toes: "This little piggy went to market, this little piggy stayed home . . ." Being silly makes you laugh, and no one needs to see you. But playing with your dog, silly or not, is a great way to bond with him.

## WATER

It may seem simplistic to say so, but your dog needs clean water to drink. Unfortunately, too many dog owners don't seem to understand how much water a dog needs and how often he may need to drink. Have an unspillable water dish or two in the house and outside, and keep them filled at all times.

Outside, you may want to use something even larger than a dish; a galvanized tub works well, especially if you have a medium, large, or giant breed dog. Don't let algae or dirt accumulate in this tub; dump it and rinse it daily.

Don't let your dog drink out of the toilet. Although all the comic strips with dogs seem to make fun of this canine trait, it really isn't very sanitary. Plus, if you use the sort of cleaner that remains

Playtime and exercise are necessary for your dog's physical and mental well-being. In addition, it's a great time to have fun with your dog. Teddy, a German Shepherd Dog, owned by Petra Burke; and Ludwig, a German Shepherd Dog, owned by Sally Kayser; both bred by Joel Towart, Bellington GSDs.

in the toilet all the time and releases a certain amount when the toilet flushes, that product could be toxic to your dog.

## BASIC CANINE NUTRITION

When you brought your new dog home, you should have had on hand a supply of the dog food he was eating at the breeder's, the shelter, the rescue group, or his foster home. Hopefully, this was a good food, but if you decide to change it, do so gradually. Feed one-third of the meal using the new food and using two-thirds the old food. After a week, change the ratio to 50/50, and then, in another week, feed two-thirds the new food and one-third the old food. By making the change gradually, your dog's system should adjust without any gastrointestinal upset.

Deciding what to feed your dog can be tough; the choices are many. Commercial dog foods are designed to supply all of a dog's nutritional needs, including proteins, amino acids, enzymes, fats, carbohydrates, vitamins, and minerals. The companies that produce commercial dog foods have fed multiple generations of dogs. However, not all dog foods are of the same quality.

The quality of a dog food is based on multiple factors, including the ingredients contained in the food. Poor quality meats or meat byproducts are less able to nourish your dog than foods made with better quality ingredients. As a general rule, less expensive foods contain inexpensive and less nourishing grains and less of the more expensive meats. In dog foods, you have a tendency to get what you pay for.

The actual ingredients in the food you feed are important—not just the quality of those ingredients, but also what those ingredients are. Allergies are a big problem today; many dogs are allergic to wheat, corn, rice, beef, and even lamb. If your dog scratches at the base of his tail and licks his feet constantly, talk to your vet about allergy tests so you can find out exactly which foods your dog should not eat.

Certain foods also have been linked to canine behavior. Many puppies and young dogs have been found to show symptoms of a type of hyperactivity when they eat foods high in cereal grains. When switched to foods containing more meat, fruits, and vegetables instead of cereal grains, the behaviors lessen significantly.

There are many forms of dog food today:

+ **Dry kibble:** These dry, crunchy foods come in a bag, typically have a good shelf life, and usually are eaten well by most dogs. They may contain meats, meat byproducts, cereal grains, fruits, and vegetables. Depending on quality, they can be very inexpensive to more expensive.

+ **Canned foods:** Canned foods are often called "wet" foods. They are primarily meats or meat recipes packed in water or gravy. They have a long shelf life unopened, but once opened must be used right away. Pound for pound, compared to dry foods, canned foods are quite expensive.

+ **Semi-moist foods:** These foods have a higher moisture content than dry foods but significantly less than canned. Most dogs eat them quite readily because these foods have a higher sugar and salt content than others. They often have more additives (food colorings and preservatives) than other foods, too. Semi-moist foods usually are moderate in price.

+ **Dehydrated foods:** These foods are raw foods that have been dehydrated. The dehydration process loses fewer nutrients in the foods than does baking and some of the other high-temperature processing. These foods contain meats, fruits, and vegetables. Some contain cereal grains. You rehydrate these foods prior to feeding. Initially, these foods seem quite expensive, but rehydrated, they are comparable to good quality dry foods.

+ **Frozen foods:** Frozen foods can be either frozen cooked meats, vegetables, and fruits or frozen raw meats, fruits, and vegetables. These foods are as good (or as bad) as the foods they are made from. Prices vary, also, depending on the ingredients used.

Photo by Sheri Wachtstetter

A well-nourished dog looks healthy, with a shiny coat, bright and alert eyes, and an active mind. Sasha, a Rottweiler, owned by Katy Silva.

+ **Raw foods:** Some dog owners firmly believe that dogs should eat as natural a diet as possible, which means that they should eat raw meats (bones included) and raw vegetables and fruits. Although some dogs do thrive on this diet, there are definitely risks. Raw meats can contain bacteria, parasites, diseases, and growth hormones. Bones can be a problem for many dogs, too. It's also very difficult for someone other than a canine dietician to formulate a balanced diet. If you're interested in feeding a raw food diet, you might want to take a look at dehydrated raw foods first, and then talk to your veterinarian.

No matter what you choose to feed your puppy, pay attention to make sure that your dog is doing well on that food.

+ Is he growing well?
+ Are his eyes bright?
+ Is he alert and attentive?
+ Is his coat healthy and shiny?
+ Is he too fat? If so, cut back on how much you are giving him.
+ Is he too skinny? If so, increase his food portions a little.
+ Does he have plenty of energy to play without acting hyperactive?

Once you have found a food that your dog likes and eats well—a food that you think is a good quality food you can afford—stick with that food. Changing foods can be very upsetting to your dog; many dogs experience gastrointestinal upset (including diarrhea) when foods are changed abruptly. If you want to offer your dog a little variety that won't upset his tummy, keep him on his normal food but add a little yogurt. A teaspoon for a small dog or a heaping tablespoon for a giant dog will add a new taste, with good nutrition to boot. You can give your dog a carrot, an apple slice, or a piece of raw pumpkin as a snack. You can add vegetable juice or meat broth to the food for variety. Just keep in mind that too many additives or supplements can upset a previously balanced and complete diet.

# When to Call the Veterinarian

Knowing when to call the veterinarian can be a stressful and confusing decision. No one wants to take up the veterinarian's time and pay for an office call if it isn't necessary, yet we don't want to deny our dog care should it be needed. Most veterinarians say, "If in doubt, call," and that's good advice.

Before anything happens, you need to make a habit of paying attention to your dog. Know what is normal behavior for him and what isn't. How hard does he normally breathe after playtimes? How quickly does he eat? How much water does he drink each day? In addition, give him a gentle massage everyday so you know what his body feels like. Then when something happens, you know exactly what is different.

Here are some problems you should watch for and call the vet for her recommendations:

+ Diarrhea that lasts more than a day or that contains blood or a lot of mucus.
+ Vomiting that doesn't stop after a couple of hours.
+ Refusal to eat and missing two meals.

- A rectal temperature lower than 100 degrees F or higher than 102.5 degrees F.
- Bleeding that doesn't stop with direct pressure on the wound.
- Cuts or wounds that gape open.
- A snakebite of any kind. Get a good look at the snake so you can describe it to the vet.
- A bite by a bat, rat, or other rodent, or a bite by another wild animal, such as a fox or coyote.
- Breathing difficulties, including gasping, heavy panting, coughing, or repetitive sneezing.
- Breathing with a gurgling sound, or a running nose, or a liquid cough.
- Any eye injury.
- A potential allergic reaction, with red skin, welts, or swelling, especially around the face.
- Suspected poisoning, especially antifreeze, rodent poison, ant poison, or snail poison.

When you call your veterinarian, she will ask you some specific questions. Have this information at hand so you don't have to fumble around for it or call back:

- How old is your puppy?
- What is the specific problem?
- What made you pay attention to it?
- What are the symptoms?
- When did the puppy eat last? How much? How does this differ from normal? Did he throw up afterward?
- Is the puppy drinking water? Is this normal or different from normal?
- Is there any diarrhea? What does it look like?
- Has the puppy gone anywhere or gotten into anything that might have caused this problem?

Tell your veterinarian anything that might tie into this problem. It's better to give too much information rather than too little; she can wade through it and pick out the important pieces.

Once your dog has seen the veterinarian, follow through with all recommended care at home. Unfortunately, far too many dog owners don't follow through and will stop giving prescribed medication once the dog is feeling and acting better. In too many cases, this could cause a relapse or a severe infection.

# Emergency First Aid

Unfortunately, accidents do happen. Sometime during your dog's life, you may have to deal with an emergency. If you know how to handle it and can keep your cool, hopefully you and your dog will weather it well.

Before any accident happens, make sure you know your veterinarian's emergency procedures. Some vets take emergencies at any time; they just prefer you call first so they know you're on the way to the clinic. Other vets do not take emergencies and prefer you go to a neighborhood emergency clinic. So check with your vet, understand the policies, and have all necessary phone numbers and directions. Put this information in your purse, wallet, cars, and first-aid kit.

When your dog is hurt, he may react out of fear and try to bite you, the vet, or the veterinary technician. Although you may not want to muzzle him, it's important to make sure no one gets

A length of soft gauze can make an effective muzzle. Always watch your dog to make sure he's breathing well. Teddy, a German Shepherd Dog, owned by Petra Burke, bred by Joel Towart, Bellington GSDs.

hurt. You can make a muzzle out of just about anything. A leash works well, as does one leg of a pair of pantyhose or a length of gauze. Make a circle out of the material, wrap it around the dog's muzzle twice, and then pull the ends behind his neck and tie it. Keep a close watch on your dog to make sure he's breathing well. Remember, he can't pant with the muzzle on.

## CANINE CPR

Cardiopulmonary resuscitation (CPR) is a combination of external heart massage and rescue breathing. It has saved thousands of people's lives and can do the same for dogs. Knowing how to perform CPR correctly could potentially save your dog's life someday. The Red Cross often offers pet CPR classes, so check in the branch in your area.

Once you begin CPR, continue with it until your dog begins breathing on his own again, or until you can get your dog to help, or until it is obvious that your efforts are in vain. Just don't stop too soon; many dogs have been saved by CPR.

1. When you see a dog lying still, make a quick evaluation. Check for a heartbeat and check to see if the dog is breathing. Never perform CPR on a dog that is breathing and has a heartbeat.
2. If the dog is not breathing, clear his mouth of anything foreign. Pull his tongue out and to one side of his mouth so it doesn't block the airway. Close his mouth, letting his teeth hold the tongue in place. (If the dog is resisting, he doesn't need CPR!)
3. Inhale a big breath and then exhale into the dog's nose, cupping your hands around the dog's muzzle and nose. Watch his chest to make sure it rises after you blow. Repeat one breath per second for ten seconds for a large dog and more often for smaller dogs. Pay attention to yourself as you do this, don't hyperventilate.
4. After ten rescue breaths, roll the dog over on his side. Place your hands, one above the other, over his heart. Lean over and push down in short bursts. Compress five times and then repeat the rescue breathing. Repeat in a cycle of ten breaths and five chest compressions.

## SHOCK

Dogs, like people, can go into shock after an injury. Shock is life-threatening by itself; when combined with the initial injury, it is extremely serious.

The symptoms of shock include:

+ Faster than normal, often irregular heartbeat.
+ Rapid breathing, panting, or even gasping for air.
+ A staring look in the eyes with no recognition of you; eyes dilated, or even no eye response to movement.
+ Pale gums.

The only treatment you can provide a dog in shock is to keep him warm and get him to the veterinarian right away. Never assume that a dog will recover from shock on his own.

## HEATSTROKE

A dog who has gotten too hot, either via the environment or from too much activity in hot conditions, may pace back and forth, looking very uncomfortable, or may throw himself to the ground. He will pant heavily, and his muzzle may be frothy. His body temperature will rise rapidly, and if he's not cooled off, he will go into shock and may die.

The first thing you must do is call your veterinarian. He will probably advise you to cool down your dog before transporting him to the vet's clinic. Run water from a hose over your dog, if the water in the hose is cool, or drape him in a wet towel and keep cool water running over him. As soon as you have him wet, transport him to the vet's clinic.

## BLEEDING

There are several types of bleeding. Some are more serious than others, but all require some care.

+ A bruise occurs when blood vessels under the skin are damaged or broken and the skin remains intact. The blood will pool under skin. Place an ice pack on the bruise for fifteen minutes and then remove. After fifteen minutes with the ice pack off, repeat. Continue the fifteen-minute cycle on and off until it appears that the bleeding under the skin has stopped.
+ Bleeding from small scrapes, scratches, and cuts is not life threatening but these still need care. Wipe off the wound with clean water. Make sure no hair or dirt is in the wound. If the wound is still bleeding, apply direct pressure with a clean gauze pad. When the oozing has stopped, apply an antibiotic ointment. If the wound is gaping, call your veterinarian to see if stitches are needed.
+ If a wound is oozing blood and direct pressure does not stop the bleeding, your veterinarian will need to see it. Use several layers of clean gauze and put direct pressure on the wound. Have someone drive you and your dog to the vet's clinic.
+ Bleeding in spurts is very dangerous; a blood vessel has been damaged. A small dog can bleed to death very quickly and even a large dog can be in danger faster than you can imagine. Although in the past tourniquets were used to stop or slow this type of bleeding, today most veterinarians do not recommend them, as damage to the limb can be equally dangerous with no blood flow. Instead, use pressure with a gauze pad and get the dog to a veterinarian as quickly as possible.

+ Internal bleeding is very difficult to detect and yet is very dangerous. If your dog has had a traumatic injury, such as a kick to the body by a horse, or has been hit by a car, assume that he's been injured and get him to the veterinarian right away. Symptoms may include restlessness, panting, a distended abdomen, bloody saliva, bloody vomit, or bloody diarrhea.

## BLOAT

Gastric torsion (also called *bloat*) is more common in giant and large breeds with a deep chest, although just about any dog can experience bloat. The first symptom of bloat is discomfort; the dog usually paces back and forth and can't settle down. He may salivate and gag but not throw up. The abdomen will eventually become distended and hard.

If you suspect bloat, call the vet right away. With quick treatment, most dogs survive. Without treatment, the stomach can turn *(torsion)*, and the dog will go into shock and die.

## BITES AND STINGS

Puppies are very curious and want to figure out what's going on in the world. That means they will chase bees, snap at wasps, and stick their nose into spider webs. Bites and stings happen, unfortunately. If your puppy has been stung by a bee, do not grab the stinger to pull it out, that will squeeze more venom into the wound. Instead, scrape the stinger out with a fingernail. Wasps do not usually leave a stinger behind; nor do spiders. The first symptoms of a bite or sting are usually whining or crying, pawing or scratching at the spot, followed by redness. If you see swelling at the site, extreme redness or whiteness, or if it progresses to a fever, vomiting, or diarrhea, call your vet. She may recommend you give your puppy an antihistamine. Follow the vet's directions.

Animal bites can be dangerous, too, especially bites from wild animals that could potentially be carrying rabies, such as bats, skunks, raccoons, and foxes. Call your veterinarian right away after a wild animal bite.

The majority of North American snakes are not aggressive and want nothing to do with dogs. Unfortunately, many dogs think snakes are great toys, so they harass the snake until it bites. If the snake is non-venomous, simply clean the wound, apply an antibiotic ointment, and keep an eye on the wound to make sure it doesn't get infected. If the snake is venomous, call your vet's office right away to let them know you're coming and get there as quickly as possible.

## POISONS

The symptoms of poisoning can vary, depending upon what your dog has gotten into. If you need to induce vomiting, you can do so by feeding him several teaspoons of hydrogen peroxide.

+ **Antifreeze:** Induce vomiting, call your veterinarian to notify her you're on your way, and then get there right away.
+ **Chocolate:** Induce vomiting, call your vet, and follow instructions.

- ✦ **Ibuprofen:** Induce vomiting, call your vet, and follow instructions.
- ✦ **Insecticides:** Do not induce vomiting except on the vet's instructions, which will depend upon the type of insecticide. Bring the container with you to the vet's office.
- ✦ **Rodent or roach poison:** Induce vomiting and get to the vet's office immediately.
- ✦ **Snail or slug poison:** Induce vomiting and get to the vet's office immediately.

## BURNS

Puppies and dogs can be burned in several ways, depending upon the circumstances.

- ✦ Thermal burns are caused by heat. A dog who touches a lit cigarette or the outside of the cooking grill will burn his nose.
- ✦ Electrical burns can occur if the dog chews on an electrical cord or an electrical appliance that is plugged into an outlet.
- ✦ Chemical burns can occur if the dog is exposed to a corrosive substance, such as bleach, gasoline, drain cleaner, paint thinner, or road salt.

Chemical burns should be rinsed off right away. Be thorough with this rinsing. Treat the burn as a potential poisoning, too, and call the vet's office right away. All other burns can be ice packed, using the fifteen minutes on, fifteen minutes off routine. If the burn is not severe and simply produces red skin, keep it clean and watch for any signs of infection. If the burn has damaged some layers of skin, producing blisters or bleeding, cover it lightly and get your dog to the vet's clinic right away. Do not put butter, honey, petroleum jelly, or other substances on the burn; these hold in heat and will cause more damage.

## TALK TO YOUR VETERINARIAN

If you have any doubts about how to care for your dog, whether in an emergency or in day-to-day living, call your veterinarian. That's her job and she's not going to laugh at you, no matter how silly you may think your question is. Veterinarians much prefer caring owners who ask questions to those who let health threats go without care.

# A First-Aid Kit for Your Dog

A first-aid kit (or two) is a necessity. You'll be amazed how often you may need it. Put together one for the house and one to carry in your car. You can use a fishing tackle box to carry these supplies; just mark the outside very prominently "First-Aid Kit."

Essential supplies include:

- ✦ Two pair of scissors, one pair with rounded tips and one pair with pointed tips
- ✦ Tweezers
- ✦ Disposable razor

Photo by Sheri Wachtstetter

A well-stocked first-aid kit should be easily available in your house and in your car. Check it often to replace used supplies. Rey, a Rhodesian Ridgeback, owned by Brett and Caroline Dorson.

- ✦ Nail clippers for dogs
- ✦ Thermometer
- ✦ Rolled gauze
- ✦ Rolled bandages
- ✦ Several rolls of elastic bandage
- ✦ Several rolls of tape
- ✦ Antiseptic cleaning wipes
- ✦ Sterile saline eyewash
- ✦ Antihistamine tablets
- ✦ Diarrhea medication

You may also wish to carry a spare leash and collar and a muzzle. A pen and paper could be useful if you need to make notes or need to jot down a veterinarian's instructions. Check the supplies every couple of months so you can rotate out any expired materials and medications, and so you can replace anything that has been used.

# Disaster Planning

We must be prepared for disasters of all kinds because they are going to happen. Whether the disaster is man-made or natural—earthquakes or wildfires, tornadoes or hurricanes, floods or automobile accidents—disasters happen. We must be prepared to take care of ourselves, at least for a few days, because we cannot count on someone else to be there for us.

This is especially true of pet owners. Most shelters do not accept pets, and some rescue organizations will not allow pets on their boats, helicopters, or buses. It is imperative that dog owners make plans to keep their dogs safe in an emergency. That means making plans ahead of time and being willing and able to follow through when an emergency happens.

Know where you will go. Have the names, addresses, and phone numbers of motels that accept pets, or campgrounds, and have the phone numbers of friends and relatives that might allow you and your pets to stay with them. Make sure you have your veterinarian's phone number on hand, too.

To prepare, keep your dog's first-aid kit well stocked. In addition, make up a disaster kit. This can be one for all your pets, or can be combined with one for your family. A trash can with a locking lid works well. In it, have a blanket or two, food and water bowls, canned food (which has a long shelf life), a can opener, extra leashes and collars with identification, and several gallon jugs of water. Throw in a couple of old towels and some grooming tools. If your dog is on any medication, have some of this in the kit, too, and rotate it often so the medication doesn't expire. Have this kit easily accessible so that if you are called to evacuate, you can grab it quickly. Or better yet, have two kits: one in the house and one in your car.

# Grooming Your Dog

All dogs need toenail care, ear and teeth cleaning, and protection from fleas and ticks. Other than that, the type of grooming your new dog needs will depend on her coat: its length, type, thickness, and whether or not it is a double coat. Short-haired dogs such as Doberman Pinschers, German Shorthaired Pointers, and Miniature Pinschers need twice-weekly brushing with a soft-bristled brush, teeth and ear cleaning, nail trimming, and a bath once in a while—that's about it. On the other hand, poodles, spaniels, and schnauzers have hair that grows continuously and need regular haircuts to keep it under control. Other breeds, like German Shepherd Dogs and Siberian Huskies, have a thick double coat that sheds regularly, so they need daily brushing.

Grooming is much more than keeping your dog looking good, although looks are important, too. Grooming is also ensuring that her ears are clean and healthy, teeth are sparkling white, and skin and body are healthy. If you smell a bad odor from her teeth or ears while cleaning them, you should get your dog into the veterinarian's office before a huge problem develops. Similarly, if a bump develops under the skin or you find an open sore while brushing your dog, get help before a bigger problem arises. Grooming is a vital part of keeping your dog healthy.

## Caring for the Coat

### COAT TYPES

Just as dogs are found in a variety of shapes and sizes, so are coats. Doberman Pinschers, Greyhounds, and Miniature Pinschers have what is called a smooth coat. This short coat has hairs that are ½ inch long or shorter that lie very close to the skin. Many dog owners feel these dogs don't need grooming, or worse yet, don't shed, but they do. Short coats need regular brushing, combing, and bathing.

Labrador Retrievers, Corgis, and Rottweilers have short coats with hairs that are between ½ inch and about 2 inches long. These coats do not lie as flat and straight as the smooth coat and may have some wavy textures. These dogs may also have longer hairs on the back of the rear legs and on the tail. These coats do shed and need regular brushing and bathing.

Many breeds have medium-length coats. German Shepherd Dogs, Australian Shepherds, Golden Retrievers, Flat Coated Retrievers, and Border Collies all have medium-length coats with hairs that are usually between 2 and 3 inches long, sometimes up to 4 or 5 inches long on the belly, around the ruff of the neck, on the back of the rear legs, and on the tail. Dogs with this type of coat shed, sometimes very heavily, and need thorough brushing, combing, and bathing. In addition, the longer coat may tangle or mat.

Long-haired dogs have coats longer than 4 to 5 inches overall and include the Afghan Hound, setters, Pekingese, Rough Collie, Rough Chow Chow, and many more. These coats vary in type, including whether or not the coat tangles and mats, and how much undercoat the dog may have, if any. All of these factors will influence how much and what kind of grooming the dog may need. Potential owners should discuss coat care with a breeder prior to committing to a dog of that breed.

Many breeds have single coats, which means that the hairs are the same from the skin on out. Breeds that have double coats have two types of hairs. The outer hairs, called the *guard coat* or *outer coat,* are coarse and long. The *undercoat* is soft, and the hairs are more downlike and fluffy. German Shepherd Dogs have a double coat. The outer hairs have the traditional colors we're used to seeing in a German Shepherd, and the undercoat is usually lighter colored (gray is common). The undercoat is very soft and, in the spring and fall, sheds tremendously, whereas the outer coat sheds a little bit year-round. Dogs with undercoats must be thoroughly brushed on a regular basis to keep the undercoat from matting. During shedding seasons, the undercoat must be brushed well to help remove the dead coat.

The variety in coat textures is tremendous, too. Papillons, Japanese Chins, and long-haired Chihuahuas have a silky coat that is soft under the hands when you pet the dog. These coats need combing to keep them from tangling. German Wirehaired Pointers, Wirehaired Dachshunds, and many terriers have a coarse, almost curly, wiry coat. Most of these coats need hand-stripping; a breeder can show potential owners how to do this correctly. Poodles and Bichons Frises have a curly yet soft coat that brushes out fluffy. These dogs often need professional grooming to keep them looking wonderful. Komondors and Pulis have a coat that forms into cords (dreadlocks). A breeder can explain the specialized care needed for these coats. Malamutes, Siberian Huskies, and Samoyeds have a thick double coat with an undercoat thick enough to protect the dog in freezing temperatures. And don't forget hairless dogs! Several breeds are naturally hairless. Chinese Cresteds have tufts of hair on the head, each paw, and the tail, yet the rest of the body is hairless. The American Hairless Terrier is exactly that: naked!

# GROOMING TOOLS

If you go to your local pet store and walk down the grooming supplies aisle, you might be overwhelmed by all the tools and products. There are combs, rakes, and brushes of all sizes and styles, scissors, clippers, shedding blades, and more. Then there are all different kinds of shampoos and conditioners. Grooming dogs is big business, and all these supplies support the industry.

You don't need all that to get started, though. Listed below are some basic tools, along with a description of how each tool should be used and the coat types on which it can be effectively used.

- **Pin brush:** This brush has a solid handle and head, with metal or plastic pin-type bristles set into a rubber base. The pins may have flat ends or tiny rubber balls on the ends. Those with balls are gentler on sensitive skin. This brush can be used on any coat type except hairless dogs and those with cords (dreadlocks). It is most effective on long, silky coats and long double coats. Brush the coat in the direction it grows or falls, from the base of the hairs all the way to the ends. Sometimes parting the hair with one hand while you brush with the other is most effective. This brush is not effective at removing mats and tangles.

- **Bristle brush:** A bristle brush is like a pin brush except that it has natural or synthetic bristles instead of pins. A soft bristle brush is very good on smooth and short coats, and even some medium-length silky coats. The hair should be brushed in the direction it grows and falls, from the skin all the way to the ends. This brush is not effective at removing mats and tangles.

- **Slicker brush:** This brush has a handle and head of hard plastic with curved metal pins set into a rubber base. The pins are very fine, with a lot of them set close together. This brush can be used on most coat types—short, medium, and long coats, both silky and double coats. It also can be used on curly coats. This brush should be used in the direction the hair grows and falls. Part the coat with one hand so the brush can reach into the coat, down to the skin, and then brush outward. Be careful not to scratch the skin. This brush alone will not get out tangles and mats.

- **All-purpose combs:** There are a variety of comb types. These are for specific coat types or just to suit the needs of the individual groomer. Rat-tailed combs, for example, are great for parting hair, and stripping combs pull out excess undercoat. In most cases, the all-purpose comb is used after a brush. The brush gets most of the dirt and debris out of the coat, as well as the hair that is clumped together (but not mats). The comb can then be run through the coat, removing any mats or tangles, giving a clean, finished look.

- **Flea comb:** This is a small metal or plastic comb with very small teeth placed close together. The comb is run through a smooth or short coat, dragging any fleas out of the coat. It will not go through heavy double coats, so it's most effective on the face of heavily coated dogs.

- **Hound glove:** This glove is usually made of rubber and is designed to pull dead hair out of a smooth or short coat. Although it can be used on a dry coat, it works best during a bath. Wet the dog, lather in the shampoo, and then, using the glove in a circular motion, rub the dog all over. The shampoo will provide lubricant for the glove and all the shedding, dead hair will come out.

## Show-Dog Grooming

In conformation shows, each individual breed must be shown in a certain way—which includes how the dogs in each breed must be groomed. Australian Shepherds, for example, are called a natural breed and must be shown as natural as possible, although the whiskers on the face are usually trimmed, and the paws are trimmed to make them look nice and neat. Poodles, on the other hand, have a very elaborate grooming regimen.

Although pet owners can certainly keep their dogs in a show-dog cut and condition, for some breeds that can be very time-consuming. Most pet dog owners find a happy medium, keeping their dog in a cut or condition that lets the dog look like its breed but in an easier-to-maintain condition.

Dogs being shown in dog shows, especially conformation competition, must be shown (and groomed) in a specific way. Bailey, an English Springer Spaniel, owned by Kelly Rodrigues.

Photo by Sheri Wachstetter

---

- ✦ **De-matter:** This brush has three or four blades in place of bristles or pins. The blades are sharp on one side. When pulled through the coat, even a heavy, tangled coat, the blades will split any tangles or mats.
- ✦ **Shedding blade:** This U-shaped blade has a plastic handle. It is designed to be run over the outside of a short or medium coat. The teeth on the blade catch shedding hair and pull it out. Although it may catch some undercoat, it is primarily designed for the outer coat, or guard hairs, when they are being shed.

Other grooming tools include a set of clippers with blades and guards. Learning to clip your dog is definitely an art, and first attempts are rarely attractive. But the hair will grow out in time! Even if you don't clip the entire dog, you can use clippers to clean up paws and to remove the hair from around the genitals and under the tail. Coarse terrier coats can be clipped (for pets) or more correctly stripped. Stripping a coat is just as much an art as clipping, so ask your dog's breeder for help in learning to do it correctly.

# A Daily Massage

It's important to establish a grooming routine. Not only will this ensure that things are done in a timely manner (and, as a result, make it more difficult to procrastinate), but dogs thrive on routine.

Your dog will learn that things happen at certain times and will look forward to it. Your routine can be daily, with those grooming chores that should be done every day, and weekly, with those that only need to be done once a week.

Every day, you should give your dog a massage. When during the day you do it is up to you, but it does need to be done daily. When you massage your dog, you can feel for any health problems on or under the skin, such as lumps and bumps, ticks, and cuts or scrapes. You can also find any tangles in the coat, dirt or mud caked in the paws or legs, and any other grooming problems.

As you massage your dog, you are also spending quality time with her. This is great for bonding, and it's relaxing for both of you.

1. If you have a medium, large, or giant dog, sit on the floor and invite your dog to lie down in front of you. Small dogs can lie in your lap as you sit in a comfortable chair.
2. Turn your dog's paws away from you so she can't paw and scratch you.
3. Begin at her head, running your hands over her muzzle and lifting her lips to look at her teeth. Look at her eyes, running your hands over her eyelids, and check out her ears.
4. Massage her neck, running your fingers through the coat at her neck, under her collar, and down to her shoulders.
5. Continue down the shoulders to one front leg, rubbing down the leg to the paw. Check out her paw, looking between each toe and touching each toenail.
6. Massage her chest, back, and body, working to her hips and back legs. Don't forget her tail.
7. Flip her over and repeat on the other side.

If your dog has a thick coat, especially a double coat, make sure your fingers feel all the way through the coat to her skin. After several massages, your fingers will learn what she feels like and will be able to detect problems you might not be able to see. Make sure, too, that you feel her all over.

# Keeping Eyes, Ears, and Teeth Clean and Toenails Trimmed

## WIPING EYES

For most dogs, keeping eyes clean is easy. You can gently wipe a damp paper towel over the eyelids daily, wiping away any dirt or crustiness. However, for some breeds, such as Toy and Miniature Poodles and Bichons Frises, eye care takes a little more time. Some dogs just seem to produce more tears, and the dampness around the eyes can cause problems. The eyelids and skin around the eyes can be wiped with an antibacterial wipe (the kind made for use by people are fine), but then the skin and coat should be dried with a small hand towel. Don't let the skin and coat remain damp; it's not healthy.

If the hair under the eyes, especially between the eyes and the muzzle, turns color (often a rust-red), take your dog to the veterinarian to make sure that the eyes are healthy. Sometimes eyelids turn in toward the eyes, causing eyelashes to rub up against the eyes, resulting in irritation and eventually eye damage. This can cause excess tearing, and surgery is often required to correct it. However, if the eyes and eyelids get a clean bill of health, talk to your groomer about products to remove the discoloration from the coat.

# CLEANING EARS

Although some dogs protest having their ears cleaned, cleaning doesn't have to be a horrible chore, especially if you introduce it when your dog is young and you clean the ears very gently. Begin with cotton balls or the cotton pads used to remove makeup. You will also need witch hazel or a commercial ear-cleaning solution.

Before cleaning, lift the ear flap and take a sniff of each ear. The ears should smell slightly damp but should not smell bad. If you detect a dirty or yeasty smell, do not clean the ears but instead take your dog to the veterinarian so he can see the ears as they are. An early ear infection often can't be seen but will smell different, often yeasty.

To clean the ears:

1. Make sure that the witch hazel or ear-cleaning solution is at least room temperature. Never use it cold from the refrigerator.
2. Dampen several cotton balls or pads with the cleaning solution and then squeeze out the excess.
3. Lift the dog's ear flap up and fold it over the top of the dog's head.
4. Holding the dog's head with one hand, use the other hand to gently wipe out the ear with the cotton ball.
5. Wipe all the crevices of the ear but do not force the cotton ball into the ear canal; just get those areas that you can easily reach.
6. If the ears are dirty, change cotton balls as soon as they are soiled.

Photo by Sheri Wachtstetter

A healthy ear should have a damp but healthy smell. Teddy, a German Shepherd Dog, with owner Petra Burke, bred by Joel Towart, Bellington GSDs.

If your dog is anxious about ear cleaning or is protesting, don't try to wrestle with her. That will turn it into a hated chore. Instead, get a spoonful of peanut butter and, as you begin to work on her ears, scrape the peanut butter onto the roof of her mouth. She'll be so busy licking the peanut butter that she won't care what you do to her ears. In addition to distracting her, the peanut butter will serve as a reward, so ear cleaning becomes a more pleasurable activity.

Some breeds, such as Poodles and Schnauzers, grow hair in their ears. This hair needs to be removed, as it will get gummed up with earwax, potentially leading to ear infections. You can pull the hair out gently with your fingers or with forceps. If you have any questions about how to do this, or how much hair to pull out, make an appointment with a professional groomer to show you how to do it correctly. This can be quite painful if done incorrectly.

Unless your dog gets really dirty when playing, the ears only need to be cleaned weekly. If your dog gets an ear infection, her ears may need to be treated daily. Ask your veterinarian for guidance.

## BRUSHING CANINE TEETH

Keeping your dog's teeth clean is just as important to her good health as it is for you to keep your own teeth clean. Many studies have shown that disease in the gums, teeth, and mouth can travel through the body, primarily through the bloodstream, and can affect other organs. One study in particular found a direct link between a dirty mouth and heart disease in older dogs.

The tools for teeth cleaning need not be elaborate; you can use a child's small toothbrush and some baking soda. Although there are toothpastes made specifically for dogs, sometimes these taste too good, and it's tough to keep the dog's tongue out of the way—he's trying to eat the toothpaste! Don't use toothpaste made for people; the taste is much too strong for dogs, and not all the ingredients have been tested for safety on dogs.

1. Before you begin, mix a little baking soda (maybe a tablespoon) with just enough water to make a paste. You will dip the toothbrush in this paste and use it as you would toothpaste.
2. Invite your dog to sit in front of you or in your lap, depending on her size. You can wrap a towel around her neck or drape it over your lap.
3. Dip the toothbrush in the dampened baking soda, lift your dog's lips on one side of her muzzle, and gently begin brushing as you steady her head with your other hand.
4. Every few strokes, pick up some more baking soda.

If your dog is very unhappy with this process, stop after brushing the outside of the teeth of one-quarter of her mouth. Offer her a drink of water, and then tell her how brave she is and what a wonderful dog she is. Later, or even the next day, you can do some more. Gradually, by doing a little each day, you can get the entire mouth cleaned and, at the same time, get her used to this necessary chore.

Some dog owners have found battery-powered toothbrushes with moveable heads to be very effective. They make it easier to remove plaque build-up from their dogs' teeth. Wait until your dog is used to the teeth-cleaning process, though, before introducing a moving toothbrush, as some dogs are very sensitive to the sound of it.

## TRIMMING TOENAILS

Most dog owners hate trimming their dog's toenails, probably because they worry about cutting into the quick, making their dog bleed, and causing pain. Although this can happen, letting the nails grow too long isn't good for the dog, either. Long nails can cause the paw to become painful as the toes are stretched into awkward positions. If the toenails remain too long for an extended period, the paw can actually become deformed.

There are several types of toenail trimmers on the market, but the two easiest styles are the scissors type and the guillotine type. Ask for help at your local pet store to find the correct size for your breed of dog. You will also need some styptic powder on hand (also available from the pet store) in case you do make one of your dog's nails bleed.

To trim the nails:

1. If you are nervous and afraid, you might make your dog nervous, too. Have some peanut butter on hand so you can distract her, as you did during ear cleaning.

2. Take one paw, separate one toe, and pull all the hair away from the nail. If the nail is clear or white, you will be able to see the pink quick inside. If you cut into the quick, the dog will cry and the nail will bleed. The nail beyond the quick has no feeling at all—just like your nails—and this is where you should cut.

A white nail shows where the quick ends. Trim past that point. Hatcreek's Doctor Bashir, an Australian Shepherd, owned by Liz Palika, bred by Karen Russell.

*Photo by Sheri Wachtstetter*

3. If your puppy has black nails, check all her toenails. If she has even one white nail, you can use that nail as a trimming guide.

4. If there are no white nails, look at the nail from the side. The top of the nail is evenly curved but the underside has a small curve under the tip and then bulges down a little under the quick. You can safely cut the tip off.

5. If you do cut into the quick, dip the bleeding nail into styptic powder and hold the paw still until the bleeding stops. Then, continue with your trimming.

Trim the nails weekly so that you and your puppy get used to it. You may need to trim only the tips of the nails, but that's okay. You will become more skilled and sure of yourself, and your dog will learn to trust you.

# Combating Fleas, Ticks, and Mites

## FIGHTING FLEAS

Fleas, ticks, and mites are external parasites that feed on your dog. In addition to taking a drop of blood each time they feed, they can also transmit diseases—some quite serious—and can cause significant discomfort. A dog infested with fleas will scratch and chew until her skin is raw, and secondary infections will follow. Controlling these pests is essential for your dog's good health.

Fleas are tiny, crescent-shaped insects. They have flat sides so they can move through animal hair easily. They have a small head and a large abdomen. Fleas are the intermediate host for tapeworms and can cause anemia from blood loss, especially in small puppies or older dogs. Fleas feed on your dog and then move away. They actually spend most of their time in the dog's environment—in the house or yard, hiding in the dog's bed, or in your carpet.

New products introduced in the past decade have made flea control considerably easier. Some of these products kill adult fleas (which are the only ones that bite), while others are insect growth regulators that stop immature fleas from maturing. Some of the newer products do both.

If your dog is infested with fleas, you will want to approach flea control with a three-pronged attack:

+ **On your dog:** Talk to your veterinarian about a prescription for a systemic product such as Program or Sentinel. As the flea bites your dog, it will take a drop of blood that will be carrying the flea-control product.
+ **In the house:** Spray carpets, dog beds, baseboards, cracks, and crevices with an insect growth regulator and a quick-kill ingredient designed for indoor use. Make sure you read and follow the directions.
+ **In the yard:** Use a spray designed for outdoor use that contains an insect growth regulator.

Don't mix flea control products. Using a systemic product and then spraying your dog or putting a flea collar on her could potentially be deadly. Instead, talk to your veterinarian or groomer about which products are working best in your area, and then use them as instructed.

## TICKED OFF ABOUT TICKS

Ticks are eight-legged insects that bury their heads in a dog's skin to feed. They will stay on the dog until gorged, when they will drop off to breed and lay eggs. Like fleas, ticks can pass along diseases to dogs and people. The most deadly right now is Lyme disease, so ask your veterinarian if Lyme disease (or any other tick-carried disease) is prevalent in your area.

Some systemic flea control products are advertised as being effective at killing ticks as well, but nothing is as effective as a daily examination. If you massage your dog each day, you can feel with your fingers for bumps on your dog's skin. Or visually check the favorite hiding spots, which include the "armpit" areas of the legs, in and around the ears, the neck, and under and around the base of the tail.

When you find a tick, use tweezers or forceps to grab the tick and slowly pull it straight out of the skin. Twisting can break the head off, leaving it in the skin. Check the tick to make sure that the head is still attached; if the head has broken off in the skin, try to pull it out. If retained in the skin, an infection could result. Put some antibiotic ointment on the wound. Burn the tick or drop it in some alcohol. Do not flush it down the toilet; it will live!

## MIGHTY MITES

Mites are everywhere. Experts say that we clean, well-groomed people are exposed to mites all the time. Dogs have their own mites, even though we can't see them. There are two types of mites found on dogs: demodetic and sarcoptic.

Demodectic mites are on dogs all the time and usually cause no problems. But sometimes, when a dog is under stress or in puberty, the mites get out of hand. Small bald spots show up, usually on the face first, and then spread. The spots rarely itch, and the dog doesn't seem bothered at all. Unfortunately, this demodectic mange can cause severe problems in older dogs, although with treatment young dogs usually recuperate easily. Any unexplained bald patches should be seen by a veterinarian; never try to treat demodex on your own. Demodectic mites do not live on people.

Sarcoptic mites cause severe itching, and dogs will scratch continually, even to the point of drawing blood. Like demodectic mange, this problem requires veterinary care. Sarcoptic mange is contagious to other pets and to people.

# Grooming Basics

Although many breeds have very specific grooming requirements, some basic techniques apply to almost all dogs. Follow this list in order before giving your dog a bath:

Photo by Sheri Wachtstetter

1. Clean the dog's eyes, ears, and teeth first, as these can be a little messy.
2. Trim the dog's toenails.
3. Completely brush the dog next, before bathing her, as you want all the dead coat out; no need to wash that!
4. Make sure all tangles and mats are out before the bath, since getting them wet will only make the tangles worse.

## Bathing Your Dog

Once your dog is thoroughly brushed, gather together all the tools you will need. You need shampoo, conditioner (if your dog's coat is dry or tangles easily), several absorbent towels, and, if it's cool, a hair dryer (many hair dryers have a cool setting). If your dog is anxious about baths, have a few good treats within reach.

Brush your dog thoroughly prior to bathing. Nyssa, a Shetland Sheepdog, owned by Bruce and Margaret Reinbolt.

1. Test the water before putting your dog in the tub. It should feel warm but not hot.
2. Lift your dog into the tub, praise her for being brave, and pop a treat into her mouth.
3. Put a cotton ball in each of her ears to prevent water from running in.
4. Using a handheld spray nozzle, wet your dog thoroughly.
5. Begin working shampoo into her coat, starting at the head and working down her back toward her tail and down each leg. Don't forget under the chest, the belly, and between the back legs.
6. When she's covered with shampoo, give her a quick massage all over to loosen the dirt.

7. Begin rinsing at her head, tilting the head so that the water runs away from her eyes and ears. Work the coat with one hand as you rinse with the other. Make sure all the soap is rinsed out.

8. If you're using a conditioner, rub it into the coat now. Again, use your hands to give the dog a massage so the conditioner spreads evenly throughout the coat. (Conditioner is most effective on coats that can tangle; it makes the hair coat slicked and easier to brush out.)

9. Rinse out the conditioner, using the same technique you used for the shampoo.

10. Use one of the towels to blot the excess water off the dog before you take her out of the tub.

11. Put that damp towel on the floor or table, lift the dog out of the tub, and place her on that towel. Using a dry towel, get her as dry as possible.

12. Use the hair dryer to get her as dry as you can, especially if the house is chilly. If your dog is worried about the hair dryer, use it in short spurts and keep a supply of treats at hand. Praise her for being brave.

13. Once the dog is dry, brush and then comb her.

Most experts recommend bathing a dog only when she needs it. If she gets into something dirty, rolls in the mud, or smells doggy, bathe her. Sometimes dogs need to bathed more often. Dogs participating in dog shows, for example, must be freshly bathed and groomed prior to each show. Therapy dogs must be clean before each visit. Frequent bathing can dry the skin, so choose a gentle shampoo and conditioner that will keep the skin and coat healthy.

## Special Problems

The saying is that curiosity killed the cat, implying that cats are curious creatures. They are, but dogs are right up there in position number-two, especially if you're involved in the activity. Dogs want to be with us, even if that means getting into situations they really should avoid. As a result, dog owners have to clean up the resulting mess.

Here are ways to clean up some special messes:

+ **Gum and other sticky things:** Using your fingers, work vegetable oil into the coat around the gum, trying to loosen the gum. Then bathe the dog to get the oil out. If the gum has really worked its way into the coat and has gathered dirt and other debris, you will probably have to trim it out. Cut carefully, placing your fingers between the gum, scissors, and skin.

+ **Paint:** If the paint is water soluble, use soap and water to wash it away. Do not use paint solvents on your dog; most are toxic.

+ **Motor oil:** Dishwashing detergent will get out oil. Rinse well.

+ **Burrs, foxtails, and other grass seeds:** Most can be combed out or picked out with your fingers. If the seed is tangled in the coat, a little vegetable oil or hair conditioner can help smooth things and loosen the hair and grass seed. If the seed is really tangled, trim it out, cutting carefully.

+ **Quills and spines:** Quills and spines can be very painful. Call your veterinarian, as your dog will probably have to be sedated during the removal process.

+ **Skunk spray:** Nothing totally removes the odor of skunk spray, but you can lessen it. First, bathe the dog thoroughly in dishwashing detergent. This will not remove the smell but will remove any of the skunk's oils that contain the smell. Rub the dishwashing detergent into the coat really well, being generous with the soap. Rinse well. Then thoroughly rub vinegar or tomato sauce into the dog's coat, again being very generous. Let the dog sit for several minutes. Rinse well.

If your dog gets into something that sticks to her coat, a simple rule to follow is don't use anything on her skin or coat to remove the substance; that will cause even more problems. Once you are through treating her, your dog is going to lick that spot, so don't use anything even mildly toxic. If you have doubts, read the label. If you're still in doubt, don't use it. You can always trim whatever it is out of the coat. The hair will eventually grow back.

# Professional Grooming

A professional groomer is someone who has gone to school to learn how to care for the skin and coats of dogs. He knows how to brush out the coat and, when possible, untangle mats. He's familiar with the products available, including shampoos, conditioners, and flea and tick products. You can find a good groomer by asking for referrals. If your neighbor's dog is groomed regularly and looks handsome and well done, ask your neighbor where he takes his dog. You can also ask your veterinarian for a referral.

When your dog goes to a groomer's facility, the groomer will ask you what you want done. Do you want your dog trimmed for cleanliness? He can trim each foot around the pads, trim around the genitals, and trim under the tail. Or, would you like a short cut? A show cut? Just as you must convey your likes and dislikes when you get your own hair cut, you must communicate with the groomer.

When you leave your dog with the groomer, she will first be brushed out. The groomer can check on the health of your dog's skin and coat at that point. She will get her ears cleaned and anal glands expressed, and then will be bathed. She will be thoroughly dried and then brushed again. Her nails will be trimmed, and if she's going to have a haircut, she will get it now. She will then get any finishing touches.

If your dog's coat is too much for you to handle, call a professional groomer for help. Rookie, a Shetland Sheepdog, owned by Judy Davis.

# Training for Life

Although almost all training begins with teaching your dog to sit and lie down, training is much more than repeating simple rote exercises. Training is the process of teaching you how to communicate with your dog and teaching your dog to be compliant with you. When the two of you reach an understanding, wonderful things can happen.

## Canine Communication

As your dog's owner and trainer, it's up to you to learn how to communicate with your dog. Sometimes this can be a challenge. Although dogs are very good at studying people and figuring out what is wanted, there is often a communication gap. Keep in mind that this is communication between two different species. Dogs live in our homes and are our companions, but they were not born understanding English, Spanish, French, or any other human language, including human body language. Therefore, it's important that you learn as much as possible about canine communication so that you can understand and then teach your dog.

### BODY LANGUAGE

Your dog has complex body language. The movements, postures, and positions of his head, ears, eyes, mouth, tongue, tail, and entire body can convey a variety of meanings. For example, a dog standing tall yet relaxed, with upright ears, open mouth, relaxed tongue, and wagging tail, exudes confidence without aggression. Each body part, alone or with others, demonstrates what the dog is feeling.

Those feelings and postures can be enhanced by colorings or markings, especially on the face and tail. For example, when the eyes are outlined in black, with tan spots above the eyes, any movement of the eyes is exaggerated. This can make communicating with other dogs easier. Dogs lacking some of these markings, such as all-white or all-black dogs, are somewhat at a disadvantage and could potentially be misunderstood. A tailless dog, whether naturally tailless or docked, loses all the communication that a tail provides. Misunderstandings in the dog's world are often minor, primarily because dogs use more than one body part to convey emotions, but occasionally a fight can ensue.

When you understand what your dog is trying to convey to you through his body language, you can communicate better with him yourself. You can tailor your training techniques when you see that he's worried or frustrated; you can give him more confidence when you see that he's insecure or afraid; and you can applaud his efforts when he's accomplished something and is proud of himself.

Bowing is a play invitation that can be given to canine or human playmates. Sandstorm November Rain JC, CGC, a Saluki, owned and bred by Kathy Morton.

Photo by Kathy Morton

+ If your dog is fearful, he will lower his body almost to the ground, with elbows and hocks bent. His tail will be lowered, as will his head and ears. The tip of the tail may be wagging slightly. He may lick his nose.
+ Very fearful dogs—those so afraid that they may bite if cornered or pushed too hard—will also have a lowered body posture. The head and ears will be lowered, and the back of the lips will be pulled back, making the dog almost look like he's smiling. The eyes may look forward at the potential threat and then glance away. The tail will be tucked, even up against the belly, and will be still.
+ A submissive but not necessarily fearful dog may roll over and bare his belly. The tail may be tucked and still (if worried) or tucked and wagging (if simply submissive). The eyes will look away.
+ A dominant dog—one with the potential to take his dominance too far (with the possibility of a bite or fight)—will have all his body language moving forward. He will be on the tips of his toes leaning forward, with his head forward and eyes staring hard at his object of interest. The ears will be lifted and facing forward, and the tail will be up and wagging slowly or stiffly, or still. His hackles will probably be up.

- A confident dog who is interested or alert but has no need or desire to bite or fight will stand tall but also be relaxed. He will not be leaning forward. His head will be high but relaxed, with ears up and forward, and his hackles will be down. His tail will be wagging.
- An eager dog will not be standing still; he will dance, circle, or bounce up and down. His eyes will be toward you; his ears will be up and down, with openings toward you; and his tail will be wagging happily. He may lower his front end to bow, an invitation to play.

This is just a brief example of some body postures. Every breed and every individual dog has its own characteristics. For example, many herding breeds stare. This technique is used to control sheep and cattle, but herding dogs also learn to use it on their owners. Staring is usually an attention-getting device, because, when stared at, most owners respond, "What do you want?" and the dog could end up going for a walk or playing ball. In other breeds or dogs (such as guard and guardian dogs), a stare such as this could be a direct threat or the first step in aggression.

As you train your dog, you will learn to recognize other gestures. If your training is getting too serious, your dog may yawn at you. This is called a calming signal; your dog is basically saying, "Relax!" Some dogs, when they are getting frustrated or bored, will look away from you. This is the time to take a training break for a few minutes and rethink your training technique so that you can approach it from another angle. Watch your dog, get to know him, and use his means of communication to your advantage.

You may be using some of your dog's body language without knowing it because some stances are very similar to our own. A person who is confidant but not aggressive or pushy stands tall yet relaxed. A bully or pushy person who is trying to get his way stands tall and leans into people, invading personal space. A worrier pulls into himself, looks away without making eye contact, and uses small hand gestures.

You can communicate more easily with your dog if you copy some of your dog's body language, but just be careful that you are conveying the message you wish to share.

- If your dog is having a hard time with a new lesson, take some pressure off him. Instead of facing your dog straight on, turn so that you are at an angle, facing toward him and to the front. Make sure that your body language is relaxed, look at your dog (his paws, body, tail, face) without staring into his eyes, and smile. This conveys to him, "Hey, it's okay. No pressure!"
- If your dog is getting into trouble, especially when he understands that he's doing something your don't want him to do, stand tall, look him in the eye, and don't flinch. You have just conveyed your position as the dominant family member. Don't assume this position with a potentially aggressive dog, however; he will read it as a challenge!
- At the end of a training session, lift your hands high over your head, and then, with a big smile on your face, bring both hands down to your knees as you bend your body at the waist. You can also hop at the same time. You have just invited your dog to play!

# VERBAL COMMUNICATIONS

Dogs are very verbal creatures. They whine, warble, howl, bark, and growl to communicate with one another and with us. We don't even have words to describe many of their sounds. An

Australian Shepherd male named Riker makes a sound that can only be mimicked: a "woo woo woo." Riker found that this sound made his owner laugh, and when she laughed, she paid attention to him. So, he uses it!

Sounds vary from breed to breed and among individuals. The howl of northern breeds is quite different from the howl of a coonhound treeing a raccoon, and the alarm bark of a Chihuahua certainly differs from the alarm bark of a Rottweiler. But miscommunications among dogs are rare, even though many seem to be speaking different languages, primarily because verbal sounds are never used alone; they are always used in conjunction with body language.

Dog owners can use verbal communications in much the same way.

+ When asking your dog to do something, use a normal speaking voice; do not change your normal, comfortable body language.
+ When the dog does something you have asked him to do, praise him in a happy "ice cream" tone of voice. Your dog language should be relaxed. Move your hands and arms up and down a little: a small play-bow. Keep eye contact soft, allowing your eyes to move naturally.
+ If you catch your dog in the act of doing something he knows is wrong (not afterward, but as it is happening), deepen your voice (growl) and turn to look directly at your dog.

The goal of all verbal communication is to teach your dog to listen to you—not just when he wants to, but whenever you direct anything toward him. You want him to listen, not just when giving him commands but also when you need to tell him something to keep him from getting into trouble or to keep him safe.

# Training Tools and Techniques

Training techniques and styles have changed over time, just as any profession changes. Thirty years ago, almost all trainers used chain slip collars (often called choke chains), and food rewards or lures were not used at all. Dogs were praised enthusiastically for good work, and collar corrections (some quite severe) were used to let the dog know when he made a mistake.

Today, food is commonly used as both a lure and a reward, and the variety of training tools is growing almost daily. The techniques used to train dogs are much more varied today, too. Although this makes it difficult for dog owners to decide which technique to use, it's wonderful for the dogs themselves. The variety today provides a technique for dogs of every personality.

Some of the training tools being used today include:

+ **Leashes:** Leashes can range from 6- and 4-foot-long nylon, leather, or rope leashes used in obedience training, to short traffic leads used while training in off-leash work and many dog sports.
+ **Buckle collar:** This is the collar your dog should be wearing with his identification tag on it. Many dogs, especially once they understand what is being asked of them, need only this collar.
+ **Chain and nylon slip collars:** These collars have gotten a bad reputation because they are often misused. When used correctly, however, a slip collar should not hurt a dog. Instead,

the snap of the collar should convey only enough force to get the dog's attention. These collars should never be pulled tight by the owner (which could choke the dog), and the dog should never be allowed to pull on the collar.

+ **Head halters:** There are several makes and styles of head halters, and they all work on basically the same premise: Where the dog's head goes, the body will follow. As with any tool, these have been misused, too, and when misused (such as by yanking on the head halter with a leash, thereby jerking the dog's head), the dog can suffer neck and back injuries. However, when used correctly, with a gentle guiding motion and other training skills, this training tool can be very effective.

+ **Prong collars:** Although many people abhor these collars, it is primarily because of their look. However, the prongs are not sharp and do not dig into the dog's neck. Many expert trainers prefer this type of collar, especially for strong-willed dogs just beginning their training and who have taken control of their owners. Most of these trainers emphasize that the prong is not necessarily for long-term use, but just to control the dog until the owner can teach him.

+ **Food:** Although thirty, and even twenty, years ago, food simply was not used in dog training, trainers today have found that food can be a powerful training tool. It is a strong motivator, lure, and reward. The size of the food used should be appropriate to your dog. Toy dogs can work for tiny pieces, even crumbs, while a giant dog needs something a little bigger. And, of course, the dog must like the food being offered.

+ **Toys:** If your dog is not motivated by food, you can use other things instead. Tennis balls are great for many dogs, as are toys with a squeaker inside, or for terriers, furry mice made as cat toys. Just make sure that the toy is safe before you use it as a training motivator.

+ **Clickers:** Clickers are small, handheld contraptions that, when pressed, make a clicking sound. Originally used with dolphins that could not be trained using a leash and collar, the click is used to mark good behavior. When the dog realizes that the click equals good, which equals a food treat, he understands and can learn. Although the clicker is an effective training tool, it requires precise timing to work well. In addition, some dogs and people simply do not like the sound, and for them, this tool will not work.

+ **Your voice:** As mentioned earlier in this chapter, your voice is the most important training tool you have. Your voice helps your dog pay attention to you, guides him, and rewards him.

There are other training tools, such as citronella collars to stop barking, leashes that make a noise when the dog pulls, and harnesses that slow down dogs who pull when they go for a walk. Electronic collars are also gaining in popularity. Many of these tools, especially electronic collars, should be used only under the guidance of a trainer experienced in their use.

## TRAINING TECHNIQUES

Most trainers today use a much more positive method than those used many years ago. Trainers have found that the more compulsive training techniques, which were forceful ("You *will* do it!")

and used leash corrections and a harsh verbal correction when the dog made a mistake, weren't much fun for dog or owner. The dogs usually disliked the training sessions and, as a result, were rarely compliant or cooperated out of fear. Of course, owners rarely enjoyed the training, either.

Today, there is a wide variety of training techniques, but the two most prevalent ones are:

+ **Positive training:** Many trainers use what is often referred to as purely positive training. No corrections at all are used, and the dog is helped to do the right thing and then rewarded for it. Most positive trainers use a clicker, and all use either food or other motivators, depending on the dog.
+ **Balanced training:** Balanced training uses techniques from both positive trainers and compulsive trainers. They feel the positive techniques can be powerful training tools and use them eagerly, but also feel that dogs can learn from making a mistake. Letting the dog know that he has made a mistake may range from withholding a treat and praise to giving a verbal correction or a snap and release of the leash.

No matter which techniques are used, almost all trainers agree that dogs need to be taught what to do rather than simply be corrected for bad behavior. When a dog knows what acceptable behavior is and is consistently rewarded for doing it, he no longer needs to engage in the "bad" behavior.

Photo by Sheri Wachstetter

A group class can be full of distractions but can be fun, with dogs and owners all getting to know each other. Group class photo at Kindred Spirits Canine Education Center in Vista, California.

# Discipline Is Not a Bad Word

Many dog trainers and owners who embrace purely positive training techniques seem to feel that discipline is a bad word. But behaviorists and psychologists agree that discipline is not about corrections or punishment, and it's not about withholding rewards; instead, discipline is about leadership. Your dog needs a leader, and that leader must be you.

You, as your dog's leader, should have a vision of what you want the dog to grow up to be. Do you want him to sit for petting instead of jumping on people? Good! Do you want him to walk nicely on the leash? Wait for permission to go through open doors? Lie nicely on his rug while people eat? That vision can then be broken down into smaller, short-term, achievable goals.

Good leadership is all about high expectations and good communication. With those things in mind, you help your dog help himself. For example, a long-term goal could be that your dog will not jump on people. You then can teach him to sit for petting and praise. When he jumps up, use your voice: "Ack! No jump!" and help your dog sit. When he sits on his own, you praise and reward him.

Your body language, voice, and eye contact all convey to your dog that you have expectations for his good behavior and you expect him to comply. That's leadership. And discipline.

For example, dogs jump on people out of excitement and to greet people face to face—a very natural behavior for dogs. They don't understand, however, that jumping on people ruins clothes and knocks people down. A dog can be corrected in any number of ways not to jump up, but if he is only corrected, he will continue to jump up because he doesn't know what to do to get the attention he wants. In addition, with the corrections, he will become more and more anxious. However, if he is taught to sit and is greeted and petted in the sitting position, he no longer needs to jump up. The jumping will disappear.

To find a trainer in your area, ask for referrals. The veterinarians in your area will know who is good and who isn't because their clients tell them. If you see a nicely behaved dog walking down the sidewalk, ask the owner where they went for training. After you collect a few referrals, call and ask if you can come watch one of the trainer's classes. Leave your dog at home and just go and watch. Would you be comfortable with that trainer's techniques? Would you be able to learn in that class? Would these techniques suit your dog's personality?

Some trainers teach group classes, while others do private training. In a group class, you and your dog attend. The trainer is teaching you and then in class, you and your dog practice together. Group classes can be chaotic, with several other dogs and people attending, but at the same time, your dog can learn to behave himself with those distractions. The classes can be fun, too, as dogs and owners all get to know one another over time.

With private training, the trainer meets with you and your dog alone. Although this training is more expensive than group classes, some dog owners prefer this style of training because they like having the trainer's undivided attention.

## SIMPLE SKILLS FOR SUCCESSFUL TRAINING

Dog training is not a mysterious skill known only to a few; most dog owners, with a little help, can become successful dog trainers. Here are some skills that will make your training easier:

- Know what you want your dog to do. Set both short-term and long-term goals.
- Find a technique that is comfortable for both you and your dog, and then stick with it. Don't change techniques each time something doesn't work; you and your dog will both be confused.
- Give a command only once. If you repeat the command over and over, which one should he listen to? The first or the sixth?
- Show your dog exactly what you want him to do, help him do it, and reward him when he does it correctly.
- Timing is critical to success. Praise your dog as he does something right. If you use corrections, let him know as he makes a mistake.
- Remember that any behavior that is consistently rewarded will be repeated.
- Praise or corrections after the fact are not effective and can confuse your dog.
- Consistency is important—in your training and in enforcing the rules you have established.
- Always finish training sessions on a high note. Have the dog do something well and then reward him for it.

Training is a learning process for both you and your puppy. Don't rush it; take your time and watch your dog. When he's confused, worried, or fearful, take a break and think about what you're doing. Why is your dog reacting the way he is? How can you communicate with him in a better way? When he does get it, don't be stingy with the praise!

# Teaching the Basic Commands

All the training you do with your dog throughout his lifetime will begin with these basic commands. In addition, the basic commands can help enforce good behavior at home, on walks, and in public. Many of the basic commands can help bad behaviors disappear because they work as alternative behaviors. For example, as mentioned earlier in this chapter, sitting is an excellent alternative behavior for jumping up on people.

The techniques taught here are easy to learn. They use food as a lure with your voice and as a reward.

# WATCH ME

This command teaches your dog to pay attention to you. When your dog can pay attention to you, he can focus on you and ignore distractions, plus he can follow any additional commands you give him. To teach this command, have your dog on leash and hold the leash close to the dog with one hand (to keep the dog from jumping on you or dashing away). Hold a treat in the other hand and let your dog smell it. Then tell him, "Fido, watch me!" and take the treat from his nose to your chin. As his eyes follow the treat to your face, praise him—"Good boy to watch me! Yeah!"—and then pop the treat in his mouth.

Photo by Sheri Wachstetter

Hold the leash close as you use a treat to get your dog's attention, "Fido, watch me!" Ben, a Great Pyrenees, owned by Janine Staudt.

Repeat five times for this training session and then quit. Come back later and do it again five times. When your dog seems to understand, hold his leash loosely, stand up, and ask for a Watch Me. After about a week of practice, do the Watch Me as you walk one or two steps (and that's all for now) with your dog. When he understands and is doing it well, gradually add more distractions. When you find him looking at you and you haven't given him a command, praise him anyway!

# RELEASE

As you begin training your dog, he needs to understand when you are going to ask him to do something. That can begin with his name or with his name plus Watch Me. He also needs to know when a training exercise is finished. By teaching him what is called the Release command, he knows exactly when he's done and can then move, stretch, sniff the grass, and relax.

With your dog on leash, ask him to do a Watch Me. When he does, pop a treat in his mouth and praise him. Then tell him, "Fido, release!" and, using the leash, move him several steps, praise him, and pet him. From now on, every time he performs a command for you, tell him "release" when he's finished. If he doesn't move on his own, use the leash to get him up and moving, and then praise him.

# SIT

The Sit position, where your dog's hips are on the ground while his shoulders remain up, is the foundation of everything else your dog will do. Sit is also the replacement action for jumping up on people. With your dog on leash and the leash held in one hand, show your dog the treat held in the other hand. Let him sniff the treat. As he's sniffing, tell him, "Fido, sit," and move the treat back over his head. As his head comes up, his hips will move down. When he's sitting, praise him— "Good to sit!"—and pop the treat in his mouth. After a few seconds, tell your dog, "Fido, release," and encourage him to get up.

Practice the Sit five times and then take a break. Come back later and do it again. When your dog is beginning to Sit nicely on command, start using it. Have him Sit at the door before you let him go outside; sitting nicely will stop him from charging through the door. Have him Sit before he comes inside for the same reason. Plus, if the weather is bad outside, you can towel him off before you let him inside. Have him Sit before you feed him so he doesn't try to jump on you for his food. Look at your routine with your dog and have him Sit in any situation where you could use more control.

Use a treat in front of the dog's nose to help shape him into a Sit position. Then praise and pop the treat in his mouth. Ben, a Great Pyrenees, owned by Janine Staudt.

Photo by Sheri Wachtstetter

# DOWN

When you ask your dog to lie down, you want him to lie down on the ground yet be comfortable, and to remain in that position until you release him. Eventually your dog will be able to lie down and hold the position with distraction for up to half an hour at a time. This exercise is wonderful in situations where your dog should remain quiet and still, and when he needs to control himself.

Begin with your dog on leash, and then have him Sit. After you praise him for sitting, show him a treat. As you tell him, "Fido, down," move the treat from his nose to his paws. As his nose follows the treat, move the treat forward until he's lying down. Give him the treat and praise him. After a few seconds, release him.

Practice the Down five times and then take a break. Come back later and do five more. When he's doing the Down without too much fuss, have him lie down at your feet while you're relaxing in the evening. Give him something to chew on, but have him lie still while you relax. Or, when you're out on a walk and meet a neighbor, have your dog lie down while you're chatting.

# STAY

The Stay command is used with both the Sit and the Down. When the dog is in either position, tell him "Fido, stay," and show him the flat of your hand as a signal. Take a step or two away while holding onto the leash. Wait a few seconds and then go back and praise him, pop the treat in his

Keep one hand on your dog's shoulder as he Sits, and then, with the treat in the other hand, bring his nose down as you tell him, "Fido, down." Cobalt, a Shetland Sheepdog, owned by Dan Townley and Nancy Mueller.

mouth, and release him. If he gets up from the position before you release him, tell him, "No," put him back where he started, and repeat the exercise. Practice a few times in the Sit and a few in the Down, and then take a break. Come back later and do it again.

The Stay should never be released from a distance (don't call your dog from a Stay); instead, always go to your dog. Doing so helps create a reliable Stay that you can eventually (with practice) depend on.

## COME

The Come is a very important command, one that makes day-to-day living with a dog easier but also could be a lifesaver. You want to teach your dog that the word *Come* means to come to you, as fast as possible, every single time you call him. To do so, you want a really good treat or toy that your dog really likes. You also want a long leash, not a retractable one that has tension on it but a simple leash—even a length of clothesline. Holding the leash so that your dog is 8 to 10 feet away, show him the treat or toy and call him, "Fido, come!" Back away so that he has to chase you. If he's moving toward you, praise him, let him catch up to you, and give him the treat or toy. Praise some more: "Yeah! Good boy! Yes, you are!"

If he doesn't appear interested, continue to back up and then reel in the rope, helping him Come even if he doesn't particularly want to. While you reel him in, praise him, but don't give him the treat or toy. Next time, make sure that you are more exciting to him, either with your voice or with the treat or toy. Make him *want* to Come to you.

Repeat the training five times and then take a break. Come back later and do it again. As your dog learns the command, continue using the long leash but extend the distance. Then add some distractions. First have him Come when there's another dog around, and then some kids playing. Have him Come when a squirrel is out in the grass. Make sure that he will Come when you call no matter what the distraction.

## Jackpot!

Jackpot is a name for an extra-special treat or reward. When your dog does something very good, has put forth extra-special effort, or has mastered something he's had trouble with, give him an extra-special reward. Pop a handful of treats in his mouth as you tell him how wonderful he is, jump up and down, and pet him enthusiastically. A jackpot is supposed to both reward him and cause him to remember what caused it. Do *not* jackpot every effort; it will lose its effectiveness. Save it for special efforts.

## LET'S GO!

This exercise teaches your dog to walk nicely on a leash without pulling. The Heel position (dog's shoulder next to your left knee, which I discuss in the following section) is not emphasized; instead, keeping the leash loose is the goal. Have your dog Sit in front of you. Show him the treat and ask him to do a Watch Me. As soon as you have his attention, take a step backward, smile, tell him, Let's go!" praise him, and encourage him to step toward you. When he does, praise him and pop the treat in his mouth.

When your dog will take several steps following you while watching you, turn so that the two of you are walking forward together. Stop, have him Sit, and praise him. If he pulls away or pulls ahead of you, stop, get his attention with a Watch Me, and start again at the beginning, backing away from him. If your dog has a problem and really enjoys pulling on the leash, you will have to make sure that his Watch Me is very, very good, and you will have to keep this exercise short and sweet, praising each step that he takes with you.

## HEEL

This is a more formal walking position than in the previous exercise. Whereas the goal of Let's Go is to keep the leash loose, the Heel emphasizes a position in regard to you. The dog should walk with his shoulder next to your left leg. He should maintain that position whether you walk slowly, walk quickly, zigzag through a crowd, or even decide to jog to get out of the rain.

Begin by repeating the Let's Go exercise. When you and your dog are both walking forward, use a treat as a lure to focus your dog's attention on you while he's walking by your left side. At that

## Making the Treats Disappear

Sometimes people get the feeling that their dog is working for the treats rather than for them. That's a distinct possibility. But keep in mind that treats are a training tool just like your voice, the leash, and anything else you may use. At some point, however, you can begin to decrease the number of treats your dog receives.

When your dog knows a command or exercise well and will do it reliably every time you ask, even with distractions, you can begin to make the treat disappear. First, begin giving the treat only when the exercise is particularly good. For example, if you want to decrease the treats given for a Sit, begin giving a treat only when the response to the Sit is quick. Continue praising all Sits, but give a treat only when Sits are quickly carried out. Then give treats only when the Sits are quick and the dog's position is neat, with his hind legs tucked in (rather than sloppy and leaning). Gradually stop giving treats altogether for this exercise, but keep them for exercises that are not as strong, or when introducing a new exercise.

moment, tell him, "Fido, heel, good job!" After just a few steps, stop, have him Sit, and pop the treat in his mouth. This requires quite a lot of concentration, so keep the praise coming when he's in the correct position, and use a good lure to help him maintain it.

# Using These Commands

The obedience commands and exercises you're teaching your dog should not be used only during your training sessions. Your best results will be found when you incorporate them into your daily routine.

Have your dog Sit:

- ✦ When greeting people so that he doesn't jump on them.
- ✦ When you hook up his leash so that he's holding still.
- ✦ Before coming in from outside so that you can towel him off or brush him if he needs it.
- ✦ Before going outside so that you can give him permission to go out, and so that he doesn't charge through the door.
- ✦ When you give him a treat so that he doesn't jump up on you or grab for the treat.

Have him Sit and Stay:

- ✦ When you're fixing his meal so that he isn't underfoot, begging, or jumping for his dish.
- ✦ At the door when you're bringing something into or out of the house so that he doesn't dash out.
- ✦ At the gate when you take the trash cans out to the curb so that he doesn't dash out without permission.

Have him Down and Stay:

+ When you're eating meals so that he isn't begging under the table.
+ When guests come over so that he isn't pestering them.
+ When you want some peace and quiet in the evening.

Take a look at your normal routine in the house, when you're out for a walk, or even when you walk out to get the mail or newspaper. How can you make these training skills work for you? How can they make life with your dog easier?

Once you decide, share this information with everyone in the family so that everyone uses these skills in the same way. Remember, consistency is important.

Photo by Sheri Wachtstetter

Once you have learned how to train your dog, there is a whole new world out there. There is so much you and your dog can do together, for fun and for competition. Molly, a Standard Poodle, owned by Beverly Hodges, pictured with Beverly's grand-kids—Natalie, Mason, Caleb, and Rebekah Hill.

# Have Fun as You Continue Training

If you and your dog are having fun with your training, there is still much more you can do. The basic obedience skills are just the beginning. Find a trainer in your area who offers basic obedience classes so that your dog gets a chance to use the commands you've taught, but with the distractions of many other dogs and people. After he satisfactorily completes a basic obedience class, enroll for more training. He can learn to Come when called off leash, to finish back to the Heel position, to Stand and Stay, to Heel in a figure-eight pattern, and more.

Many dog sports might appeal to you and your dog, too. You can compete for titles in many sports, or train and participate just for the fun of it. You might decide to participate in a volunteer activity, such as therapy dog work or search and rescue. There's so much you can do!

## CONFORMATION COMPETITION

The American Kennel Club (AKC), United Kennel Club (UKC), Canadian Kennel Club (CKC), and other registries award championship titles to purebred dogs who successfully compete in their dog shows. The requirements for each registry's competitions vary, but basically the dogs must compete against other dogs of the same breed. Judges choose the dog(s) who, on that day, best represent all that is correct about the breed according to the breed standard. (The *standard* is a description of the breed usually written by the national breed club.) The dog's physical conformation (how he is put together) is being judged, as well as how he gaits (moves, usually in a trot) and, to a lesser extent, his temperament.

This is a very simplistic explanation of dog show competition. There is much more to it—so much so that entire books have been written on it. To get started, you will need a copy of the breed standard for your dog. You can go to the AKC's website (www.akc.org), the UKC's website (www.ukc dogs.com), or the registry that governs your dog's breed. You can print the breed standard for your dog.

The websites also have information about conformation competition as well as upcoming dog shows. Go watch a few shows, watch the dogs, and talk to people before entering your first show. To succeed, your dog must be an excellent representative of his breed; you may want to have some people who are knowledgeable of the breed (not friends and neighbors!) take a look at him. Showing can be a fun activity, but it is also very competitive; many people, especially breeders, take it very seriously.

## OBEDIENCE TRIALS

Many registries, including the AKC, UKC, and CKC, sponsor dog obedience trials. Dogs and their owners can compete at a variety of classes (levels), from novice through utility and on, to earn obedience titles and championships. In each class, dog and owner must perform a number of different exercises. For example, in the AKC's Novice class, the dog must Heel on leash and off leash, allow the judge to touch him in a Stand for exam, Come when called across the ring, and do a timed Sit-Stay and Down-Stay. When a dog and owner successfully compete at the Novice level according to the AKC's competition guidelines, the dog is awarded the title "Companion Dog." As the dog continues to compete, he can earn additional titles and even Obedience Trial Champion. The best obedience competition dogs have a strong desire to please, cooperate with training, and want to work with you.

The guidelines and competition rules for obedience are quite specific and require training prior to entering a trial. As with the conformation competition, go to the AKC, UKC, or CKC website and read through the obedience competition rules. You may also want to find a trainer in your area who specializes in competition training to assist you.

Photo by Sheri Wachtstetter

Once your dog knows the basic commands, there is so much more you can do. Although dogs today may learn to pull a cart for fun, many dogs have done so as an occupation throughout history. Kona, an Australian Shepherd, owned by Petra Burke, bred by Kathy Usher; and Kealy, a Pomeranian, owned by Cayla Horn.

## CANINE GOOD CITIZEN

The Canine Good Citizen (CGC) program was introduced by the AKC in an effort to promote and reward responsible dog ownership and, at the same time, to get well-behaved dogs some positive media attention. After all, too many times the only media attention dogs get is negative because something awful has happened. Since its introduction, many therapy dog programs have adopted the CGC test as a standard for evaluating new members.

To earn a CGC, the dog must pass a number of exercises, including sitting nicely when greeted by a friendly person, walking nicely on a leash, and demonstrating that he knows the Sit, Down, and Stay. For a list of all the CGC exercises and to find a trainer in your area who offers the CGC tests, go to the AKC's website, www.akc.org.

## RALLY-O

Rally-O is the newest sport offered by the AKC. At a Rally-O event, signs lead dog and owner through a series of exercises. The dog must perform one before going on to two, and so forth. The dog can do the exercises on leash or when well-enough trained, off leash. The exercises can be as simple as having the dog Sit, and then increase in difficulty. Many trainers are now offering Rally-O training. This is a great introduction to competition—it's fun, there's little to no pressure, and anyone can do it with some pre-training. Go to the AKC's website, www.akc.org, for more information.

## AGILITY

Agility is a great sport, with the dog running through tunnels, jumping over jumps of various kinds, and climbing obstacles, all against the clock. It takes quite a bit of training to be competitive and win. However, agility can also be a fun sport just to do, even if you have no desire to compete. Many trainers incorporate agility into their training programs as confidence builders for puppies.

To compete, the dog must be in great physical condition; an out of shape dog will be slow and prone to injury. Dogs perform off leash, so they need a good foundation in obedience. Owners must also be in shape (some running is involved), and dog and owner must work well together as a team.

If you decide to compete, there are several organizations that offer competitions and titles. The AKC, UKC, Australian Shepherd Club of America, and United States Dog Agility Association are the most popular.

Agility is a great sport for dogs of all sizes. Chasan's Noble Lovejoy CGC RN NJP, therapy dog, a Basset Hound, owned by Marianne Lovejoy.

## FLYBALL

Flyball is a popular sport that combines running and jumping, two things dogs excel at, with tennis balls, every dog's favorite toy! This is a team sport, with two teams of dogs running and jumping along side each other. The dog leaves his owner, jumps over four hurdles, then jumps on the side of a wall, triggering a mechanism that throws out a tennis ball. The dog grabs the ball, turns back and returns to his owner over all the hurdles. The team that gets all its dogs over the course first wins. The North American Flyball Association awards titles for competing dogs.

## LURE COURSING

Only sighthounds can compete in this event, which uses the breed's natural instincts to follow prey by sight rather than scent. A plastic bag is hooked to a pulley mechanism that makes the plastic bag move quickly and "flash" like a rabbit's tail. Sighthounds participating in this sport should have a desire to run, be in good shape, and have a foundation in basic obedience, as you will need to call your dog to Come at the end of the race.

Photo by Sheri Wachtstetter

Therapy dogs can be of any size, breed, or mixture of breeds. They must have a solid foundation in obedience training. A group of Love on a Leash therapy dogs.

## Therapy Dogs

Therapy dogs are privately owned dogs who, with their owners, visit people in nursing homes, hospitals, day care centers (for kids and for the elderly), and provide warmth and affection, a break from the daily routine, and laughter. Therapy dogs can be of any breed or mixture of breeds; they simply must love people and be well socialized to people of all ages, sizes, and ethnic backgrounds. A solid foundation of basic obedience is required.

## There Is More!

Obedience competition will challenge your training skills, and agility is great fun, but there is still more you can do with your dog. If he is of a herding breed, he can learn to work sheep and compete for titles. If he's a terrier bred to hunt vermin, he can participate in earthdog trials, going down a tunnel to find a caged rat (which is not harmed by the way). Dogs with good scenting abilities can learn to track. Those dogs bred to work and be protective can train and compete in Schutzhund trials, which test the dog in tracking, obedience, and protection. If you enjoy training and having fun with your dog, check out some of these sports and see which one would suit you (and your dog) best.

# Preventing and Solving Problems

*A*lthough most dog owners would love to have a relationship with their dog in which nothing ever goes wrong, unfortunately, at some point in their lives, most dogs do get into trouble. Dogs jump on people, smearing them with dirt or mud and knocking down small children or the elderly. They bark, creating bad feelings between neighbors. Dogs destroy things that don't belong to them and dig holes in the lawn. And there's more, such as food guarding, mouthing, leg lifting, mounting, and trash-can raiding. At times, dogs can seem downright uncivilized!

It is important to remember that dogs are dogs. They are not people in fuzzy dog suits. All the behaviors we feel are problems are very normal behaviors for dogs. They bark to communicate, jump up on people to greet them face to face as they would other dogs, urinate to mark territory, and so on. However, just because dogs do these things normally doesn't mean that we have to tolerate these actions.

## What Can You Do?

The key to controlling most problem behaviors is to manage your dog and her environment so that you can teach her more desirable behaviors. It is much easier to make a few changes in your dog's life and yours, perhaps even to your home or your schedule, so that you can prevent problems from occurring. Then, simultaneously, teach your dog something she *can* do, and will enjoy doing, in

Good aerobic daily exercise is good for all healthy dogs but is more important to dogs prone to bad behaviors. Silken Windhounds, Ch. Talisman's Byzantine Empire, owned and bred by Joyce Chin, and Kristull Rhett Ronan, owned by Stephanie Gallenson, bred by Francie Stull.

place of the problem behavior. At the same time, though, it's important to understand that many things can lessen the incidences of problem behaviors.

## HEALTH PROBLEMS

Many trainers and behaviorists feel that as much as 20 percent of all behavior problems may have some root in physical or health-related problems. Thyroid or hormone imbalances can cause behavior problems, as can many medications. Seizure disorders may have a relationship with unpredictable aggression. A bladder or urinary tract infection can cause housetraining difficulties. An ear infection can cause enough pain that the dog will snap when her head is touched. Many, many physical and health problems can cause behavior problems or changes in normal behavior.

When your dog's behavior changes, especially if the changes are sudden, call your veterinarian before you call a trainer. Tell your veterinarian you want to rule out a health problem first, before consulting with a trainer, and ask for a thorough exam and physical for your dog. During the exam, give your veterinarian as much information as you can think of, even if you're not sure it has any bearing on the problem. Let him sort through the information. If he finds a problem, then treat it and see if the behavior disappears. If no problem is found, then call your trainer or behaviorist.

## EXERCISE

Very few dogs get as much exercise as they should. Even though a dog home alone in a big backyard might dash back and forth a few times, she is not going to do enough for the movement to be considered aerobic activity. Aerobic activity for most dogs is a fifteen-minute game of chasing the tennis ball, or a run alongside a bicycle, or a jog with you. Obviously, a Basset Hound's exercise needs will differ from a Doberman Pinscher's, but both need aerobic exercise of some kind every day.

Photo by Sheri Wachtstetter

Play can be exercise, too, but the most important part of play is your participation. Kealy, a Pomeranian, owned by Cayla Horn.

When a dog doesn't get enough exercise, she's more apt to look for stuff to do, and very often that ends up a problem behavior. She may run back and forth along the fence, barking, or she may chew up your landscaping. Just keep in mind that a tired dog is a happy dog.

If your dog is very young, or elderly, or has some physical problems, talk to your veterinarian about an exercise program before you begin. Your vet may suggest a lower-impact form of exercise, such as swimming, rather than running and leaping for a ball. No matter which form of exercise you do, begin it gradually. Sore muscles are no fun for anyone, human or canine.

## PLAY

Your dog needs time to play with you every day. The playtime may happen while you're exercising, or it can be later, in the house. The key ingredient to play is laughter, and that's what makes it so special. When you play with your dog and laugh with her (with her, not at her!) you feel better, and the relationship with your dog—the bond you have with her—is strengthened. This is especially important when your dog has some behavior problems and you feel that she's always in trouble.

Play doesn't have to be structured. Give your dog a tummy rub and scratch her. Laugh while she wiggles around and kicks a back leg. Play hide-and-seek, hiding her favorite ball, and then encourage her to find it. Do some trick training and laugh as you help her succeed. You and your dog can make up your own games; after all, it doesn't matter what you do as long as you both are having fun.

# NUTRITION

Nutrition can definitely affect your dog's behavior. If your dog is eating a food that she cannot digest well, or is eating a less-than-good-quality diet, her body may be missing some vital nutrients. Dogs lacking something in their diet might eat dirt, chew on rocks or wood, or even try to gnaw the stucco off the side of a house. Other dogs seem almost desperate and will chew on anything within reach, in a frenzy almost, to try to find that ingredient needed.

Other dogs may be eating the best commercial foods on the market, the super-premium foods, and will react with a type of hyperactivity. They can't sit still, can't control themselves, and certainly can't follow directions for training. In these situations, the food may be awesome but is too much for these dogs.

In many instances, a more natural food is needed, one that includes meats and fish, cheeses, tubers (potatoes, sweet potatoes, and yams), and fruits. Avoid cereal grains, as these can cause allergic reactions and hyperactivity in many dogs. You can put together a diet yourself or check into one of the dehydrated foods now available. See chapter 4 for more on nutrition.

# TRAINING

Training can teach your dog what she is supposed *to do*. It provides her with guidelines for behavior that is acceptable to you. For example, a big dog that jumps on people is potentially dangerous, never mind annoying. If you simply yell at her for jumping up, or you correct her constantly for jumping, she is still going to need to jump because greeting you face to face is natural for her. When she gets worried about all the corrections, she's going to be even more anxious and will jump any time she can. However, if you have her Sit every time you greet her, bending over to pet her while she's sitting and giving her that opportunity to greet you face to face, you will remove her need to jump.

Photo by Sheri Wachtstetter

Training helps teach your dog good skills but also enforces your leadership role. Practice your training skills often. Ludwig, a German Shepherd Dog, pictured with owner Sally Kayser.

Although some dog owners think of training as simply teaching the dog some "tricks"—Sit, Down, Stay, Come, and Heel—it is really much more than that. You are also providing alternative behaviors that she will be praised and rewarded for doing.

Keep your training as positive as possible, focusing on helping your dog do what you wish her to do. However, remember discipline is not a dirty word and when used correctly, can be a valuable aid to training. Withholding a potential reward is discipline. If you want Lady to sit nicely by your side when you're talking to your neighbor, have some training treats in hand (or pocket). If Lady sits nicely, doesn't bark, and waits patiently for you, she should get a treat every so often, depending upon her age and level of training. However, if she's pushing the envelope, is wiggling, whining, moaning, and otherwise being disruptive, the treats stay in the pocket and you should have her lie down and Stay. Review chapter 6 for more training help.

## MANAGE THE DOG'S ENVIRONMENT

One of the most important things you can do to help curb some behavior problems is to manage your dog's environment so that you can prevent the problem from occurring. By managing her environment, you can ensure that some behaviors simply do not happen at all, or you can limit other behaviors. For example, if your dog spends the day outside while you're at work but has been digging up your backyard, chewing on the trees, and ripping up your garden, build her a dog run. Make it big enough so that she can play, relieve herself, and move around. Make sure there is shade and sun, and unspillable water. Let her do what she pleases here, and then when you come home and can supervise her, let her out of the run to spend time with you. By managing the environment, you have stopped the behavior from occurring. Later, when she's grown up, well trained, and is on a good exercise schedule, you can then begin allowing her more freedom. But that may be months or even years from now.

Managing the environment may mean using baby gates in the house to restrict your dog's access to parts of the house. It may mean taking the trash cans out before they are full, or closing bedroom doors. By managing the dog's environment, you are setting her up to succeed.

## INTERRUPT BAD BEHAVIOR

When you catch your dog in the act of doing something you don't want to continue, interrupt her. Your voice, "Ack!" can be a good interruption. If she's too excited or doesn't listen well, use a squirt bottle as you use your voice. The leash can also be used as a back up to your voice. Once you have interrupted the behavior, give her some directions—what should she do instead?

For example, when someone comes to the door, she will run to the door barking hysterically when she hears the doorbell. Tell her, "Thank you, Lady, that's enough." (After all, her job is to tell you that someone is there.) Have a leash in hand and clip it on her collar and have her Sit. Let your guest in. If your dog loses her mind, interrupt the behavior, "Ack! Quiet!" and enforce the Sit, "Lady, sit! Good job!" When she behaves herself, don't ignore her by paying attention to your guest, but praise her, "Good girl to sit and be quiet! Yeah!"

## Corrections After the Fact Do Not Work

What happens when you come home from work and find that your dog has chewed up a sofa cushion or has dug a huge hole in the middle of your lawn? Do you drag your dog over to the problem and yell at her? Do you shake her as you point to the mess and scream? Many dog owners do. Does it work? No.

Corrections after the fact, or corrections given after the behavior is completed, do not teach a dog what not to do. What these corrections will do is cause your dog to be submissive to you, to slink and even urinate when you come home, and perhaps even fear your unpredictable behavior. Your dog will understand that you're angry about the sofa stuffing or the hole in the backyard, but she will not put that together with the action she performed hours ago.

Instead of correcting the dog, look upon this as your mistake.

# Specific Problems

This section gives guidelines for some specific problem behaviors. Keep in mind, though, that every dog is an individual and although these guidelines do work and have been tested on hundreds of dogs, you may need more help than is provided here. If you follow these guidelines and find you're still having trouble, call a trainer or behaviorist for more help. You should also call for help if your dog is showing any signs of aggression toward you or other people. It is especially important to call for help right away if you have a feeling that your dog may bite, or if she has already bitten. Don't hesitate; call for help immediately.

## MOUTHING

All puppies use their mouths to manipulate the world. They chew on toys, on their food, on their littermates, and when they can, on people. Puppies don't have hands and so their mouths become their tools to control things in their environment. Unfortunately, puppy teeth are very sharp and can draw blood, and dogs that grow up and continue to use their teeth on people will be in a great deal of trouble. A dog that bites for any reason can be taken from you and euthanized, while you could face criminal and civil procedures. See chapter 8 for more on biting dogs.

Puppies must learn when they are very young that biting is not allowed in any situation. If your puppy tries to bite during playtime, simply tell your puppy, "Ack! No bite!" and stand up and walk away. Stop the playtime immediately at the first attempt at mouthing. You must make this very clear to your puppy. If you allow some mouthing and stop other mouthing, your puppy will never be reliable. Instead, be very clear; it simply is not allowed.

## Temper Tantrums

Puppies (and young adult dogs) can throw temper tantrums when things don't go their way. Perhaps you took a chew toy away from your dog or told her that she wasn't allowed on the sofa, and she began barking, crying, growling, and throwing herself around. A temper tantrum is bad behavior. You do not want to ignore a temper tantrum, nor do you want to give your dog what she wants. You need to handle this carefully; if you are aggressive to your dog, you could make it worse. Calmly remove your dog from the situation (away from the toy or away from the sofa) and put her in a quiet place to calm down. Her crate is fine. Leave her for fifteen minutes or so, and let her out with the leash hooked to her collar. If she behaves herself, great. If she's still angry and tries to get her way again, use the leash to control her and have her do a Down-Stay or some other obedience commands. If she throws another tantrum, put her back in her crate.

If the puppy attempts to mouth or bite during grooming, hold the puppy by the scruff of the neck by one hand as you close her mouth with the other hand as you tell her, "Ack! No bite!" Don't be rough; don't be aggressive; simply convey what you want the puppy to learn.

Supervise all play with the puppy and the children in the family (and their friends). When the puppy gets too stimulated and wants to chase and mouth the kids, take the puppy away. Put her in her crate for a timeout and let her relax a while. Never leave the puppy (or dog) and young kids alone.

If you have an older puppy or dog who tries to bite either you, your family, or other people, don't waste any time—call a professional trainer or behaviorist for help. A biting dog is a major problem that must be dealt with right away.

## JUMPING ON PEOPLE

Dogs jump on people to greet them face to face. Young or subordinate dogs lick the muzzle of older more dominant dogs; it's a greeting and a sign of respect. Unfortunately, dogs don't realize that jumping on people can ruin clothes and that hard nails can scratch skin. In worst case scenarios, a jumping dog can knock down a person, potentially causing injury.

If a dog is continually corrected for jumping, perhaps by being kneed in the chest, yelled at, or even by having his paws grabbed and held tightly, his anxiety about greeting this person or persons is going to increase. It's important to teach the dog how to greet people in an acceptable way where she can perform her greeting rituals and be greeted in return. When this happens, her need to jump up disappears.

If the dog is off leash, as she runs toward you, make sure your hands are empty (drop your purse or briefcase). As she begins to jump, grab the scruff of her neck; all that loose skin is a great handle and does not cause her any discomfort. Tell her, "Lady, no jump. Sit!" and using the scruff as a handle, shape her into a sitting position. Keeping one hand on her scruff so she doesn't jump up, pet her and praise her for sitting. "Good girl to sit! Yeah!" Let her greet you, too, so she feels she has done her part. Keep a hand on her until she relaxes. Turn away as you let go of her (she'll be less likely to jump on your side). Do not try to rush this, especially in the beginning. If the dog feels rushed or that she hasn't been able to greet you properly (in her mind), she will continue to jump.

When the dog jumps on other people, it's usually easier to have the dog on leash. That's easy when you're out for a walk, but at home that means you need to leash the dog before people come in the house. You might want to post a sign, "Knock, please, but don't walk in until I leash the dog." If your dog likes to jump on guests, they will be very happy to wait until she's leashed! With your dog on leash, have her Sit as your guests walk in. Tell your guests not to pet her until she can Sit without jumping. That might mean you have to hold her collar in the beginning to help her hold the Sit position. Again, give her a chance to greet the people, too, as they pet her. Use the same technique when you're out on a walk; have the dog Sit before she's allowed to greet people or people are allowed to pet her.

# EXCESSIVE BARKING

Dogs bark; that's how they communicate. Your dog may bark to let you know someone is approaching the house or that a family member has pulled into the driveway. Unfortunately, many dogs also bark when someone is walking down at the other end of the block, or when a neighbor sneezes. Dogs also bark when they are lonely, bored, or hear another dog bark. Excessive barking, especially nonstop barking, causes more problems among neighbors than just about anything else.

The first step in controlling barking is to make sure that the dog is getting plenty of aerobic exercise every day. A tired dog who is getting plenty of owner attention is less likely to be bored, even if left alone for several hours each day.

Then, take a look at your dog's environment; why is she barking? You might want to stay home from work one day and pay attention to the times and places where your dog barks. Does the school bus drop the kids off near your

Photo by Sheri Wachtstetter

The Sit is an alternative action that helps dogs learn not to jump on people; they cannot jump up if they're sitting! Chante, a Standard Poodle, with owner Mary Moore; Quimby, an Airedale Terrier, with owner Maggie Moore; and Sailor, a Standard Poodle, with owner Mary Katherine Moore.

house? Do any of the kids tease your dog? Or, does the neighbor's dog bark, causing yours to answer? When you know what triggers the barking, it's easier to try and prevent it.

Most barking can be stopped by interrupting the behavior. You can do so personally, "Lady, quiet!" or there are mechanisms available commercially that make a high pitched sound when the dog barks. The dog must be praised when she stops barking, however, for the interruption to continue to work. You cannot ignore the quiet, you must praise her for it. "Good girl to be quiet! Yeah!" and then toss her a treat or throw the tennis ball for her.

Hard-core barkers may need more help than this. If your neighbors are complaining, animal control or the police have been out to your house, and you've either been cited or threatened with a citation, then call for professional help. There are lots of gadgets that are advertised as excellent for stopping barking, including citronella collars and electronic collars, but all should be used only under a trainer's supervision. These gadgets do not address the root of the problem; why is your dog barking in the first place? If you are able to stop the barking but do not solve the underlying problem, your dog will most likely misbehave in another way.

## DESTRUCTIVE CHEWING

Destructive chewing can be an expensive bad behavior. After all, the cable repair guy will charge you each time he has to come to the house to repair the cables your dog chewed! It can also be a dangerous behavior, should your dog chew live wires or swallow some of the stuff she's chewing up.

To curtail chewing, you need to first teach your dog what is appropriate for her to chew. Hand her a toy and praise her, "Here's your toy! Good!" Do this often, and when she picks up her toy on her own, praise her even more. Make her wiggle with happiness!

You also need to limit your dog's access to places where she can chew stuff. That means in the house, she should be in the room with you and nowhere else. If you go to another room, she goes with you. If she has access to the garage from the backyard, fence off areas where she can get into trouble. *Never* think that something is unchewable or unattractive to your dog—we simply cannot second guess what a dog will chew on.

Then, make sure your dog has vigorous aerobic activity every day. A tired dog will be less likely to get into trouble than a dog who is full of energy.

## THE LANDSCAPE ARTIST

Some dogs can be incredibly destructive in the backyard: digging up the lawn, chewing on plants and trees, and uprooting the garden. These behaviors can have several different sources. First of all, if your dog likes to uproot plants, don't let her watch you dig holes and plant new plants. After all, if you can do it, why can't she? Also, those new plants probably have good smelling dirt in their pots, most likely with some bone meal or manure. That's an invitation to a dog, "Come dig here!" Dogs dig for many reasons, from chasing that gopher in your yard to trying to bury a toy or bone. The things that we call problems in the yard are all very natural behaviors.

Have you heard the adage "Good fences make good neighbors"? Well, good fences also can protect your garden. Put up some decorative fencing around your special gardens or plants. You may think they look out of place initially, but you'll get used to them, especially if they teach your dog to leave your garden alone.

Photo by Sheri Wachtstetter

Digging is not only unsightly in your yard but can also be dangerous should someone step in the hole. Hatcreek's Doctor Bashir, an Australian Shepherd, owned by Liz Palika, bred by Karen Russell.

The landscape artist also needs good, vigorous, aerobic activity every day. If she's tired—good and tired—she's not going to have any energy left over to ruin your garden! She also needs training on appropriate backyard behavior. When she approaches a garden fence, tell her to leave it alone, call her away and praise her.

If your landscape artist must be left alone for many hours each day, seriously consider building a dog run. It should be large enough for her to run back and forth, play, and still have a spot to relieve herself. It should have shade and a source of unspillable water. The dog run will prevent her from getting into trouble so that when you come home, you won't be mad at her and can then let her out to spend enjoyable time with you.

## DASHING THROUGH OPEN DOORS AND GATES

Dashing out the front door, garage door, gate, or even an open car door can be very dangerous. If the dog takes off at a run, she could easily end up in the street where she could be hit by a car. Luckily, this habit can be easy to break for most dogs.

Start with refreshing your dog's training. She needs to Sit quickly on command, and on leash, and hold her Sit-Stays. Practice in the house and outside so she can do her Stays with distractions.

## A Place of Her Own

If you have a dog who really enjoys digging or a breed that is known to dig (most terriers, German Shepherds, and Labrador Retrievers, to name just a few), you may want to give your dog a place where she can dig to her heart's content. Find a spot in your yard where the digging won't bother you, such as behind the garage or in an out-of-the-way spot. Dig up that area well, making the dirt soft. Take a handful of dog biscuits and stick them in the dirt so that the ends are sticking out. Invite your dog to find them. When she's eaten them, while she's watching, take a few more and bury them in the dirt—not very deep—but just so they are covered with dirt. Encourage your dog to find them. Every once in a while, bury another handful so your dog knows that this is the fun place to dig.

At the same time you're refreshing these commands, begin giving your dog permission to go through any door in the house, as well as gates and car doors. If your dog wants to go outside, have her Sit and hold her collar as you tell her, "Lady, wait." Open the door and have her hold her Sit. Then tell her, "Lady, go ahead," as you release her. You must be consistent with this exercise; she needs to learn to control herself and wait for permission.

When she's had a couple of weeks of practice, put the leash on, have her Sit at the door she goes in and out of the most, and tell her to Sit. Praise her for sitting. (Don't forget the basic training skills!) Then tell her to Stay and take a step away from her and open the door. If she dashes out, just hold on to the leash; she may hit the end of it. You can also tell her she made a mistake, "Ack!" and bring her back to the original position and have her Sit-Stay again, closing the door. Repeat the exercise several times, stopping when she succeeds and holds her Sit-Stay.

Eventually move around the house to all doors, and then go outside to the garage door and gate. When she does that well, train in the car, having her wait before she jumps into or out of the car doors.

If she makes it past you and is dashing around, don't chase and never ever correct her when you catch her. If you do, next time she'll make sure you never catch her! Instead, use your Come command in a very positive tone of voice, make things look like great fun, and even shake a box of dog treats. Make your dog *want* to Come to you. Then, look at where the mistake happened and begin training again.

# SEXUAL BEHAVIORS

Sexual behaviors are very normal; they are a part of reproduction. However, some dogs will perform them inappropriately—almost to the point of being obsessive about it—and others seem to feel the best time to perform is with an audience. Other behaviors are sexual in nature but are used to assert dominance over other dogs, or worst case scenario, over people.

The most commonly seen behaviors include leg lifting, mounting, and masturbation. Leg lifting to urinate on vertical surfaces is called marking, and although done primarily by male dogs, is sometimes also done by very dominant females. Mounting behaviors (humping, grasping with the front legs and moving the hips) is also primarily done by males, but as with leg lifting, can sometimes be performed by dominant females. Masturbation is almost always done by male dogs, very rarely by females.

Spaying the female and neutering the male usually will decrease all these behaviors, though not overnight. It takes a few weeks before any noticeable change will be seen.

Unfortunately, these behaviors usually have a root in the relationship between the dog and owner, or dog and another family member. There may be a relationship where the dog is treated as a person rather than a dog. Sometimes a dog is the answer to the empty-nest syndrome or is providing company for someone who lost a spouse, child, or other family member. Although this is fine, the dog must still be treated as a dog rather than a person. When the dog is overly demanding, gets everything she wants, and is never asked to do anything, she can develop a greatly inflated ego. Invariably this leads to behavior problems.

Many dog owners also seem to feel that because leg lifting is natural—just something male dogs do—it should be allowed to continue. No! Male dogs can learn, with an owner's guidance, that they lift their leg to urinate and that's all. Marking every vertical surface on a walk or in the backyard is rude! If allowed to continue, it invariably gets worse and can eventually begin to happen indoors. Eventually, the dog cannot be trusted not to lift his leg anywhere and can no longer go to the pet store for a treat or to a friend's house.

To solve this problem, the dog should first be spayed or neutered, if that hasn't already been done. Then the dog and owner (or family) relationship should be evaluated by a neutral third party, a trainer or behaviorist, to make sure there are no underlying problems. The dog's training should be refreshed, with emphasis on the basic commands. Although the training should be fun, there must also be some emphasis on encouraging the dog to comply with the training.

The environment must also be managed. Any surfaces that have been urinated on should be removed or cleaned thoroughly with a cleaner made for removing urine. Carpet should be pulled up or cleaned professionally. If the dog uses any cushions or toys for humping, those should be thrown away. Then, the dog's access to the house should be limited to the room where you can supervise him. If he isn't with you, he's in his crate or outside.

Any instances of sexual behavior should be interrupted immediately. Any leg lifting, mounting, or masturbation should be stopped cold. The interruption can be verbal if the dog will listen, or it can be verbal backed up by a squirt from a spray bottle.

# When You Need Professional Help

Asking for professional help is not an acknowledgment of failure or a sign that you've given up on your dog, nor should it be embarrassing. After all, you take your car to a professional mechanic when it's broken, and you go to the dentist when you have a toothache. A professional trainer or behaviorist is there to help you with your dog. You can call her whenever you need help, whether for puppy class or obedience training, fun classes like trick training, or when your dog has a behavioral problem.

There are some very specific times when you should call for help:

- ✦ When your puppy or dog throws temper tantrums that worry you, and when they escalate in frequency.
- ✦ When you feel overwhelmed by your dog's behavior—when you feel you can't handle her and when you think she's smarter than you are.
- ✦ When your dog has been doing well but suddenly regresses and is doing several bad behaviors that have not been allowed in the past.
- ✦ When your dog guards her food, treats, or toys; or growls, barks, or snaps at anyone who comes close.
- ✦ When your dog growls or snaps when you ask her to get off the sofa or bed.
- ✦ Whenever your dog acts aggressively toward any member of the family.
- ✦ When your dog acts aggressively toward unthreatening people while out on a walk or out in public.
- ✦ When your dog shows signs of being aggressive toward other friendly, nonthreatening dogs.
- ✦ When your dog bites you or any other person.

Far too many dogs are given up by their owners because of behavior problems. As mentioned at the start of this chapter, these problems are natural to the dog—they are not problems to her. Nor are they directed at you, personally. So before giving up, get some help.

# Responsible
# Dog Ownership
# (and the Law)

*O*wning a dog is not as simple as just picking up a dog at a shelter and feeding him. As mentioned throughout this book, dogs cannot care for themselves. They need quality food, regular veterinary care, daily grooming, playtime, exercise, and training. Dogs need to be a part of the family and feel as though they belong. With the help of caring owners, dogs can be a wonderful part of our lives and communities.

Unfortunately, not everyone who has a dog is willing to go to these lengths. As a result, the word *dog* has developed a negative connotation in many communities. When cities or counties (and even some countries!) outlaw dogs of certain breeds or types, our very ability to own dogs is put into question. The AKC instituted its Canine Good Citizen program to help generate good publicity for dogs and responsible dog owners, and to a certain extent, it has been successful. (Go to the AKC's website, www.akc.org, for more information.) Unfortunately, the problems often overshadow the positives. It is up to individual dog owners everywhere to be responsible—to show the world that dogs can play a positive role in our lives.

Photo by Sheri Wachtstetter

Requiring that a dog be on leash when out in public doesn't mean that the dog can't have fun; it simply means that he must be leashed. It's up to the owner to make things fun! Dogs at Kindred Spirits Canine Education Center in Vista, California, playing a training game.

# Leashing Your Dog

Three and four decades ago, allowing dogs to run loose was much more acceptable than it is today. Although some inevitably would get hit by cars, neighborhoods expected to see dogs running and playing or following children as they played. Today, that freedom is rarely allowed—most communities (and states) have leash laws. The reasoning behind these laws is that being on leash protects both dogs and people. Dogs on leash will not get hit by cars or stray off. People are also protected, as dogs on leash can be prevented from jumping on people, chasing them, or biting them.

Although some people believe that leash laws are too restrictive, there are places where dogs can run and play. Private property is still under the control of the property owner as long as the dog does not stray from the property. Many communities have established dog parks and dog beaches where dogs can run free and play.

# Keeping Your Dog Safe

When leash laws came into effect, it became necessary for dog owners to figure out how to keep their dogs at home. A fence around the backyard was the most obvious solution then and still is today. However, fences are not cheap, and many dog owners still chain or tether their dogs to a stake in the ground or a tree.

Leaving a dog chained or tethered, though, is not a good solution. These dogs are vulnerable to teasing by kids or strangers. A dog who has been teased many times will begin to react aggressively whenever anyone approaches his chain limits, and should someone get within his reach, he is likely to bite. Chained and tethered dogs also are vulnerable to attacks by other dogs or predators, with no way of escaping.

With so many dog bites pointing to chaining and tethering as a potential problem, many communities have made it illegal to confine a dog in this way. Most experts prefer that a dog be behind a fence, either a fence around a yard, or a fence creating a dog run. The fence should be secure so that the dog cannot go through or under it, and high enough (or roofed) so that the dog cannot go over it.

# Protecting Dogs in Vehicles

We've all seen dogs riding in cars with their heads out the window, hair blowing in the wind and nose twitching as they soak up all the scents. A dog may love riding in the car like this, but it sure isn't good for him. Bugs smacking into his eyes at high speed will cause major eye damage, perhaps even blindness. A sharp turn or brake could send the dog flying, either out the window or into the dashboard or windshield. As with so many things in life, the things we love are often not the things that are the best for us.

Dogs must be secure in the car when the vehicle is moving. That means the dog is in his crate, which is fastened down with a seatbelt, or the dog is wearing a specially made harness that the seatbelt clips into. The window can be partway down, if you wish, but the dog should not hang his head out the window.

Dogs riding in the backs of trucks must be restrained, too, so that they can ride safely. The leash restraining the dog must be short enough that the dog cannot jump out of the truck bed. Far too many dogs have been thrown from truck beds. Some were restrained, but not enough, and hung from the truck bed until they died or were rescued.

Dogs should never be left in a car alone while you go into a store or run errands. Even if the windows are open a few inches, the air in the car will heat up very quickly. On a sunny 70-degree day, the air in a car parked in the sun will reach more than 100 degrees within ten minutes and 120 degrees or more in a half-hour.

# The Wastes Dogs Leave Behind

Picking up what your dog leaves behind is simply the act of a responsible dog owner. Bailey, an English Springer Spaniel (pictured with Cayla Horn), owned by Kelly Rodrigues.

Dog urine and feces can be unsightly, cause odor problems, and, in some cases, even be a part of disease transmission. Feces not picked up can attract disease-carrying pests (primarily flies) and can seep into groundwater as they dissolve. When many dogs live in a small area, as in a large city, the amount of feces produced can be mind-boggling. Most cities and counties, plus many states, now have laws stating that the owner of a dog, or the person who has control of the dog (such as a dog walker), must pick up any feces produced by that dog. Fines for not doing so can range from $25 to even $500, depending on the city.

Dog urine is also a problem. A lamppost or fire hydrant that has become a neighborhood marking post will quickly become unbearable to people walking by. In addition, the urine is corrosive, causing problems with the lamppost and the fire hydrant. Male dogs should not be allowed to lift their legs and urinate on every vertical surface; it's not necessary, and it's rude. See chapter 7 for training tips.

# When Dogs Bark (and Bark and Bark)

Dogs who bark excessively cause more problems among neighbors than just about any other single neighborhood issue. A dog barking on and on can disrupt sleep, wake babies, cause other dogs to bark, and create innumerable other headaches. This is very sad because when a dog is barking continually, it is a sign that there is something wrong; either the dog is alone too much, is ignored, or is not getting enough training or exercise.

Barking dogs usually fall under city or county noise ordinances, although some localities have specific barking-dog laws enforced by the animal control department. Dog owners are normally cited once or twice, with fines escalating each time. If the problem isn't resolved, more drastic steps can be taken. In some cities, the dog will be confiscated, while in others, the owner may be arrested. The owner of a barking dog should contact a professional trainer or behaviorist for help in solving the problem.

# When Dogs Bite

The nation reeled when we heard about the horrible mauling and death of a woman in San Francisco by her neighbor's dogs. We would like to think that such incidents are a rarity, but unfortunately, they are not. The very next day, a headline in San Diego read, "Boy, 3, Killed by Neighbor's Pit Bull." It happens way too often.

The Centers for Disease Control in Atlanta, Georgia, has stated that the United States is in the midst of a dog-bite epidemic. Although dog ownership has increased only 2 percent over the past decade, dog bites have increased by more than 35 percent. More children are hurt by dog bites than by any other single childhood activity, including inline skating or even skateboarding.

## WHAT WENT WRONG?

Dogs were domesticated to be our friends and companions, so what went wrong? Why are dogs biting, mauling, and even killing people?

+ **Little or no bite inhibition:** Most dogs are born with the ability to be aware of using their jaws; they bite too hard on a littermate, the littermate cries, and the puppy doing the bit-

  ing learns to be gentler in play the next time. When a dog has never learned this lesson (such as an orphaned or bottle-raised puppy, or a puppy taken from his mother and littermates at too young an age), he may be too rough with people. If the puppy's parents did not have the inhibition, he may not have inherited it. When people play too rough with a puppy, they teach him to ignore this instinct.

+ **Genetic predisposition to bite:** If a dog comes from a parent or parents who were aggressive to people, he, too, may be aggressive to people.

+ **Little or no training:** When a dog has not had any training or has had too little training, he may not look upon people as leaders. When someone then tells him to do something, especially if he doesn't want to do it, he may bite.

Photo by Sheri Wachstetter

A well-trained, well-socialized dog is much less apt to bite than a dog with no leadership or guidance. Rebel, a Doberman Pinscher, owned by Chris Downs.

- **Fearful personality:** A dog who was born with a fearful personality may bite when pushed too hard to do something he's worried about. A fearful dog also will bite when cornered.
- **Illness or injury:** A dog who is hurt or sick may bite out of fear or pain, even when well-loved family members are trying to help him.
- **Hormones:** Most bites are made by intact (not neutered) male dogs. Although some intact (unspayed) females and some spayed females and neutered males will bite, intact males as a whole seem more willing to bite.
- **Means of restraint:** Dogs who are chained or tethered and vulnerable to people walking by are more apt to bite than dogs protected by a secure and solid fence.
- **Dog not restrained:** Dogs running loose (especially a pack of three or more dogs) have inflicted many serious, and often fatal, bites.
- **People gone wrong:** When people treat a puppy roughly, are aggressive to him, or ignore and neglect him, even the nicest puppy can learn to dislike people.

Dog bites have happened in a variety of ways and for many different reasons. Some people blame breeders, saying that they have produced inferior dogs, while others blame permissive parenting, saying that its philosophies have trickled down into dog training. There is no one reason why dogs are biting more today.

## KEEP YOUR DOG FROM BECOMING A STATISTIC

To prevent your dog from becoming a statistic, here are some suggestions:

- If possible, get your dog from a reputable breeder and meet the mother of the litter. If the mother is shy, fearful, or aggressive, do not buy the puppy.
- If adopting a dog, find out as much as you can from the shelter volunteers or rescue group. Do not buy a shy or fearful dog because you feel that you can "save" him.
- Spay or neuter your dog.
- Socialize your dog well and continue socializing him throughout his life. Do not isolate and ignore your dog.
- Do not play aggressive games with your dog, and never encourage him to fight you in any way.
- Train your dog. Begin early, keep the training fun, and continue it into your dog's adulthood.
- Keep your dog securely confined, making sure that your fence is escape-proof, and do not allow him to run free.
- Be your dog's leader. Every dog needs a leader. Think and act like your dog's parent, providing rules and guidance for behavior.

If you ever feel that your dog might bite you, call for professional help right away. The sooner you act, the better your chances of preventing the behavior. If you wait until your dog has bitten you, it may well be too late.

# PROTECT YOURSELF

If you feel threatened by a dog and fear that you may be attacked, follow these tips to protect yourself:

+ Never run from a dog, even a small one.
+ Stand still and turn slightly so that you aren't facing the dog directly. Never try to stare down a dog; that's issuing a challenge. Don't turn your back on the dog.
+ Tell the dog to go home; many who run loose know what that phrase means.
+ If you're on a bicycle, stop, get off, and use it as a shield between you and the dog.
+ If you have a backpack, purse, or briefcase or are carrying something, use it as a shield.
+ If a dog attacks you, try to stuff the purse or briefcase in his mouth. If at all possible, try not to scream. A high-pitched scream is the sound of prey.
+ If you are knocked down by a dog, curl up in a ball and protect your neck and head with your arms. Play dead if you can.

Always seek medical help after a dog bite. Dogs can have a lot of bacteria in their mouths, and your doctor will probably prescribe antibiotics after scrubbing and soaking the wound. The doctor will also report the bite, even if you don't, so you will need to able to describe the dog. If you know where the dog lives, report that, too. The doctor will want to make sure that the dog has been vaccinated, especially for rabies. By reporting the bite, animal control or police officials can intervene, especially if the dog is a stray or the owner refuses to take responsibility for the dog.

# RULES FOR CHILDREN

A child of any age should never be left alone with a dog, even for just a few minutes. Too many disasters have occurred when a parent left the dog and child, especially an infant, alone, coming back to find that the dog had attacked the child.

Children are very vulnerable to dog bites. Not only does their small stature make them easier targets, but kids have high-pitched voices that sound like prey, and they often have food or other interesting things with them. Kids also move fast and unpredictably—again, just like prey.

It's very important, then, to teach children skills that can help keep them safe, both with a dog at home and with other dogs they meet.

+ Never run from a dog, even your own.
+ Never scream at or flail about with a dog, even your own.
+ Never poke a dog's eyes or nose, pull ears, stick fingers into a dog's mouth, or pull a dog's tail.
+ Do not step on a dog's tail, kick him, hit him, poke him with things, or otherwise torment him.
+ Never pet a strange dog; always ask the dog's owner's permission before petting. Not all dogs like kids.

- Pet a dog on his back; do not hug his head or neck.
- Do not stare into a dog's eyes, lean into his face, or kiss him on the nose.
- If a dog growls at a child, snaps, or barks, tell the parent about the incident—even if a bite doesn't result. The next time, it could turn into a bite.

Dogs who don't like kids are not necessarily bad dogs. They may not have been socialized to kids, or perhaps a child has treated the dog wrongly. Dogs who don't like children should simply be kept away from and protected from kids.

# Breed-Specific Legislation

The most serious issue facing dog owners today is that of breed-specific legislation, or laws targeting one or more specific breeds. Breed-specific legislation originated with Pit Bulls. Pit Bulls—American Pit Bull Terriers or other breeds, or simply mixed Pit Bull–type dogs—have often been owned by uncaring or ignorant owners. They have been badly bred, badly trained, and involved in incidents in which another dog or person was bitten, mauled, or even killed. Such attacks are horrible and require serious action; the reaction, however, has unfortunately been a knee-jerk one: "Let's make those dogs illegal!" rather than looking at the individual problem that has caused the attack or taking into consideration the number of wonderful Pit Bulls not causing trouble in any given community.

Because of breed-specific legislation, Pit Bulls today (and those breeds related to Pitties or that bear a superficial resemblance to them) are illegal in many localities, including Denver, Colorado, and Ontario, Canada, as well as many places in between.

Breed-specific legislation has quickly moved to outlaw other breeds. Rottweilers, German Shepherds, Doberman Pinschers, and Akitas were quickly targeted, primarily because of the breeds' reputations and heritages as working guard dogs. Belgium has banned not only Pit Bulls, but also American Staffordshire Terriers, Staffordshire Bull Terriers, and Bull Terriers, as well as Rottweilers, Rhodesian Ridgebacks, and Akitas.

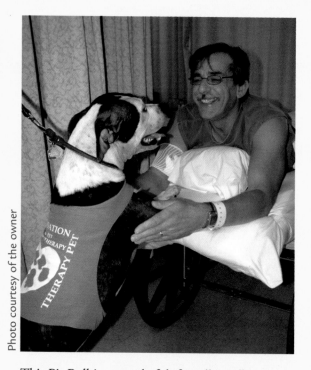

Photo courtesy of the owner

This Pit Bull is a wonderful, friendly, well-trained dog. He is also a working therapy dog, visiting military veterans at a veterans' hospital and care facility. In some places, breed-specific legislation would make him illegal. Jake, an American Pit Bull Terrier, owned by Nicole Rattay.

This type of legislation has even moved into private business. Many insurance companies will not cover renters or homeowners who have specific breeds of dogs. Some landlords will not allow tenants to own some breeds.

Obviously, breed-specific legislation is not fair. This type of law punishes a group of dogs when the blame should be put upon the individual dog and owner. Not all dogs of a given breed are dangerous. However, an irresponsible dog owner can make just about any dog dangerous, given the situation. Legislation should target dogs and dog owners, not breeds.

Dog owners—all dog owners, not just the owners of banned breeds—should pay attention to local and state legislation targeting dogs. Let your representatives know that you do not agree with breed specific legislation and that you are a voter! The AKC has also been very active in combating breed-specific legislation.

# Part II

# Breed Profiles

# ffenpinscher

ffenpinschers are one of the oldest toy breeds. In the 1600s in Germany, these little dogs were used as mousers and ratters on farms or in food businesses. Their name means *monkey dog* in German.

An alert, sturdy little terrier standing 9.5 to 11.5 inches tall and weighing 8 to 10 pounds, he is known by his cute, monkeylike face. With a round head, short muzzle, round and dark expressive eyes, and erect ears (natural or cropped), the Affenpinscher has a distinct look. The rough coat is about an inch long. There is slightly longer hair on the face to emphasize his features. The coat can be black, gray, silver, red, or black and tan. The tail may be docked or natural.

Grooming the Affenpinscher takes some skill. Show dogs must be hand-stripped. If you would like to do this, talk to your dog's breeder for guidance. Most pet dogs are groomed with scissors and clippers by a professional groomer.

This breed is playful and full of energy—very terrierlike. A brisk walk morning and evening plus a playtime (or two or three) in between will keep most Affenpinschers happy. They also enjoy games and canine sports; trick training is always fun, as the breed is a natural showoff!

Housetraining these dogs can be a challenge, but with patience and consistency it can be accomplished. The Affenpinscher Club of America recommends that these dogs attend puppy training classes for socialization, basic obedience training, and, if you should need it, help with the housetraining. The training should be structured yet fun; keep in mind that Affenpinschers may cooperate with training or they may not. They do have a quirky sense of humor!

Affenpinschers are funny little dogs and do best with active people. The breed is fine with children as long as they treat him with respect. The breed is also good with other pets, although most Affenpinschers need to learn not to chase the family cat. Health concerns include hip and knee problems, and they can have breathing problems during hot, humid weather.

## Breed in Brief

**Registries:** AKC, UKC, CKC
**Occupation:** Ratter, companion
**Size:** 9.5 to 11.5 in tall; 8 to 10 lbs
**Longevity:** 14 to 16 years
**Exercise:** Active dog
**Training:** Easy; hard to focus
**Grooming:** Hand-stripping or professional groomer

# Afghan Hound

The Afghan Hound originated in the wilds of Afghanistan. When Westerners first saw the breed in the 1800s, they found a fast, sure-footed sighthound who would chase and bring down hare or deer and would corner predators, such as wolves and jackals.

The Afghan has a regal appearance, standing 25 to 27 inches tall and weighing between 50 and 60 pounds, with females smaller than males. The head is held high, and the eyes are dark and almond-shaped. The ears are long. The body is that of a runner with long legs, a strong back, and a deep chest. The tail is long and has a curve at the end. The coat is long and silky and may be of any color.

The coat requires daily combing and brushing to maintain it without tangles. The Afghan Club of America recommends bathing adult Afghans once a week. Bathing and blow drying the coat and brushing and combing it as it dries requires two to three hours. Many pet owners choose to keep the coat significantly shorter for ease of care.

The Afghan enjoys a chance to stretch his legs at least once each day. The Afghan should always run in a fenced yard because if he is off leash and happens to flush a rabbit, he will be gone in a heartbeat. Afghans also appreciate comfort and will enjoy a snuggle on the sofa once the exercise is over.

Training the Afghan can be a challenge. Bred to work independently, he prefers his own agenda to someone else's and can have quite a stubborn streak. In the house, young Afghans are known to be destructive chewers if given too much freedom and not allowed enough exercise. With the right motivation, the Afghan can learn to enjoy training and to go along with household rules. Training should be structured yet fun.

This is a fun breed for people who understand it. Afghans are good with children if raised or well-socialized with them. Bred as hunting dogs, they are not good with small pets. Health concerns include hip dysplasia and eye and heart problems.

## Breed in Brief

**Registries:** AKC, UKC, CKC
**Occupation:** Hunter, companion
**Size:** 25 to 27 in tall; 50 to 60 lbs
**Longevity:** 10 to 12 years
**Exercise:** Daily run
**Training:** Challenge
**Grooming:** Difficult

# Airedale Terrier

Most breeds have specialties, but Airedale Terriers have a broad range of skills. They can hunt birds, retrieve downed birds, and track and tree mammals, both large and small. Airedales were also the first breed used as police dogs in both Great Britain and Germany, and in wartime, served as guards and messengers. They were prized by both law enforcement and military because they retained their training well and would work through harsh conditions and discomfort.

The breed was developed in Aire, England, probably from the English Terrier. Some experts feel the Otterhound was crossed with the English Terrier to help create a waterproof coat and to add to the first breed's hunting abilities. After the mid-1800s, the breed was known as the Working Terrier, Waterside Terrier, and Bingley Terrier.

Male Airedales stand about 23 inches tall at the shoulder, with females slightly shorter. Both males and females are well-muscled and sturdy, with an athletic appearance. The black and tan coat is wiry with a slight wavy texture. Airedales stand tall, on straight front legs, with their heads held high. The ears are V-shaped, folded at the side of the head, and alert. The eyes are dark and expressive, with an alert, intelligent expression. The tail is carried high.

The Airedale's coat requires daily brushing and combing to keep it clean and free of debris. The coat grows continually, and a visit to a professional groomer every six to eight weeks is necessary to keep the coat looking as it should. Airedales competing in conformation dog shows are hand-stripped (rather than having the hair cut with clippers). If you wish to show your dog, ask your dog's breeder to show you how to do this type of grooming.

Athletic, active dogs, Airedales need vigorous daily exercise. A casual walk morning and evening is nowhere near enough for a young, healthy Airedale. Instead, these dogs need a brisk jog or run alongside a bicycle, a twenty-minute game of tennis ball fetch, or a workout on the agility course (or all of the above) every day.

Airedales are intelligent dogs and retain what they have learned quite well. Puppies should attend puppy kindergarten classes to begin their training. The socialization in these classes is also important. Airedales can be hardheaded when they get bored, and very stubborn if the training is not fair. You must figure out what motivates your dog, and keep one step ahead during the training process. Keep the training fair and structured and lots of fun, and the Airedale will always be looking for more to do.

The Airedale today is a strong, active, and very physical dog. The breed retains its hunting instincts, so a gopher or squirrel in the yard could cause great excitement. They have excelled in many sports, including obedience, agility, tracking, search and rescue, and carting. Many are still used for hunting. As hunters, Airedales should not be trusted with small pets, and interactions with the family cat should be supervised. Although Airedales can be great family dogs, they are rambunctious and must learn to behave around small children. The primary health concerns include hip dysplasia and hypothyroidism.

## Breed in Brief

**Registries:** AKC, CKC, UKC
**Occupation:** Hunter, police and military dog
**Size:** 23 in tall; 50 lbs
**Longevity:** 11 to 13 years
**Exercise:** Vigorous daily exercise
**Training:** Easy; retains what is learned well
**Grooming:** Difficult

# kbash Dog

## (Medium Coat and Long Coat)

The white Akbash Dog is from Turkey and claims both sighthounds and Mastiffs as ancestors. The breed was imported into the U.S. in the late 1970s as a livestock guardian, and by 1986, had established itself as one of the most successful livestock guardian breeds, protecting livestock from predators, including coyotes and bears.

The Akbash Dog stands 27 to 32 inches tall and weighs 75 to 140 pounds. It is white with a double coat. The undercoat is dense and soft. The outer coat comes in two lengths: either a medium coat that lies flat or a long coat that has a distinct ruff and profuse feathering. The Akbash Dog should show features of both the sighthound, with his long legs and deep chest, and the Mastiff, with his broad head, height, and weight.

Grooming the Akbash is not difficult; the breed is not prone to matting. However, the coat sheds a little all the time and heavily in the spring and fall. Daily brushing can reduce the hair in the house.

The Akbash is a calm dog in the house but is an athletic breed. Walks alone are not enough; a daily run is necessary to use up excess energy. Although puppies and young Akbash like to play, this is a serious breed; adult Akbash usually forego games.

Early and continuing socialization is very important, especially for those kept as family pets. Bred to be protective and wary, the Akbash does not like strangers. Training can be challenging because as a livestock guardian, he is supposed to think for himself. With motivation, the Akbash can be trained, but he will question each command and respond as he wishes.

This is a loyal breed, one that would give his life for his family, but he can be a difficult dog for a first-time dog owner. Because he can be opinionated and pushy, he's best with kids over 8 to 10 years of age. Bred to ward off predators, the Akbash can be dog-aggressive. Health concerns are few but include cardiomyopathy and hip dysplasia.

## Breed in Brief

**Registries:** Akbash Dogs International, UKC
**Occupation:** Livestock guardian
**Size:** 27 to 32 in tall; 75 to 140 lbs
**Longevity:** 9 to 10 years
**Exercise:** Daily run
**Training:** Challenge
**Grooming:** Easy

# kita

The Akita was bred as a versatile hunting dog in Japan and, over the years, has assumed a place of honor in the hearts of the Japanese people. When a child is born, the parents are often given a small statue of an Akita as a symbol of happiness, health, and longevity.

The Akita stands 24 to 28 inches tall and weighs between 65 and 115 pounds, with females smaller than males. The head is broad, with a deep muzzle, upright ears, and small, dark eyes. The body is longer than the dog is tall at the shoulder, the chest is deep, and the tail is large, full, and carried over the back with a curl. The coat is double, with the undercoat soft and dense. The outer coat is straight and stands out from the body. Colors include white, pinto, or brindle.

During most of the year, the Akita can be brushed twice a week. During spring and fall when shedding is heaviest, daily brushing is needed. Akitas do not have a doggy odor and are catlike in their ability to help keep themselves clean.

Akitas are not an overly active breed. A couple of long walks each day plus a quick jog alongside a bicycle will satisfy the needs of most. Puppies can be bouncy, silly, and like to play games, but adult Akitas can be quite serious.

Akitas have strong guardian instincts. To grow up confident and well-adjusted, they must meet a variety of people early in life. Training is also important; the Akita is a powerful dog who could take advantage of his owner. Training should be firm, yet fair and fun.

Akitas can be a difficult dog for a first-time dog owner. Loyal and devoted to a fault, they can also be stubborn and dominant. Although good with children who respect them, they are intolerant of teasing. They are not always good with visiting children or rough kid's play; it may be misinterpreted as something harmful. As hunters, they are not good with small pets. Health concerns include hip and elbow dysplasia, knee and eye problems, and cancer.

## Breed in Brief

**Registries:** AKC, UKC, CKC
**Occupation:** Hunter, guardian
**Size:** 24 to 28 in tall; 65 to 115 lbs
**Longevity:** 9 to 11 years
**Exercise:** Active puppies; calm adults
**Training:** Difficult; can be stubborn
**Grooming:** Lots of brushing

# Alapaha Blue Blood Bulldog

Although often confused with the American Bulldog, this is a separate breed. The breed originated in the American south in the 1800s as a plantation dog. As the large plantations disappeared, so did the breed. Ms. Lana Lou Lane, a third-generation owner of the breed, has worked with the Animal Research Foundation to save the breed from extinction.

Alapahas have definite bulldog characteristics and should convey an aura of nobility and pride, hence the "blue blood" name. They stand 20 to 25 inches tall and weigh between 65 to 110 pounds, with females smaller than males. The head is broad and flat across the top, and the jaws are heavily muscled. The eyes are prominent and the ears are folded. The coat is short and stiff. Colors include white with patches of color, including brindle, blue merle, or chocolate.

This breed is easy to groom. Twice a week the coat can be brushed with a soft bristle brush or curry comb.

The breed needs vigorous daily exercise. A long walk morning and evening plus a couple of good games of fetch will keep most happy. Puppies are very silly but both puppies and adults enjoy games. Adults can enjoy carting and weight pulling.

The breed is protective of both property and people. Early and ongoing socialization is needed to ensure the dog grows up well-adjusted. Training is also important, not just because this is a powerful dog but also to give the dog a job. These are bright, inquisitive dogs, and if they don't have something to keep them busy, they will get into trouble.

These dogs are protective and devoted; they will give their lives to protect their owners. This, as well as the breed's size and power, makes them a difficult dog for first-time dog owners.

## Breed in Brief

**Registries:** Alapaha Blue Blood Bulldog Club
**Occupation:** Guardian
**Size:** 20 to 25 in tall; 65 to 110 lbs
**Longevity:** 10 to 13 years
**Exercise:** Vigorous daily exercise
**Training:** Moderate
**Grooming:** Easy

They usually love children and are willing playmates. Although they won't start fights with other dogs, they won't back away from a fight, either. The biggest health concerns today are the problems associated with the breed's very small gene pool.

# laskan Klee Kai

## (Toy, Miniature, and Standard)

Linda Spurlin developed the Alaskan Klee Kai (AKK) in the 1970s and '80s, using the old Alaskan Husky as the foundation breed. She also used a Siberian Husky and some smaller dogs of similar conformation. Her goal was a smaller-sized husky-type breed that would be an excellent companion dog.

Today's Alaskan Klee Kai has the appearance of a northern breed, with a wedge-shaped face, prick ears, a sturdy body, and a tail that curls over the back. The face has a distinct and striking mask. The coat is a double coat, with a dense undercoat and longer guard hairs. The toy stands up to and including 13 inches at the shoulder; the miniature is over 13 inches and including 15 inches; and the standard is over 15 inches and including 17 inches.

During most of the year, this breed can be brushed two or three times a week; however, during spring and fall when shedding is at its heaviest, daily brushing may be needed.

With his sled dog heritage, the AKK can be quite busy. Without daily exercise, he may be prone to trouble. A couple of good walks every day and a jog with you or alongside a bicycle will keep him happy. This breed is also quite playful and thrives in many canine sports, including sledding, skijoring, agility, flyball, and flying disc. Many have also made excellent therapy dogs.

Although training is important and should begin young, dogs of this breed will never be as compliant as some other breeds. They do enjoy the attention that training provides. Early and continuing socialization is vital, as these dogs can be wary of strangers.

The AKK is an excellent watchdog, yet is affectionate and loyal to his family. He will do best with an owner who understands the northern breeds. He is good with children who treat him gently and with respect; he will not tolerate rough handling. He has a strong prey drive and should not be trusted with smaller pets. The breed tends to be healthy.

---

### Breed in Brief

**Registries:** UKC, ARBA
**Occupation:** Companion
**Size:** Toy: under 13 in tall
  Mini: 13 to 15 in tall
  Standard: 15 to 17 in tall
**Longevity:** 13 to 15 years
**Exercise:** Required daily
**Training:** Moderate
**Grooming:** Sheds!

# laskan Malamute

Alaskan Malamutes are natives of northwest Alaska, where they served as hunting partners, pack dogs, and sled dogs for the Mahlemut people, an Innuit tribe. The dogs were vital to the peoples' survival. In the mid-1900s, Malamutes were used in many of the Artic exploratory expeditions and also served in World War II.

This breed is large and substantial, standing 23 to 25 inches tall and weighing between 75 and 85 pounds, although many are larger. His head is broad and deep, ears are upright, and eyes are medium-sized, almond-shaped, and dark brown. With a deep chest, powerful shoulders, heavy bones, strong legs, and good feet, this is a breed designed to work hard. The outer coat is thick and coarse; the undercoat is dense. The tail is a plume that is carried low when working.

Malamutes need brushing at least twice per week, but during the shedding seasons, primarily spring and fall, daily brushing is needed to keep the hair under control.

Exercise is important; this breed is a working dog bred to carry packs or pull sleds. A long, brisk walk morning and evening and a play session in between is the least exercise this dog can tolerate. A Malamute would be thrilled to have an owner who does skijoring, sled dog training, carting, hiking, or backpacking.

Although they were bred to work, and Malamutes love to have something to do, they can also be a little independent and often have a touch of stubbornness. The key is to make training interesting and fun. Don't battle a Malamute; intrigue him instead and teach him compliance. Socialization is also important and should begin early.

This breed is a wonderful companion for people who are leaders; he can be domineering over people who are too soft. The breed may be dog-aggressive; males especially may be aggressive toward other male dogs. All interactions with small pets should be carefully supervised. Health concerns include hip dysplasia, bloat, and torsion.

## Breed in Brief

**Registries:** AKC, UKC, CKC
**Occupation:** Sled dog
**Size:** 23 to 25 in tall; 75 to 85 lbs
**Longevity:** 10 to 12 years
**Exercise:** Vigorous daily exercise
**Training:** Moderate
**Grooming:** Lots of brushing!

# merican Bulldog

*I*n early England, blood sports were very popular with both the working class and royalty. The old English bulldogs were developed for blood sports, fighting bulls and bears, and later, other dogs. After blood sports were made illegal, the dogs were used for a variety of purposes. In the U.S., they accompanied settlers across the unknown frontiers as guardians, hunters, and at times, even herding dogs.

This breed should convey a sense of power. Standing between 20 and 26 inches tall and weighing 60 to 120 pounds, with the females smaller than the males, this is an all-purpose working dog. The head should show its bulldog heritage, broad with a slightly shortened muzzle. The coat is short, harsh, and white with patches of brindle, brown, red, or tan.

Grooming this breed is easy; use a curry comb or soft bristled brush twice a week to brush out the dead hairs.

The Bulldog is quite active. Long, brisk walks are good, as are a few games of catch and fetch, but he also needs a job to do where he can burn some calories—either pulling a wagon or running on the agility course.

The breed needs early and ongoing socialization. Because they are still used as guardians of people, livestock, and property, these dogs are aggressive toward strangers and socialization can temper this reaction. Training should begin early, too, and continue into adulthood—not just for this physically powerful breed to learn self control but also to give the dogs a job to do. This breed also thrives in dog sports, including carting and weight pulling.

## Breed in Brief

**Registries:** UKC, ARBA, American Bulldog Registry
**Occupation:** Farm dog, guardian
**Size:** 20 to 26 in tall; 60 to 120 lbs
**Longevity:** 12 to 14 years
**Exercise:** Active dog
**Training:** Easy; hard to focus
**Grooming:** Easy

The American Bulldog requires an active owner who is a leader and is dog savvy. He is affectionate, loyal, and good with older children. (He can be too rough for young kids.) He will be a willing playmate for lots of childhood adventures. The breed can be dog-aggressive. Health concerns include hip dysplasia and allergies.

# $\mathcal{A}$merican Eskimo Dog

## (Toy, Miniature, and Standard)

$\mathcal{A}$merican Eskimo Dogs, or as they are commonly known, Eskies, are descended from several European spitz-type dogs, including the Pomeranian, Italian Spitz, German Spitz, and Keeshound. Some experts even feel the Japanese Spitz may be a part of the breed's ancestry. The early dogs of the breed served both as watchdogs and companions. In the late 1800s, the breed was known as the American Spitz and was very popular in traveling road shows and circuses, performing tricks. The breed's intelligence, agility, and unique white coat caught the American public's attention during this period, and the breed's popularity grew. In 1917, the name was changed to American Eskimo Dog, although the reasons why have been lost.

Eskies are bred in three sizes. Toys are 9 inches up to and including 12 inches at the withers (point of the shoulder); miniatures are more than 12 inches up to and including 15 inches; and standards are 15 inches and up to 19 inches at the withers. All Eskies of all sizes have the same look: upright ears, alert expression, plumed tail, and wonderful coat. Eskies are pure white, although some may have some biscuit cream in the coat. The coat is straight and is a double coat with a thick undercoat. All sizes should present the appearance of alertness, strength, and agility.

The Eskie's lush coat requires a minimum of twice weekly brushing. Although not prone to heavy matting (tangles), the dense undercoat will shed, and brushing can keep that under control. The heaviest shedding is usually in the spring and fall, although some shedding will take place throughout the summer and, depending upon your climate, sometimes year-round. The coat requires no trimming.

These dogs need vigorous daily exercise. Although daily walks are a great idea, they are not enough. A brisk jog, game of fetch, session of flyball, or training session on the agility course will keep them satisfied. Without enough exercise, Eskies can be quite mischievous and will amuse themselves, often to the owner's dismay!

All Eskie puppies should attend a puppy kindergarten class where they can socialize with puppies of other breeds and meet a variety of people. Continuing the training after puppy class is imperative for Eskies, not because they are bad—they're certainly not—but because they are alert, intelligent, and need something to occupy their mind. The training program should be structured yet fair and fun. Teach your Eskie tricks, too; he loves it!

Eskie's make alert watchdogs; trespassers will be met with a flurry of barking. Wary of strangers, the breed is very loyal to family and friends. The standard size Eskies make great companions for children and are usually quite tolerant of some roughhousing. The toy and miniature Eskies are too small for rough childhood play. If treated too roughly, these small dogs will protest. Most Eskies are quite tolerant of other small pets, including cats, although few can resist the chase of a running cat, so interactions should be supervised. The primary health concerns include Progressive Retinal Atrophy (PRA), knee problems, and hip dysplasia.

## Breed in Brief

**Registries:** AKC, CKC, UKC
**Occupation:** Companion, watchdog, performer
**Size:** Toy: 9 to 12 in tall
Mini: 12 to 15 in tall
Standard: 15 to 19 in tall
**Longevity:** 13 to 15 years
**Exercise:** Vigorous daily exercise
**Training:** Easy; hard to focus
**Grooming:** Twice weekly brushing

# American Foxhound

Foxhounds were brought to the American colonies from England in the mid-1600s. The dogs known today as American Foxhounds descend from those dogs and from others imported from England, Ireland, and France. The American Foxhound is recognized by both the AKC and UKC, but many foxhounds are not registered with either and may be mixtures of other foxhounds. Many hunters simply want a foxhound who will hunt in a specific way or who can handle certain terrain or conditions. Claudia Bazinet, of Foxhound Relocation and Retirement, says, "There are about two dozen strains of American Foxhounds, and they vary widely in type."

She continues, "The American Foxhound was bred from the English Foxhound but has a medium build and is faster. They have a shorter neck and longer legs. The American Foxhound has longer ears, but again, that can vary according to the strain." As a general rule, American Foxhounds stand between 21 and 25 inches tall and weigh between 40 and 70 pounds. The coat is short and can be any color but is often the typical hound white and red or rust with a black saddle or cape.

Grooming this Foxhound is easy; simply brush him with a soft bristle brush or curry comb a couple times a week to loosen the dead hairs.

## Breed in Brief

**Registries:** AKC, UKC, CKC
**Occupation:** Hunter
**Size:** 21 to 25 in tall; 40 to 70 lbs
**Longevity:** 10 to 12 years
**Exercise:** Daily aerobic exercise
**Training:** Challenge
**Grooming:** Easy

Foxhounds need daily aerobic exercise. Many will not play catch or fetch games, so a long, vigorous walk or a jog beside a bicycle will be needed. Never allow a Foxhound to run off leash outside of a fenced yard; as a hunter, if a rabbit or other critter is flushed, he will be gone and no amount of calling will bring him back.

Although American Foxhounds can be kept as pets and can be quite calm and gentle in the house, the breed is first and foremost a hunter. Training can be a challenge. They are good with other dogs (although they should never be trusted with small pets) and can be quite tolerant of children's antics. They do bay and may cause neighborhood complaints. Health concerns include ear problems.

# $\mathscr{A}$merican Hairless Terrier

## (Toy and Miniature)

$\mathscr{I}$n the early 1970s, a hairless puppy was born in a litter of Rat Terrier puppies. That puppy was the origin of the American Hairless Terrier (AHT) breed. In fact, for many years, the breed was known as Rat Terrier—Hairless Variety. In January, 2004, the breed was renamed.

The breed has two sizes: toy and miniature. The toys are 7.5 to 11 inches tall and weigh between 4 and 8 pounds. The miniatures are 11.5 to 16 inches tall and weigh between 8.5 to 16 pounds. In both sizes, the dogs strongly retain their Rat Terrier heritage and appearance. They are well-balanced and muscular. Although puppies are born with short, fuzzy hair, by 8 weeks old, they have lost it. Their skin is soft, smooth, and warm. They have freckles or spots of black, brown, or red.

Grooming is very easy. The skin can be washed with a damp rag. They can sunburn so they must be protected from too much sun exposure.

This is a high-energy breed. They can go for a long walk morning and night and will enjoy several games of catch and fetch. As befitting their terrier heritage, they also enjoy hunting for small critters in the backyard. They excel at agility training.

This breed needs early socialization, as these dogs can be wary of strangers. Early training is a plus, as AHTs have a quick, bright mind and if you don't set some rules, they will. After basic obedience, have some fun. AHTs love trick training.

AHTs are devoted and loyal to their family. They are active and can be great with older children who respect them and are not too rough. They can be good with other dogs, although play with larger dogs should be supervised. They are not always good with smaller pets. Health concerns include knee problems, hip and elbow dysplasia, and allergies. The small gene pool in the breed is concern to some.

## Breed in Brief

**Registries:** UKC, AHT clubs
**Occupation:** Companion
**Size:** Toy: 7.5 to 11 in tall;
4 to 8 lbs
Mini: 11.5 to 16 in tall;
8.5 to 16 lbs
**Longevity:** 12 to 14 years
**Exercise:** Active dog
**Training:** Easy
**Grooming:** Easy

# American Pit Bull Terrier

$\mathscr{B}$lood sports (pitting a dog against bulls or bears) were very popular in ancient Britain. These sports provided entertainment for both the working class and royalty, and dogs who fought well were treasured. Blood sports were outlawed in England in 1835, but illegal dog fighting continued in backyards, cellars, and the back rooms of pubs. Today's American Pit Bull Terrier, or APBT, is probably descended from the bulldog and terrier crosses used in these fights. The dog that developed in America in the 17th and 18th centuries was a bigger dog; settlers needed

a larger, more powerful dog to protect their homesteads. Although illegal dog fighting has continued, with the APBT and APBT crosses in the midst of it, APBTs have also found a home in the hearts of many owners as courageous yet gentle companions.

An APBT is a medium-sized dog whose muscular build makes him appear larger than he actually is. Males are normally between 18 and 22 inches tall at the shoulder and between 40 and 60 pounds, with females slightly smaller. The head is blocky with strong, muscular jaws, round eyes, and either cropped ears or natural half-pricked ears. The body is strongly muscled, giving the appearance of great strength. The coat is short and is stiff to the touch, but shiny and glossy. APBTs can be any color.

Grooming an APBT is easy; the short coat can be brushed once or twice a week with a bristle brush or curry comb.

APBTs require daily exercise. A long, brisk walk is good, as is a session of weight pulling, a game of retrieve, or a session on the agility course. Although APBTs can run, and can run quite quickly, they do not have the body build of a long-distance runner, so their exercise should not be centered around that type of activity. To prevent the dog from running off and to make sure problems with other dogs do not occur, all exercise should be within a fenced-in yard, or the dog should be on leash.

The ancestry of APBTs includes dogs who were bred to fight, often with other dogs. Therefore, not all APBTs can be social with dogs outside of their own family. However, if APBT puppies are socialized well to puppies of other breeds, sizes, and colors, then they often can learn to enjoy other dogs' company and learn to play nicely. All APBTs must be supervised when interacting with other dogs, though, and those that show aggression should no longer be allowed to socialize.

Training should be a part of every APBT's upbringing, not just because a powerful breed such as this needs to learn manners, but because the breed is bright and enjoys learning. The training should be firm yet fair, and lots of fun.

APBTs are excellent watchdogs. With the bulk to stand behind their bark, they can be quite imposing. However, to their family, APBTs are gentle, affectionate, and silly clowns. They love to be the center of attention. They are also very tolerant of kids and take roughhousing well. When raised with other pets, they can be very gentle and patient, although interaction with other animals should always be supervised. APBTs can suffer from allergies, and hip dysplasia can be a problem. Incorrect, overly aggressive, or overly fearful temperaments are the biggest problem within the breed today.

## Breed in Brief

**Registries:** UKC, ARBA
**Occupation:** Fighter, guardian, companion
**Size:** 18 to 22 in tall; 35 to 60 lbs
**Longevity:** 11 to 13 years
**Exercise:** Moderate
**Training:** Easy; hard to keep focused
**Grooming:** Easy

# American Staffordshire Terrier

The early history of the American Staffordshire Terrier was not recorded, but many experts feel the Am Staff and the Staffordshire Bull Terrier share some of the same ancestors, especially the old English Bulldog and perhaps the white English Terrier. These dogs were used in the blood sports of bull and bear baiting. The Am Staff and American Pit Bull Terrier separated into two different breeds many years ago when the Pit Bull was recognized by the UKC and the Am Staff was recognized by the AKC.

The Am Staff is a medium-sized dog standing between 17 and 19 inches tall and weighing between 55 and 70 pounds. The head is blocky with muscular jaws, dark, round eyes, and either cropped or natural ears. The body is muscular, with a deep, wide chest, straight front legs, and a tapered, rather short, but not docked tail. The coat is short and may be any color.

Grooming the Am Staff simply means brushing the dog with a soft bristle brush or curry comb twice a week.

This is an active breed who needs vigorous daily exercise. They do not have the body build of a long-distance runner, however, so the exercise should be long, quick-paced walks, weight-pulling exercise, carting training, or a game of catch and fetch.

The ancestry of Am Staffs includes dogs who were bred to fight and sometimes to fight other dogs. Because of this, Am Staffs often do not get along with other dogs, especially dogs of the same sex. Although early socialization can often temper this reaction, interactions with other dogs should always be closely supervised, and those who show aggression should no longer be allowed to socialize. To prevent potential problems, all exercise should be on leash or within a fenced yard.

## Breed in Brief

**Registries:** AKC, CKC
**Occupation:** Fighter, guardian, companion
**Size:** 17 to 19 in tall; 55 to 70 lbs
**Longevity:** 11 to 13 years
**Exercise:** Vigorous daily exercise
**Training:** Moderate
**Grooming:** Easy

Am Staffs are excellent watchdogs. They are also gentle and affectionate family dogs who are tolerant of children's rough play. When raised with other pets, they can be gentle and patient. Health concerns include hip dysplasia, allergies, and thyroid problems.

# merican Water Spaniel

This breed developed in the American midwest as a working gun dog. He may have some Irish Water Spaniel in his background or some Curly-Coated Retriever. Today, although seen occasionally in dog shows, he is still a prized working gun dog, retrieving small game of any kind.

The AWS is a medium-sized dog, standing 15 to 18 inches tall at the shoulder and weighing 25 to 45 pounds. The dog should be in proportion and well-balanced. The eyes are slightly rounded and may be yellow brown to brown, hazel, or dark to harmonize with the coat. The ears are dropped and long. The coat is wavy to curly with a weatherproof undercoat. The coat should be solid liver, brown, or dark chocolate.

The coat should be brushed two or three times per week, and the dog should be bathed every other week. Professional grooming is recommended every six to eight weeks.

These dogs need daily exercise and playtimes. Paul Morrison of Little Brownies Kennel says, "The breed loves to play. They will bring toys to the owner and set them in the lap to initiate play. They will then dance around in front to encourage the owner to throw the toy."

Although the breed standard calls for a friendly dog, some timid dogs are seen. Early socialization is very important for these dogs. These are quick, intelligent dogs who like to work; they need those traits channeled productively, so early training is imperative. Linda Ford, an AWS breeder, says, "The AWS is easy to train but will shut down if he feels you are being unnecessarily harsh. If trained with encouragement, he is a joy to train." The AWS can become protective of toys or food.

The AWS can be a wonderful family companion, although some bond more strongly with one family member. He is good with children when the kids treat him with respect. When raised with other pets he is fine with them, although he should never be trusted with birds. Some health concerns include baldness and heart and eye problems.

## Breed in Brief

**Registries:** AKC, UKC, CKC
**Occupation:** Gun dog
**Size:** 15 to 18 in tall; 25 to 45 lbs
**Longevity:** 11 to 13 years
**Exercise:** Moderate
**Training:** Easy; keep training fun
**Grooming:** Moderate

# Anatolian Shepherd Dog

This is an ancient breed that originated in Turkey as a livestock guardian dog. His job was to protect the flock from predators. Today, he is prized as a deterrent for both livestock rustlers and animal predators of every kind.

The Anatolian is a large, impressive, powerful dog looking fully capable of defending a flock from wolves or bears. Females should be 27 inches tall or taller and males 29 inches tall or taller. Weight can range from 80 to 160 pounds. The coat varies in length, from about 1 to 4 inches long. Color can vary, too, with all colors acceptable.

Grooming is not difficult at all; the coat should be brushed twice a week.

Anatolians need daily exercise. A long walk or a nice jog beside a bicycle will suffice. Although puppies are playful, adults are quite serious and few enjoy games.

Gary Jakobi, President of the Anatolian Shepherd Dog Club of America, says, "Anatolians are highly territorial and possessive of their charges, whether four-legged or two-legged." Although early socialization is good, and the dogs are not aggressive, it will not change their nature. The same applies to obedience training. This breed is very intelligent and learns quickly; however, they were bred for thousands of years to think on their own. They may comply with most commands, but they may also decide to ignore commands. Someone who wishes to have an obedient, compliant dog should not get an Anatolian.

Jakobi says, "Anatolians think of children the same way they think of lambs—something small to be protected." As such, they are very tolerant but will not be a child's playmate. They are also good with other pets and dogs that were raised in the family. This breed can be a good family dog for people who truly understand what the breed is. These dogs are "hard-wired" to be who they are, and no amount of training (or anything else) will change them. This is a healthy breed.

## Breed in Brief

**Registries:** AKC, UKC
**Occupation:** Guardian
**Size:** 27 to 29+ in tall; 80 to 160 lbs
**Longevity:** 11 to 13 years
**Exercise:** Active puppy; calm adult
**Training:** Intelligent and independent
**Grooming:** Easy

# ppenzeller Sennenhunde

The Appenzeller Sennenhunde, or Appenzeller, is one of four related Swiss breeds. The other three are the Greater Swiss Mountain Dog, the Bernese Mountain Dog, and the Entlebucher. The breed was, and still is, a livestock guardian, draft dog, and versatile farm dog.

This is a medium to large dog, standing 19 to 23 inches tall and weighing between 50 and 60 pounds. He has a broad head, small dark eyes, and dropped ears. His body is powerful, with a deep chest and well-muscled shoulders. The tail is carried over the back. The short coat is always tricolored—black with rust and white markings.

Grooming this breed is not difficult. A twice weekly brushing will suffice.

This is an active working breed that needs exercise every day. A long morning and evening walk is good, as is a long, slow jog alongside a bicycle. Puppies can be very playful, but adults can sometimes be too serious for games. Without daily exercise, the Appenzeller is prone to finding something to do to amuse himself and you may not like what he does.

The breed can be wary of strangers, so early socialization is important. Training is also very important. As a working breed, Appenzellers need guidance and rules; otherwise they will make their own. Luckily, the breed is easily trained and thrives on training that is fun and not too repetitive. This breed is also a good choice for many canine sports; he is happy, athletic, and has the desire to do things with you. Obedience competition, herding trials, agility trials, and carting are all good activities for this breed.

This is not a city dog; he does best in a place where he can have a nice yard (or farm) to play and work. He is affectionate with family, protective of his home, and good with children who treat him well. He can also be good with other pets, although interactions should be supervised. There are few health concerns—hip dysplasia is one.

## Breed in Brief

**Registries:** AKC FSS, UKC
**Occupation:** Versatile farm dog, guardian
**Size:** 19 to 23 in tall; 50 to 60 lbs
**Longevity:** 10 to 12 years
**Exercise:** Moderate to high activity level
**Training:** Easy
**Grooming:** Easy

# ustralian Cattle Dog

The Australian Cattle Dog (ACD) was developed in Australia in response to the growing beef industry. The herding dogs available were unable to manage the herds of wild cattle. The breed was derived from crossing the native dingo (a silent hunter with incredible stamina) with a Dalmatian (for horse sense), Highland Collies (for herding ability), and the Black and Tan Kelpie (a herding breed). The breed has been called a blue heeler, red heeler, and Queensland heeler.

ACDs are compact and powerful. They stand between 17 and 20 inches tall and weigh between 35 and 50 pounds. The eyes are oval and alert, ears are upright, and the tail reaches the hocks with a slight curve. The coat has a dense undercoat and a close outer coat no longer than a 1.5 inches. Colors include red speckle, blue, blue speckle, and blue mottle.

Twice weekly brushing will keep the ACD in nice shape, except during shedding season (spring and fall) when daily brushing is needed.

The ACD needs vigorous daily exercise. Although long brisk walks will be appreciated, that is not enough exercise for this breed. The ACD will also need to go for a run alongside a bicycle, do herding training, run the agility course, or play a fast game of flying disc. Without enough exercise, the ACD will become bored and develop bad habits. The breed excels at many canine sports and should participate in at least one.

Early socialization and training are also needed, as this breed is very bright and able to think for himself. Training can teach good habits and household rules and can motivate the dog to want to be good. Without mental stimulation, as well as exercise, the ACD will get into trouble.

This can be a difficult breed for a first-time dog owner. He can be wary of strangers but is affectionate with his people. He's good with kids but will try to herd them, often nipping at heels. Health concerns include hip and elbow dysplasia and deafness.

## Breed in Brief

**Registries:** AKC, CKC, UKC
**Occupation:** Cattle dog
**Size:** 17 to 20 in tall; 35 to 50 lbs
**Longevity:** 12 to 14 years
**Exercise:** Vigorous daily exercise
**Training:** Hard to keep challenged
**Grooming:** Easy

# ustralian Kelpie

This is an Australian breed that is most likely a descendant of several old English herding breeds. Although many believe dingos may have been used in the breed's development, this is still being debated. The breed has been used in Australia and North America as a versatile, sturdy working dog able to do anything needed on a farm or ranch.

The Kelpie stands 17 to 20 inches tall and weighs between 25 and 50 pounds. They are strong for their size, with a body that is slightly longer than tall at the shoulder. He has prick ears, almond-shaped eyes, a broad chest, and a long tail. The undercoat is thick and the outer coat is short. Colors include black, blue, or red, all with or without tan markings.

Grooming this breed is easy; twice weekly brushings will suffice. During spring and fall when the shedding is at its worst, you may wish to brush a little more.

This is a very active, high-energy breed with a strong desire to work. He needs vigorous exercise each and every day without fail. A bored Kelpie will get into trouble. He needs to herd sheep, run alongside a bicycle, train on the agility course, or play flyball. Or better yet, let him do all of those things! This breed is the ultimate workaholic.

Training should begin early, as this intelligent breed deserves a chance to use his brain. After basic obedience, keep training him. Teach him tricks and get him involved in dog sports. Early socialization will get him used to a variety of people and other dogs. The Kelpie can be a protective watchdog.

This breed needs an active owner who wants to do things with him, whether it's farm work, dog sports, or hiking and backpacking. The Kelpie has a strong tendency to be a one-person dog and, in a family situation, may ignore the other members of the family. Kelpies are usually good with other dogs and pets when raised with them. Cats may dislike being herded. Health concerns include eye problems.

## Breed in Brief

**Registries:** CKC, UKC
**Occupation:** Versatile ranch dog
**Size:** 17 to 20 in tall; 25 to 50 lbs
**Longevity:** 12 to 14 years
**Exercise:** Vigorous daily exercise
**Training:** Easy; hard to keep busy
**Grooming:** Easy

# *A*ustralian Shepherd

The Australian Shepherd, or Aussie, is not from Australia but instead is a native of the American West. When gold miners flocked to the American West in the 1800s, food became scarce and sheep were imported from Australia. Basque sheep herders managed these flocks and brought their dogs to assist them. Although the true origin of the name is unknown, most breed experts assume that people thought the dogs came with the flocks of sheep, hence, Australian Shepherd. The dogs became very popular with western ranchers and farmers; they were versatile, hardy, and able to master any job required of them. Jay Sisler, a rodeo performer, brought the breed to the public's attention in the 1950s when his Aussies performed amazing tricks at rodeo performances.

Aussies are medium-sized dogs, with males standing 20 to 23 inches tall at the shoulder and females slightly less. Aussies are quick, athletic, and agile and can work all day. An Aussie's expression is very intelligent, bright and alert, with eyes that can be brown, amber, blue, or any variation

or combination. The coat is medium-length, straight to wavy, with an undercoat. The coat can be black, red, blue merle, or red merle, all with or without copper and white points. (The merle color is patches of darker color on a lighter, but not white, background.) The breed has a docked or naturally bobbed tail.

Grooming an Aussie takes only a little time. The coat requires brushing at least twice weekly—more during the spring and fall when shedding is heaviest. Tangles can form in the soft coat behind the ears or in the pantaloons (the hair on the back of the rear legs). The coat requires no trimming.

A breed developed to work hard, the Aussie needs vigorous daily exercise. A run alongside a bicycle, a jog with you, a game of flying disc, or a run through the agility course can all be part of the breed's daily routine. Aussies also need a job, whether it's herding sheep, keeping track of the family children, bringing in the morning paper, or learning tricks; Aussies need to be needed. Without exercise and a job to do, Aussies will find something to amuse themselves. Because of this trait, Aussies rarely do well in a home where they are alone for many hours each day.

The socialization of a puppy kindergarten class is important for Aussies, as they are naturally reserved with strangers. As puppies, Aussies need to meet people of all ages, sizes, and ethnic backgrounds. Continuing training after puppy class is vital to challenge the Aussie's mind and to teach household rules and good social behavior.

Aussies are excellent watchdogs, although once you're a friend, you will always be recognized and greeted with exuberance. Aussie owners will never find a more loyal companion. Aussies can be great with children, although puppies can be quite exuberant and need to be taught how to behave. Many children get frustrated, though, with the breed's tendency to herd (or circle) kids, trying to keep the kids in one spot as they would sheep. The breed is usually very good with other pets, although the herding instinct can be quite strong and cats rarely enjoy being herded. Major health concerns include eye disorders, hip dysplasia, and seizure disorders.

## Breed in Brief

**Registries:** ASCA, AKC, UKC, CKC

**Occupation:** Herder, versatile farm dog, performance sports

**Size:** 20 to 23 in tall; 45 to 60 lbs

**Longevity:** 14 to 16 years

**Exercise:** Vigorous daily exercise

**Training:** Easy; hard to keep challenged

**Grooming:** Easy to moderate

# Australian Terrier

A native to Australia, this tough little terrier was bred to be versatile. Most likely descended from Irish Terriers, Yorkshire Terriers, Cairn Terriers, and a few other terriers who had the qualities the settlers needed, this little dog was used to control rodents and snakes, warn of trespassers and predators, and at times, even tend the sheep.

The Australian Terrier is a small dog standing 10 to 11 inches at the shoulder and weighing 12 to 14 pounds. He is sturdy, with dark eyes, upright ears, and a docked tail. His body is longer than he is tall at the shoulder, and his coat is about 2.5 inches long. He can be three colors: blue and tan, sandy, and red.

Grooming this breed is easy. He needs twice weekly brushing, and you might want to trim the hair on his paws to keep them neat. Twice a year, he needs to be hand-stripped.

Aussies need a long brisk walk morning and evening and a chance to hunt for critters in the yard a couple of times a day. They enjoy games, including hide-and-seek, and some may retrieve thrown toys. Without enough exercise, they can be destructive, and they love to dig. They should never be allowed to run off leash outside of a fenced-in yard; these dogs have strong hunting instincts and will be off after a rabbit, squirrel, or cat in a flash.

The Australian Terrier Club of America says, "Puppy kindergarten classes are an excellent way to socialize your new puppy and provide you, the new owner, with guidance in helping your new puppy become a well-trained addition to your family." Aussies are not bad little dogs, but instead, are active physically and mentally and need to know what is acceptable and what is not. The training should be firm yet fun, and should avoid too much repetition.

The Aussie can be a good family dog if he's kept busy. He will tolerate children if they respect him. He is not to be trusted with other small pets; remember, he is a hunter. This is a healthy breed.

## Breed in Brief

**Registries:** AKC, UKC, CKC
**Occupation:** Vermin hunter
**Size:** 10 to 11 in tall; 12 to 14 lbs
**Longevity:** 13 to 15 years
**Exercise:** Vigorous daily exercise
**Training:** Moderate
**Grooming:** Easy

# Azawakh

This is an ancient sighthound breed that has lived for thousands of years with the cattle breeding nomads of the south Sahara in Africa. His job has been to protect the camp, the people in the camp, and the cattle from predators and trespassers. Also known as the Sahel hound, he howls and growls to warn of intruders and, should they continue into the camp, he will charge and can be aggressive.

The Azawakh stands 23.5 to 29 inches tall and weighs between 35 and 55 pounds. His head is long and thin and his muzzle even thinner. His eyes are almond-shaped and dark, and his ears are pendant. He is very lean; there is nothing extra on his body. He stands square, with his body as long as it is tall. His chest is deep, with room for a large heart and lungs. His muscles are evident under the skin. His coat is very short and thin.

Grooming this breed is very easy. The coat is very short and thin and may be brushed with a soft bristled brush once a week.

The Azawakh is a sighthound. His long legs, deep chest, and agile body are made so he can run with the wind. Although he can walk on a leash, he prefers to run and will need a daily run in a safely fenced yard.

In his natural state, the Azawakh learns what to do from the other dogs in camp. Obedience training is unnatural to him. However, when kept as a companion, even the Azawakh must learn some rules. Early socialization and training can help him learn to walk on a leash, to understand that all people outside his family are not necessarily intruders, and to abide by some household rules.

The Azawakh has often been called more catlike than doglike. He will allow petting when he's ready to be petted, and although he may never come the first time you call him, you are still vitally important to him. He can be good with children as long as they treat him with respect, and can be trusted with the family cat only if raised with her. The breed can suffer from heart problems and hip dysplasia.

## Breed in Brief

**Registries:** AKC FSS, UKC
**Occupation:** Guardian
**Size:** 23.5 to 29 in tall; 35 to 55 lbs
**Longevity:** 10 to 14 years
**Exercise:** Daily run
**Training:** Challenge
**Grooming:** Easy

# Basenji

There is documented evidence of Basenjis 5,000 years ago in Egypt, where they were known as "the pharaoh's dog." In Africa, the breed was used as a hunting dog. Although it has been known as the "barkless dog," it is not noiseless. Instead of barking, these dogs yodel and shriek and can be quite noisy.

The Basenji stands 16 or 17 inches tall and weighs 20 to 25 pounds. She is very much an athlete, lightly built but muscular. She has a wrinkled forehead, upright ears, and almond-shaped, dark eyes. The tail is high and curled. The coat is short and may be red, black, tricolored, or brindle.

The Basenji's short coat should be brushed twice weekly with a soft bristle brush.

Although a walk morning and evening will be enjoyed, that's not enough exercise. The Basenji needs to run inside a safely fenced area where she can sniff for critters and run until she's tired. Although she doesn't look like a sighthound, she has many characteristics of a sighthound, including the joy of running and the hunting of prey by sight.

Enrolling in a puppy socialization class can help Basenjis be more comfortable with people outside their families. Early training that is fun can teach her important household rules. Keep in mind, though, that during training many people feel Basenjis are more like cats than dogs. Although the breed is quick and intelligent, it is not necessary compliant, so training can be a challenge. However, with lots of positive reinforcement, the Basenji can learn to enjoy training, and many have succeeded in a variety of canine sports.

This breed can be very difficult for a first-time dog owner or for an owner who wants a compliant dog. A Basenji's owner needs a sense of humor. The Basenji can be good with children when they treat her with respect. She may chase cats and can be dog-aggressive. Health concerns include eye, kidney, and thyroid problems and anemia.

## Breed in Brief

**Registries:** AKC, UKC, CKC
**Occupation:** Hunter
**Size:** 16 to 17 in tall; 20 to 25 lbs
**Longevity:** 12 to 14 years
**Exercise:** Needs to run
**Training:** Challenge
**Grooming:** Easy

# Basset Hound

The Basset Hound originated in France (*bas* in French means *low-set*) in the mid-1500s. The Basset was developed by friars of the French Abbey of St. Hubert. They wanted a slower-moving hound who could be followed by men on foot. For centuries, the Basset was used to track and hunt rabbits, hare, and deer, as well as any other game that could be trailed on foot.

The Basset Hound is a large dog, of heavy bone, with short legs. She should stand no taller than 14 inches at the shoulder, and most weigh between 40 and 60 pounds. She is powerful and has great stamina, able to work in the field day after day. The head is large, with very long ears and dark, soft eyes. The chest is deep, the body is long, and the tail is carried gaily in hound fashion. The skin is loose, while the coat is short and may be any hound color.

The Basset's coat is not difficult to groom; it may be brushed with a soft bristle brush twice a week to loosen dead hair. The ears should be cleaned at least twice a week also, as the heavy ears can get dirty.

A young, healthy Basset will have plenty of energy to go for walks or to play. Unfortunately, the breed is prone to obesity, and as a Basset gets heavier, she also gets lazier. Bassets need exercise. A good walk morning and evening is great, but a play session midday is also good.

Although training can be a challenge, Bassets can participate in some canine sports, including tracking and therapy dog work.

Bassets are one of the most amiable breeds. They are good with children, other dogs, and other pets, although Basset puppies can be rowdy and must be taught to be gentle with children. Bassets do not like to be alone, however; if they must be left alone, having another dog for companionship is a good idea. Bassets can bark and bay, which can cause neighborhood problems. The breed has some health issues, including obesity, back problems, hip and elbow dysplasia, eye problems, and bloat.

## Breed in Brief

**Registries:** AKC, UKC, CKC
**Occupation:** Trailer
**Size:** No taller than 14 in; 40 to 60 lbs
**Longevity:** 11 to 13 years
**Exercise:** Calm; low energy
**Training:** Challenge
**Grooming:** Easy

# Beagle

## (13-inch and 15-inch)

Packs of hunting hounds were being used in England long before the time of the Roman invasion. However, exactly what those hounds were is unknown, although they are thought to be the distant ancestors of the scenthounds that developed later, one of which was the Beagle. When fox hunting became popular in England in the mid-1800s, the Foxhound was developed, and one of its ancestors was said to be the Beagle. At around that same time, Beagles were gaining popularity in the United States, with the National Beagle Club forming in 1888.

Beagles are small dogs, compact and lean, with wonderfully expressive faces, large dropped ears, and dark eyes. The short coat, often tricolored with red or tan, a black saddle, and white on the legs, belly, and muzzle, is soft to the touch. As a hunting scenthound, the Beagle is strong and able to follow a trail for hours at a time. Beagles have two height categories. The smaller ones are under 13 inches at the shoulder, and the larger are over 13 but not exceeding 15 inches.

Grooming the Beagle is not difficult; the short coat can be brushed once or twice a week with a soft bristle brush or curry comb. The short coat does shed, although not heavily. The dropped ears should be checked often, as they can get dirty.

The Beagle requires daily exercise. A long, brisk walk is sufficient, although these dogs also enjoy a good run. Beagles should not be allowed to run free outside of a securely fenced yard, as they can be easily distracted by any scents they detect. Even well-trained Beagles will ignore a Come command in favor of following an interesting scent trail.

Training should definitely be a part of every Beagle's upbringing. Although Beagles by nature are social pack dogs, they still need to learn household manners. Plus, learning to walk nicely on leash can be a challenge; Beagles love to forge ahead with their noses to the ground! However, fair yet structured training that keeps things fun can help Beagles learn basic obedience skills.

Beagles are first and foremost hunting hounds. Their sense of smell is their most important sense, and they will follow it anywhere. Packs of Beagles today compete in hunt tests very successfully. Although their good-natured, friendly temperament makes them appealing family dogs, unless you understand the hound personality, you may be frustrated by them. Hounds can be quite independent, and being with people will never be as exciting as following the scent of a rabbit.

In families where they are understood, Beagles can be wonderful pets. They are sturdy and make great playmates for kids. They are clean, do not have a doggy odor, and do not mind spending time outside. As hunting hounds, they do bay, and not all neighbors appreciate their melody! They should not be trusted alone with small pets (they *are* hunters!), although they are very social with other dogs. Beagles are, unfortunately, prone to several serious health problems, including hip dysplasia, hypothyroidism, dwarfism, seizure disorders, knee problems, and reproductive disorders.

## Breed in Brief

**Registries:** AKC, UKC, CKC
**Occupation:** Pack hunter
**Size:** Under 13 in tall and between 13 and 15 in; 15 to 30 lbs
**Longevity:** 14 to 15 years
**Exercise:** Moderate to vigorous
**Training:** Challenge
**Grooming:** Easy

# earded Collie

The Bearded Collie is one of England's oldest breeds. In the past, the breed was also known as the Highland Collie or Mountain Collie; it is said to be an ancestor of the Australian Cattle Dog as well as other hard-working herding breeds.

The Beardie stands 20 and 22 inches tall and weighs between 40 and 60 pounds. She has a broad skull, large dark eyes, and dropped ears. The body is strong but not heavy. The tail is long. The Beardie's coat is her crowning glory; the outer coat is long, flat, and follows the line of the body. The undercoat is soft and close. All Beardies are born black, blue, brown, or fawn, and as the Beardie grows, the coat lightens.

This lovely coat does need some care to keep it looking its best. It needs be brushed and combed at least every other day—daily if the dog runs and plays outside and gets wet or dirty. In the spring and fall when shedding is at its worst, daily brushing is needed. Many pet owners have the coat trimmed to a shorter length for ease of care.

Beardies are active, playful, and often silly dogs. They need time to run, play, and exercise. Although walks are enjoyable, they are not enough to use up this breed's excess energy. Games of fetch and hide-and-seek are good, as is a daily run alongside a bicycle. Beardies also enjoy canine sports, including agility, herding, and flyball.

Early training can help teach this boisterous dog what behavior is acceptable and what isn't. Although Beardies are bright and intelligent, they are also freethinkers. Training should be structured yet fun.

The Beardie can be a good watchdog, but she's too social to be overly protective. She does best in an active household where people enjoy doing things with her. She is good with kids, but as a puppy, she may be too boisterous for young children. She can be good with small pets but may try to herd the family cat. Health concerns include eye problems, hip dysplasia, and Addison's disease.

## Breed in Brief

**Registries:** AKC, UKC, CKC
**Occupation:** Herder
**Size:** 20 to 22 in tall; 40 to 60 lbs
**Longevity:** 13 to 15 years
**Exercise:** Active and playful
**Training:** Easy to train; hard to keep focused
**Grooming:** Difficult

# Beauceron

The Beauceron is a herding dog from France with a documented history going back to the 1500s. The breed was used to herd both sheep and cattle and to protect livestock from predators and thieves. An intelligent, bold, and trainable breed, she has also been used extensively by the military and law enforcement agencies.

The Beauceron stands 24.5 to 27.5 inches tall and weighs 80 to 110 pounds, with females smaller than males. The head is carried proudly, with either natural dropped ears or cropped upright ears. The double coat is short and coarse and is usually black and red, although there is also a harlequin (gray, black, and tan).

This breed's coat requires brushing twice a week, except during spring and fall when shedding is heavier.

The Beauceron does not tolerate a quiet, calm lifestyle well. She needs activity, exercise, and a job to do. If she is not living on a farm herding, then she needs vigorous daily exercise. She should also participate in dog sports.

Training should begin early and continue into adulthood, as this intelligent breed needs mental challenges. She will enjoy advanced obedience, trick training, tracking, air scenting, Schutzhund, and search and rescue training. The Beauceron Club of Canada says, "It must be stressed the Beauceron is not the dog for everyone. They are not suitable for the first-time dog owner unless that person is prepared to seek the guidance of a professional dog trainer." Without an owner who is a leader, the Beauceron will assume that position, with less-than-pleasant results.

With training, leadership, and a job to do, the Beauceron can be a wonderful family companion. Although rowdy as puppies, adults are good with children. They are great with other dogs in the family but can be assertive with strange dogs. When raised with other pets, they are fine, but they will herd the family cat. Health concerns include hip dysplasia and bloat.

## Breed in Brief

**Registries:** AKC, UKC
**Occupation:** Herder
**Size:** 24.5 to 27.5 in tall; 80 to 110 lbs
**Longevity:** 11 to 13 years
**Exercise:** Very active
**Training:** Easy; hard to keep challenged
**Grooming:** Easy

# Bedlington Terrier

Although this small terrier looks like a stuffed toy, she is a game little hunter. In England, the breed was used to kill badgers, foxes, and other vermin. Named for the mining village where the breed was popular, this dog did not reach the public's attention until the late 1800s when the National Bedlington Terrier Club (England) was formed.

Bedlingtons stand 15.5 to 16.5 inches tall and weigh 17 to 25 pounds. They have narrow heads crowned by a topknot of coat, which is lighter in color than the rest of the coat and tapers down the face to just behind the nose. The eyes are small, and the ears are triangular and hang flat. The chest is deep, and the back arches to the hips. The coat has a mixture of both hard and soft hairs and has a tendency to curl. It may be blue, sandy, or liver-colored, with or without tan markings.

This breed can be a challenge to learn to groom, and most pet owners would do well to ask their dog's breeder to show them how. The topknot on the face must be shaped, and the coat must be trimmed on the body. Show dogs can have no more than 1 inch of coat on the body, although the legs can have a slightly longer coat.

Bedlingtons are not as active as many other terriers. A good walk morning and night, with a playtime in between, will keep most of these dogs happy. If allowed to run off leash, they must be in a safe, fenced-in yard. These dogs can be enthusiastic hunters and will chase rabbits, squirrels, or running cats.

Training should begin early so that dog and owner can bond and the terrier can be socialized to other dogs. Training is often a challenge, so the owner should be patient and keep the training structured yet fun.

The Bedlington is a scrappy little dog, yet she enjoys the comforts of home, too. She can be dog-aggressive, especially to dogs of the same sex. She can be good with cats but cannot be trusted not to chase them. Health concerns include copper toxicosis, eye problems, and kidney disease.

## Breed in Brief

**Registries:** AKC, UKC, CKC
**Occupation:** Hunter, companion
**Size:** 15.5 to 16.5 in tall; 17 to 25 lbs
**Longevity:** 10 to 12 years
**Exercise:** Moderate
**Training:** Moderate
**Grooming:** Difficult

# $\mathcal{B}$elgian Laekenois

The Belgian Laekenois is one of, and probably the oldest of, four related varieties of Belgian Shepherd Dogs. The Laekenois originated in the mid- to late 1800s in Flandres, where the dogs herded sheep and guarded flax fields. In the early 1900s, the Brussels police force and Belgian army used these versatile dogs.

The Laekenois stands 22 to 26 inches tall and weighs between 40 and 80 pounds, with females smaller than males. The head is strong, the eyes are almond-shaped and dark brown, and the ears are upright and large. The body is as long as it is tall at the shoulder. The tail is long. The coat is wiry and can be fawn to mahogany, usually with a touch of black.

Grooming the weather-resistant wire coat is not difficult. It should be brushed twice a week.

The Laekenois is a very active, high-energy breed. Vigorous daily exercise is very important; without exercise or a job to do, this breed will get into trouble. Long walks are great, but she will also need a jog alongside a bicycle, an agility training session, or a fast game of fetch.

Early socialization is necessary, as the breed is reserved with strangers. Early training that continues into adulthood will not only teach household rules and social manners, but will give the dog mental stimulation. These alert, intelligent dogs were bred to work and will not be happy unless they have a job to do. They also excel at canine activities and sports, including agility, obedience competition, herding trials, and flyball.

The Laekenois are watchful and protective. They are affectionate with their people but tend to bond more closely with one family member. They can be good with older children but will tend to try to herd them. They can be good with smaller pets if raised with them but, again, will try to herd cats. Health concerns include hip and elbow dysplasia, eye and thyroid problems, and epilepsy.

## Breed in Brief

**Registries:** AKC FSS, UKC, CKC
**Occupation:** Herder
**Size:** 22 to 26 in tall; 40 to 80 lbs
**Longevity:** 12 to 14 years
**Exercise:** Vigorous daily exercise
**Training:** Easy; needs to work
**Grooming:** Easy

# Belgian Malinois

The Belgian Malinois is one of four varieties of Belgian Shepherd dogs. This breed was developed in Belgium in the mid- to late 1800s as both sheep herding and guardian dogs. In the early 1900s, they were used by both the Brussels police and Belgian army.

The Malinois stands between 22 and 26 inches tall and weighs between 40 and 80 pounds, with females smaller than males. The head is strong, and the eyes are almond-shaped and dark brown. The ears are pricked and large. The body is as long as the dog is tall at the shoulder, and the legs are strong. The tail is curved and reaches the hock. The coat is short and hard and is fawn to mahogany, with black tips, mask, and ears. There is a dense undercoat.

The Malinois needs twice weekly brushing for most of the year, but during spring and fall when shedding is at its worst, the coat should be brushed more often.

The Malinois is a high-energy, active breed. Vigorous daily exercise is an absolute must. Jogging alongside a bicycle, plus a game of flying disc and a couple of walks, is the minimum. This breed excels at canine sports and does best in a home where people are active and want to play games with her every day.

## Breed in Brief

**Registries:** AKC, UKC, CKC
**Occupation:** Herder
**Size:** 22 to 26 in tall; 40 to 80 lbs
**Longevity:** 12 to 14 years
**Exercise:** Vigorous daily exercise
**Training:** Easy; needs to work
**Grooming:** Easy

The Malinois is the most driven of the four Belgain Shepherd varieties; she has an innate drive to work. Her training should begin early and continue into adulthood so that she has a focus and a job to do. She can also be very wary of strangers and quite protective, so socialization should start early, too, and continue into adulthood.

The Malinois is too much dog for a first-time dog owner; she requires an active, experienced owner who understands what she needs. She can be a good family dog but tends to bond more closely with one person in the family. She may not be good with other dogs; she wants to be in charge. She should not be trusted with small pets; she has a strong prey drive. Health concerns include hip and elbow dysplasia and eye and thyroid problems.

# Belgian Sheepdog

The Belgian Sheepdog is one of four breeds that make up the Belgian Shepherd family. The breed can credit its existence to Nicolas Rose, who established the first known kennel of the breed. His foundation pair, Picard d'Uccle and Petite, can be found in the lineage of most Belgian Shepherds today. These are superb working dogs.

The breed has a very distinct look. All black (or with just a touch of white on the forechest), the dog stands tall, with head up and with pricked ears. The coat is luscious, with a heavier ruff around the neck and a plumed tail wagging slowly. Males are 24 to 26 inches tall and about 55 to 75 pounds; females are slightly smaller.

The Belgian Sheepdog's coat is long, of medium harshness, and has a very dense undercoat. Although the coat is not prone to matting, tangles can form behind the ears or in the pantaloons. The coat should be brushed at least twice a week, although during the spring and fall, daily brushing can keep shedding under control.

## Breed in Brief

**Registries:** AKC, UKC, CKC
**Occupation:** Herder, farm dog, police dog, performance sports
**Size:** 22 to 26 in tall; 50 to 75 lbs
**Longevity:** 12 to 14 years
**Exercise:** Vigorous daily exercise
**Training:** Easy; hard to keep challenged
**Grooming:** Easy to moderate

This breed was designed to work and likes to be active. Daily aerobic exercise is very important—running alongside a bicycle, jogging with you, playing a vigorous game of retrieve, or a quick run through the agility course.

All Belgian Sheepdogs should attend a puppy socialization class when they are young so they get to meet a variety of people. Training should be introduced early, in puppy class, and continued through adolescence, as the breed is very intelligent but can also be somewhat independent. Training should be structured yet fair and fun and should keep the dog challenged.

Belgian Sheepdogs are excellent watchdogs, yet are affectionate and loyal to family and friends. They can be good with children, although they often try to herd (circle) and control rambunctious kids. The breed can be good with other dogs and small pets, although these interactions should always be supervised. Health concerns include hip dysplasia, thyroid problems, and seizure disorders.

# Belgian Tervuren

The Belgian Tervuren is one of four varieties of the Belgian Shepherd. All four varieties originated in Belgium as herding and guardian dogs and became recognized in the late 1800s. In Europe, all four varieties form one breed with different coat types; only in the U.S. are they separated into four breeds.

The Tervuren is the most elegant of the four varieties. Although the size and body type are very much the same, the Tervuren's wonderful coat and proud head carriage set her apart. The Tervuren stands between 22 and 26 inches tall and weighs between 40 and 80 pounds, with females smaller than males. The eyes are dark brown and expressive; the ears are upright. The body is strong, and the tail reaches the hock. The coat is elegant. The outer coat is long with a thick undercoat. The coat can be fawn to mahogany, with black tips and a black mask and ears.

The coat needs regular brushing, especially during the spring and fall when shedding is at its heaviest.

The Tervuren is an active breed that needs vigorous daily exercise. She can take a couple of long walks every day but also needs to train on the agility course, chase tennis balls, or run alongside your bicycle. Without enough exercise she will get into trouble.

## Breed in Brief

**Registries:** AKC, UKC, CKC
**Occupation:** Herder
**Size:** 22 to 26 in tall; 40 to 80 lbs
**Longevity:** 12 to 14 years
**Exercise:** Vigorous daily exercise
**Training:** Easy; needs to work
**Grooming:** Moderate

The Tervuren is the most sensitive of the four varieties of Belgian Shepherd and should begin puppy socialization classes early so that she meets many different people. Training should begin early, too, to challenge the Tervuren's mind and to give her a job to do. The training should be structured yet fun. The Terv excels at many canine sports.

The Tervuren should have an active, experienced owner who knows what she needs. She can be a good family dog but tends to bond more closely with one family member. She is usually good with other dogs but may not be good with dogs of the same sex. She will try to herd the family cat. Health concerns include eye and thyroid problems.

# Bergamasco Sheepdog

The Bergamasco Sheepdog is an old breed that probably originated in the Italian Alps. As sheep and shepherds spread through Europe and Asia, especially in the Alpine regions, so did the dogs who served them.

The Bergamasco stands 22 to 25 inches tall and weighs 60 to 85 pounds. She is solid and large-boned, with a long head and thin dropped ears. Although her eyes are rarely seen, they are dark and intelligent. The breed's unique characteristic is the corded coat. The coat is made up of long black, silver, or gray hairs that mat into long cords that fall from the dog's body to the ground. It takes about five years for the coat to fully grow out and cord.

The cords require minimal care once they form. The dog can be bathed occasionally, but the cords must then be dried. Many owners keep the hair trimmed under the tail, around the genitals, and on the feet.

This breed requires only moderate exercise. A walk daily, a chance to play in the yard, and maybe a run through the agility course will be fine. Although not a high-energy breed, the Bergamasco does best in a home with a yard; this breed enjoys spending time with family but does not do well inside all the time.

Training this breed can be a challenge. They are bright and learn quickly; however, they were bred for thousands of years to think for themselves while tending flocks of sheep. When given an obedience command, the dog may or may not respond, depending upon how important she feels it is. Owners who want a very compliant dog should not get this breed. All training should be fun and very positive, and there should be minimal repetition.

This breed does best in a rural home with an experienced dog owner. The dog will be happiest if a flock of sheep is present. She is wonderful with children, great with cats if raised with them, and good with other dogs as long as she doesn't perceive them to be a threat. This is also a very healthy breed.

## Breed in Brief

**Registries:** AKC FSS, UKC
**Occupation:** Livestock guardian
**Size:** 22 to 25 in tall; 60 to 85 lbs
**Longevity:** 12 to 14 years
**Exercise:** Moderate
**Training:** Easy; compliance is hard
**Grooming:** Long, corded coat

# Berger des Pyrenees

## (Smooth Face and Rough Face)

The Berger des Pyrenees, or Pyrenean Shepherd, is an ancient breed; it is known to have been used as a herding dog in the Pyrenees Mountains for as long as men have been herding sheep there. The shepherds used two different breeds for two purposes. The Great Pyrenees were livestock guardians and protected the flocks from predation, while the smaller, more active herding dogs, the Berger des Pyrenees, were used to move the flocks. This breed is also thought to be the ancestor of several modern herding breeds, including the Australian Shepherd.

The Berger stands 15 to 20 inches tall and weighs 25 to 30 pounds. The eyes may be blue, brown, or marble; the ears may be cropped or fold naturally. The tail is a natural bob or may be docked. The coat is wavy, long, and may be corded or brushed. The smooth-faced variety has short hair on the face. The rough-faced variety has longer hair on the muzzle and cheeks. The coat may be gray, blue merle, black, or black with white markings.

If the coat is allowed to cord, ask a breeder for a demonstration on coat care. If the coat is to be brushed, it requires twice weekly brushing.

This active herding breed needs daily exercise and a job to do. That could be herding, running the agility course, trick training, or running alongside a bicycle. This is not a good dog to leave alone for hours each day; if bored, she will get into trouble.

Bergers are wary of strangers, so socialization should begin early, as should training. The training needs to be fun and varied; repetition is not good for this breed. Training should continue on into adulthood so she has a sense of purpose.

The Berger is good with an experienced dog owner. She is affectionate, silly, and playful with her own family and is great with the children she is raised with. She is reserved with other dogs. Health concerns include hip dysplasia and knee problems.

## Breed in Brief

**Registries:** AKC FSS, CKC
**Occupation:** Herder
**Size:** 15 to 20 in tall; 25 to 30 lbs
**Longevity:** 12 to 14 years
**Exercise:** Very active
**Training:** Easy; needs a job
**Grooming:** Moderate

# Berger Picard

The Berger Picard, or Berger de Picard, originated in the Picardie region of France and is known to have been in existence for at least 1,000 years. This herding breed nearly disappeared after the devastation of World Wars I and II but is making a comeback in France, Germany, and, to a lesser extent, North America.

The Berger Picard stands 21.5 to 25.5 inches tall and weighs between 50 and 75 pounds. This dog has a broad head, long muzzle, and large upright ears. Her eyes are dark, and she has a terrierlike face with a mustache, beard, and eyebrows. The tail is long. She has a double coat with a dense undercoat. The outer coat is coarse and wiry and is about 2.5 inches long. The coat is gray, silver, or gray with reddish touches.

The coat is easy to care for and needs brushing only once a week. The breed sheds lightly and has no doggy odor.

The Berger Picard is a perimeter herding dog, one who runs the perimeter of the area in which the sheep are grazing, like a canine fence. Therefore, this is a very active dog who loves to run. She will need vigorous exercise every day. Running alongside a bicycle will be great, or take her jogging with you.

She will need early and ongoing socialization. Like most herding dogs, she can be reserved with strangers. She is very receptive to training, which should be firm yet fun. She will thrive in continued training, especially games or activities that challenge her. Train her in agility, flyball, or flying disc.

The Berger Picard is quite protective of her family and property and is very affectionate and loyal. She's great with children and is fine with smaller pets if raised with them. She can be a barker, and that can cause neighborhood problems. As a perimeter herding dog, she can also be a fence runner in the backyard, barking at people or dogs going past. This can cause fence-fighting issues. The breed has few health issues, although these dogs can have eye problems.

## Breed in Brief

**Registries:** UKC, CKC
**Occupation:** Herder
**Size:** 21.5 to 25.5 in tall; 50 to 75 lbs
**Longevity:** 13 to 15 years
**Exercise:** Vigorous daily exercise
**Training:** Moderate; needs a job
**Grooming:** Easy

# Bernese Mountain Dog

The Bernese Mountain Dog, also known as the Berner Sennenhund, is one of four breeds under the umbrella known as the Swiss Mountain Dogs. The other breeds are the Greater Swiss Mountain Dog, the Entlebucher Sennenhund, and the Appenzeller Sennenhund. All four share the distinctive tricolor markings, but the Bernese is the only one with a long coat.

The Berner is an old breed in Switzerland—her ancestors were brought to the region by Roman soldiers 2,000 years ago—and throughout her history has been an all-purpose farm dog. These dogs drove cattle, both on the farm and to market, pulled wagons, protected the farm, and of course were family companions.

This is a large breed, with males standing 25 to 27 inches tall at the shoulder and weighing between 90 and 120 pounds. Females are slightly smaller. Dogs should give the impression of stockiness and power; they should appear able to work hard. The coat is moderately long, straight to slightly wavy, with a thick undercoat. The dog is black with copper/rust and white markings on the face, chest, all four legs, and under the tail. Her expression is alert and good-natured. The ears are folded and move with the dog's expression.

Grooming the Berner's coat is not difficult but takes time. Brushing twice weekly is needed to keep the coat clean, but during shedding seasons, usually spring and fall, daily brushing will keep the loose hair in the house somewhat under control. Although Berners are shown in dog shows with a natural coat, many owners prefer to trim the long hairs on the feet and ears to help keep their dogs neat and clean.

As working farm dogs, Berners need daily exercise. However, this breed is not designed for fast running; instead, this is a strong, powerful breed. A long, brisk walk followed by a game of tennis ball retrieve will keep most Berners happy. Other activities, such as trick training, agility, and carting, can help keep body and mind challenged.

Although Berners can be a little cautious with strangers, they were not bred to be overly protective or watchful. As a whole, they are even-tempered, good-natured, and friendly. Socialization during puppyhood can make sure you're taking full advantage of the breed's wonderful temperament.

Training should begin early with these large, powerful dogs. Training should be fair and fun and should continue even after a basic obedience class. Bred to work, a bored Berner will get into trouble. However, a Berner who learns how to pull a cart, works as a therapy dog, or performs tricks will have a job to do and, as a result, will feel needed.

Berners are wonderful with children, usually very patient and tolerant. Activities should be supervised, of course, as Berners are large dogs and sometimes don't know their own strength. Berners are usually very tolerant of other pets. Family-oriented Berners do not like being isolated and should never be considered backyard dogs. Major health issues include hip and elbow dysplasia, bloat, von Willebrand disease (a bleeding disorder), eye disorders, and cancer.

## Breed in Brief

**Registries:** AKC, UKC, CKC
**Occupation:** Versatile farm dog, carting, drover
**Size:** 23 to 27 in tall; 90 to 120 lbs
**Longevity:** 8 to 10 years
**Exercise:** Moderate
**Training:** Easy
**Grooming:** Moderate

# Bichon Frise

hese adorable white fluffy dogs originated in the Mediterranean regions of Italy, Spain, and the Canary Islands. Descended from the Barnet (or water spaniel), they were often called Barbichon, which was shortened to Bichon, and later were called Bichon Teneriffe. The breed's small size, happy personality, and appealing coat made the dogs wonderful companions. In the 1300s, sailors brought the dogs aboard ships as companions and as barter for other goods at ports of call. Using them as barter spread the dogs' popularity throughout the Mediterranean and into Europe. In the 1500s, Henry III was a fan of the breed, as was Napoleon III.

The Bichon Frise stands between 9.5 and 11.5 inches tall and weighs between 10 and 16 pounds, with females smaller than males. The eyes are dark and expressive, the tail is carried happily over the back, and the white fluffy coat draws your hands—you simply must touch it. Although the Bichon is a small dog, she is sturdy, with a strong little body. At one point during the breed's history, in the late 1800s, she was known as the circus dog or organ grinder's dog and danced and performed tricks for the amusement of onlookers. Bichons today still retain those athletic abilities.

The breed's fluffy white coat is very appealing but does require regular grooming to keep it in shape. If the coat is ignored, it will mat (tangle). If matting is not taken care of right away, the entire coat could become matted, requiring a professional groomer's services to shave the dog. Therefore, the coat should be brushed and combed daily. Although the Bichon's coat does not shed, it does grow continually and requires trimming. If you wish to trim your Bichon yourself, talk to your dog's breeder for guidance. Most Bichon owners find a professional groomer who knows the breed and then bring their dogs in for grooming every four to six weeks.

The Bichon's exercise requirements are not extreme. Older puppies and young adult dogs are the most active, but a good walk morning and night with a game of catch at midday will keep most of them happy. Bichons do like to play, are always open to a challenge, and have participated in obedience competitions, agility, and flyball.

Early socialization is important for all Bichons. Although the breed is, for the most part, happy and extroverted, some puppies can be quite reserved. With socialization, even these puppies can learn that the world is really a wonderful place. Training is important as well; this is a bright breed, and if not trained, they can easily train their owners to do exactly what they wish. Housetraining can be a challenge; set up a routine, use a crate, watch the dog carefully, and be patient and consistent.

Bichons are alert watchdogs, barking when anyone approaches the house. With family and friends, they are very affectionate and playful. Although they are sturdy, have a happy temperament, and enjoy children, they can be too small for rough childhood play. They are good with other pets, although interactions with small animals should be supervised. Primary health concerns include knee problems, eye disorders, and allergies.

## Breed in Brief

**Registries:** AKC, UKC, CKC
**Occupation:** Companion
**Size:** 9.5 to 11.5 in tall; 10 to 16 lbs
**Longevity:** 13 to 15 years
**Exercise:** Low activity level
**Training:** Easy to obedience train; challenge to housetrain
**Grooming:** Difficult

# Black Mouth Cur

The term *cur* has a negative connotation for some people; perhaps they believe it means a mixed-breed dog or a bad dog. Curs originated in rural America, primarily in the South, and were bred specifically to do a job. They were most often mixed-breed dogs, and in most cases no attention was paid to breed; these were working dogs. However, over time, some have evolved into breeds that now breed true.

The Black Mouth Cur is a medium-sized to large dog, 16 to 25 inches tall and weighing between 50 and 100 pounds. She has a black muzzle (hence the name) and a short coat that is fawn, yellow, or brindle. She is muscular and strong with dropped ears and a tail that is docked or naturally short.

The short coat requires weekly brushing with a soft bristle brush or curry comb.

As with many hunting breeds, the Black Mouth Cur is very active. She needs a good long run every day. Although many hunting dogs do not understand the joys of agility training or some of the other canine sports, she can learn to do them and wear off excess energy in the process. She should be allowed to run off leash only in a fenced-in area; this devoted hunting dog loves to hunt, and no amount of calling will bring her back in mid-chase.

Training this dog can be a challenge. She will not tolerate rough or harsh training, and yet even with positive training, she will think before responding. As a hunter of large game, she must think for herself, and your commands will be followed only after she thinks it's appropriate to do so. If you want a compliant dog who follows orders well, do not get this breed.

The Black Mouth Cur, however, is utterly and totally devoted to her family. She is wonderful with children and will place herself between a child and danger with no thought of the threat to herself. She may even place herself between a child and an angry parent. She should not be trusted with smaller pets; remember, this is a hunting dog.

## Breed in Brief

**Registries:** UKC, American Black Mouth Cur Breeders Association
**Occupation:** Herder, hunter
**Size:** 16 to 25 in tall; 50 to 100 lbs
**Longevity:** 10 to 12 years
**Exercise:** Energetic
**Training:** Challenge
**Grooming:** Easy

# Black Russian Terrier

This breed was developed by the Russian military as a versatile, trainable, working dog. The Airedale Terrier, Giant Schnauzer, and Rottweiler were the primary breeds used, but Newfoundlands and the Caucasian Ovtcharka were also a part of the mix. The Black Russian Terrier was recognized as a breed by the USSR Ministry of Agriculture in 1981.

This large, powerful breed stands 26 to 30 inches tall and weighs 90 to 150 pounds. The head is large and broad, the eyes are small and dark, and the ears are dropped. The body is slightly longer than the dog is tall at the shoulders. There is a thick undercoat. The outer coat is black and is straight to wavy. The dog has a terrier beard, eyebrows, and mustache.

This breed's coat does need some grooming upkeep. It must be brushed regularly, and every four to six weeks it needs to be trimmed. The beard is often wet and may need drying, combing, or special care.

Black Russian Terriers need daily exercise. They will enjoy a couple of walks a day but also need time to run, play on the agility course, or chase a ball. Without exercise, and if left alone too much, they are prone to making their own fun.

## Breed in Brief

**Registries:** AKC, UKC, CKC
**Occupation:** Versatile working dog
**Size:** 26 to 30 in tall; 90 to 100 lbs
**Longevity:** 10 to 12 years
**Exercise:** Active
**Training:** Moderate
**Grooming:** Difficult

This breed is very watchful and protective, so early training and socialization are very important. The training should be structured and firm yet fun. There shouldn't be too much repetition; this breed is designed to be highly trainable. Black Russians can have fun with training, too, though they can be mischievous and a bit stubborn. Training should continue in some form (obedience, trick training, canine sports) into adulthood.

The Black Russian Terrier can be a great family dog for an experienced dog owner who understands the breed's needs. She is good with older children who treat her with respect. She may not be good with other dogs, especially those of the same sex. She is usually good with smaller pets. Health concerns include hip and elbow dysplasia and eye problems.

# Black and Tan Coonhound

The Black and Tan Coonhound has a long history dating back to early England. Descended from the Bloodhound (which was known as the St. Hubert Hound) and the Talbot Hound, the ancestors of today's Black and Tan were treasured as early as the 11th century. In the United States, the Black and Tan was bred both for her distinctive color and her ability to hunt raccoons and opossums. She is not limited to small game, however. The breed has also been used to trail larger game, including deer, bears, and mountain lions. The Black and Tan is not a fast hunter, but instead trails her game as her Bloodhound and Virginia Foxhound ancestors do. She is a deliberate, persistent hunter, giving voice (baying) when her quarry is found (or chased) up a tree.

The Black and Tan is first and foremost a hunting dog. This breed stands 23 to 27 inches tall at the shoulder, weighing between 50 and 70 pounds, with females slightly smaller than males. They should give the impression of alertness, power, and stamina. This dog is well-muscled yet not blocky or heavy; she must be able to run for hours. The eyes are round, dark brown, and expressive; the ears are hanging and, if pulled forward, reach beyond the tip of the nose. The coat is dense but thick, so as to be impervious to brush and brambles during a hunt. The coat is black with rich tan markings on the muzzle, over the eyes, and on the chest, legs, and toes.

Grooming a Black and Tan is easy. The short but dense coat needs twice weekly brushing with a soft bristle brush or curry comb. Although these dogs do shed, primarily in the spring and fall, regular brushing will help keep the shedding under control. The breed's heavy ears require weekly cleaning, or more if the dog is outside a lot.

The Black and Tan requires daily exercise. A long walk morning and evening, a run alongside a bicycle, and a chance to chase squirrels in the backyard will keep most dogs happy. They are not known to be retrievers, so fetch is not a favorite game. Hide-and-seek games are great favorites, though. Hide a toy (or one of the family kids) and send your Black and Tan after it. During exercise, the Black and Tan must be leashed at all times when outside of a fenced-in yard, as the breed's hunting instincts are strong. If she catches a scent, she will be gone, and no amount of calling will bring her back.

Black and Tans are social animals, both with people and other dogs. A puppy class with socialization opportunities to other people and other puppies will bring out the best in a Black and Tan

## Breed in Brief

**Registries:** AKC, UKC
**Occupation:** Hunter, trailer
**Size:** 23 to 27 in tall; 50 to 70 lbs
**Longevity:** 10 to 12 years
**Exercise:** Moderate to vigorous daily exercise
**Training:** Challenge; never trust off leash
**Grooming:** Easy

puppy. Training can be a challenge, however, as Black and Tans have minds of their own. They are naturally fairly well-behaved but can also be stubborn and independent. A puppy class followed by a basic obedience class is always a good idea, although motivating this hound to follow directions can keep an owner on his toes.

Black and Tans can be good family dogs; they are patient with children and good with other dogs. They can bay and howl, though, which can cause problems with neighbors. All interactions with other small pets should be supervised; remember, this is a hunting hound! Major health problems include hip and elbow dysplasia and hypothyroidism.

# Bloodhound

In the 3rd century, Claudius Aelianus wrote about dogs with scenting abilities far better than those of ordinary dogs. These dogs were determined to follow a trail and would never give up. Those scenting dogs were probably the ancestors of the dogs that later became known as St. Hubert Hounds. In fact, in French-speaking countries, Bloodhounds are still known as St. Hubert Hounds.

Bloodhounds are known for their scenting abilities, as they should be, because they have the best noses in the canine world. Several individual Bloodhounds have brought about more arrests and convictions than the best human police officers. Some dedicated dogs have followed trails of more than 100 miles. But unlike German Shepherd Dogs and other law enforcement dogs, the Bloodhound does not bite or take down the person she has trailed; as far as she is concerned, her job ends when she finds the person she was trailing. Search and rescue organizations also treasure the breed's abilities.

The Bloodhound is large, with heavy bones and long hanging ears. The breed stands between 23 and 27 inches tall and weighs between 90 and 130 pounds. The head is long, and the ears are very long and hang in folds. The nose is large, and the flews are deep. The skin hangs loose and looks as if there is enough extra skin for another dog to fit inside. The chest is deep, the body is strong and fit, and the tail is long. The coat is short and is either black and tan or liver and tan.

The Bloodhound's short coat is easy to groom; it needs only twice weekly brushing with a soft bristle brush or curry comb. The heavy ears need regular cleaning, however, to prevent ear infections.

Although the Bloodhound isn't as active as some other breeds, she still needs daily exercise. A brisk long walk morning and evening is fine, but she also needs a chance to run and play. These playtimes should be only within the confines of a fenced-in yard; if the Bloodhound catches a scent she wishes to follow, she could be gone faster than you can catch her.

Training the Bloodhound can be a challenge. Although many Bloodhounds have successfully competed in obedience and other canine sports, the Bloodhound's owner must first figure out what

motivates his dog to want to learn. Then, and only then, can the dog be trained. The training should be firm and structured, yet fun. The dog's owner must be patient and persistent.

A Bloodhound needs a very special owner. The Canadian Bloodhound Club says, "Not everyone should own a Bloodhound. The swing of a Bloodhound's head can spread saliva across a 20-foot room, and years of antiques can be destroyed by her stroll across your living room." The same dog who slobbers all over you and knocks your knickknacks to the floor with one sweep of her tail will adore you and your children with all her heart, showing that love in her eyes for the world to see. She is not a good dog to leave in the backyard; she needs to be with her people. The Bloodhound is usually good with other dogs and small pets. Health concerns include hip and elbow dysplasia, ear and eye problems, bloat, and torsion.

## Breed in Brief

**Registries:** AKC, UKC, CKC
**Occupation:** Scenthound
**Size:** 23 to 27 in tall; 90 to 130 lbs
**Longevity:** 9 to 11 years
**Exercise:** Moderate
**Training:** Challenge
**Grooming:** Easy

# Bolognese

The Bolognese is related to several other small companion breeds, including the Bichon Frise, Maltese, Havanese, and Coton de Tulear. The breed was prized by nobility as long ago as the 11th century, and many Bolognese can be seen in old paintings.

The Bolognese is a small dog who stands between 9 and 12.5 inches tall and weighs between 8 and 15 pounds. The breed has dark round eyes, dropped ears, and a dark nose. The body is as long as the dog is tall at the shoulder. The coat is long all over the body, falls in flocks, and is white without any shadings or markings.

Grooming this breed does take some time, as it must be brushed and combed on a regular basis to prevent matting—how often will depend upon the dog. If the dog runs and plays outside and gets wet, or if she trains in agility and is running, jumping, and climbing, then the coat may need to be brushed and combed daily. A sedate, stay-at-home dog may need to be groomed two or three times a week. The coat is not trimmed and does not have an undercoat.

Bolognese will enjoy a couple of walks each day, with a play session in between. They are playful and energetic without being overly active.

Early training and socialization will help this companion breed learn household rules and social manners. Most Bolognese are wary of strangers and will bark; early training can control this tendency prior to it becoming a problem. Housetraining can sometimes be a challenge, but with patience and persistence, these dogs can learn what is expected. Bolognese enjoy agility and therapy dog work.

This breed was bred to be a companion and makes a wonderful pet. They are good with children they are raised with but will not tolerate rough handling. Bolognese can be good with other dogs but should be protected from larger dogs who play roughly. They are good with the family cat but should not be trusted with smaller pets. This is a healthy breed.

## Breed in Brief

**Registries:** AKC FSS, UKC, ARBA
**Occupation:** Companion
**Size:** 9 to 12.5 in tall; 8 to 15 lbs
**Longevity:** 12 to 14 years
**Exercise:** Moderate
**Training:** Easy; hard to housetrain
**Grooming:** Difficult

# Border Collie

The ancestors of today's Border Collie probably developed in Scotland, as the word *collie* is a Scottish dialect word meaning *sheep-dog*. The Border Collie is recognized worldwide today as one of the best sheep-herding breeds in existence.

The Border Collie is a medium-sized dog, between 18 and 23 inches at the shoulder and 35 to 50 pounds. The breed has two varieties of coat. The rough coat is medium to long, with a flat to slightly wavy outer coat. The hair on the face is short and smooth. The short coat variety has a short, smooth coat over the entire body, although dogs may have feathering on the back of the forelegs. The breed has many acceptable colors, including black with or without white markings and the classic tricolor with white and copper markings on a black dog.

Grooming a Border Collie is easy. She should be brushed and combed twice weekly.

Border Collies are workaholics. If there are no sheep to herd, then there should be an agility course to run, a newspaper to be retrieved from down the driveway, and tricks to learn. A Border Collie can be tough to live with because she won't get comfy on the sofa and stay there until you're ready to do something.

Training a Border Collie can also be a challenge; not because training is difficult—it's not—but because Border Collies are very intelligent. Instead, the challenge is staying one step ahead! All Border Collies should attend puppy and basic training and then go on to more advanced training. Keep her mind busy and active and make training fun.

The Border Collie can be a wonderful family pet in a busy, active household that can meet her needs. She is patient with children and loves to play games with them, but may frustrate some kids when she tries to herd them. She is also fine with other dogs when well-socialized as a puppy, but other dogs may not understand the breed's stare. Interactions with small pets should be supervised. Health concerns include hip dysplasia and eye defects.

## Breed in Brief

**Registries:** AKC, UKC
**Occupation:** Sheep-herder, performance sports
**Size:** 18 to 23 in tall; 35 to 50 lbs
**Longevity:** 13 to 15 years
**Exercise:** Vigorous daily exercise
**Training:** Easy; hard to keep challenged
**Grooming:** Easy

# Border Terrier

The Border Terrier was developed as an all-purpose hunting terrier who was long-legged enough to follow the hunters on horseback yet small enough to crawl into burrows after prey. Her ancestors are all working terriers. The hill men of the border regions of England bred these dogs for performance rather than along breed lines.

The Border Terrier stands 12 to 14 inches tall and weighs between 11 and 15 pounds. Her head is otterlike, eyes are dark, and ears are dropped. Her body is sturdy and narrow. The undercoat is dense and the outer coat is wiry. She has whiskers and a beard. The coat may be red, wheaten, blue and tan, or grizzle and tan.

The coat requires hand-stripping, which can be tough to learn. Ask your dog's breeder for instructions. The coat does shed and should be brushed two to three times a week.

This active breed needs vigorous daily exercise. Although morning and evening walks will be enjoyed, walks alone are not sufficient. These dogs also need to play some catch and fetch games, train on the agility course, or participate in canine sports. All exercise, games, and training should be on leash or in a fenced yard. The Border Terrier Club of America says, "The Border Terrier is an instinctive hunter and cannot be trusted off leash in an unfenced area at any time."

Early training can help channel some of the breed's tendency to be busy. This is also a very bright breed who will thrive with varied and fun training.

The Border Terrier does well with an active owner who likes canine games and sports or at least enjoys playing with the dog. This breed is also good with children, as long as the kids are not too rough. Border Terriers usually get along with other dogs and can live nicely with the family cat if raised with the cat. This breed should never be trusted with strange cats, however, or other small pets. Health concerns include heart defects, eye problems, and hip and knee problems.

## Breed in Brief

**Registries:** AKC, UKC, CKC
**Occupation:** Vermin hunter
**Size:** 12 to 14 in tall; 11 to 15 lbs
**Longevity:** 12 to 15 years
**Exercise:** Vigorous daily exercise
**Training:** Easy; loves sports
**Grooming:** Hand-stripping

# Borzoi

The aristocracy of Russia created the Borzoi, also known as the Russian Wolfhound, as a sporting yet serious hunter who was prized for speed and courage. The first breed standard is known to have been created in 1650, but at that writing, the breed had already existed for two to three centuries.

The Borzoi is a tall dog, standing 26 to 32 inches and weighing 60 to 110 pounds. She has a long, narrow head with dark eyes and strong jaws. She has a runner's body, long and narrow, with a deep chest and a long feathered tail that acts as a rudder when she runs. Her legs are strong and feathered. Her coat is of medium length, silky, and can be any color.

The Borzoi Club of America recommends using a pin brush to groom this breed; a slicker brush can damage the coat. Borzoi should be brushed two to three times weekly.

Borzoi adults are calm in the house, although puppies can be more active. Twice-daily walks and a chance to run will be enough exercise for this breed. The Borzoi Club of America says, "Being sighthounds, they are apt to chase anything that moves. They should always be in a fenced area or on a leash. It is never advisable to allow a Borzoi to run loose."

Training a Borzoi can sometimes be a challenge. Although these dogs are sweet and sensitive, they can also be independent and a touch stubborn. Training should be structured yet fun and positive. Avoid too much repetition. The trainer must also be very patient. If you want a quick-learning, compliant dog, do not get a Borzoi. This breed enjoys lure coursing, and many have made excellent therapy dogs.

Borzoi are elegant, attractive, fun dogs and can be wonderful pets for those who understand sighthounds. If raised with children, they can be very good with them. They should never be trusted with smaller pets, as they are instinctive hunters and will chase and catch anything that runs. Health concerns include bloat, torsion, and hip and shoulder dysplasia.

## Breed in Brief

**Registries:** UKC, UKC, CKC
**Occupation:** Sighthound
**Size:** 26 to 32 in tall; 60 to 110 lbs
**Longevity:** 10 to 12 years
**Exercise:** Loves to run
**Training:** Challenge
**Grooming:** Easy to moderate

# Boston Terrier

Developed in the U.S. in the late 1800s from English Bulldogs, white English Terriers, French Bulldogs, and a few other breeds, the Boston Terrier has received many accolades from fans. These dogs have been called "American Gentlemen" because of their fine manners and American roots. The Boston Terrier was the first American breed recognized by the American Kennel Club and, for many years in the early 1900s, was one of the most popular breeds. One of the breed's first nicknames was "roundhead," for its round skull shape.

The Boston Terrier stands 15 to 17 inches tall at the shoulder and weighs between 15 and 25 pounds. She has a round head with a shortened muzzle; large, round, dark eyes; and ears that can be either cropped or left natural. The body is short, the legs strong, and the tail either straight or twisted. Unlike many other terrier breeds, the tail is not docked. The short, smooth coat is brindle, seal, or black with white markings.

This breed is easy to groom; it requires twice weekly brushing with a soft bristle brush. If the dog has skin wrinkles on her muzzle, those should be cleaned daily.

The Boston Terrier is not a high-energy dog. She will be happy with a good walk and a playtime or two. Most Bostons enjoy playing fetch, and some will do so for as long as someone will throw the ball. Exercise should be avoided during the heat of the day in hot climates or in the summer, as her shortened muzzle can cause breathing difficulties. In cool weather, the Boston enjoys agility. Many Bostons have also served admirably as volunteer therapy dogs.

This friendly breed enjoys the socialization aspects of a puppy kindergarten class. Training should begin early, as some Boston puppies have housetraining challenges, but with patience and persistence, they do learn what is expected of them. Leash training is also important, as Bostons are strong for their size and love to pull. Training should be structured yet fun; when motivated, Bostons love to learn, but they can be a touch stubborn.

The Boston will bark when people approach the house but is not known for being protective. This barking can cause a problem with neighbors, so it should be addressed early with training.

This is a great family dog who will become very attached to her people. She enjoys playing with children as long as they are not too rough. Many Bostons have been dressed up in doll clothes and wheeled in doll carriages, and they put up with it all with great patience. Bostons generally get along well with other dogs, although playtime with larger dogs should be supervised; Bostons have no idea that they are are small, and larger dogs could hurt them inadvertently. If a strange dog challenges a Boston, she will not back away from a scuffle. Interactions with small pets should be supervised. Health concerns include breathing disorders, deafness, and thyroid and knee problems.

## Breed in Brief

**Registries:** AKC, UKC, CKC
**Occupation:** Companion
**Size:** 15 to 17 in tall; 15 to 25 lbs
**Longevity:** 11 to 13 years
**Exercise:** Moderate
**Training:** Moderate
**Grooming:** Easy

# Bouvier des Flandres

The Bouvier des Flandres originated in France and belonged to people who worked with cattle, such as farmers, drovers, and butchers. These people were more concerned with the dog's ability to work than with uniform physical characteristics, so the dogs varied in size and color.

Today, the Bouvier is a large dog standing 23.5 to 27.5 inches tall at the shoulder and weighing between 65 and 110 pounds. She is strong and compact. Her head is large, eyes are oval and dark, ears may be cropped, and face features a full beard and mustache. The Bouvier has a double coat. The undercoat is soft and dense, and the outer coat is harsh. Colors range from fawn to black, although black, salt and pepper, and brindle are most common.

This breed needs to be brushed every other day. The coarse outer coat will catch most of the shed undercoat, but in doing so, the undercoat can form mats. For show dogs, the coat can be slightly trimmed to follow the body's outline. Many pet owners keep the coat short.

The Bouvier is a breed developed to work, so those kept as companions require regular daily exercise and need to participate in canine activities. Bouviers enjoy agility, carting, weight pulling, search and rescue work, and herding.

The American Bouvier des Flandres Club says, "We can't recommend too strongly the importance of socialization and basic obedience training." The Bouvier is a large dog who, in adulthood, can easily overpower her owner. She is also wary of strangers. Early training and socialization can give the owner control and teach the dog social rules.

This active, smart, protective dog needs a job (or two or three) and should have an owner who is actively involved with her. Bouvier puppies can be rough with small children, but older kids will enjoy playing with her. Bouviers are good with other pets when raised together. Health concerns include bloat, torsion, and eye problems.

## Breed in Brief

**Registries:** AKC, UKC, CKC
**Occupation:** Cattle dog
**Size:** 23.5 to 27.5 in tall; 65 to 100 lbs
**Longevity:** 12 to 13 years
**Exercise:** Active; good in sports
**Training:** Easy; hard to keep busy
**Grooming:** Regular brushing

# oxer

The Boxer is said to be descended from a variety of European breeds, including the old English Bulldog and the French Dogue de Bordeaux. The breed came to maturity in Germany and was one of the first breeds selected for police training there. Their name is derived from their tendency to stand erect on hind legs and box with the front legs.

The Boxer is a medium-sized dog, 21 to 25 inches tall and 50 to 80 pounds, with females smaller than males. The body is compact, muscular, and powerful. The tail is docked and carried high. The head is also carried high and has the short muzzle typical of bull breeds. The ears naturally drop but are often cropped. (Although cropped ears are required for AKC competition, many owners prefer the natural ears.) Boxers are fawn with a black muzzle and mask and white on the chest, legs, and feet. The coat is short and smooth.

Grooming is easy; the coat should be brushed twice a week with a soft bristle brush or curry comb.

Exercise is very important. Boxers enjoy performance sports. The breed should not be exercised in the heat of the day during hot weather, especially in humid climates, as they can have breathing difficulties due to the shortened muzzle.

Young Boxers should meet and play with a variety of other puppies, as adult Boxers do tend to be aggressive toward strange dogs. Socialization can often keep this behavior in check.

Boxers should attend puppy and basic obedience classes and ideally continue training. A Boxer can be stubborn at times, but when she wants to learn, she learns easily and retains training well. Training should be firm and structured, yet fair and fun.

Boxers are happiest when with their people. They are excellent with children, although puppies can be quite rambunctious and need to learn how to play with kids. They are usually quite good with other pets, although they do need to be taught not to chase cats. Health concerns include breathing problems, bloat, torsion, cardiomyopathy, and hip dysplasia.

## Breed in Brief

**Registries:** AKC, UKC, CKC
**Occupation:** Guardian, companion
**Size:** 21 to 25 in tall; 50 to 80 lbs
**Longevity:** 9 to 11 years
**Exercise:** Moderate to vigorous
**Training:** Easy
**Grooming:** Easy

# $\mathcal{B}$oykin Spaniel

The Boykin Spaniel is an American breed developed in South Carolina as a multipurpose retriever. Ancestors include the Chesapeake Bay Retriever, as well as several different spaniels and a stray of uncertain parentage who was a versatile hunting dog. The breed has been used to flush game, retrieve on land and in the water, and track wounded deer. The breed is the official state dog of South Carolina.

This small retriever stands only 15 to 18 inches tall and weighs 25 to 45 pounds. She is smaller than the Cocker Spaniel (one of her ancestors), has a straighter muzzle, and has ears set higher than the Cocker's. The tail is docked, and the coat is wavy to curly and is brown or liver-colored.

The Boykin's coat needs regular brushing to prevent matting. If the dog gets wet, she should be dried and brushed; otherwise, brushing every other day is fine. Her ears need regular cleaning to prevent ear problems. Her coat will need trimming every four to eight weeks.

This breed is active and energetic. When hunting, the Boykin will go all day long; as a pet, she will need vigorous daily exercise. If not provided with enough exercise, she will amuse herself in ways that rarely please her owner. The breed loves water. Many dogs participate in a variety of canine sports.

Boykins are known for their pleasant disposition. Early training can help channel their energies, but for the most part, this breed is more compliant than defiant. Keep in mind, though, as an instinct-driven hunting breed, the Boykin can become distracted by the sight and scent of critters, so all off-leash exercise and training should be in a fenced yard.

The Boykin is not a city dog; the breed does best in a rural environment, preferably one where her owner likes to hunt. With plenty of exercise and room to run, she is also a good family dog and is very tolerant of children. She should not be trusted with smaller pets. Health concerns include hip dysplasia and allergies.

## Breed in Brief

**Registries:** AKC FSS, UKC
**Occupation:** Gun dog, retriever
**Size:** 15 to 18 in tall; 25 to 45 lbs
**Longevity:** 13 to 15 years
**Exercise:** Vigorous daily exercise
**Training:** Easy
**Grooming:** Difficult

# Bracco Italiano

This breed has been popular since the Renaissance. The breed (which is also called the Italian Pointer) was originally used to drive game, primarily birds, into nets. However, with changing times the breed was able to change, too, and today is used to find, point, and flush birds and then retrieve them.

There are two types of Bracco Italiano. One body type is heavier and more houndlike and predominantly white and brown. The other is lighter-bodied, more pointerlike, and is white and orange. The Italian Kennel Club recognizes both types. The breed stands 21 to 26.5 inches tall and weighs between 60 and 90 pounds, with females smaller than males. The head is large but narrow, with long, low-set ears, deep flews, and loose skin on the head and neck. The chest is broad and deep, the body is longer than it is tall, and the tail is long. The coat is short.

This breed is easy to groom; a twice weekly brushing will keep her shiny. Her heavy ears should be cleaned regularly, though, to keep them healthy.

The Bracco Italiano is usually calm in the house but requires vigorous daily exercise. She will enjoy walks, play sessions, and catch-and-fetch games. If she doesn't get enough exercise, she will amuse herself and can be a destructive chewer.

## Breed in Brief

**Registries:** AKC FSS, ARBA, UKC

**Occupation:** Gun dog

**Size:** 21 to 26.5 in tall; 60 to 90 lbs

**Longevity:** 12 to 14 years

**Exercise:** Moderate

**Training:** Firm but fun

**Grooming:** Easy

Training should begin early. Although the breed is intelligent and sensitive, these dogs also have a touch of independence and stubbornness. Training should be firm and structured but should also be fun. Avoid too much repetition and heavy-handed training. Their affectionate nature makes them wonderful therapy dogs, and their scenting abilities make them superb tracking dogs.

The Bracco Italiano is still used as a hunting dog in Italy, although many in the U.S. are family pets. They do best in homes where people will be involved with the dogs; they are not good backyard dogs. The breed is great with children but should be supervised with smaller pets. Health concerns include bloat, torsion, and hip dysplasia.

# **B**riard

The Briard is a very old French breed. Its portrait has been found in old tapestries and other works of art, some dating back to the 8th century. Briards have served as livestock and property guardians, as perimeter sheep-herders, and, during the World Wars, as military sentries and guards. They were also used to find wounded soldiers on the battlefield. So many Briards were used during the war that the breed was threatened with extinction. Today, the breed is still used as a herding dog.

This is a big dog, standing 22 to 27 inches tall and weighing 70 to 90 pounds. The Briard's head is long, the eyes are large, and the ears are natural or cropped. The body is slightly longer than tall, and the chest is broad and deep. The breed has two dewclaws on each rear leg. The identifying characteristic is the coat; even the head and ears are well-covered with a long, coarse coat. The coat is a double one; the undercoat is fine and tight. The coat is usually tawny, with deeper colors preferred, and often darkens with age.

The Briard requires constant care to keep the coat in good shape. Without daily brushing and combing, it will mat. Daily brushing also lessens the amount of coat shed in the house. The hair in the ears and between the pads of the feet needs regular trimming, and many owners trim the hair over the eyes so they can see their dogs' eyes. Some pet owners have the coat trimmed short, especially in the summer months.

Briards need vigorous daily exercise, and a walk or two every day is not nearly enough. A Briard is great for an active owner and can run alongside a bicycle, go jogging, herd sheep, play agility, or catch flying discs. Bred to work, they will get into trouble if they don't have something to do and a chance to burn off excess energy.

Early socialization is vital, as this is a watchful, protective breed. Socialization to a variety of

people, places, sounds, sights, and things can help her adjust to her surroundings. Unfortunately, some Briards—especially those who are not well-socialized—are overprotective, which can lead to aggressive behavior.

Training should begin early, too, and continue into adulthood. This breed is bright and intelligent and enjoys a mental challenge. Training should be structured and firm (but not heavy-handed), yet fun and challenging. Briards enjoy many dog sports, including agility, herding, trick training, and flyball.

This breed is not for a first-time dog owner; even many experienced dog owners may find her to be a handful. The Briard needs an owner who can also be her leader. She is not good when left alone for many hours every day, and when bored will get into trouble. With company and leadership, she is an affectionate, loyal, and devoted companion. She can be good with children when raised with them but will not tolerate teasing or disrespect. She can be dog-aggressive if not socialized with other dogs early. The breed tends to herd anything that moves, including kids and the family cat. Health concerns include bloat, torsion, and hip dysplasia.

## Breed in Brief

**Registries:** AKC, UKC, CKC
**Occupation:** Livestock guardian, herder
**Size:** 22 to 27 in tall; 70 to 90 lbs
**Longevity:** 10 to 12 years
**Exercise:** Vigorous daily exercise
**Training:** Moderate; hard to keep challenged
**Grooming:** Difficult

# *B*rittany

*O*riginally called the Brittany Spaniel (and still called that by some registries), this French breed is derived from crossing French spaniels with English Setters. Showing traits of both spaniels and setters, the breed hunts more like a setter, so the name was officially changed with the American Kennel Club in 1982.

The Brittany is a medium-sized dog standing 17.5 to 20.5 inches tall and weighing between 30 and 40 pounds. Her body length is equal to her height at the shoulders. The eyes are expressive, and the ears are dropped but not pendulous. The tail can be naturally bobbed, nonexistent, or docked to 4 inches in length. The coat is medium in length, flat or wavy but never curly, and orange and white or liver and white in color.

The Brittany's coat needs twice weekly brushing and combing. It can mat, but that can be prevented with regular grooming.

This is a high-energy breed. Bred to work all day in the field, the Brittany needs regular aerobic exercise. She will enjoy long walks, a jog with you, or a run alongside a bicycle. Many Brittany owners have also found their breed to be enthusiastic about dog sports, including agility and flyball. A Brittany who doesn't get enough exercise will amuse herself, much to her owner's dismay.

## Breed in Brief

**Registries:** AKC, UKC, CKC
**Occupation:** Gun dog
**Size:** 17.5 to 20.5 in tall; 30 to 40 lbs
**Longevity:** 12 to 14 years
**Exercise:** Very active
**Training:** Easy
**Grooming:** Moderate

The Brittany is a friendly dog who will enjoy the socialization of a puppy class. Early training will teach the Brittany household rules, but training should continue into adulthood. This intelligent breed will thrive with fun yet challenging training.

The Brittany is still a versatile hunter and is one of the most popular hunting breeds in the U.S. If not hunting, the Brittany needs an active owner who will spend time with her. Puppies and young dogs can be too rowdy for small kids, but adult dogs are playful and patient. Most are good with other dogs and pets. Health concerns include hip and elbow dysplasia, heart defects, epilepsy, and eye problems.

# Brussels Griffon

## (Rough Coat and Smooth Coat)

*I*n the 1800s, it was very common all over Europe for a terrier-type dog (or dogs) to reside in stables to help control vermin. In Belgium and particularly in Brussels, the Griffons d'Ecurie (or wire-coated stable dog) was the most popular. This breed's ancestry is unknown, but at some point in the mid-1800s, the Pug and the English Toy Spaniel were introduced, and the ratter moved out of the stable and into the house to become a companion dog.

The Brussels Griffon is a toy breed, standing 8 to 10 inches tall and weighing 8 to 12 pounds. The head is large and round; the eyes are very large, dark, and expressive; and the muzzle is very short. The nose should appear to be set between the eyes. The body is thick and short. The smooth coat is short and glossy; the wire coat is coarse. The coat can be red, black and red mixed, black and tan, or solid black.

The smooth coat is very easy to groom. A twice weekly brushing with a soft bristle brush will suffice. The rough coat will need twice weekly brushing as well, but also needs to be hand-stripped on a regular basis; owners of the rough coat variety can ask their dog's breeder for instructions.

This bright, active little dog will enjoy walks and play sessions. She is not overly active, however, and enjoys cuddling with her people.

Socialization and training should begin early. The Brussels Griffon can be wary of strangers, so socialization can help her accept new people. She can be stubborn, especially in regard to leash training, but is intelligent and quick to learn once the owner understands how to motivate her.

This companion dog does not do well when left alone for long hours every day. She will thrive with someone who can spend a lot of time with her. She is too small for rowdy children or those who do not treat her gently. She is good with other dogs and cats when raised with them, but should not be trusted with small pets. Health concerns include breathing disorders and reproductive problems.

## Breed in Brief

**Registries:** AKC, UKC
**Occupation:** Companion
**Size:** 8 to 10 in tall; 8 to 12 lbs
**Longevity:** 13 to 14 years
**Exercise:** Low activity level
**Training:** Moderate
**Grooming:** Easy to moderate

# Bulldog

The original bull breeds were fighting dogs: tough, courageous, and tenacious. They fought bulls and, later, bears and other ferocious animals, even other dogs. However, in the mid-1800s, blood sports were declared illegal in England, and the bull breeds, including the Bulldog, faced extinction unless they could change, and change they did. Breed fanciers bred for traits other than aggression and produced the breed we know today.

The Bulldog (or English Bulldog) is a medium-sized dog, with a heavy body and large head on sturdy legs, standing 12 to 16 inches tall and weighing 40 to 50 pounds. The chest is broad and deep, with the front legs set wide apart. The muzzle is very short, the eyes are round, and the ears are set high on the head. The tail is straight or screwed. The coat is short and fine and may be one of several colors, although red brindle is preferred.

The coat should be brushed a couple of times each week with a soft bristle brush. The wrinkles of the face need to be cleaned daily to prevent dirt build-up and skin problems. Some dogs' faces may need to be washed after every meal.

The Bulldog is not a very busy dog. She will enjoy a walk daily and needs some playtime each day, as obesity can be a problem in the breed, but she is also a great lover of comfort, and the sofa cushions will call to her.

Early training is important, as Bulldogs can be quite powerful as adults. But the breed has a gentle and stable temperament and, with training, these dogs rarely try to get into trouble, although puppies can be mischievous.

Living with Bulldogs can be a challenge. They snort, snore, and grumble; they drool and most have trouble with flatulence. They are affectionate with children and are usually very good with other pets. Some males may challenge other male dogs. They do not breathe well in hot, humid weather. They are prone to many health problems, including allergies, breathing difficulties, and reproductive problems.

## Breed in Brief

**Registries:** AKC, UKC, CKC
**Occupation:** Fighter, companion
**Size:** 12 to 16 in tall; 40 to 50 lbs
**Longevity:** 10 to 12 years
**Exercise:** Low activity level
**Training:** Moderate
**Grooming:** Easy

# Bullmastiff

*I*n the late 1800s, strong, protective dogs were used to protect England's large estates from poachers. When the old English Bulldogs were crossed with the Old English Mastiff, the result was a dog who could remain quiet as poachers approached and then take the poachers down and hold them until help arrived. Because most poaching happened at night, the breed was also known as the Gamekeeper's Night Dog.

The Bullmastiff is an imposing dog, giving the impression of great strength. Standing 24 to 27 inches tall and weighing between 100 and 130 pounds. The head is broad, the eyes dark and expressive. The ears are V-shaped and dropped. The body is longer than the dog is tall at the shoulders, with a deep, wide chest and heavy-boned legs. The tail is long, reaching the hocks. The coat is short and smooth and may be red, fawn, or brindle, with a black mask.

The Bullmastiff's short coat can easily be groomed with a soft bristle brush or curry comb a couple of times per week. Having a small towel at hand is usually wise, as Bullmastiffs do drool.

The Bullmastiff does not need a lot of exercise. Although these dogs can move quickly when they wish, this is not a breed made for running. Puppies may want to play some games with you, but adults usually outgrow such silliness.

Keep in mind that the breed was designed to protect property against poachers and remains wary of strangers. Early exposure to a variety of people will help establish a good relationship with the human race. Training is needed, too, as these very large, strong dogs could easily overpower a person. Bullmastiffs have a stubborn streak, though, so training can be a challenge.

Bullmastiffs are calm companion dogs. They can be good with children when raised with them. If not raised with kids, they tend to think children are something other than people. Bullmastiffs are not always good with other dogs; males especially can be dog-aggressive. When raised with other pets, Bullmastiffs will be good with them, but interactions should be supervised. Health concerns include bloat, torsion, hip dysplasia, and hypothyroidism.

## Breed in Brief

**Registries:** AKC, UKC, CKC
**Occupation:** Guardian, companion
**Size:** 24 to 27 in tall; 100 to 130 lbs
**Longevity:** 8 to 10 years
**Exercise:** Easy
**Training:** Moderate; can be stubborn
**Grooming:** Easy

# Bull Terrier

## (Colored and White)

The Bull Terrier is descended from the old White English Terrier. Crossed with the old English Bulldog, Spanish Pointer, and some say even Dalmatian, this Bull Terrier was a gentleman's dog and was called the White Cavalier. The dog was friendly and mannerly but would not refuse if a challenge was thrown her way.

The breed went through many changes during its development, and many people were instrumental in bringing these changes about. James Hicks is credited with producing all-white dogs, or dogs who were all white with a patch of color on the head. Ted Lyon brought about the colored Bull Terriers, especially the brindle. Harry Monk has been given credit for producing dogs with the preferred tulip ear. Monk also worked to produce the egg-shaped head for which the breed is now known. Billie Tuck

worked to perfect that skull shape. The Bull Terrier today may not look like the dogs of 150 years ago, but the breed is unique and handsome.

The Bully today is a muscular, athletic dog standing between 21 and 22 inches tall and weighing between 45 and 65 pounds. (The Miniature Bull Terrier is a separate breed and is profiled on page 296.) The distinguishing characteristic of this breed is the egg-shaped head. Seen in profile, the head curves downward from between the ears to the nose. The body is strong and fit, with a deep, broad chest and a short coat. The white variety is all white, although patches of color on the head are allowed. The colored variety is predominantly another color (brindle is preferred), with or without white markings.

This breed should be brushed twice a week with a soft bristle brush.

Bull Terriers are quite playful. They love to play games, chase toys, and, as very social dogs, will encourage you to walk every day. The breed is known for its ability to chew, however, so toys for their games must be chosen wisely. All exer-

cise should be within a fenced yard or on leash. If a Bully takes off after a squirrel, she could easily run off, become lost, or be hit by a car.

The Bull Terrier Club of America says, "Obedience and socialization classes are a must for Bull Terriers. Proper training will provide good manners, socialization skills, and bond the dog to you." They continue by saying, "The Bull Terrier must be handled firmly but with patience and positive reinforcement." Although the Bull Terrier has a much different look from most other terriers, she is still very much a terrier. She is active, intelligent, sometimes stubborn, and quite independent when she wants to be. Continued training into adulthood can help channel those characteristics.

This breed will thrive in a busy home where people will spend time with her. Although young Bullies can be quite rough and rambunctious, adults are great with kids—playful and tolerant. When raised with them, she will be good with the family cat but will chase any stray cats who come into her yard. She may try to hunt smaller pets. Male Bullies are often intolerant of other male dogs. Health concerns include deafness; kidney, heart, and knee problems; and allergies.

## Breed in Brief

**Registries:** AKC, UKC, CKC
**Occupation:** Companion
**Size:** 21 to 22 in tall; 45 to 65 lbs
**Longevity:** 12 to 14 years
**Exercise:** Very playful and active
**Training:** Challenge; hard to keep focused
**Grooming:** Easy

# Cairn Terrier

The Cairn Terrier is from the Isle of Skye, Scotland, and is a working terrier. Traditionally, this breed's job was to protect small farms from foxes and other vermin. He would squirm his way into piles of rocks, called *cairns,* to get to a hiding fox or badger. He would then either flush the vermin or hold it there so the farmer could dispatch it. Originally classified as a Scotch Terrier and then as one of the Skye Terriers, he became known as the Cairn Terrier in 1912. The breed is closely related to the West Highland White Terrier, and in early years the two were cross-bred.

The Cairn Terrier today is still a game, hardy, working terrier. Size is of utmost importance, with males weighing 14 pounds and females weighing a pound less. These dogs are short-legged but should be proportional, with most standing between 9.5 and 10 inches tall. The skull is broad, muzzle strong, eyes hazel, and nose black. The ears are upright and small. The tail is short and carried upright. The coat is double, with a hard outer coat and a soft undercoat. The coat may be any color except white.

The Cairn Terrier Club of America recommends weekly brushing and combing to keep shedding to a minimum. They also recommend trimming the hair from the tips of the ears, tail, and feet. Many Cairns are allergic to fleas, so keeping the dog free of these pests is important.

Cairn Terriers are active little dogs who love to play. Although they enjoy a walk morning and evening, walks are not enough exercise for this spunky little dog. A Cairn also needs a chance to play on the agility course, chase a ball, or jump for a small flying disc. All off-leash exercise should be within a fenced-in yard, because Cairns love to chase squirrels and other small animals. If your terrier takes off after a small animal, all the calling in the world will not bring him back.

The Cairn Terrier Club of America recommends kindergarten puppy classes for young Cairns, saying, "Be sure to train your puppy with firmness and consistency. Harsh punishment is not necessary. Be sure, though, that your Cairn knows you are in charge. Like children, they will test your limits, but need discipline to turn out well." Training should continue on into adulthood to keep this bright breed's mind active. Cairn Terriers are also quite good at many canine sports, including agility, obedience trials, tracking, and terrier go-to-ground competitions.

Cairn Terriers are great family dogs. They are affectionate and enjoy children and their games. They are sturdy enough to take some rough play, but kids should be taught to treat them with respect. Cairns prefer to be with people; when left alone for too many hours, they are prone to get into trouble. Most Cairns also get along well with other dogs. They are fine with cats when raised with them but will chase strange cats who come into their yard. Cairns should not be trusted with smaller pets; a Cairn will have a hard time differentiating between a pet rat and a wild rat. Health concerns include eye problems, liver shunt, and knee problems.

## Breed in Brief

**Registries:** AKC, UKC, CKC
**Occupation:** Vermin hunter
**Size:** 9.5 to 10 in tall; 13 to 14 lbs
**Longevity:** 13 to 15 years
**Exercise:** Busy and active; playful
**Training:** Moderate
**Grooming:** Easy

# Canaan Dog

The Canaan Dog is the native dog of Israel. Drawings on tombs at Beni-Hassan, which date to 2200 B.C., depict dogs that look like the Canaan Dogs of today. When the Romans invaded and scattered the Israelites, the native dogs escaped extinction by becoming feral. They lived wild in the Negev Desert for centuries. Some dogs also served the Bedouins as both guard dogs and herding dogs.

The Canaan Dog stands between 19 and 24 inches tall and weighs 35 to 55 pounds. The head is wedge-shaped, the ears are upright, and the eyes are almond-shaped and dark. The tail is often curled over the back when the dog is excited. The double coat has a harsh, flat outer coat and a soft, short undercoat. Canaan Dogs are predominantly white with patches of color, or a solid color with or without white trim.

## Breed in Brief

**Registries:** AKC, UKC, CKC
**Occupation:** Guardian, herder
**Size:** 19 to 24 in tall; 35 to 55 lbs
**Longevity:** 13 to 15 years
**Exercise:** Moderate
**Training:** Moderate
**Grooming:** Easy; does shed

The Canaan Dog does shed, although the heaviness of the undercoat varies according to climate. Twice weekly brushing will suffice for most of the year; daily brushing may be needed during shedding.

A native desert breed, the Canaan Dog is most active in the morning and evening and is content to sleep during the heat of the day. He enjoys walks, games, and many dog sports, including agility, herding, search and rescue, and tracking.

Naturally protective, early socialization can temper the Canaan Dog's responses. He also needs early socialization to other friendly dogs because he can be dog-aggressive. The Israel Canaan Dog Club of America says, "The Canaan Dog is a survivor because of his self-reliance and his adaptability. He is not a dog for everyone. His independence requires that his owner be loving but firmly in charge."

This breed needs an experienced dog owner who is patient and affectionate, yet firm and willing to establish household and social rules for the dog. He is good with kids who respect him. His interaction with other dogs and animals should be closely supervised. The primary health concern is hip dysplasia.

# Canadian Eskimo Dog

The ancestors of today's Canadian Eskimo Dog arrived in the Arctic regions around 1200 A.D. The dogs were the companions and working partners of the Inuit people. The dogs pulled sleds, carried backpacks, hunted, and warned of polar bears. However, as the modern age intruded into the Arctic, the dogs were replaced with modern tools. By 1970, the breed was facing extinction. Although efforts are underway to save the breed, its future is still in jeopardy.

These dogs stand between 23 and 27.5 inches tall and weigh 60 to 100 pounds. The ears are erect but not large. The eyes are usually dark; blue eyes are not allowed by the breed standard. The coat is dense, with a heavy undercoat and a long outer coat. Any coat color is permitted. The tail is long and is usually carried curled over the back.

The coat should be brushed at least twice a week, although daily brushing may be needed when shedding is at its worst.

This breed was designed to work. If there is no work to do (weight pulling, sledding, skijoring, or agility), then these dogs need vigorous exercise. When there is no snow, they can run alongside a bicycle. Without work or adequate exercise, they can get into trouble.

Training should begin early. The Canadian Eskimo Dog Club of Canada says, "Firm training is essential for this breed, as they are very determined." Training can also provide the breed with a job to do.

Unlike the Siberian Husky, the Alaskan Malamute, and other northern breeds, this breed is relatively unknown to pet owners, which may have led to its present predicament. However, pet owners who enjoy northern breeds can still help save the Canadian Eskimo Dog. When provided with training and exercise, this dog can be a good pet. He is patient with children who treat him respectfully. He should not be trusted with other small pets; his hunting instincts are too strong. This is a healthy breed.

## Breed in Brief

**Registries:** CKC, UKC, ARBA
**Occupation:** Sled dog, hunter
**Size:** 23 to 27.5 in tall; 60 to 100 lbs
**Longevity:** 11 to 13 years
**Exercise:** Needs exercise and a job to do
**Training:** Needs firm training
**Grooming:** Sheds!

# Cane Corso

The Cane Corso is an old Italian breed, with evidence to its use during the Roman Empire. However, after World War II, changes in how people hunted and raised livestock led to the breed's decline, so much so that it was facing extinction. Fanciers, however, have saved the breed.

The Cane Corso is 23.5 to 27 inches tall, weighs 90 to 120 pounds, and has a large head, short muzzle, and muscular jaws. The ears are either naturally dropped or cropped upright. His body is strong and powerful, and his tail is docked. His coat is short and stiff and may be black, gray, or fawn.

Grooming consists of twice weekly brushing with a soft bristle brush or curry comb.

The Cane Corso is not an overly active breed but does need daily activity. Walks that provide socialization opportunities are good, as he needs to continue to meet people. He will also enjoy games, especially with kids, but he is not good at amusing himself—he prefers to do what the family is doing.

Shauna de Moss of CastleGuard Cane Corsos says, "The Corso is a dominant guardian breed that requires extensive socialization, thorough obedience training, and confident owners who understand how to establish pack order." This dog is intelligent and responsive to training, and if bonded to his owner, is willing to please. The Cane Corso Association of America says, "It is strongly recommended that training become a permanent part of your life."

de Moss says, "This is a complicated, intelligent breed and is not for most pet owners. Anyone considering the breed should do considerable research on the breed temperament and meet several dogs." Those who understand living with a dominant dog will find the Corso affectionate, loyal, and protective. When raised with kids who treat him with respect, the Corso is awesome. He can be good with other pets when raised with them. Health concerns include eyelid problems, bloat, torsion, and hip dysplasia.

## Breed in Brief

**Registries:** AKC FSS, CKC
**Occupation:** Versatile guardian
**Size:** 23.5 to 27 in tall; 90 to 120 lbs
**Longevity:** 10 to 12 years
**Exercise:** Moderate
**Training:** Difficult
**Grooming:** Easy

# Cardigan Welsh Corgi

The Cardigan Welsh Corgi is an old breed descended from dogs the Celts brought to Wales more than 3,000 years ago. The two Corgi breeds are related, although the Cardigan (the breed with a tail) is much older than the Pembroke Welsh Corgi (the breed without a tail). Originally a ratter and a cattle herding dog, the Cardigan today is primarily a companion dog.

The Cardigan is a long-bodied, low-slung, sturdy dog with heavy bone and a deep chest. Standing 10.5 to 12.5 inches tall and weighing between 25 and 38 pounds, he should give an impression of both speed and endurance, even with very short legs. The head is wedge-shaped, with large upright ears and brown eyes. The front legs are bowed. The tail is long and bushy. The double coat has a soft undercoat and a medium-length outer coat. Coat colors include black, blue merle, sable, red, and brindle.

The coat should be brushed two to three times a week, although daily brushing might be needed in the spring and fall when shedding is at its worst.

This Corgi is not an overly active dog, but he is far from sedate. He loves to play games and enjoys daily walks. Without enough exercise, he will find ways to amuse himself that could get him into trouble.

The Cardigan needs early socialization so that he can meet a variety of people, as he is naturally protective and wary of strangers. A very intelligent breed, early training can teach him household rules. Training should continue on into adulthood, as this breed thrives with mental challenges. He also enjoys many dog sports, especially herding and agility.

The Cardigan is very much a companion dog who enjoys his family and likes to do things. He may try to herd the children and the family cat. He is wary of strange dogs and should not be trusted with small pets; he is still an efficient ratter. Health concerns include eye problems and hip dysplasia.

## Breed in Brief

**Registries:** AKC, UKC, CKC
**Occupation:** Herder, companion
**Size:** 10.5 to 12.5 in tall; 25 to 38 lbs
**Longevity:** 12 to 14 years
**Exercise:** Moderate
**Training:** Easy; hard to keep challenged
**Grooming:** Easy

# arolina Dog

arolina Dogs, also called American Dingos, are free-ranging dogs who have lived in remote areas of South Carolina, Georgia, and other parts of the American Southeast. Written descriptions by some of the first European settlers to the area suggest that these dogs were in the region even then. Captive breeding has shown several primitive behaviors, including pack hierarchy and cooperative hunting. Unlike many other wild canines, Carolina Dogs, when bred in captivity and raised with people, make great family pets when their needs are known and understood.

The Carolina Dog usually stands between 17 and 24 inches tall and weighs between 40 and 60 pounds, but there is some variety in size. This breed has a primitive look. These dogs have large erect ears, almond-shaped dark eyes, and a long tail. The body is muscular without being bulky. The coat is short, with a dense undercoat in the winter. Coat color may be ginger, black and tan, or piebald.

Twice weekly brushing is sufficient, except the undercoat sheds heavily in the spring and fall and at those times needs more frequent brushing.

Carolina Dogs are active but not overly so. Two walks a day with a playtime in between are fine for most dogs. These dogs do enjoy more playtime, however, and will willingly participate in hikes, camping, agility training, flying disc, and running alongside a bicycle. Exercise should be on leash or inside a fenced yard; this breed does hunt naturally, and if a rabbit or squirrel is flushed and the dog is off leash, he'll be gone.

Carolina Dogs are, by nature, reserved with strangers. Early socialization is very important, as is early training. The breed thrives on gentle, positive training and enjoys learning.

Carolina Dogs can be very good with children when raised with them and when the children are kind and gentle. The breed is not normally destructive in the house and not prone to escaping from the yard. This is a healthy breed.

## Breed in Brief

**Registries:** UKC, ARBA
**Occupation:** Primitive dog
**Size:** 17 to 24 in tall; 40 to 60 lbs
**Longevity:** 12 to 14 years
**Exercise:** Active
**Training:** Easy; needs positive methods
**Grooming:** Easy

# Caucasian Ovtcharka

The Caucasian Ovtcharka (or Ovcharka), also known as the Caucasian Shepherd, is a livestock guardian breed from the region that includes Georgia, Armenia, and Turkey. The breed has also been used as a versatile military dog in Russia.

Males are 25.5 inches at the shoulder, weighing more than 100 pounds. Females are slightly smaller. The head is wedge-shaped, the eyes are dark, and the ears may be cropped. The strong body is longer than it is tall. The coat is double with a dense undercoat. The most common color is gray, but other colors include rust, straw, earth, spotted, piebald, and brindle.

The Caucasian's coat sheds all the time, but brushing two to three times a week will keep it manageable. However, when the dog begins his annual shed, daily brushing is definitely in order.

This is a low-energy breed. He will be happy with a walk morning and evening and dozing during the heat of the day, but should a trespasser walk into his house or yard, he will be up in a flash. Puppies are more playful than adults.

Caucasian Ovtcharka International recommends a puppy kindergarten class for all puppies, followed by more obedience training: "Obedience training helps establish the bond between you as pack leader and your dog as a respected member of the pack." As guardian dogs, early socialization will help the dogs of this breed fit into society.

Caucasian Ovtcharka International says, "This breed is not the dog for everyone. They demand time, attention, frequent training, and handling. They are strong, willful, and cannot be expected to like everyone. Without proper training, they can be very aggressive to both people and dogs." Like most other guardian breeds, they also bark a lot, which can annoy neighbors. The breed can be good with kids with training, but will not necessarily be good with your kids' friends. (They don't understand rough play.) This is a healthy breed.

## Breed in Brief

**Registries:** AKC FSS, UKC, ARBA
**Occupation:** Livestock guardian
**Size:** 25.5 in tall; 100+ lbs
**Longevity:** 10 to 12 years
**Exercise:** Low activity level
**Training:** Challenge
**Grooming:** Sheds

# Cavalier King Charles Spaniel

The Cavalier King Charles Spaniel got its name as the favorite pet of Britain's King Charles I, but the breed itself has been around for even longer. Many old portraits show dogs that look like today's Cavaliers.

The Cavalier is an adorable, friendly toy spaniel. He stands between 12 and 13 inches tall and weighs 13 to 18 pounds. He has a rounded skull, large dark eyes, and a full muzzle. The ears are long and dropped, and the tail is long. His coat is silky and is medium to long, with feathering on the ears, legs, and tail. The Cavalier may be black and tan, red (ruby), white with chestnut markings (Blenheim), or tri-colored (black, red, and white).

The Cavalier does require regular grooming, as the long, silky coat can mat. He should be brushed and then combed every other day. Daily grooming is needed if he runs through wet grass or brush.

This breed enjoys daily walks and playtimes but is also willing to cuddle. He is adaptable; if you are active and enjoy dog sports, he will do them with you. If you are more sedate, he can do that, too. All exercise should be on leash or in a fenced yard, as Cavaliers are still spaniels; if a bird or rabbit is flushed, they will be off in a flash!

The breed is friendly and affectionate but needs early socialization; without it, some dogs can be shy. Training is needed, too, as housetraining can be a challenge. Training is also important for the owner, as this breed is easy to spoil yet needs the same guidance and rules that other breeds require.

The Cavalier needs a gentle, affectionate owner. He does not tolerate rough handling well, and as a companion breed will not thrive when left alone for many hours. Most breeders will not sell a puppy to a family with very young children. The breed is good with other dogs and is usually trustworthy with other pets. Health issues include deafness; heart, eye, and knee problems; and hip dysplasia.

## Breed in Brief

**Registries:** AKC, UKC, CKC
**Occupation:** Companion
**Size:** 12 to 13 in tall; 13 to 18 lbs
**Longevity:** 13 to 15 years
**Exercise:** Calm to moderately active
**Training:** Challenge to housetrain
**Grooming:** Moderate

# Chart Polski

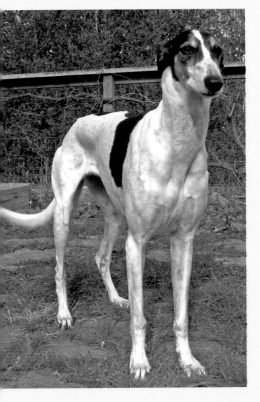

Although the Chart Polski, or Polish Sighthound, resembles the English Greyhound, it is actually a much older breed and developed separately. It is descended from Asiatic sighthounds and was first written about in 1600. The breed was used to hunt hare, deer, and wolves and has great endurance over rough terrain.

This large sighthound stands 27 to 32 inches, with males larger than females. The head is long and narrow, with folded ears, large amber eyes, and a dark nose. The chest is deep, the body compact, and the legs strong. The dog should look like an athletic running dog. The coat is short and hard and may be any color.

This breed's coat is easy to groom. A twice weekly brushing will keep it in shape.

These dogs need daily exercise. A good run in a fenced-in yard is excellent. Chart Polski can also run alongside a bicycle. All exercise should be on leash or in a fenced yard, though, as these dogs retain their hunting instincts and will be off in a flash if a small animal dashes away.

Lynda Mulczynski, a Chart Polski breeder, says, "Obedience training should be an absolute requirement for all Chart Polski and their owners." She continues by saying that training should be positive, fun, and interesting. "Some individual dogs are very dominant and can take the upper hand over an unsuspecting owner, creating an unhappy situation in the home." Socialization is also very important, as this is a highly protective breed that will courageously protect home and family.

Mulczynski says, "The Chart Polski loves and adores his whole family and usually extends his friendliness to their friends." They are wary and aloof toward strangers. These dogs can be wonderful with children, although young dogs are rowdy and exuberant. Many can be dog-aggressive, especially males. They can be good to cats when raised with them, but will chase any animal that runs. This is a healthy breed.

## Breed in Brief

**Registries:** UKC, CKC
**Occupation:** Sighthound
**Size:** 27 to 32 in tall; no weight standard
**Longevity:** 12 to 15 years
**Exercise:** Daily run
**Training:** Moderate
**Grooming:** Easy

# Chesapeake Bay Retriever

This is an American breed, bred and developed along the eastern seaboard, particularly (as the name implies) around the Chesapeake Bay. In 1807, a British brig was lost during a storm, with the ship sinking and all hands evacuated. An American ship, the *Canton,* picked up survivors, among whom were two puppies the ship had picked up in Newfoundland. The male, named Sailor, the female, Canton, and their individual progeny became well-known for their abilities in the water and as superior hunting dogs and retrievers. Duck hunters along the Chesapeake Bay crossed the two original dogs and their offspring with local hunting dogs, including yellow hounds and Irish Water Spaniels, to improve the local breeds. By the late 1800s, the Chesapeake Bay Retriever was an established breed.

This is a physically tough breed, built to withstand the harsh conditions of the Chesapeake Bay region. The breed is 21 to 26 inches tall, weighing between 55 and 80 pounds, with females smaller than males. The head is broad, the eyes are yellow to amber, and the ears are dropped. The chest is deep and wide, the back is short, and the tail is of medium length. Dewclaws on the front legs may be removed; any on the back legs must be removed. The coat is thick and short, with a dense undercoat. The coat is oily, which enables the dog to work in cold, harsh conditions, including retrieving birds in the ice-packed Chesapeake Bay. Color may be any shade of brown, dead grass, or sedge.

The undercoat does shed, so the dog should be thoroughly brushed twice a week. The oil in the coat can also create a doggy odor, but bathing the dog destroys the protective oils.

The Chesapeake can be quite active. Chesapeake owner and trainer Debbie Founds says, "Chesapeakes play hard and sleep hard. Sydney, my Chessie, swims in our pool three to four times a week. She also runs hard every day." She adds, "A bored Chesapeake will quickly make confetti out of favorite footwear, unattended mail, and magazines." Chesapeakes were bred as hunting dogs and retrievers and still perform those tasks today, but they also enjoy other dog sports, including agility, flyball, tracking, and search and rescue.

The American Chesapeake Club recommends early training for all dogs: "Training should begin with puppy classes, which provide socialization as well as the foundation for command (obedience) training." Founds says, "This is a very intelligent breed that learns quickly and loves to please. However, the breed is also very strong-willed and will readily adopt 'bad' behaviors if instruction is neglected."

This breed does best with an experienced dog owner, as he can be strong-willed and independent at times. Founds compares a Chesapeake to a 4-year-old child with four legs and a tail. "They love to tease and are full of mischief," she says. Although affectionate and loving with his family, the Chesapeake is wary of strangers. He is good with kids who respect him. He can be great with cats when raised with them but should be supervised with other small pets. Chessies, especially males, can also be aggressive toward other dogs. Health concerns include hip and elbow dysplasia, eye disorders, bloat, and torsion.

## Breed in Brief

**Registries:** AKC, UKC, CKC
**Occupation:** Gun dog, retriever
**Size:** 21 to 26 in tall; 55 to 80 lbs
**Longevity:** 10 to 12 years
**Exercise:** Moderate
**Training:** Easy; hard to keep challenged
**Grooming:** Easy

# Chihuahua
## (Smooth Coat and Long Coat)

The Chihuahua's history has been hotly debated. One group feels that the breed originated in China before being introduced to Central America by Spanish explorers. Others firmly believe that the Chihuahua is a native of Central America, descended from the Techichi, a small dog who was a companion to the Toltecs as far back as the 9th century. Small dogs much like the Chihuahua have been found in the pyramids of Cholula, which were built before the 1500s. No matter where the breed originated, it has become a popular pet in Central and North America, Europe, and the Mediterranean, as well as other parts of the world.

The Chihuahua is a very small dog, never to exceed 6 pounds, with a bright, alert expression. Other than weight, there are no size classifications. The Chihuahua Club of America states on its website, "Teacup, Pocket Size, Tiny Toy, Miniature, and Standard are several of the many tags assigned to this breed." They caution that the use of these terms is actually incorrect and misleading. There are only two varieties of Chihuahua, and those are the coat types. The long coat Chihuahua has a soft, flat, or slightly wavy coat, while the smooth coat (or shorthaired) Chihuahua has a short, close, glossy coat. Both varieties may have an undercoat. Coat colors include black and

tan, tricolored, red, fawn, sable, and brindle. The Chihuahua's head is rounded, with full but not protruding eyes, large erect ears, and a jaunty curved tail that is carried gaily and loops over the back.

Grooming this little dog is not difficult. The long-haired coat should be combed every other day and checked for tangles, especially behind the ears and in the pantaloons. The smooth variety can be brushed twice a week with a soft bristle brush.

Chihuahuas are not sedentary lap dogs. They like to cuddle, but they also need exercise and playtime. Edna St. Hilaire, the president of the Chihuahua Club of Canada, says, "Chihuahuas are moderately active, playful, lively, and alert." She adds that two hours of exercise and playtime are needed each day. The breed's small size makes this easy, as Chihuahuas can chase a ball or toy across the room or go for a nice walk for lots of exercise.

Socialization is important for this breed. St. Hilaire says, "They are very loyal to one person, although they will accept other family members and close friends." With early socialization to people of all ages, Chihuahuas can become more comfortable with people outside the home circle.

## Breed in Brief

**Registries:** AKC, UKC. CKC
**Occupation:** Companion
**Size:** Not to exceed 6 lbs
**Longevity:** 14 to 18 years
**Exercise:** Active
**Training:** Challenge
**Grooming:** Easy

Even though this is a very small dog, training is very important. Chihuahuas are bright dogs and quick thinkers. Without training, they can take advantage of a permissive owner. Training can be a challenge, but with fair yet fun training techniques, these dogs will learn and will have fun doing it.

Chihuahuas are alert little dogs and try to be watchdogs; sometimes they take their job too seriously. This breed is not necessarily the best choice for children, as the dogs can be fragile. St. Hilaire comments, "They prefer older folks; however, they will accept children who have been taught to be gentle and to respect them." Health concerns include an open fontanel (soft spot on the skull), knee problems, and hypoglycemia.

# Chinese Crested

## (Powderpuff and Hairless)

The Chinese Crested is an old breed, and as is so often the case, its history has been lost over time. Some experts feel the breed most likely descended from hairless dogs in Africa, with the Chinese developing the smaller version of the breed. Pictures created in the 1500s and 1600s show Chinese Cresteds involved in Chinese life. Chinese sailors kept the dogs aboard ship as vermin hunters and, in doing so, spread the dogs to ports throughout the world. They were known as Chinese Sailor Dogs, and many of the small dogs were used for barter. The dogs were especially prized during times of the plague, as the hairless skin didn't harbor fleas. The breed was also known as the Chinese Edible Dog, which can give you a clue as to the breed's other purpose in China.

The Chinese Crested is found in two varieties—Powderpuff (with hair) and Hairless. These dogs stand 11 to 13 inches tall and weigh between 6 and 12 pounds. This small, fine-boned dog has a tapered muzzle, almond-shaped eyes, and large, erect ears. The Hairless variety has hair on the head and crest of the neck, the feet, and the tail. When running, with the coat flowing behind them,

they look like tiny horses. The Powderpuff variety has a normal coat of long, silky guard hairs over a silky undercoat.

Grooming the Hairless consists of bathing the dog, using moisturizers on the hairless skin to keep it healthy, and applying sunscreen to prevent sunburn. The Powderpuff requires twice weekly brushing to prevent tangles and mats.

The Chinese Crested is not overly active but does enjoy walks and playtimes. He does well in agility but also likes to cuddle. The Chinese Crested enjoys therapy dog work, and although the Powderpuff will be eagerly petted, the Hairless will always create conversation. As with all toy breeds, during therapy dog visits, these dogs should be protected from hard hugs that might injure the dogs.

As with many toy breeds, it is very easy to spoil Chinese Cresteds, so early training is a good idea. With puppy training and socialization classes, the dog learns how to learn, is introduced to the basic commands, and gets to meet a variety of people and other puppies. In addition, the dog owner learns how to teach her dog and establish household rules. Housetraining can be a challenge.

## Breed in Brief

**Registries:** AKC, UKC, CKC
**Occupation:** Vermin hunter, companion
**Size:** 11 to 13 in tall; 6 to 12 lbs
**Longevity:** 12 to 13 years
**Exercise:** Moderate
**Training:** Moderate; challenge to housetrain
**Grooming:** Easy

However, this breed is very clean, and with patience and consistency, housetraining will happen.

The Chinese Crested makes a wonderful companion for many different people. If you are active and want to do agility, he can do that. He can also be a terrific pet for a housebound senior. He is good with older children as long as they treat him with respect. He is too small for very young kids, and many breeders will not sell puppies to families with young children for this reason. When well-socialized, he is good with other dogs, although playtimes should be carefully supervised. The Chinese Crested is small, but he doesn't realize that he is small, and could be hurt by a larger dog. The Hairless variety can have jaw and dental problems, including malformed teeth and early tooth loss. The breed can also have liver and eye problems.

# Chinese Foo Dog

## (Toy, Miniature, and Standard)

The Chinese Foo Dog is an old spitz-type breed that is probably a descendant of Chow Chows crossed with Northern European hunting dogs. History shows that the Tong, a Chinese association or fraternity, believed the Chinese Foo Dog would bring them luck, and so they kept and bred the dogs. The breed evolved into a versatile utility dog that could hunt, herd, carry packs, pull, and guard.

The Chinese Foo Dog is found in three sizes: toy (10 inches or less), miniature (over 10 inches up to and including 15), and standard (over 15 inches). The breed can also be classified by weight, with small dogs weighing up to 20 pounds, medium dogs weighing 21 to 50 pounds, and large dogs weighing over 50 pounds. A typical Nordic-type dog, the head is broad, the ears are upright, and the eyes are dark. These dogs often have a dark blue tongue. The tail is set high and curled over the back. Some breeders dock the tail. The coat is double, with a thick, dense undercoat and an outer coat that is hard and stands away from the body.

With the heavy coat, grooming is very much a part of life with these dogs. This breed needs brushing at least twice a week, although when the heavy undercoat is shed, daily brushing will help keep the hair in the house somewhat under control.

Foo Dogs are moderately active. They enjoy a walk morning and evening and can be quite playful. Breed expert Brad Trom says, "Chinese Foo Dogs are appealing to the sense of humor and continue to be playful on into adulthood."

One of the original uses of Foo Dogs is as guard dogs, and the breed continues to be wary of strangers. However, unlike some other watchful breeds, this one does not bark unless there is a reason to do so. Early socialization and training is important, and teaching the dog to accept regular grooming should be a part of that.

The Chinese Foo Dog is an affectionate, intelligent, playful breed. They are good with well-behaved children but will not tolerate disrespectful behavior. The breed is good with other dogs, although interactions with other pets should be supervised. This is a healthy breed with few problems.

## Breed in Brief

**Registries:** Chinese Foo Dog Club of America
**Occupation:** Watchdog
**Size:** Toy, mini, standard from under 10 in to 15+ in tall; from under 20 lbs to 50+ lbs
**Longevity:** 12 to 14 years
**Exercise:** Moderate
**Training:** Easy
**Grooming:** Regular brushing; sheds

# hinese Shar-Pei

The Chinese Shar-Pei originated in the southern provinces of China and has been known since 200 B.C. The communist government of the People's Republic of China has on more than one occasion tried to eradicate dogs, and although these efforts have, at times, driven the Shar-Pei close to extinction, breeders in Hong Kong and Taiwan kept the breed alive prior to its introduction to the western world.

This breed has a unique look. The head is large, the muzzle is padded (or meaty), the eyes are small, and the ears are small and folded against the head. The body is square, while the tail is set very high and curls over the back. Puppies' skin is loose and wrinkled, while adults keep wrinkles on the head, neck, and forequarters. The coat is harsh, short (up to 1 inch in length), and stands out from the skin. Solid colors are acceptable, with some shading down the back and on the ears.

The Shar-Pei is easy to groom. The Chinese Shar-Pei Club of America says, "Shar-Pei are clean dogs that require little more care than an occasional bath, regular ear cleaning, and toenail clipping."

The Shar-Pei is usually quiet in the house but loves to run and play outside. Long, brisk walks morning and evening and a chance to play will keep this breed satisfied.

Early socialization is important to this breed, as the Shar-Pei is wary of strangers. Training should also be started young. The Chinese Shar-Pei Club of America says, "An obedient dog is a happy dog." This bright breed can be independent and stubborn; training can help the dog become more compliant. The breed was initially a peasant's dog—versatile and hard-working, used for guard duty, hunting, and herding.

The Chinese Shar-Pei needs an experienced dog owner who understands this breed's temperament. The breed can be good with children who treat the dog with respect. The breed is not social with other dogs. Health concerns include cancer and immune system problems.

## Breed in Brief

**Registries:** AKC, UKC, CKC
**Occupation:** Guard dog
**Size:** 18 to 20 in tall; 45 to 60 lbs
**Longevity:** 12 to 14 years
**Exercise:** Moderate
**Training:** Early socialization needed
**Grooming:** Easy

# hinook

The Chinook got its name from the breed's founding sire. The original Chinook was born in 1917 in Wonalancet, New Hampshire, and became his owner's idea of a perfect sled dog. Arthur Walden, Chinook's owner, bred his dog so that the breed would have the strength of the larger weight-pulling dogs and the speed of the smaller racing-sled dogs.

Chinooks stand 21 to 27 inches tall and weigh between 50 and 75 pounds. The head is broad with a tapering muzzle. The eyes are almond-shaped, and either dropped or pricked ears are acceptable. The body is strong, powerful, and athletic. The tail is long and sickle-shaped. The double coat is tawny-colored.

The coat does shed and needs twice weekly brushing.

Chinook owner Amanda Bays says, "Chinooks are moderately active. They do best with daily exercise but prefer to be doing what their owners are doing. They can

be a jogging partner or a couch potato." Without enough exercise, though, Chinooks can become bored, and when bored, they find ways to amuse themselves, sometimes destructively. All exercise should be within a fenced-in yard.

This breed needs early and continued socialization throughout puppyhood to prevent shyness. When exposed to a variety of people, places, things, and other friendly dogs, they will grow up to be confident, well-adjusted dogs. Training is also important. Bays says, "The Chinook is smart and easy to train but can also be headstrong. They require consistent training." This sensitive breed does well with firm yet fun training—not too repetitive and not heavy-handed.

The Chinook needs an owner who is home most of the time, as the breed does not do well when left alone for many hours each day. A lonely Chinook may develop separation anxiety or destructive behaviors. They are wonderful family dogs and get along great with kids and other dogs. They should not be trusted with smaller pets. Health concerns include hip dysplasia, cataracts, allergies, and seizures.

## Breed in Brief

**Registries:** AKC FSS, UKC
**Occupation:** Sled dog
**Size:** 21 to 27 in tall; 50 to 75 lbs
**Longevity:** 10 to 12 years
**Exercise:** Moderate
**Training:** Moderate
**Grooming:** Moderate

# Chow Chow

## (Rough Coat and Smooth Coat)

The Chow Chow originated in China, where it was known as Lang Gou (wolf dog) or Xiong Gou (bear dog). The breed is known to have been in existence 2,000 years ago but might be even older. Some experts say that the breed resulted from a cross between the Tibetan Mastiff and the Samoyed, although other experts claim the Chow Chow is one of the founding breeds of dogs and is the parent breed for Samoyeds, Keeshonds, and several other similar breeds.

The Chow Chow is a sturdy dog, standing 17 to 20 inches tall and weighing between 50 and 75 pounds. The head is carried high and is large with almond-shaped eyes. The ears are small and upright. The tail is carried over the back. Both the rough and smooth coats have a thick, dense undercoat. The rough coat is straight and stands out from the body. There is an abundant ruff around the head and neck. The tail is well-feathered. The smooth coat is shorter, with no ruff, and is hard and dense. Coat colors include red, black, blue, cinnamon, and cream.

Grooming the Chow Chow requires some work. The undercoat on both coat types does shed and can shed a lot! Thorough brushing is needed at least every other day, although when shedding is at its heaviest, daily brushing is better.

## Breed in Brief

**Registries:** AKC, UKC, CKC
**Occupation:** Hunter
**Size:** 17 to 20 in tall; 50 to 75 lbs
**Longevity:** 10 to 12 years
**Exercise:** Low activity level
**Training:** Challenge
**Grooming:** Daily brushing recommended

The Chow Chow is not an active breed. A walk morning and evening will suit this breed quite well. Puppies appreciate a couple of playtimes throughout the day.

The Chow Chow is a dignified breed, aloof and reserved. Early socialization is needed so that the dog can connect with people. During socialization, he should meet people of all ages, especially children. Early training should be firm and structured yet fun and upbeat.

The Chow Chow does better with an experienced dog owner who understands the breed's temperament. With socialization, he can be good with kids who treat him with respect. He may not be good with other dogs or pets. Health concerns include hip and knee problems, eyelid defects, and sensitivities to anesthesia.

# Clumber Spaniel

No one really knows where or how the Clumber Spaniel came to be. The breed got its name from Clumber Park in Nottinghamshire, England, where the Duke of Newcastle's gamekeeper hunted with these dogs. The breed is also portrayed in many old paintings, some from the 1700s, looking remarkably like today's Clumbers. The Basset Hound is thought to be one of the breeds used to develop the Clumber.

The Clumber Spaniel is a rectangular-shaped dog, with a long body and short, thick legs.

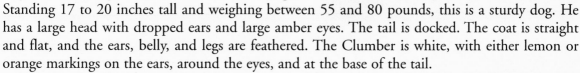

Standing 17 to 20 inches tall and weighing between 55 and 80 pounds, this is a sturdy dog. He has a large head with dropped ears and large amber eyes. The tail is docked. The coat is straight and flat, and the ears, belly, and legs are feathered. The Clumber is white, with either lemon or orange markings on the ears, around the eyes, and at the base of the tail.

This breed sheds year-round. To control some of the hair in the house, daily to every-other-day brushing is needed. The feathering on the belly and legs needs combing and brushing to keep it free of mats. It's advisable to keep the feet trimmed for ease of cleaning. The heavy ears need regular cleaning to prevent problems.

The Clumber is a slow, steady dog and is not the right breed for someone who wants a jogging partner. These dogs do need exercise, though, and enjoy walks and a game of fetch.

The Clumber is not a watchdog. He may initially be standoffish with strangers, but is affectionate and friendly with people he knows. Early, upbeat, and fun training is a good idea for all Clumbers. Avoid heavy-handed techniques and too much repetition. This intelligent breed will shut down if training is too rough. Clumbers enjoy several dog sports, including agility, obedience, and hunt tests.

The Clumber Spaniel loves to spend time with the family. Although he can be left alone occasionally, he does not like to be left at home alone for long hours every day. He is great with kids and loves to play games. The breed is also good with other dogs and pets. One drawback to the breed is the drool; Clumbers do drool, often in great quantities, especially when anticipating food or treats. Health concerns include hip dysplasia, allergies, and eye, ear, and back problems.

## Breed in Brief

**Registries:** AKC, UKC, CKC
**Occupation:** Gun dog
**Size:** 17 to 20 in tall; 55 to 80 lbs
**Longevity:** 12 to 14 years
**Exercise:** Low activity level
**Training:** Keep it fun
**Grooming:** Moderate

# Cockapoo

The Cockapoo (or Cockerpoo) is a mixed-breed dog, the cross between a Cocker Spaniel and a Poodle, and has been popular in the United States for more than thirty years. Although many cute, fuzzy dogs of dubious ancestry have been called Cockapoos, as the North American Cockapoo Registry states, "A true Cockapoo is *only* a purposeful, planned crossing of a purebred Cocker Spaniel with a purebred Poodle." However, many breeders are now breeding Cockapoos to Cockapoos with the goal of creating a new breed. Several registries keep records of breedings, and at some point there may be a motion to have Cockapoos recognized as an official breed with one or all breed registries.

Cockapoos are still mixed-breed dogs, and this makes describing the breed a little difficult. As with any mixed breed, some of the offspring will be more like the Poodle and some more like the

Cocker Spaniel. However, most Cockapoos from a Cocker Spaniel and a Miniature Poodle cross are Cocker Spaniel height (14 to 16 inches tall) but slighter in build. The coat is usually wavy to curly but without tight curls. Although the tail is sometimes docked, some breeders leave it naturally long. The face and expression usually show the mixed ancestry with characteristics of both breeds. Most are bright-eyed, intelligent, and ready for anything that comes their way.

Since both the Poodle and Cocker Spaniel have coats that grow continually and require regular grooming, so does the Cockapoo. Unless the dog is shaved short, the coat needs daily brushing and combing to keep it from matting. The hair needs to be trimmed every four to six weeks. The hanging ears can be quite heavy with long hair on them and require regular cleaning.

Cockapoos vary in temperament and need for exercise. Some are calmer, more like their Cocker Spaniel ancestors, while others are quite busy—more like Poodles. The majority of Cockapoos need a vigorous walk morning and evening and a boisterous playtime in between. Without exercise, Cockapoos are smart enough to get into trouble and may use up all that excess energy doing something you'd rather they didn't do!

Socialization is very important. Young Cockapoos should meet people of all ages and ethnic backgrounds and get to play with puppies of various breeds. Training should also begin early, as Cockapoos are usually very quick and bright. The training should be structured yet fun. These dogs often get bored if training is too repetitive, so trick training and other activities can be incorporated. Many Cockapoos are serving as wonderful volunteer therapy dogs.

The variety within this mixed breed applies to many characteristics; some Cockapoos are wonderful with children, while others are not. Some are excellent with other dogs and small pets, and others are not. Each Cockapoo is an individual, and that's one of the characteristics many people enjoy. Cockapoos are, for the most part, healthy dogs, but problems can be inherited from both parent breeds, including knee problems, eye defects, and allergies.

## Breed in Brief

**Registries:** Cockapoo registries (see appendix)
**Occupation:** Companion
**Size:** Varies; usually 14 to 16 in tall; 20 to 25 lbs
**Longevity:** 14 to 16 years
**Exercise:** Daily walks and games
**Training:** Easy; hard to keep focused
**Grooming:** Moderate to difficult

# ocker Spaniel

The spaniel family of dogs is a very old one, dating back as far as the 14th century. Cocker Spaniels are the smallest of the sporting dog breeds, and legend has it they got their name from their proficiency at flushing woodcocks. The breed as it is now known developed in the United States. To handle the hunting conditions in the U.S., the breed developed a shorter back and longer legs. Today, the American Cocker Spaniel is visibly a different breed from the English Cocker Spaniel.

Cocker Spaniels stand between 13.5 and 15.5 inches tall and weigh between 24 and 30 pounds, with females smaller than males. The American Cocker's face is one of the most recognizable in the canine world, with round, full, intelligent eyes, a rounded head, a broad muzzle, and hanging ears. The Cocker's body is sturdy and compact; he is an athlete and should be ready for action at all times. The coat is short on the head and medium-length on the body. The legs are well-feathered. The acceptable colors include black, black and tan, cream, red, brown, and even parti-colors. The tail is docked.

Grooming is a big part of Cocker ownership. The silky coat requires daily brushing and combing; ignoring the coat will result in a matted mess. Many pet owners keep the coat trimmed short for ease of care. You will also need to check and clean the ears on a regular basis, at least twice weekly. The coat requires trimming every four to six weeks. If you wish to learn how to do this yourself, ask your breeder for guidance. If you would prefer not to do it, a professional groomer will be happy to help you.

Cocker Spaniels are active dogs; bred to run in the field, they need a long, vigorous walk or a good run every day. Cockers shouldn't be allowed to run free outside of a fenced-in yard, however, as many have retained their hunting instincts. If a rabbit or squirrel dashes past, they will be off after it. Most Cockers enjoy a game of fetch and canine sports, especially agility and flyball.

Early socialization is important. Although Cockers should be happy extroverts, some can be a little on the shy and fearful side. When they are introduced to a variety of people, other dogs, and the sights and sounds of the world, this tendency can be diminished. Training is important for both the Cocker and his owner, as Cockers are excellent at manipulating their owners. That wonderful head and those expressive eyes can get to anyone, but Cockers, just like all other dogs, need to learn household rules and social manners.

A well-trained, well-socialized Cocker Spaniel can be a wonderful playmate for kids. Sturdy enough to play yet small enough not to be overpowering, Cockers will play with the kids and then take a nap curled up with them. Most Cockers are also good with other family pets, although interactions should be supervised; many Cockers want to chase anything that runs. Major health concerns include eye defects, knee problems, cardiomyopathy, hypothyroidism, and hip and elbow dysplasia.

## Breed in Brief

**Registries:** AKC, UKC, CKC
**Occupation:** Hunter, performance sports
**Size:** 13.5 to 15.5 in tall; 24 to 30 lbs
**Longevity:** 13 to 15 years
**Exercise:** Moderate
**Training:** Moderate
**Grooming:** Difficult

# Collie

## (Smooth Coat and Rough Coat)

In the 1800s in Scotland, the breed was used to herd and guard sheep and to drive the sheep to market, but it was in England in the late 1800s that the breed we know today began to take shape. The breed didn't catch the public's eye until the publication of Alfred Payson Terhune's (1872–1942) stories and books about his treasured Collies: Lad, Wolf, and Bob. When Lassie was introduced in movies, books, and on television, the public was reminded of these beautiful dogs, and their popularity soared again.

The breed's long wedge-shape head is unique and instantly recognizable. Standing 22 to 26 inches tall and weighing 55 to 75 pounds, with females smaller than males, the Collie should be lean with no extra weight. The rough coat has a long double coat with a lush mane, well-feathered legs, and a plumed tail. The smooth coat has a short, dense double coat with no feathering. Collies may be sable and white, tricolored, blue merle, and white.

The smooth Collie needs twice weekly brushing, but the rough Collie's coat takes considerably more work. Both the smooth Collie and rough Collie shed, and shed a lot during the spring and fall. In addition, the rough coat can tangle and mat. A daily brushing and combing can keep the coat looking good, keep the hair in the house to a minimum, and prevent mats from forming.

A vigorous walk morning and evening and a fast game of catch will keep most Collies happy. A bored Collie who is not exercised regularly will get into trouble.

The Collie Club of America strongly recommends that every Collie and owner attend a basic obedience class together. You may want to continue your training, attend advanced training, or learn how to participate in dog sports.

A well-trained Collie can be a wonderful family companion. Collies are loyal to a fault, great with children, and watchful of the home. As dedicated watchdogs, some Collies bark too much, which is annoying to neighbors, but training can help temper that trait. Health problems include a sensitivity to heartworm preventatives, eye defects, gastric bloat, and torsion.

## Breed in Brief

**Registries:** AKC, UKC, CKC
**Occupation:** Herder, companion
**Size:** 22 to 26 in tall; 50 to 75 lbs
**Longevity:** 10 to 12 years
**Exercise:** Moderate
**Training:** Easy to moderate
**Grooming:** Easy for the smooth coat; difficult for the rough coat

# oonhound

There are a few different coonhound breeds. The Black and Tan Coonhound is profiled individually in this book, but other coonhound breeds share a common purpose and ancestry. Although often used on fox and other game, their primary purpose was to hunt raccoons.

The vast majority of coonhound breeds in existence today (excluding the Plott Coonhound) are descended from English Foxhounds. Bluetick Coonhounds are descended from English Foxhounds and French hounds used to hunt big game. The English Coonhound was bred from English Foxhounds and other hounds imported to the American colonies from England in the 1600s and 1700s. The Redbone Coonhound is the result of several crosses, including English Foxhounds, a red dog of unknown ancestry, a Bloodhound, and some Irish hounds. Treeing Walker Coonhounds are descended from English Foxhounds and a dog of unknown ancestry called Tennessee Lead.

Although many people today are breeding coonhounds for breed type according to a breed standard, it's important to remember that for most of their history these dogs were bred for their ability to hunt and for their physical soundness. Most coonhounds stand between 23 and 30 inches tall and weigh between 50 and 100 pounds. The dogs have a hound appearance, with long legs, an athletic body, large eyes, and dropped, hanging ears. The coat is usually short and flat. The tail is long.

Although quiet in the house, these dogs were bred to run and hunt and need vigorous daily exercise. They must be exercised in a fenced-in yard, because if a small animal appears, they could be gone in a flash!

Although most of these dogs are compliant with people, training is sometimes a challenge, as everything these dogs smell will be more important to them than any obedience commands. They can also be quite destructive as puppies. They are good with kids and other dogs but should not be trusted with smaller pets. There are few health concerns.

## Breed in Brief

**Registries:** Registries vary by breed
**Occupation:** Hunter
**Size:** 23 to 30 in tall; 50 to 100 lbs
**Longevity:** 12 to 14 years
**Exercise:** Vigorous daily exercise
**Training:** Challenge
**Grooming:** Easy

# Coton de Tulear

The Coton de Tulear is one of five breeds in the Bichon family, which includes the Bichon Frise, Bolognese, Havanese, and Maltese. The ancestors of these five breeds were popular companions and barter items for sailors in the Mediterranean. The dogs that would one day become the Coton eventually landed in Madagascar, where they became the favorites of royalty.

This is a small breed, standing 8.5 to 12.5 inches tall and weighing 8 to 12 pounds. The eyes are round and dark, the ears are dropped, and the nose is dark. The coat is long, soft, and dense. Although the white coat is the most popular, the Coton may also be black and white or tricolored. The breed standards vary slightly between registries, both as to size and weight and as to coat colors.

This breed should be thoroughly brushed and combed daily, as the coat can mat. Many pet owners keep the feet and under the tail trimmed short for cleanliness.

The Coton can be quite playful but is generally a calm dog. He prefers snuggling to playing in the backyard. Walks are always welcome, though, as every walk turns into a social event; people are drawn to this adorable breed.

## Breed in Brief

**Registries:** AKC, UKC
**Occupation:** Companion
**Size:** 8.5 to 12.5 in tall; 8 to 12 lbs
**Longevity:** 14 to 15 years
**Exercise:** Low activity level
**Training:** Challenge to housetrain
**Grooming:** Daily brushing

Training should begin early. Although this breed is bright and intelligent, housetraining can be a challenge. However, with a good schedule, patience, and consistency, housetraining will happen. Obedience training is also a good idea for both dog and owner, as this breed is easily spoiled.

The Coton de Tulear needs an owner who wishes to have a canine shadow. The owner should also enjoy grooming the dog. This breed is good with children, as long as the kids treat him with respect; he will not tolerate rough handling. He can be good with other dogs, although playtimes with larger dogs should be supervised to prevent injuries. He is usually good with smaller pets, as he has a very low prey drive. Health concerns include knee problems and thyroid disorders.

# Curly-Coated Retriever

The Curly-Coated Retriever is the oldest of the breeds now known as retrievers. Originating in England, this breed has many well-known breeds in its ancestry, including Irish Water Spaniels, Poodles, and the St. John's Newfoundland. Excellent bird dogs, Curlies can note where a bird has fallen and find it no matter how difficult the retrieve. As the breed's heritage would suggest, this breed loves water and will retrieve fallen birds in the water as well as on land.

The breed stands between 23 and 27 inches tall and weighs 60 to 80 pounds. This is an athletic breed, with a strong body and legs. The ears are dropped and the tail is long. The defining characteristic is the tightly curled, weatherproof coat that covers the dog from the top of the head, down over the body, down the thighs, and over the tail. The face, front of the forelegs, and feet have a shorter, smooth coat. The coat is either black or liver-colored.

The Curly should be brushed twice a week, or more if the dog is in the water often. The hair on the paws, under the tail, and around the ears can be trimmed to keep the dog clean and neat.

Curlies can be quite active, especially as puppies. They need vigorous daily exercise and enjoy a good run, swim, or training session on the agility course.

The Curly-Coated Retriever Club of America says, "Early obedience training, geared toward puppies, is recommended, as Curlies are highly intelligent and bore easily. Without training they will teach themselves their own games, to the possible woe of their owner." Curlies are slow to mature, so this training should continue throughout puppyhood.

This breed is still used for hunting and does best in a home where the dog can use these instincts. When not hunting, the Curly is a wonderful family dog, great with children, and usually calm in the house. He is affectionate and loyal but reserved with strangers. Health concerns include hip and elbow dysplasia and eye defects.

## Breed in Brief

**Registries:** AKC, UKC, CKC
**Occupation:** Gun dog
**Size:** 23 to 27 in tall; 60 to 80 lbs
**Longevity:** 10 to 12 years
**Exercise:** Vigorous daily exercise
**Training:** Moderate
**Grooming:** Moderate

# Dachshund

## (Miniature and Standard; Smooth Coat, Long Coat, and Wirehaired Coat)

Dachshunds originated in Germany and have a documented history going back as far as the 15th century. Most breed experts feel that Basset Hounds and some unknown terriers were the ancestors of the breed. The Bassets provided the long body, short legs, strength, good nose for scenting, and smooth coat. The terriers provided tenacity, stamina, the drive to hunt, and the wire coat to that variety. Other experts feel the Dachshund is simply a short-legged version of the German Schweisshund. In any case, the name Dachshund wasn't given to these long-bodied, low-slung hunting dogs until the 17th century; the name reflects both the breed's hunting ability and its prey drive (Dachshund means *badger hunter*).

In the United States, Dachshunds are found in two sizes: standard and miniature. Standards weigh between 16 and 32 pounds, while miniatures weigh less than 11 pounds. In Germany, there are three sizes that are determined by the dog's chest measurement. The dwarf Dachshund measures no more than 13.8 inches around the chest, while the rabbit Dachshund measures no more than 11.8 inches. The standard is the largest, measuring more than 13.8 inches.

All sizes have three coat varieties. The smooth coat is shiny and slick. The longhaired is silky and slightly wavy with feathers on the legs and tail. The wirehaired has a rough, coarse, wiry coat with a softer undercoat. In all varieties, the dog is long-bodied and muscular, with short legs and a long tail that continues the line of the spine. The head is carried high and boldly, and the eyes are almond-shaped and expressive. The ears are dropped and of moderate length.

Grooming the Dachshund depends upon the coat type. The smooth coat is easy to groom; it should be brushed twice weekly with a soft bristle brush or curry comb. The longhaired coat needs a little more work, as the feathers can get tangled. Every other day the coat should be brushed and combed. The wirehaired coat should be brushed twice weekly, and several times a year it needs stripping to remove dead hairs. If you don't know how to strip the coat, talk to your breeder or call a professional groomer.

Don't let the short legs fool you; these hunting dogs are athletes and need daily exercise. They need a good walk morning and evening, a chance to play ball, and a chance to run around the yard looking for squirrels. Because of their long backs and the potential for injury, exercise should not include any jumping onto, off of, or over high obstacles or leaping to catch a ball or flying disc.

Dachshunds are very devoted to their families and quite wary of strangers. It's important that Dachshund puppies attend a puppy class where socialization is incorporated into the lesson plans. Dachshunds can also be barkers; a training class begun when the dogs are young can help prevent or control this tendency. Dachshunds can be good with children who are not overly rough. Interactions with small pets should be supervised; after all, Dachshunds are still tenacious hunters. Health concerns include back problems, knee problems, and obesity.

## Breed in Brief

**Registries:** AKC, UKC, CKC
**Occupation:** Hunter, companion
**Size:** No height standards
Mini: under 11 lbs
Standard: 16 to 32 lbs
**Longevity:** 12 to 14 years
**Exercise:** Moderate
**Training:** Challenge
**Grooming:** Easy to moderate, depending on coat type

# Dalmatian

The origin of the Dalmatian is shrouded in mystery. Although most experts agree that the name comes from the Eastern European region of Dalmatia, it's not known whether the breed originated there or not. Spotted dogs with a similarity to today's breed were painted on tomb walls in Egypt, portrayed running after chariots, and a fresco painted around 1360 in Italy shows a spotted dog. Later, spotted dogs accompanied the Romany gypsies as they traveled throughout Europe. During the 18th century, the breed was introduced to England, where it developed a reputation as a natural coach dog. The breed's affinity for horses, ability to keep up with them, and willingness to protect the horses, carriage, and passengers gained the Dalmation an enthusiastic following. It was in England, too, where Dalmatians were first used as mascots at fire stations, first running with the horses and later riding on the firetrucks.

The Dalmatian today is a medium-sized to large dog, muscular and strong, with the appearance of an athlete, standing 19 to 23 inches tall and weighing between 45 and 60 pounds. The recognizable coat is pure white with either black or liver-colored spots. The spots can range from the size of a dime to the size of a half dollar. The Dalmatian's expression is alert and intelligent. She has dropped ears, round dark eyes, and a long tapered tail.

Even though they have fine, short coats, Dalmatians do shed—not a lot, but a little year-round. Brushing the coat with a soft bristle brush or curry comb will reduce the hair in the house.

Exercising the Dalmatian is a very important part of caring for this breed. Bred to run with carriage horses, fire wagons, or gypsy wagons, this breed must get in a good hard run every day. A walk, even a vigorous one, is not enough. A daily brisk run alongside a bicycle or a run with a horse, if you happen to own one, will keep a Dalmatian happy. If a Dalmatian doesn't get enough exercise, she will find something to amuse herself, and that could very easily be destructive to your house or yard.

Early training is important. Although Dalmatians are intelligent and enthusiastic, they can also be independent and stubborn. The trainer will need to find something that catches the dog's interest to keep her motivated and attentive. Socialization is also necessary, as Dalmatians are wary of strangers. Many dogs of this breed have enjoyed advanced training and performance sports. Dals do great in agility and flyball. Many serve as excellent volunteer therapy dogs.

Because Dalmatians are active dogs and are sometimes quite exuberant, they can be too rowdy for very young children. However, once the kids are big enough to play with the dogs, Dalmatians are great companions, never getting tired or bored of the kids' games and adventures.

This breed has some special health concerns. The Dalmatian Club of America estimates that about 8 percent of Dalmatians are totally deaf and about 22 percent are deaf in one ear. The breed also has a problem with urinary stones.

## Breed in Brief

**Registries:** AKC, UKC, CKC
**Occupation:** Carriage horse, companion
**Size:** 19 to 23 in tall; 45 to 60 lbs
**Longevity:** 11 to 14 years
**Exercise:** Vigorous daily exercise; needs to run
**Training:** Bright; hard to motivate; a challenge to train
**Grooming:** Easy

# Designer Dogs

Paige (at right) is a Goldendoodle. She is tall, the height of a standard Poodle. She is wavy-coated, with dropped ears, a bearded face, and a wiggling body. She is cute, charming, and quite appealing. But what is she, really? It depends on who you talk to. To purebred dog fanciers, Paige is a mixed-breed dog, a cross between a Poodle and a Golden Retriever. To the breeders of these dogs and their owners, Paige is a designer dog: a whole new world in dogdom!

Designer dogs are produced by a purposeful crossing of two unrelated breeds. Although mixed-breed dogs have been around as long as there have been dog breeds, and Cockapoos (the first designer breed) have been around for more than thirty years, the designer dog era probably began with the Labradoodle in Australia. In 1989, John Grosling, manager for the GDAV Guide Dog Services, bred a litter in response to a request from a vision-impaired woman whose husband was allergic to dogs. A Poodle and a Labrador Retriever were bred and produced three puppies, one of which became her guide dog, and luckily her husband was able to tolerate him.

Other breedings between Labrador Retrievers and Poodles have occurred since then in both Australia and the U.S., and the results have varied tremendously. Some of the resulting dogs shed (like the Lab), and others are nonshedding like Poodles. Some are allergy friendly, while others are not. Sizes vary, too, as the Poodle is sometimes a standard and sometimes a miniature.

The success of the Cockapoo, Labradoodle, and the more recent Goldendoodle has led to a number of different designer dogs. There are Puggles, which are a cross between Pugs and Beagles. Roodles are Standard Poodles crossed with Rottweilers. Maltepoos are Maltese and Toy Poodles;

Schnoodles are Miniature Schnauzers and Miniature Poodles; and Pugapoos are, obviously, Pugs and Poodles. The prices asked (and paid) for some of these dogs have been higher than many people pay for purebred dogs with registration papers, pedigrees, and guarantees.

The temperaments, personalities, behavior, and trainability of designer dogs vary tremendously. The offspring will have a tendency to have some of the traits of each parent, but as with all mixed breeds, that can be unpredictable. Paige, for example, has many of the friendly, extroverted characteristics of a Golden Retriever but is sensitive and intelligent—traits common to Poodles.

Breeders of designer dogs have been promoting their benefits, one of which is their hybrid vigor. Breeders say that designer dogs do not have the health problems of purebreds, but that isn't necessarily so. The offspring of any breeding will be genetically healthy or not depending upon their parents' (and grandparents') genetic health. Labradoodle owners have found many of the same health concerns as those found in both Labs and Poodles, including a tendency toward ear infections, allergies, and hip dysplasia. Designer dogs have their enthusiasts, and that's wonderful as long as their owners know exactly what they are getting and are not expecting something entirely different.

# Doberman Pinscher

oberman Pinschers were created by Louis Dobermann, of Apolda, Germany, in the 1890s. Dobermann wanted a medium-sized dog who could be a companion dog and yet still serve as a guard dog. It is believed that Dobermann used German Pinschers, Rottweilers, a black and tan Manchester Terrier, and a shorthaired shepherd to create his new breed. Some experts believe that there might also be some Greyhound mixed in. No matter what the ancestry, Louis Dobermann created a versatile working dog who has served ably in many capacities. The U.S. Marine Corps has used many breeds, including the Doberman. In World War II, dogs were integral to the success of so many operations that a war dog platoon was required to serve with every Marine Corps division. A life-sized bronze statue of a Doberman stands in Guam, labeled "Always Faithful," in honor of the many war dogs who served and died there.

The Doberman Pinscher today is a medium-sized dog who stands tall and carries herself proudly, making her look larger than she actually is. Dobies stand between 24 and 28 inches tall and usually weigh between 60 and 85 pounds, with females smaller than males. The head is wedge-shaped, the eyes almond-shaped and expressive, and the neck well-arched so that the head is carried proudly. For the show ring in the U.S., the ears are cropped, although today many people retain the natural ears, which are folded. The Doberman's chest is broad, back is straight, and tail is docked. The coat is smooth, short, hard, and thick. The Doberman can be black, red, blue, or fawn; all four colors will have rust marking above the eyes, on the muzzle, throat, forechest, and all four legs, and below the tail.

Grooming the short coat is easy; brush it twice a week with a soft bristle brush or curry comb. During spring and fall, when shedding is at its worst, daily brushing will help keep hair in the house to a minimum.

Dobies need exercise, and a walk is certainly not enough. A run alongside a bicycle will be better, as will a vigorous game of catching a tennis ball or a good workout on the agility course. Vigorous daily exercise is needed to keep her fit and to prevent problem behaviors that will crop up when she's bored.

Although Dobies today are much softer that those of years past, they are still excellent watchdogs and protectors. It's very important that puppies attend a puppy class where socialization is emphasized, especially to a variety of people. An over-protected and undersocialized Dobie can be worried and fearful, neither a good trait for this proud breed. Training should begin young, too, not just to teach household rules and social manners—although both are important—but also to keep that intelligent, inquisitive mind busy! The breed thrives on canine sports.

Doberman Pinschers are dedicated, loyal companions, excellent with people of all ages, although puppies can be rowdy and need to be taught not to play roughly with children. They can be good with other pets and, when taught not to chase, with the family cat. They can be aggressive toward unknown dogs. Health concerns include cardiomyopathy, wobbler's syndrome, and von Willebrand's disease.

## Breed in Brief

**Registries:** AKC, UKC, CKC
**Occupation:** Guard dog, military dog, companion, performance sports
**Size:** 24 to 28 in tall; 60 to 85 lbs
**Longevity:** 10 to 12 years
**Exercise:** Vigorous daily exercise
**Training:** Easy; hard to keep challenged
**Grooming:** Easy

# Dogo Argentino

The Dogo Argentino, or Argentinian Mastiff, is the only native breed from Argentina. The breed was created by Dr. Antonio Martinez in the early 1900s when he crossed several breeds with the old fighting dogs from Cordoba. He was looking for a strong, vigorous, balanced athlete who could be both a hunting companion and a fighter.

This is a large dog, standing between 23.5 and 27 inches tall and weighing from 85 to 100 pounds or more. The head is broad, the muzzle short, and the ears either cropped or left natural. The chest is deep and broad and the body strong. The coat is white and short.

Grooming this breed is easy and consists of a twice weekly brushing with a soft bristled brush or curry comb.

Breed expert Tim Parr says, "This is an active breed that needs daily exercise. Consider that on hunts, the dog may cover ten to twelve miles." Daily exercise can consist of walks plus runs alongside a bicycle, agility training, hunting, or weight pulling. All off-leash exercise must be in a fenced area, as the dog will forget all training if a prey animal is sighted or scented.

Early socialization and training are very important for this breed. Parr says, "Training must be kept fun and gamelike, as Dogos tend to be sensitive to corrections from their owner. They usually respond well to a sharp verbal correction when needed." Because they are natural guard dogs, Parr says, "Dogos need extensive socialization in order to develop a sense of judgment as to who is a threat and who is not."

This breed should never be kept just as a family pet. This is a dedicated, loyal working dog with all her hunting and working instincts still intact. Dogos require experienced dog owners who will work with them on a daily basis. Some Dogos are very patient with children, while others may not be. The breed is dog-aggressive, and Parr says two Dogos of the same sex should never be housed together. Health concerns include deafness, hip dysplasia, immune system problems, and heart problems.

## Breed in Brief

**Registries:** AKC FSS, UKC
**Occupation:** Hunter, guardian
**Size:** 23.5 to 27 in tall; 85 to 100+ lbs
**Longevity:** 10 to 15 years
**Exercise:** Daily
**Training:** Needs an experienced owner/trainer
**Grooming:** Easy

# Dogo Canario

The Dogo Canario (also known as the Presa Canario, Perro de Presa Canario, or Canary Dog) was developed in the Canary Islands and is a descendant of Mastiffs brought to the islands by Spanish explorers. The dogs were used to control and herd cattle and to protect farms, businesses, and property. During the years since the explorers, the Mastiffs were mixed with other breeds and at times were also used for blood sports. After the prohibition of blood sports, the breed almost disappeared, but in the 1970s and 1980s fanciers banded together and saved it.

The breed stands 22 to 25.5 inches tall and weighs 90 to 115 pounds. The body is slightly longer than the dog is tall at the shoulder. The head is broad with a short muzzle. The ears can be cropped or left dropped. The chest is wide, the body strong, and the tail saberlike.

The coat is short, and there is no undercoat. These dogs are fawn with a dark mask or brindle. The coat needs twice weekly brushing with a soft bristle brush or curry comb.

This breed needs moderate exercise. A walk morning and evening and a playtime in between will satisfy most, although puppies can be more active. Ewa Ziemska, a breed expert from Poland, says, "This is a very serious breed. It will play, but in most situations it prefers to watch its territory."

This is a watchful and protective breed. Early socialization is very important so the dog learns to live in her world. Training is very important, too, as this highly intelligent breed needs a job to do. She needs firm, structured, yet fun training.

Ziemska says, "This breed will always protect its owner, even to the point of putting itself at risk." The breed, therefore, needs an experienced owner who can train and control the dog. Dogos Canarios are good with the children they've been raised with but may not understand or tolerate rough play with other children. They may not be good with other dogs or small pets. Health concerns include hip and elbow dysplasia and eyelid and knee problems.

## Breed in Brief

**Registries:** AKC FSS, UKC
**Occupation:** Guardian
**Size:** 22 to 25.5 in tall; 90 to 115 lbs
**Longevity:** 10 to 12 years
**Exercise:** Moderate
**Training:** Moderate
**Grooming:** Easy

# Dogue de Bordeaux

The Dogue de Bordeaux is an ancient breed whose history is more legend than fact, as written records are nonexistent. What is known, however, is that these early dogs were incredibly versatile. At various times during their early history, they were used as protectors of homes and businesses, as guardians for livestock, and as herding dogs. They also hunted and were prized for their ability to hunt boars. They were fighters, too, and were used to bait bears, bulls, and big cats.

The Dogue was popular in France in the mid- to late 1800s. There were three varieties: the Toulouse, the Paris, and the Bordeaux. The modern Dogue has the genetics of all three types, but most experts feel that today's Dogues are primarily Bordeaux. During the French Revolution, the breed almost disappeared, as it was associated with royalty and the wealthy.

Dogues de Bordeaux were virtually unknown in the United States until 1986, when Touchstone movies released the movie *Turner and Hooch*. The co-star, "Beasley," was a handsome red Dogue de Bordeaux who drooled copiously in the movie and destroyed everything he touched.

Today's Dogue de Bordeaux is a very large, Mastiff-type breed standing between 22.5 and 26.5 inches tall and weighing 90 to more than 100 pounds. The head is very broad, with a short muzzle and small dropped ears, and the expression always appears to be scowling due to facial wrinkles. The chest is wide and deep, the body is strong, and the legs sturdy. The tail is long. The coat is short and smooth and can be any shade of red or fawn.

This breed's coat is easy to care for and requires brushing once or twice a week. Dogs with deep wrinkles on the face will need those wrinkles cleaned regularly.

The Dogue is not a high-activity breed but does need regular exercise. Many, especially puppies, can be quite playful, although adults are calmer and more dignified. This breed can run but is not a long-distance runner; instead, they do well at activities where they can use their strength, including carting and weight pulling.

Early socialization is very important, as this is a watchful, protective breed. Training should begin during puppyhood so that the Dogue grows up understanding household rules and social manners and is well-versed in basic obedience skills. This is a powerful dog who can, if she wishes to, overpower her owner. Although normally calm, affectionate toward her people, and quiet, the Dogue is also naturally watchful, protective, and powerful, so she needs an owner who is in complete control; training can help achieve that.

These dogs need experienced owners, as they can be quite dominant and pushy and will take advantage of an inexperienced or passive owner. They are good with children when raised with them. They may not, however, be good with strange children and may interfere if the kids' play gets too rough. They are often dog-aggressive. The breed does drool and can drool a lot, especially when the dog is anticipating a treat or meal. Health concerns include breathing problems, bloat, torsion, thyroid problems, mange, and hip dysplasia.

## Breed in Brief

**Registries:** AKC FSS, UKC
**Occupation:** Versatile working dog
**Size:** 22.5 to 26.5 in tall; 90 to 100+ lbs
**Longevity:** 10 to 12 years
**Exercise:** Low to moderate
**Training:** Vitally important
**Grooming:** Easy

# Dutch Shepherd

## (Short Coat, Long Coat, and Rough Coat)

The Dutch Shepherd originated in Holland as an all-purpose farm and herding dog. The breed was a protective guardian of the flock of sheep and the farm, as well as a herder. These shepherds are now working as search and rescue dogs, military and police dogs, and in the sports of Schutzhund, obedience competitions, and agility.

Several organizations register the Dutch Shepherd, and their standards vary slightly. The American Dutch Shepherd Club standard calls for a dog at least 21.5 inches tall but no taller than 27.5 inches, with weight in proportion to height. The dog's body is slightly longer than the dog is tall at the shoulder. The ears are upright. The tail is long.

The coat may be short (hard and smooth with a dense undercoat), long (sturdy with a dense undercoat), or rough (tousled with a dense undercoat). Brindle coloring is preferred, but some other colors are acceptable. All three coat types shed and need regular brushing, especially during the spring and fall when shedding is at its worst.

Dutch Shepherds have a strong prey drive and need to work. They require vigorous daily exercise. Although walks are great for training and socialization, these dogs enjoy a run or a training session on the agility course. A Dutch Shepherd who doesn't get enough exercise will use her energy in other ways that could be destructive.

Wary of strangers and very intelligent, this breed needs early and ongoing socialization and training. They need to meet a variety of people of all sizes, shapes, and ethnic backgrounds so they can function well in society and learn to make good choices.

The Dutch Shepherd needs an owner who can be the dog's leader and who likes to do things with his dog. This breed is not a good pet; she needs to work. She is good with kids when raised with them and when the kids treat her with respect. She can be good with other dogs but can also be bossy. This is a healthy breed.

## Breed in Brief

**Registries:** UKC, ARBA
**Occupation:** Versatile herding dog
**Size:** 21.5 to 27.5 in tall; weight proportionate to height
**Longevity:** 12 to 14 years
**Exercise:** Vigorous daily exercise
**Training:** Easy; hard to keep challenged
**Grooming:** Sheds

# English Cocker Spaniel

Spaniels originated in Spain but were prized in England (and other places) for their hunting abilities. Bred to hunt birds, the English Cocker Spaniel and English Springer Spaniel were the same breed, differentiated only by size, until the late 1800s. The American Cocker Spaniel became a separate breed in the early 1900s, although the English and American Cockers were interbred until the 1940s.

The English Cocker Spaniel stands between 15 and 17 inches tall and weighs between 26 and 34 pounds. He has a softly arched skull, long muzzle, large oval eyes, and hanging ears. The tail is docked, and the coat is medium length and silky. The coat on the head is short, but the ears, legs, and tail are feathered. The coat may be solid colored or parti-colored. Black, liver, and red are all acceptable colors.

This coat needs regular grooming to prevent tangles and mats. The coat should be brushed and combed two to three times a week—more if the dog gets wet or dirty. The coat should be trimmed every six to eight weeks.

This is a moderately active breed. Adults can be calm in the house, although puppies are quite active. These dogs will enjoy a walk mornings and evenings, a good run, a training session on the agility course, or a vigorous game of flyball. The breed is still used for hunting.

## Breed in Brief

**Registries:** AKC, UKC, CKC
**Occupation:** Gun dog
**Size:** 15 to 17 in tall; 26 to 34 lbs
**Longevity:** 12 to 14 years
**Exercise:** Moderate
**Training:** Moderate
**Grooming:** Difficult

Socialization and training are important to this breed, if for no other reason than they are friendly, social, intelligent dogs who thrive on social contact and activity. Training should continue into adulthood to keep their minds busy. English Cocker Spaniels also do well in obedience competition.

This breed needs an active owner who likes grooming. The English Cocker Spaniel is good with children who treat him with respect; he does not like to be handled roughly. He is good with other dogs and pets, although interactions with smaller pets should be supervised. Health concerns include deafness, hip and knee problems, allergies, and seizures.

# nglish Foxhound

The English Foxhound was developed in England, as its name suggests, as a pack hound (dogs who live and work together in a pack) to trail foxes. The breed's history can be traced back to the 1700s. Many of today's English Foxhound pedigrees can be traced back to that era in an unbroken line, primarily because each pack has a Master of the Hounds who manages the pack, including keeping careful records of each dog.

English Foxhounds stand 23 to 27 inches tall and weigh between 50 and 80 pounds. Although it is a pure breed in England, in North America the dogs used for hunting are often crossbred. Claudia Bazinet of Foxhound Relocation and Retirement says, "Foxhounds tend to be bred to be able to hunt in the terrain of their region." She continues, "English Foxhounds are solidly built, with very straight front legs, a straight back, long neck, and round, tight feet." The coat is short, and the coat colors are considered not important, although the traditional hound colors (white, tan, and black) are preferred.

Grooming this dog consists of a twice weekly brushing with a soft bristle brush or curry comb.

The breed needs daily aerobic exercise. Since catch-and-fetch games are usually not appealing to Foxhounds, exercise can be a long, vigorous walk or a jog alongside a bicycle. This breed should never be allowed to run free outside of a fenced yard; if a rabbit or squirrel is flushed, the dog will be gone, and no amount of calling will bring him back.

English Foxhounds can be pets, but they are first and foremost pack dogs; they do best with other dogs. Bazinet says, "English Foxhounds can be quite active in the house." They are not able to settle down and relax on the sofa. Obedience training can sometimes be a challenge; they see no need for these rules. They are good with children and enjoy the kids' antics. They do bay, which can cause problems with neighbors. The breed has few health concerns.

## Breed in Brief

**Registries:** AKC, UKC, CKC
**Occupation:** Hunter
**Size:** 23 to 27 in tall; 50 to 80 lbs
**Longevity:** 10 to 12 years
**Exercise:** Daily aerobic exercise
**Training:** Challenge
**Grooming:** Easy

# English Setter

The English Setter was bred in England more than 400 years ago. Spaniels, the Spanish Pointer, and other breeds were used in the creation of this breed. The name *setter* derives from the dogs' habit of crouching (or setting) after finding birds so that the nets used to capture the birds could be thrown without the dogs getting in the way. Once firearms were used for hunting, the dogs were bred to stand upright rather than crouch.

There are two types of English Setter—the show dog and the Llewellin (or field) type—although there is only one breed standard. (The show dogs tend to be larger.) The standard calls for a dog standing 24 to 25 inches tall. These dogs usually weigh between 50 and 70 pounds, have a long head with dropped ears, and a long tail. The coat is straight, and the ears, legs, belly, and tail are feathered. The coat is white with speckles of color, including orange, blue, lemon, and liver.

The English Setter's lovely coat needs brushing and combing at least twice a week to keep it looking nice and to prevent mats from forming.

The English Setter Association of America (ESAA) says, "They do need a considerable amount of exercise to keep both body and mind in shape. The natural exuberance of a young Setter can make him difficult to live with if he is confined without enough exercise." All exercise should be on leash or within a fenced-in area.

Training is also very important. The ESAA encourages all Setter owners to participate in basic obedience training, saying, "It establishes a bond between you and your English Setter and makes him a joy in your home and community."

This breed needs an active owner who enjoys hunting, jogging, agility training, or some other active canine sport. Although most puppies are pretty rowdy and need supervision around young children, the breed is good with kids. English Setters are usually good with other dogs. Health concerns include deafness, allergies, and hip and elbow dysplasia.

## Breed in Brief

**Registries:** AKC, UKC, CKC
**Occupation:** Gun dog
**Size:** 24 to 25 in tall; 50 to 70 lbs
**Longevity:** 11 to 13 years
**Exercise:** Daily exercise
**Training:** Moderate
**Grooming:** Moderate

# English Shepherd

The English Shepherd, also known as the farm collie or old farm collie, is a descendant of the old shepherds' dogs of England and is probably related to both the Collie and the Border Collie. Some experts feel that there is a relationship between the Australian Shepherd in the U.S. and the English Shepherd. The breed has been used in the United States as a versatile farm dog, able to protect property, guard livestock, herd all manner of domestic animals, and even round up the family children.

Even today, the English Shepherd is bred for function over appearance. He is a confident worker, able to take direction yet also able to make his own decisions. He is agile, quick, and strong, with the stamina to work all day. His ideal height is between 19 and 22 inches tall, and he should be lean and fit, usually between 35 and 65 pounds. He has brown eyes, dropped ears, a level back, and strong legs. The tail is long. His coat is medium length with an undercoat. He can be black and tan, black and white, sable and white, or tricolored. Unlike the Border Collie, Collie, and Australian Shepherd, this breed does not have the merle coloring.

Twice weekly brushing will keep the English Shepherd clean and looking nice. The undercoat does shed, and during heavy shedding, daily brushing may be needed to keep the hair in the house to a minimum.

This is a high-activity breed that needs vigorous daily exercise and a job to do. The English Shepherd will need sheep to herd or goats to look after, or, in the absence of livestock, he will need to go for a long jog or have a vigorous training session on the agility course every day. Without enough exercise, he will get into trouble. Many performance canine sport enthusiasts have found that this breed thrives in many different sports, including herding trials, agility, obedience competition, flyball, flying disc, and tracking. Many English Shepherds also serve as wonderful therapy dogs.

This breed needs early socialization and training. A watchful breed, he can be wary of strangers, and socialization will help him make better decisions. Training that begins in puppyhood will teach him household rules and social manners, but also help challenge his bright, intelligent mind and give him constructive things to think about. Breed expert Rebecca Wingler says, "The breed is extremely receptive to training, quick to learn new commands, tricks, or activities."

This breed needs an active, involved owner who enjoys training and doing things with the dog. This breed is not happy when isolated for many hours each day. Wingler continues, "The breed is warm and affectionate to the entire family, but each dog may have a favorite person." A wonderful working and herding dog, the English Shepherd can also be playful and silly. He can be great with children when raised with them and will be watchful and protective of the kids. He may not understand rough play with his kids' friends. He can be good with other pets, although he may try to herd the family cat. He will chase cats that venture into his yard. This is a healthy breed, although hip dysplasia has been found in some dogs.

## Breed in Brief

**Registries:** UKC, English Shepherd Club
**Occupation:** Herder, farm dog
**Size:** 19 to 22 in tall; 35 to 65 lbs
**Longevity:** 13 to 15 years
**Exercise:** Vigorous daily exercise
**Training:** Easy; hard to keep challenged
**Grooming:** Sheds

# English Springer Spaniel

*T*he English Springer Spaniel shares its heritage with the English Cocker Spaniel; in fact, at one time, they were the same breed. The English Springer Spaniel Field Trial Association states that in the 1800s, "In a litter of Spaniel puppies, the smaller dogs would hunt woodcocks and were called *cockers*. The larger puppies in the litter were used to flush the game and were therefore called *springers*." In the late 1800s and early 1900s, Springers and Cockers were finally recognized as two different breeds, both in England and the U.S. Today in the U.S., there are two types of English Springer Spaniel: the show dog and the field dog. Although the breed standard describes the perfect Springer and applies to all Springers, those who breed for field performance tend to view those traits as much more important than the breed's appearance.

The Springer is a medium-sized dog, between 18 and 21 inches tall and about 40 to 50 pounds, with females smaller than males. The head is classically shaped, with long, drooping ears made to look longer with the long, slightly wavy coat. The eyes are medium-sized, oval and alert, intelligent and expressive. The body is slightly longer than tall, the legs are long, and, when trotting, the dog covers ground effortlessly. The coat on the body is of moderate length, but there is profuse feathering on the legs and sides. Springers may be black or liver-colored with white markings, white with black or liver markings, blue or liver roan, or tricolored. The tail is docked.

Daily brushing and combing is needed to keep the feathers and long hair from tangling and matting. The coat will need to be trimmed every four to six weeks. If you wish to learn how to do the haircuts on your own Springer, talk to your dog's breeder for guidance, or you can have a professional groomer do it for you. The long, heavy ears need to be cleaned twice a week to prevent ear problems.

Bred to work hard in the field all day long, Springers need vigorous daily exercise. Kelly Rodrigues, the owner of two show Springers, Bix and Bailey, says, "Springers are very active and need a lot of exercise and playtime. They are very athletic, but beware of water; if any is at hand, they will be in it." Because they love water, swimming is great exercise, as is running, jogging, playing, or catch.

## Breed in Brief

**Registries:** AKC, UKC, CKC
**Occupation:** Hunter, companion, performance sports
**Size:** 18 to 21 in tall; 40 to 50 lbs
**Longevity:** 12 to 15 years
**Exercise:** Vigorous daily exercise
**Training:** Easy
**Grooming:** Moderate to difficult

Basic obedience training should be a part of every Springer's puppyhood. Training has long been a part of the breed's heritage, as field dogs had to be obedient. Rodrigues says, "Springers are affectionate and want to please." Many people interested in performance sports such as agility and flyball have found that Springers make great competitors; they want to learn and are fast and very athletic.

Springers will bark when people approach their home but are not known for being protective. The breed is a wonderful family dog, patient with children, and tough enough to take some roughhousing. They are generally good with other pets, although they need to learn that chasing the cat is not allowed. They should not be trusted with the family bird; their heritage says that birds are prey! Health concerns include hip and elbow dysplasia, eye defects, and rage syndrome.

# English Toy Spaniel

The English Toy Spaniel is a very old breed whose roots probably go back to ancient Japan or China. Some experts believe that he may be related to the Japanese Chin or Pug, or that English Spaniels were crossed with these two breeds to create the round skull and shortened muzzle that all three breeds have. Although much of the breed's history is unknown, what is known is that this wonderful spaniel has been known in England since the 16th century and, throughout much of history since that introduction, has been a favorite of the English people. For a long time, only royalty was officially allowed to own the breed, although that didn't stop many breed enthusiasts.

This is a small breed, standing 9 to 11 inches tall and weighing 8 to 14 pounds. He is compact and short-bodied, with a domed head and short muzzle. His eyes are large and dark, ears are long,

and tail is docked. His coat is straight and silky, with profuse feathering on the ears, body, chest, and legs. The Bleinheim is red and white; the Prince Charles is tricolored; the King Charles is black and tan; and the Ruby is a rich red.

The coat tangles and mats easily, so it should be brushed and combed two or three times per week, and more often if the dog gets wet. Many pet owners keep the ears, feet, and under-the-tail areas trimmed for cleanliness. The wrinkles on the face may also need regular cleaning to remove dirt and food particles and to prevent skin problems.

English Toy Spaniels enjoy daily walks and playtimes, but otherwise this is a breed who will be happy to cuddle and snuggle in the house. His activity level will mirror that of his owner. If you are up and about and active, he will be, too; if you want to relax, he will, too.

This is a friendly, affectionate dog. Although not as watchful and wary of strangers as so many breeds are, socialization is still important, as unsocialized dogs can be fearful of new people and situations. Training will teach young Spaniels household rules. Housetraining can be a challenge, but with persistence and patience, it can be accomplished.

This breed is happiest when spending time with his owner; he will not be happy spending long hours alone. He is one of the quietest of the toy breeds and does well in an apartment. He is good with children when they have been taught to be gentle with him. He will not tolerate rough handling; he will simply get up and walk away. He is also very tolerant of other pets. Health concerns include knee problems, cataracts, and heart defects.

## Breed in Brief

**Registries:** AKC, UKC, CKC
**Occupation:** Companion
**Size:** 9 to 11 in tall; 8 to 14 lbs
**Longevity:** 13 to 15 years
**Exercise:** Low activity level
**Training:** Challenge to housetrain
**Grooming:** Moderate

# Entlebucher Sennenhund

The Entlebucher Sennenhund, also called the Entlebucher Mountain Dog or Entlebucher Cattle Dog, is the smallest of the group of four Swiss dogs that includes the Bernese Mountain Dog, Greater Swiss Mountain Dog, and Appenzeller. The breed was a herding dog and guardian for livestock, people, and farms.

This breed is medium-sized, standing 16 to 20 inches tall and weighing between 50 and 75 pounds. The muzzle is long, the eyes are dark and small, and the ears dropped. The tail is often a natural bobtail, but if it isn't, it can be either docked or left long. The coat is short and hard and is a classic tricolor—primarily black with rust and white markings.

The short coat does shed and should be brushed twice weekly except during heavy shedding, when a daily brushing will help control hair in the house.

The Entlebucher Sennenhund is not overly active, although puppies can be quite rambunctious. Adults are normally calm in the house but will enjoy any activities you wish to pursue. They enjoy walks, a good run, training to pull a cart or wagon, and agility training. The breed does not tolerate hot, humid weather well.

## Breed in Brief

**Registries:** AKC FSS, UKC, CKC
**Occupation:** Herder, guardian
**Size:** 16 to 20 in tall; 50 to 75 lbs
**Longevity:** 11 to 13 years
**Exercise:** Moderate
**Training:** Moderate
**Grooming:** Easy

This breed is very wary of strangers, so early socialization is critical. Without adequate socialization, the dogs can become too reactive and will be overly watchful or fearfully shy. The breed was bred to work, so early training is important, too, to keep the mind busy. The training should be firm and structured, yet fun.

The Entlebucher Sennenhund needs an experienced owner who understands working and herding dogs. He needs a job to do and a purpose. He is friendly and loyal to family and friends but is watchful of his property and wary of strangers. He is great with children, although puppies can be rowdy and must learn the rules of good behavior around kids. When raised with them, he is very tolerant of other pets. Health concerns include eye problems and hip dysplasia.

# $\mathcal{E}$urasier

The Eurasier is a very new breed. It was developed in the 1960s in Germany by Julius Wipfel to be a family pet. The original mix included the Chow Chow, the Wolfspitz, and, later, the Samoyed. Although watchful and wary of strangers, this is not a working dog.

The Eurasier stands 18 to 24 inches tall and weighs between 40 and 70 pounds, with females smaller than males. This breed should be well balanced, with a spitz-type appearance. The Eurasier has a wedge-shaped head and prick ears. The tail is carried over the back. The coat has a thick undercoat, with a medium-long outer coat that lies flat. The legs and tail are feathered. The coat can be fawn, red, wolf gray, black, or black and tan.

The coat is easy to care for but does require regular brushing, especially during the spring and fall when shedding is at its worst.

Josee Dessouroux of MacArras Brook Euraisers says of the breed's exercise needs, "The Eurasier is very playful. They learn tricks easily and love to do them as long as you don't ask them to repeat them endlessly. They are also very agile and love to run. One to two hours a day for exercise is best, off leash when possible." Off-leash play should always be in a fenced yard, of course, so the dog doesn't dash away.

## Breed in Brief

**Registries:** UKC, CKC
**Occupation:** Companion
**Size:** 18 to 24 in tall; 40 to 70 lbs
**Longevity:** 12 to 14 years
**Exercise:** Active
**Training:** Easy; moderate compliance
**Grooming:** Moderate

Training the Eurasier takes a light touch. Dessouroux says, "This breed responds best to positive reinforcements. But don't expect an Eurasier to always be obedient; they have a certain level of independence, which sometimes makes them a little stubborn. They are not suited for sports such as agility. That doesn't mean they can't do it; they can, but they won't do it to win." She emphasizes, "They were bred as companions, not as working dogs."

The Eurasier is a family dog, devoted and affectionate, although he usually bonds more strongly with one person. He is good with children in his family who treat him with respect, and he's good with other pets. Health concerns include hip dysplasia and eye disease.

# Field Spaniel

The Field Spaniel and Cocker Spaniel were, at one time, one and the same. In any given litter, the larger pups were called Field Spaniels, and the smaller dogs were called Cockers. The relationship doesn't end there, however. The breeds known today as English Springer Spaniels, Sussex Spaniels, English Cocker Spaniels, and American Cocker Spaniels are all descended from the ancient, related spaniels that were simply called Spaniels in England.

The dogs that eventually became Field Spaniels lived through some grave disservices on the part of a few breeders. Phineas Bullock of England took some dogs of Field Spaniel heritage and

created dogs that had very low and long bodies and heavy bones. These dogs were still spaniels but looked nothing like any other spaniel in existence, and many people called them grotesque. It took considerable effort by dedicated breeders in England and in North America to re-create the balanced, athletic Field Spaniel known today.

These dogs stand 17 to 18 inches tall and usually weigh between 35 and 50 pounds. The body is slightly longer than tall, well balanced, and moderate in everything without any extremes. The ears are dropped, and the tail is usually docked. The coat is a single coat (with no undercoat) and moderately long. The chest, belly, back of legs, and ears are feathered. The coat is black, liver, or golden liver.

This breed is not as heavily coated as the Cocker Spaniel, but it does need regular brushing and combing to prevent mats. The ears, insides of the ears, paws, and under the tail should be trimmed regularly for cleanliness. Many pet owners have the dog groomed (including a haircut) to make daily care easier.

Although not a highly active breed, the Field Spaniel does need daily exercise. She enjoys a good walk but will also need a chance to run and play. Field Spaniels can train on the agility course, run alongside a bicycle, or go jogging with you. This breed has excelled in many performance sports and has become a favorite of many serious competitors.

Early training and socialization are very important. The training should begin early, both to instill a joy of working within the dog and to establish household rules, as this breed can have a stubborn streak. The breed can be wary of strangers; early socialization can help develop a trust of people and prevent shyness.

The Field Spaniel can be a good family dog and pet when she has a job to do. If someone in the family enjoys training and likes to hunt or participates in canine performance sports, this breed will suit wonderfully. Without a job or sense of purpose, the dog might amuse herself by getting into trouble.

This breed likes to spend time outside and will enjoy a large yard to run around in and investigate. She also likes to be with the people in her family and, when inside, will keep herself close. Owners often call their dogs Field Shadows. She is patient with children. When well socialized, she is good with other dogs. Health concerns include eye and eyelid problems, hip dysplasia, and hypothyroidism.

## Breed in Brief

**Registries:** AKC, UKC, CKC
**Occupation:** Gun dog
**Size:** 17 to 18 in tall; 35 to 50 lbs
**Longevity:** 12 to 14 years
**Exercise:** Moderate
**Training:** Moderate
**Grooming:** Moderate

# Fila Brasileiro

This breed originated in Brazil and counts among her ancestors English Mastiffs, Bloodhounds, Bulldogs, and even some herding dogs. Throughout the breed's history, it has been used as a guard for homes and businesses, a police dog, a hunting dog, and even a guide dog for the blind.

The Fila Brasileiro is a large, heavy, sturdy dog, standing 23.5 to 29.5 inches tall. Most weigh between 125 and 175 pounds. The Fila has a big, broad head and a deep muzzle with heavy lips and flews. The ears are dropped. The skin is thick and loose, creating folds and heavy dewlaps on the neck. The coat is short and smooth, with all solid colors accepted except white and gray.

The coat is easy to care for with twice weekly brushing with a soft bristle brush or curry comb.

This breed does not require a great deal of exercise. Breed expert Clelia Kruel says, "A half-hour of exercise per day is sufficient for adult dogs." Although the Fila is a dignified breed, Kruel says that these dogs are also playful and enjoy their owners' company.

Protective and watchful dogs, Filas need early and continued socialization. Without it, they can become overly protective and aggressive or fearful. A well-socialized dog is much more able to make good decisions as to how to protect her home and family. Early training is needed, too, to channel the breed's desire to work. Kruel says, "The Fila is very willing to please her owner and is a smart, trainable dog." Training should be firm and structured, yet fun and without too much repetition.

The Fila needs a dog-wise, experienced owner who understands the breed. Kruel says, "Before buying a Fila, you need to know if you are ready to take on the responsibility for her training. You must have a 6-foot, secure fence. You must also understand her temperament and be prepared to avoid accidents with strangers." Health concerns include bloat, torsion, and hip dysplasia.

## Breed in Brief

**Registries:** CKC
**Occupation:** Versatile working dog, guardian
**Size:** 23.5 to 29.5 in tall; 125 to 175 lbs
**Longevity:** 10 to 12 years
**Exercise:** Low to moderate activity
**Training:** Moderate
**Grooming:** Easy

# Finnish Spitz

The national dog of Finland, the Finnish Spitz is a barking bird dog. She follows the birds until they are treed, and then she barks (with a ringing, yodel-like bark) to direct the hunter to her location. She is so valuable in her native land that a Finnish Spitz cannot finish her championship until she has proven her worth in the field. Competitions are also held to find the dog with the best bark.

The Finnish Spitz stands between 15.5 and 20 inches tall and weighs between 25 and 40 pounds. She is foxlike, with a pointed muzzle, upright ears, and almond-shaped, dark eyes. Her tail is plumed and carried over her back. She has a dense, soft undercoat and a long, straight outer coat. Colors range from deep auburn to pale honey, but all are shades of golden-red.

The coat will need brushing two or three times a week. The undercoat sheds heavily in the spring and fall and will need more brushing then.

This is a moderately active breed that needs daily exercise. She will be satisfied with a couple of walks and a good run. All runs off leash should be in a fenced yard, however, as this hunting dog will take off if she flushes a bird or rabbit.

## Breed in Brief

**Registries:** AKC, UKC, CKC
**Occupation:** Barking bird dog
**Size:** 15.5 to 20 in tall; 25 to 40 lbs
**Longevity:** 13 to 15 years
**Exercise:** Moderately active
**Training:** Easy; breed does bark
**Grooming:** Double coat sheds!

Early socialization is very important to Finnish Spitz kept as pets, as these dogs can be wary of strangers. The barking can easily turn into problem behavior in an area where neighbors live close together. Early training can help control the barking, but these dogs will always bark. The Finnish Spitz is receptive to training but can be independent and just a little bit stubborn.

She has a tendency to bond more closely with one person than with the entire family. She is usually quite tolerant of children and will simply walk away if the kids get too rough. She is good with other pets in the family when raised with them but can be aggressive toward strange dogs. There are no major health concerns.

# Flat-Coated Retriever

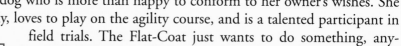

The Flat-Coated Retriever is one of several retrieving breeds that were bred from the Newfoundland in the 1800s. Other breeds (including setters, spaniels, and even sheepdogs) were crossed with Newfoundlands to create retrievers who could retrieve on land and in the water. The term "Labrador" was used to describe just about any dog from this ancestry, not to be confused with the Labrador Retriever of today who shares this heritage. The Flat-Coated Retriever became a distinct type and then a breed in the late 1800s and early 1900s.

This is a large dog standing 22 to 24.5 inches tall and weighing between 60 and 75 pounds. She has a broad head, small dropped ears, and almond-shaped eyes. The body is strong, with a level back, and the tail is long and usually wagging. The coat is medium length, straight, and weather-resistant. The ears, chest, legs, and tail are feathered. The acceptable colors are liver and black.

The coat should be brushed at least twice weekly to prevent tangles and mats. Many pet owners trim the ears, feet, belly, and under the tail for cleanliness.

This is a moderately active dog who is more than happy to conform to her owner's wishes. She can go jogging, will walk nicely, loves to play on the agility course, and is a talented participant in field trials. The Flat-Coat just wants to do something, anything, with her owner. She can be a couch potato but will not be happy doing that for long; she is happiest participating in some kind of dog sports. Gina Spadafori, a breed enthusiast, says, "A Flat-Coat is a breed who does everything well. They are friendly, smart, trainable, biddable, and birdy. They can do anything you want them to."

This breed needs an actively involved owner. She can be great with children, although young dogs may be a little too rowdy for small kids. She is good with other dogs and with cats when raised with them. Health concerns include hip dysplasia; eye, knee, and thyroid problems; and bloat.

## Breed in Brief

**Registries:** AKC, UKC, CKC
**Occupation:** Hunter
**Size:** 22 to 24.5 in tall; 60 to 75 lbs
**Longevity:** 12 to 14 years
**Exercise:** Active
**Training:** Easy; loves dog sports
**Grooming:** Moderate

# ox Terrier (Smooth)

Fox Terriers have a rich history going back at least 300 years, if not longer, and have been used as the foundation breed for several other breeds. Although the Wire Fox Terrier and Smooth Fox Terrier were shown together for many years, and in early years were bred together, experts agree that they come from different backgrounds. The Smooth Fox Terrier is probably descended from a smooth-coated black and tan terrier breed, the Bull Terrier, the Beagle, and, most likely, a dash of Greyhound.

The Smooth Fox Terrier stands 14 to 15.5 inches tall and weighs 15 to 19 pounds, although weight is less important than the dog's fitness. The head is long and wedge-shaped, the eyes small and dark, and the ears small and V-shaped. The body is strong and fit and shorter than the dog is tall. The tail is docked. The coat is short and hard and is predominantly white with patches of color.

The short coat should be brushed twice weekly.

This is a very active dog who needs vigorous daily exercise. A securely fenced yard is advisable; this dog is not particularly suited to apartment living. She enjoys daily runs, playtime on the agility course, and a chance to hunt for rodents and bugs in the woodpile. Without enough daily exercise, this dog will find something to amuse herself, and that could be destructive.

Early training is recommended. Because Smooth Fox Terriers are bright, they are able to think for themselves. Firm and structured yet fun training can help teach household rules and social manners.

The Smooth Fox Terrier needs an owner who understands the terrier temperament, their love of fun and activity, and their ability to be hardheaded at times. This breed can be good with older children but may be too rowdy for younger kids. She is not always good with other dogs, especially those of the same sex, and should not be trusted with smaller pets. Health concerns include hip and knee problems, allergies, and Cushing's disease.

## Breed in Brief

**Registries:** AKC, UKC, CKC
**Occupation:** Vermin hunter
**Size:** 14 to 15.5 in tall; 15 to 19 lbs
**Longevity:** 13 to 15 years
**Exercise:** Very active
**Training:** Challenge
**Grooming:** Easy

# Fox Terrier (Toy)

Unlike the Smooth and Wire Fox Terriers, the Toy Fox Terrier did not originate in England. This is, instead, a recently developed American breed. Smooth Fox Terriers were crossed with several toy breeds, including Chihuahuas, Italian Greyhounds, Miniature Pinschers, and perhaps even Manchester Terriers. The resulting dogs are both true terriers (with strength, stamina, and gameness) and true toys (with a more livable disposition).

Toy Fox Terriers stand 8.5 to 11.5 inches tall with weight proportionate to height. They are small yet well-balanced and strong. The eyes are dark and round, and the ears are upright and large, never dropped. The tail is docked. The coat is smooth, fine, and predominantly white with patches of color.

Brush weekly with a soft bristle brush or rubber curry comb.

This is an active dog who is playful and animated, yet not as busy or intense as the Smooth and Wire Fox Terriers. She enjoys daily walks. She is also suited to many dog sports, including agility, flyball, obedience, and terrier go-to-ground competitions. She is active enough to get into trouble, however, if left alone for too many hours.

Early socialization is important. Although normally outgoing and friendly, some Toy Fox Terriers can be reserved and wary of strangers, and early socialization can help build their confidence. Training should begin early, too, as this is a very intelligent breed. Training should be fun and not too repetitive, yet firm and structured. Toy Fox Terriers really enjoy mental challenges, so training should continue into adulthood. Teach the dog hand signals, scent discrimination, and trick training. As with some other toys, housetraining can sometimes be a challenge.

This breed can be a good family dog as long as children are not too rough. She can be a great companion for an active senior citizen. Health concerns include knee problems and allergies.

## Breed in Brief

**Registries:** AKC, UKC, CKC
**Occupation:** Companion
**Size:** 8.5 to 11.5 in tall; weight proportionate to height
**Longevity:** 13 to 14 years
**Exercise:** Active and playful
**Training:** Moderate
**Grooming:** Easy

# Fox Terrier (Wire)

The Wire Fox Terrier is descended from the old English black and tan, rough-coated terrier from Durham and Wales. Although for many years the Wire and Smooth Fox Terriers were bred and shown together as one breed with two coat varieties, they were recognized as separate breeds by the American Kennel Club in 1985.

The Wire Fox Terrier is first and foremost a hunting terrier and should be fit and fast. She stands 14 to 15.5 inches tall and weighs 15 to 19 pounds. Her head is long and wedge-shaped, with small dark eyes and V-shaped ears. Her body is shorter than she is tall. Her tail is docked. The coat is double, with a soft undercoat and a hard, wiry, broken outer coat. The color should be predominantly white with patches of color.

This coat does require dedicated grooming, including regular brushing, combing, and trimming. The undercoat does shed. Show dogs are hand-stripped, although most pets are groomed with clippers.

This is a very active breed that requires daily exercise. Walks are not enough; these dogs need to run, play, train in agility, or hunt for small animals and insects in the brush. All exercise should be in a fenced-in yard because if a small animal is flushed, Fox Terriers will be after it in a flash.

Training is very important, as Wire Fox Terriers are very bright. Training that is fun yet firm and structured can help keep the dog's mind challenged, and the dog will then be less prone to getting into trouble. When well motivated, these dogs enjoy many canine sports, including agility, flyball, and terrier go-to-ground tests.

Wire Fox Terriers do best in a home where the owner understands the terrier mindset. An active owner can best keep this breed busy and out of trouble. Wires do well with older children but may be too rowdy for very small kids. They should not be trusted with smaller pets. Health concerns include hip and knee problems, allergies, and Cushing's disease.

## Breed in Brief

**Registries:** AKC, UKC, CKC
**Occupation:** Vermin hunter
**Size:** 14 to 15.5 in tall; 15 to 19 lbs
**Longevity:** 13 to 15 years
**Exercise:** Very active
**Training:** Challenge
**Grooming:** Difficult

# rench Bulldog

Experts have debated, and continue to debate, the origins of this breed. A small English Bulldog, perhaps one as small as a toy, may be one of the ancestors, but there were probably several different breeds in France that were crossed with the Bulldogs in the late 1800s. One of the distinguishing features of the breed today is the upright bat ears; early American breeders can be credited with establishing this feature. European dogs of this time period had the rose ears of the English Bulldogs.

The French Bulldog stands 10 to 12 inches tall and generally weighs between 16 and 28 pounds. The head is large and square, with a domed forehead. The muzzle is very short. The eyes are large and dark; the bat ears are upright. The body is muscular and heavy-boned. The tail is straight or screwed. The coat is short and smooth; many colors are acceptable, but brindle and white or brindle and fawn are the most common.

This breed's coat should be brushed twice weekly. The wrinkles on the face should be cleaned daily.

Frenchies are relatively low-activity dogs, although they do like to play and enjoy long walks. Their short muzzles makes them prone to breathing difficulties, though, so exercise should be avoided during hot, humid weather.

## Breed in Brief

**Registries:** AKC, CKC, UKC
**Occupation:** Companion
**Size:** 10 to 12 in tall; 16 to 28 lbs
**Longevity:** 12 to 14 years
**Exercise:** Low activity level
**Training:** Challenge to housetrain
**Grooming:** Easy

Training should begin early. Although Frenchies are companion dogs, they can also have a mind of their own. The French Bull Dog Club of America says, "Although cute and cuddly-looking, a French Bulldog has a big personality and needs an adequate amount of training to make it a civilized companion." Housetraining can sometimes be a challenge.

This breed makes an excellent companion for a sedentary person who is home quite a bit. Although this breed can be good with children, she prefers adults to active kids. Unfortunately, as a brachycephalic (short-muzzled) and dwarf breed, French Bulldogs do have some health concerns, including breathing problems, back disorders, and difficulties with anesthesia.

# German Pinscher

Although the German Pinscher was one of the breeds used to create the Doberman Pinscher, breed experts feel it is more closely related to the much older Standard Schnauzer. The German Pinscher is thought to be a descendant of the now extinct German Rat Pinscher. Bred to protect home and family, this working breed is also a fervent vermin hunter.

This is a medium-sized breed, standing between 17 and 20 inches tall with weight proportionate to height. The head is wedge-shaped, with either upright cropped ears or V-shaped natural ears. The eyes are medium in size, dark, and oval. The body is compact and muscular without being bulky. The tail is docked. The coat is short and smooth. Colors include fawn, red, blue, and black, with or without tan or rust markings.

This is an easy-to-groom breed. The coat can be brushed weekly with a soft bristle brush or curry comb.

German Pinschers are naturally busy. Walks, jogs, playtimes with a ball, or training sessions on the agility course will all be enjoyed. All off-leash play sessions should be inside a fenced-in yard, because if a small animal is flushed, these dogs will chase!

Early socialization is extremely important. This is not a large dog but is still a very watchful and protective one. The German Pinscher is wary of strangers and willing to carry out his protective threats. Early training is also vital. This breed is bright and intelligent but can be strong-willed, manipulative, and stubborn. Training should be firm and structured yet fun, and should continue from puppyhood into adulthood.

This breed needs an experienced owner, preferably one who understands the breed's temperament. He needs supervision with children, as he will not tolerate disrespect or rough handling. He can be aggressive with other dogs, and interactions with small animals should be limited and closely supervised. Health concerns include eye problems and hip dysplasia.

## Breed in Brief

**Registries:** AKC, UKC, CKC
**Occupation:** Guardian, vermin hunter
**Size:** 17 to 20 in tall; weight proportionate to height
**Longevity:** 13 to 14 years
**Exercise:** Active and busy
**Training:** Hard to keep challenged; stubborn
**Grooming:** Easy

# German Shepherd Dog

*I*n the late 1800s, Captain Max von Stephanitz wanted a superior working dog. He used several old farm and herding breeds to produce the German Shepherd Dog or, in German, the Deutscher Schaferhund. In 1899, the parent club for the breed, the Verein fur Deutsche Scheferhunde, was formed. Under the guidance of the club and Captain Stephanitz, the breed rapidly gained popularity as a versatile and superior working dog. Today, it is one of the most recognizable breeds in the world.

The German Shepherd Dog (GSD or, in Great Britain, the Alsatian) is first and foremost a working dog; his temperament and character are his most important traits. GSDs are loyal and courageous, and their ability to learn and retain their training is legendary. The GSD's head is classic, with large upright ears; the eyes are almond-shaped, dark, and alert. Longer than tall, the body is strong and muscular. The front legs are straight, the back legs well-angled. The tail is bushy and hangs in a sickle shape. The coat has a straight outer coat and a dense undercoat. The most recognizable color pattern is the tan to rust base color with a black saddle, black muzzle, and black on the ears.

Grooming a GSD is not difficult but does require time. The coat is not prone to matting but sheds year-round, with the heaviest shedding in the spring and fall. During shedding seasons, the undercoat comes out in handfuls, and, if not brushed daily, the interior of your home will be covered in puffs of soft undercoat. The large upright ears work like radar, catching every sound, but also seem to scoop up dirt, so the ears need to be cleaned twice a week.

The German Shepherd Dog needs vigorous daily exercise. The breed is known for its effortless flying trot, so running alongside your bicycle is great natural exercise. The breed is usually a natural retriever, so games of tennis ball, catch, or flying disc are also great ways to burn off excess energy.

GSDs are naturally watchful, protective, and reserved with strangers. Early puppy socialization is very important. GSDs need to meet people of all ages, sizes, and ethnic backgrounds. An under-socialized GSD can be worried, fearful, and shy. Training should also begin early. An intelligent breed, the GSD needs the mental challenge of training long past basic obedience. Petra Burke, a dog trainer and the owner of Teddy, her second GSD, says, "GSDs are loyal, dedicated, and will give their all to protect their owner. They are very responsive to training. Their owner must structure the training, provide guidelines for the dog, and then enforce them." A German Shepherd Dog is intelligent enough to get into trouble and can be entirely too much dog for a first-time dog owner. This breed's owner must keep the dog active and busy, maintain ongoing training, and be able to channel the dog's desire to work.

A well-trained GSD can be very good with children, although puppies can be quite rambunctious. These dogs are also good with other pets. The breed does, however, have some major health concerns, including bloat, torsion, hip and elbow dysplasia, panosteitis, problems with the pancreas, and allergies.

## Breed in Brief

**Registries:** AKC, UKC, CKC
**Occupation:** Herder, versatile working dog, companion
**Size:** 22 to 26 in tall; 70 to 90 lbs
**Longevity:** 9 to 11 years
**Exercise:** Vigorous daily exercise
**Training:** Easy; difficult to keep challenged
**Grooming:** Moderate

# German Shorthaired Pointer

The German Shorthaired Pointer was developed by German hunters who wanted a versatile hunting dog who could retrieve on land or in water, work with birds of all kinds, and trail at night. As with so many breeds, the exact origins of this pointer are unknown, but experts believe that the German Bird Dog, Spanish Pointer, English Pointer, and local German scenthounds were all used to create an intelligent, attractive, utilitarian dog with excellent scenting abilities.

This breed stands between 21 and 26 inches tall and usually weighs between 45 and 70 pounds. He appears well-balanced, is muscular without being bulky, and gives the appearance of a fine athlete. He has a broad head with a long muzzle, dropped ears, and almond-shaped amber eyes. His tail is docked. His coat is short and tough and is solid liver, liver and white, or patched, ticked, or roan. This coat can be cared for by brushing twice weekly with a soft bristle brush or curry comb.

This athletic breed is active and needs vigorous daily exercise. The German Shorthaired Pointer Club of America says, "The natural exuberance of a young Shorthair can make him difficult to live with if he is kept confined and not exercised." Although these dogs enjoy daily brisk walks, they do better with a good run. The breed is also good at many canine activities, including obedience competitions, field trials, search-and-rescue work, agility, and more.

Early training is very important for this breed—both to teach him household rules and to establish some control over a rowdy young puppy. He needs structured, firm yet fun training. Young Shorthairs can have very short attention spans. If the training is in short sessions, interspersed with some playtimes, he will be more apt to cooperate.

This breed does best with an active owner. He is good with older children; young Shorthairs may be too rowdy for small kids. He's good with other dogs. The primary health concern in this breed is hip dysplasia.

## Breed in Brief

**Registries:** AKC, UKC, CKC
**Occupation:** Hunter
**Size:** 21 to 26 in tall; 45 to 70 lbs
**Longevity:** 12 to 14 years
**Exercise:** Vigorous daily exercise
**Training:** Moderate
**Grooming:** Easy

# German Wirehaired Pointer

This German hunting dog was developed in the late 1800s from crossings of the German Shorthaired Pointer, Pudelpointer, Pointer, Foxhound, and other breeds. It is an excellent hunting dog both on land and in water. This is an active, hard-working dog with a strong desire to both point and retrieve. Although there are similarities between the German Wirehaired Pointer and the German Shorthaired Pointer, and the Shorthaired Pointer is an ancestor, the Wirehaired Pointer should not be considered a Shorthair with a different coat. This is an entirely different breed.

The Wirehair stands 22 to 26 inches tall and weighs 45 to 75 pounds. He is medium-sized, lean, and athletic. He has brown eyes, a brown nose, and dropped ears. The tail is docked. His coat is wiry and weather-resistant, with a dense undercoat. The coat is liver and white, with spots, ticking, or roaning.

This breed's wiry coat needs regular grooming. A breeder can demonstrate correct grooming techniques. The undercoat does shed, and between grooming sessions, the coat should be brushed twice weekly.

The Wirehaired Pointer is an active breed who needs vigorous daily exercise. He will enjoy a run alongside a bicycle or a jog with you. All exercise should be on leash or inside a fenced-in yard, as this breed enjoys hunting and can be gone in a flash.

Training should begin young because this breed can be somewhat independent and stubborn. The breed does take to training well, however, if the training is structured and firm yet fun. Socialization should also begin young, as Wirehairs can be wary of strangers.

This breed does best with an active owner who will keep the dog active as well. Left alone too much, these dogs can get into trouble. With socialization and training, Wirehairs can be good with kids, although young dogs may be rowdy. The breed is not always good with smaller dogs, cats, or other small pets. Health concerns include hip dysplasia and von Willebrand disease.

## Breed in Brief

**Registries:** AKC, UKC, CKC
**Occupation:** Hunter, pointer and retriever
**Size:** 22 to 26 in tall; 45 to 75 lbs
**Longevity:** 12 to 14 years
**Exercise:** Vigorous daily exercise
**Training:** Moderate
**Grooming:** Moderate

# Giant Schnauzer

The Giant Schnauzer was developed in the German agricultural areas of Wurttemberg and Bavaria, as were the other two schnauzer breeds, the Standard Schnauzer and Miniature Schnauzer. The Giant Schnauzer was developed from the Standard Schnauzer and crossed with other drovers' dogs and the black Great Dane. Some experts believe the Bouvier des Flandres might also have been used in the breed's development. The Giant Schnauzer was used as a drover, helping to drive sheep and cattle to market, and as a guard dog for both farms and businesses. Rarely

seen outside of agricultural districts, it wasn't until World War I that the breed was discovered to be an excellent candidate for police and military training.

This breed is the largest of the three schnauzer breeds. Standing 23.5 to 27.5 inches tall at the shoulder and weighing between 70 and 100 pounds, with females smaller than males, this large, sturdy dog is able to work hard. The Giant should look like a larger version of the Standard Schnauzer, with a body as long as the dog is tall, a head carried erect, and medium dark eyes. The ears can be cropped or left as natural button ears carried high on the head. Giant Schnauzers are all black or salt and pepper. The tail is docked.

The Giant's coat has a hard, wiry outer coat and a soft undercoat. It needs brushing and combing two to three times a week. Dogs being shown will need to be hand-stripped every four to six weeks. If you desire to do this yourself, your dog's breeder can teach you how to do it. If you're not showing your dog, he can be trimmed with clippers; a professional groomer can groom your dog for you.

Bred to work and work hard, this breed needs vigorous aerobic exercise every day. A long walk morning and evening is great but is not enough. The Giant will also need a fast game of catch, a session of flyball, or a good agility training session. The Giant also makes a great carting dog, and pulling a load in the wagon is good exercise.

Training is very important for all Giant Schnauzers. These dogs will get into all kinds of trouble of their own making if not provided with guidelines for their behavior in the house and out in public. Training, especially advanced training, can help provide them with a job to do—something to keep the mind challenged.

## Breed in Brief

**Registries:** AKC, UKC, CKC
**Occupation:** Drover, guardian
**Size:** 23.5 to 27.5 in tall; 70 to 100 lbs
**Longevity:** 9 to 12 years
**Exercise:** Vigorous daily exercise
**Training:** Easy; hard to keep challenged
**Grooming:** Difficult

Early puppy socialization is also important for this breed. Bred to be watchful and protective, Giants need socialization to people of all sizes, ages, and ethnic backgrounds. A well-socialized dog is a well-balanced dog who is able to make a decision about protection without fear. Puppy socialization should include introductions to dogs of various sizes and breeds, too, as the breed has been known to be aggressive toward other dogs.

Giants are devoted to their family, steady, and intelligent. Young Giants can be quite rambunctious and must be taught to be gentle with younger children. They are wonderful playmates and companions for older kids. Interactions with other pets should be supervised. The breed does have some health concerns, including hip and elbow dysplasia, seizure disorders, eye problems, and hypothyroidism.

# olden Retriever

This lovely golden breed was developed in Great Britain. In the mid-1800s, Lord Tweedmouth of Guisachan bought his first yellow retriever, a male, whom he bred to a Tweed Water Spaniel in hopes of developing an even better bird dog. Through the years, cross-breedings were made to other Tweed Water Spaniels, Irish Setters, other retrievers, and, it is said, even a Bloodhound. Lord Tweedmouth's gamekeepers kept records of breedings from 1835 until about 1890. These records detailed the beginning of the breed that was later to be called the Golden Retriever.

Goldens stand from 21.5 to 24 inches tall and weigh about 50 to 80 pounds, with females smaller than males. Their expression is kind, eager, and alert, with dark, friendly eyes and soft, dropped ears. The body is strong, giving the appearance of being able to work in the field all day. The coat is dense and of medium length, not coarse or silky. There is a ruff around the neck and down the front of the chest and feathering on

the legs and tail. The undercoat is soft. Colors range throughout the spectrum of gold, from light to dark, although extremely pale and extremely dark golds are less preferable.

Grooming a Golden is not difficult but needs to be done on a regular basis, as the feathering can mat, especially if it gets wet or picks up burrs or foxtails. Brushing and combing the dog twice a week is usually fine, although additional effort might be needed in the spring and fall when shedding is at its heaviest. The ears should be cleaned twice a week, too.

Goldens are very active, and when they don't get enough exercise, they can get into trouble. Linda Hughes, a Golden breeder and owner of two certified Golden Retriever therapy dogs, says, "My dogs get two good walks a day, morning and evening, plus playtime. When it's time for their walk, they will bug me until we go!" Hughes says that even when her dogs go on a therapy dog visit with children, they still demand their exercise walks and playtime.

Goldens, by temperament, are friendly with just about everyone. Hughes says, "Goldens love all mankind! Snickers would rather you pet her than throw the ball, and the ball is her favorite toy." The breed can also be funny and silly; Goldens enjoy trick training and love to show off. Although they will bark when someone comes to the house, they cannot be counted on to be watchdogs or protectors.

## Breed in Brief

**Registries:** AKC, UKC, CKC
**Occupation:** Hunter, companion, performance sports
**Size:** 21.5 to 24 in tall; 50 to 80 lbs
**Longevity:** 11 to 13 years
**Exercise:** Vigorous daily exercise
**Training:** Easy; moderate to keep challenged
**Grooming:** Easy to moderate

Training is necessary so that the Golden puppy learns the household rules and correct social behaviors. In addition, the breed needs the mental stimulation and challenge of training. A bored Golden will get into trouble; a Golden with training and a job to do is a happy dog. Goldens also thrive in performance sports, including obedience competition, agility, flyball, flying disc, and hunt tests, as well as tracking and search and rescue. Their temperament is perfect for therapy dog work.

Goldens are excellent family dogs, although puppies can be rowdy and need to learn to be gentle with small children. They are usually quite good with other small pets. Do not trust the breed with birds! Health concerns include hip dysplasia, allergies, and eye disorders.

#  Gordon Setter

Gordon Setters are an old breed; black and tan setters were known in England and Scotland as early as the 1500s. In the early 1800s, the Duke of Gordon took a somewhat generic bird dog and created the versatile dog we know today.

The Gordon stands between 23 and 27 inches tall and weighs between 45 and 80 pounds. He has a chiseled head, long muzzle, dark eyes, and dropped ears. He is sturdy without being heavy. He has a long tail. The coat is straight or slightly wavy, with feathering on the tail, the back of the legs, the belly, the ears, and around the neck down to the front of the chest.

The Gordon's lovely coat needs at least twice weekly combing and brushing to prevent tangles and mats. The Gordon Setter Club of America recommends daily brushing for puppies to get them used to the grooming routine.

This is a busy breed who needs vigorous daily exercise. The Gordon is an athlete and will enjoy playing flying disc, training in agility, tracking, search and rescue, playing flyball, or participating in field trials. Without enough exercise, Gordon Setters will get into trouble and can be quite inventive. All exercise should be on leash or within a fenced area; when hunting, a Gordon can be gone in a flash.

Although Gordon Setters are bright and curious, they can also be a bit stubborn. The Gordon Setter Club of America says, "Gordons are highly intelligent dogs, and basic obedience will make your dog a better companion. Although Gordons are bright, they are not blindly obedient and may seem stubborn. Firmness and consistency are the keys to handling Gordons." Socialization is also important, as these dogs may be wary of strangers.

The Gordon Setter needs an actively involved owner, preferably someone who understands the setter mentality and enjoys grooming the dog. He is great with children who treat him well. He is usually good with other dogs but may not be good with smaller pets. Health concerns include bloat and hip dysplasia.

## Breed in Brief

**Registries:** AKC, UKC, CKC
**Occupation:** Hunter
**Size:** 23 to 27 in tall; 45 to 80 lbs
**Longevity:** 10 to 13 years
**Exercise:** Vigorous daily exercise
**Training:** Moderate
**Grooming:** Moderate to difficult

# reat Dane

The Great Dane is not from Denmark; rather, this breed was developed in Germany, although artwork in Egypt dating back to 3000 B.C. shows dogs looking remarkably like Great Danes. The Germans used this breed to hunt wild boar. In the late 1800s, the Germans decided that the breed was to be named the Deutsche Dogge. Where the name Great Dane originated has been hotly debated.

This is a giant breed, standing taller than 28 to 32 inches and weighing between 125 and 180 pounds. He has an elegant, regal yet strong appearance, with a rectangular head, medium-sized dark eyes, and a black nose. He has either folded ears or cropped upright ears. The chest is deep and the body strong and balanced. The tail is long, reaching to the hocks. The coat is short and may be brindle, fawn, blue, black, harlequin, or mantle (black and white).

The short coat should be brushed twice weekly.

Great Dane puppies are clumsy, silly, and playful and need regular, easy exercise and several play sessions a day. Puppies should not over-exercise; doing so can cause problems with growing bones. Adult dogs are calmer, although they appreciate a walk morning and evening and a chance to play.

## Breed in Brief

**Registries:** AKC, UKC, CKC
**Occupation:** Hunter, companion
**Size:** 28 to 32+ in; 125 to 180 lbs
**Longevity:** 8 to 10 years
**Exercise:** Moderate
**Training:** Moderate
**Grooming:** Easy

The Great Dane Club of America recommends early and continued socialization and training for all puppies. A Great Dane grows very rapidly (owners and trainers need to know that these dogs are very large physically while mentally still puppies), and training not only teaches him what is expected of him at home and out in public, but also teaches the owner how to control the dog. Training should be firm and structured, yet kind and fun.

The Great Dane does best with an owner who understands the needs and characteristics of a giant dog. The breed is good with children who treat the dog with respect, although puppies can be quite rough. Great Danes are usually good with other dogs. The breed has a number of health concerns, including cardiomyopathy, bloat, cancer, hip dysplasia, and wobbler's syndrome.

# Great Pyrenees

The Great Pyrenees is also known as the Pyrenean Mountain Dog and Le Chien des Pyrenees. This giant livestock guardian originated in the mountains of southwestern Europe, where the breed has guarded flocks of sheep for centuries.

Great Pyrenees stand between 25 and 32 inches tall and weigh 90 to 130 pounds. The head is wedge-shaped, the eyes are dark, and the ears are dropped. The body is slightly longer than the dog is tall. The tail is plumed. There are double dewclaws on each rear leg. The coat is weather-resistant and double, with a thick undercoat and a long, flat outer coat. This breed is either all white or white with markings of tan, gray, or reddish brown.

This double coat needs regular brushing (at least twice a week) to keep it neat and clean. Brushing the outer coat is not sufficient; the undercoat must be brushed, too, to prevent matting. Daily brushing is needed during the spring and fall shedding seasons.

Young Pyrenees can be quite active, although adult dogs are calmer. Pyrenees owner Janine Staudt says of her dog, Ben, "He has lots of energy and needs daily walks and playtimes." This breed is not the retrieving type; the Pyrenees does not have much interest in bringing back a ball or toy. As with so many livestock guardians, this breed is more active at night.

Early socialization is very important. The Pyrenees needs to meet a variety of people and other dogs, and if he is going to be a livestock protection dog, must also be introduced to livestock. This breed is very protective, and his verbal warnings should never be disregarded. Training should also begin early and should be firm and consistent. These dogs are large and powerful, and the owner should establish leadership early.

This breed needs an owner who understands livestock guardian dogs. They bark and, if left outside at night, will bark loudly at any sound or perceived threat. Many Pyrenees also drool. Health concerns include eyelid problems, hip dysplasia, and bloat.

## Breed in Brief

**Registries:** AKC, UKC, CKC
**Occupation:** Livestock guardian
**Size:** 25 to 32 in tall; 90 to 130 lbs
**Longevity:** 9 to 11 years
**Exercise:** Moderate
**Training:** Needs leadership training
**Grooming:** Moderate

# Greater Swiss Mountain Dog

The Greater Swiss Mountain Dog, also know as a Swissy, originated in Switzerland as a versatile working dog doing herding, carting, and guard dog duty. The breed came close to extinction when machines took away several of its ancestral duties, but Dr. Albert Heim, of Zurich, was instrumental in building enthusiasm for saving the breed.

A Swissy stands between 23.5 and 28.5 inches tall and weighs between 90 and 150 pounds. The head is broad, and the muzzle is large and blunt. The eyes are almond-shaped and dark. The ears are dropped. The body is strong and muscular, and the tail reaches to the hocks. The coat is double, with a thick undercoat and a dense 2-inch outer coat. Swissies are tricolored: black with white and rust markings.

The Swissy's coat sheds, so twice weekly brushing is needed to keep it under control. In the spring and fall, when shedding is at its worst, daily brushing may be needed.

Swissy puppies are active and playful, and although some Swissies retain that sense of play when they grow up, they can also be quite serious. They are not overly active but still need regular exercise. A long, brisk walk morning and evening and a chance to play will make most Swissies happy.

The Greater Swiss Mountain Dog Club of America recommends early and continued socialization and training for all Swissies. The training should be structured, fair, and firm yet fun. Swissies also do well in many canine sports, including carting, weight pulling, search and rescue, tracking, and agility. In puppyhood, housetraining can be a challenge and requires patience.

The Swissy is a working dog and needs an owner who will do things with him. This dog needs to feel needed, yet also needs an owner who will be his leader. He is great with kids as long as he has been well socialized with them and the kids treat him with respect. He is not always good with strange dogs. Health concerns include hip and elbow dysplasia, bloat, and epilepsy.

## Breed in Brief

**Registries:** AKC, UKC, CKC
**Occupation:** Versatile draft and farm dog
**Size:** 23.5 to 28.5 in tall; 90 to 150 lbs
**Longevity:** 9 to 11 years
**Exercise:** Moderate
**Training:** Challenge to housetrain
**Grooming:** Easy; sheds

# Greyhound

*A* running Greyhound is an elegant sight. With no wasted motion and a body uniquely suited to the effort, the Greyhound is the fastest dog on the planet. A well-conditioned racing Greyhound can run up to forty-five miles per hour. The Greyhound is an ancient breed, with a documented history going back at least 5,000 years. Carvings of Greyhounds, looking then like they do today, can be found in Egyptian tombs dating back to 2900 B.C. The breed's popularity was not limited to the Mideast; in Elizabethan England, hare coursing with

Greyhounds was popular. In the late 1700s, when the U.S. was being explored and settled, many European immigrants brought their Greyhounds with them.

The Greyhound is first and foremost a dog made for running. He is lean, with a narrow body and a deep chest with room for the large lungs and big heart. He is well-muscled and gives the appearance of a well-conditioned athlete. The head is long and narrow, the eyes are dark and full of personality, and the ears are small and folded. The tail is long and fine. The Greyhound's coat is short and smooth and can be found in any color or color pattern.

Grooming a Greyhound is very easy. The coat should be brushed twice a week with a soft bristle brush or curry comb.

Although most Greyhounds enjoy snuggling on the sofa, they are athletes. They do need daily exercise, and a long walk morning and evening should be the absolute minimum. Designed for thousands of years to run, they should be allowed to run at least once every day. However, they should not be allowed to run outside of a fenced-in area; if a rabbit or squirrel is flushed during that run, the Greyhound will forget everything in the excitement of the chase. No amount of calling the dog to Come will break off that chase.

Greyhounds who have been adopted from a racetrack are normally well-socialized to both people and other Greyhounds. Racing Greyhounds are crate (or cage) trained and know how to walk on a leash. The adoption agencies who rescue and place these dogs usually make sure the dogs are healthy prior to placing them, and often foster homes make sure the dogs are housetrained. Once adopted, the dogs need to learn the details of living in a house, including walking up and down stairs. But they usually adapt well and can make wonderful pets.

Greyhound puppies from a breeder (non-racing) should attend a puppy class for socialization and an introduction to training. Although the Greyhound is not normally a problem breed, just as with any puppy, he can get into trouble if not supervised.

Greyhounds are very oriented to people and can be quite social but can also develop a strong attachment to one person. Tammy Zybura, owner of Moose, a rescued racer, says, "Moose is very gentle, loving, and silly. He's affectionate to everyone, but he is definitely my dog." Greyhounds are good with other dogs, especially large ones, but should be closely supervised and should be on leash when interacting with small dogs, cats, and other small pets. Greyhounds can be prone to sports injuries from running. Other health concerns include sensitivity to anesthesia, bloat, and torsion.

## Breed in Brief

**Registries:** AKC, UKC, CKC
**Occupation:** Sighthound, racer, companion
**Size:** 26 to 30 in tall; 60 to 70 lbs
**Longevity:** 12 to 14 years
**Exercise:** Couch potatoes who love to run
**Training:** Easy; hard to motivate
**Grooming:** Easy

Greyhound    259

# Harrier

The Harrier originated in England and has not changed significantly in centuries. This is a pack scenthound used primarily to hunt hares, although packs occasionally hunted other game.

The Harrier stands between 19 and 21 inches tall and weighs between 45 and 55 pounds. The eyes are medium-sized and range from brown to yellow. The ears are dropped. The topline is level, and the chest is deep with plenty of room for the heart and lungs. The tail is long and carried high but not arched over the back. The coat is short and dense. Color is not regarded as important.

The Harrier's coat is not difficult to care for; a weekly brushing is fine.

Breed expert Donna Smiley-Auborn says, "Harriers are a very active breed, requiring a lot of daily exercise. A bored, lonely Harrier may very well become a loud, destructive Harrier." A hunting Harrier could easily cover between twenty and forty miles a day. Even though many Harriers today are companions rather than hunting dogs, they still need a vigorous daily run.

Training is important for all companion dogs, Harriers included. The breed is quite food-motivated, which can make training easier. Smiley-Auborn says, "Harriers are intelligent but are not naturally obedient. They bore easily if the training is too repetitive." She also says that the breed is not recommended for first-time dog owners or trainers not familiar with the challenges of training scenthounds. However, with a motivated trainer, a Harrier can succeed in obedience and agility training.

Smiley-Auborn says, "Harriers are outgoing, friendly, gregarious, affectionate, self-willed, independent, intelligent, determined, and inquisitive." As pack hounds, they are good with other dogs and do best in a home with at least one or two other dogs. They are wonderful with children and, when raised with small pets, can be okay with them, although they will chase running animals. Health concerns include hip dysplasia and eye and thyroid problems.

## Breed in Brief

**Registries:** AKC, UKC, CKC
**Occupation:** Hunter
**Size:** 19 to 21 in tall; 45 to 55 lbs
**Longevity:** 11 to 13 years
**Exercise:** Vigorous daily exercise
**Training:** Challenge
**Grooming:** Easy

# Havanese

The Havanese is one of the older breeds in the Bichon family. In the 1600s, explorers, colonists, and traders brought dogs from Tennerife to Cuba, where the dogs found favor with the local aristocracy. By the 1800s, they had been taken to Europe, where they were popular with the royal families in England, France, and Spain.

The Havanese is a sturdy toy dog who stands between 8.5 to 11.5 inches tall and weighs 7 to 14 pounds. Her body is slightly longer than she is tall, her head is wedge-shaped, eyes are dark, and ears are dropped. Her tail is plumed and carried over the back. Her crowning glory is her silky double coat. The undercoat is soft, while the outer coat is longer, abundant, and slightly wavy. Although white is the best known color, the coat may be any color.

This coat does require some care. Daily brushing and combing will prevent tangles and mats. Show dogs should be untrimmed, but many pet owners have the coat trimmed to keep it neat and clean, especially around the genitals and under the tail.

The Havanese is playful and mischievous but not overly active. She will be happy with a nice walk and a couple of playtimes each day.

## Breed in Brief

**Registries:** AKC, UKC, CKC
**Occupation:** Companion
**Size:** 8.5 to 11.5 in tall; 7 to 14 lbs
**Longevity:** 11 to 13 years
**Exercise:** Low activity level
**Training:** Moderate
**Grooming:** Moderate; lots of combing

This breed is intelligent. Havanese enjoy training, especially when interspersed with playtimes. They enjoy many canine sports, especially agility. Although these dogs are more affectionate with their owners than anyone else, they are still friendly to most people. Socialization is a good idea since the breed was at one time a watchdog, although today they are more social. Havanese make wonderful therapy dogs.

The Havanese will thrive in a home with affectionate people who like to play. She is wonderful with children who treat her gently. She is good with other dogs as long as larger dogs are not too rough. She can also be very good with smaller pets. There are several major health concerns, including chrondrodysplasia, cataracts, deafness, hip dysplasia, liver disorders, and knee and skin problems.

# Hovawart

This is an old German working breed with a history that goes back to the 13th century, although it may be even older. This versatile farm dog could herd livestock, protect them from predators, and guard the farm against predators and trespassers.

The Hovawart stands between 22 and 28 inches tall. Her weight should be in proportion to her height. Males are larger and more robust than females. The Hovawart has a broad head, amber eyes, and dropped ears. Her body is slightly longer than tall at the shoulder, with a plumed tail. She has a double coat, with a light undercoat and a medium-length outer coat that includes feathering on the legs and tail, around the neck, and down the front of the chest. The coat may be blond, black, or black and tan.

The coat should be brushed twice weekly to keep it clean and to prevent mats from forming, especially under the legs and behind the ears.

For many centuries, this breed served as a working dog with many jobs to do, and even today, the breed retains that desire to be busy. The Hovawart needs vigorous daily exercise and a chance to participate in daily activities. She will be happy to watch the kids, look for delivery drivers, and get the newspaper every morning.

These dogs are watchful and protective, so early socialization is very important. They also need early training that continues on into adulthood. Bred to work but also to think for themselves, they may have a stubborn streak, so training should be firm and structured but fun and challenging. The breed does well in many canine sports, including obedience, Schutzhund, search and rescue, tracking, and agility.

The Hovawart needs an owner who will be her leader and will challenge her with training and activities. If left alone for too many hours each day, this dog will get into trouble. She is great with kids and livestock but might not tolerate strange dogs. Health concerns are few but include hip and elbow dysplasia.

## Breed in Brief

**Registries:** UKC, CKC
**Occupation:** Versatile farm dog
**Size:** 22 to 28 in tall; weight proportionate to height
**Longevity:** 12 to 14 years
**Exercise:** Vigorous daily exercise
**Training:** Hard to keep challenged
**Grooming:** Easy

# Ibizan Hound

## (Smooth Coat and Wirehaired Coat)

The Ibizan Hound's history can be traced back to 3400 B.C. in ancient Egypt, where artifacts from many well-known tombs bear a striking resemblance to today's dogs. What is unknown is how the breed went from Egypt to the island of Ibiza where the breed got its name.

This sighthound is an athlete with a body and legs made for running. An Ibizan Hound stands between 22.5 and 27.5 inches and weighs 45 to 50 pounds. The head is long and narrow, with amber eyes, a pink nose, and large, upright, uncropped ears. The back is level, and the chest is deep. The tail is long and sickle-shaped. There are two coat types—smooth and wirehaired. Coat colors include white and red, solid white or red, or any combination.

Both coat types require twice weekly brushing to keep them neat and clean.

Ibizan puppies are very active and quite silly; they love to play. Although adults are not quite as busy, they still enjoy a good run and should get a chance to run off leash in a safe place at least once a day. Young Ibizans who do not get enough exercise will get into trouble and can be problem chewers.

This breed can be wary with strangers, so early socialization is very important. Training should begin early, too, to deter some of the puppy antics that might otherwise occur. Ibizan puppies mature quite slowly, so training should continue into adulthood. The breed's active body and bright mind make it a wonderful participant in many canine sports, including lure coursing, flyball, flying disc, and agility.

This breed needs a well-fenced-in yard to keep it safe, as it is a natural hunter. The owner should be active and want to do things with the dog; the Ibizan does not do well when left alone for hours each day. Adult Ibizans are good with children, but puppies can be rowdy. Although good with other dogs, this breed has a strong prey drive and so should not be trusted with smaller pets. Health concerns include sensitivities to medications.

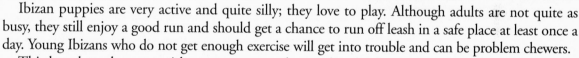

## Breed in Brief

**Registries:** AKC, UKC, CKC
**Occupation:** Sighthound
**Size:** 22.5 to 27.5 in tall; 45 to 50 lbs
**Longevity**: 11 to 13 years
**Exercise:** Moderate
**Training**: Moderate
**Grooming:** Easy

# Icelandic Sheepdog

## (Medium Coat and Long Coat)

The Icelandic Sheepdog was brought to Iceland by the Vikings more than 1,100 years ago. Descended from Nordic Spitz breeds, the Icelandic Sheepdog is now considered Iceland's native dog. The breed was (and still is) used to work the sheep and horses also brought to Iceland by the Vikings.

This is a medium-sized dog, standing between 16.5 and 18 inches tall with weight in proportion to height. The head is triangular, with medium-sized brown eyes and upright ears. The body is slightly longer than the dog is tall at the shoulder, and the tail is curled over the back. The coat is double with a thick, soft undercoat; there are two lengths of outer coat: medium and long. Colors vary from cream to reddish brown and gray to black. All may have white markings.

This coat needs weekly brushing during most of the year, although when the dog is shedding, daily brushing can help keep the hair in the house under control.

Breed expert Brynhildur Inga Einarsdottir of Iceland says, "ISDs are very individual in the amount of exercise they need. Some dogs seem to be content with a daily walk, while others can have endless energy." The breed is playful, and many dogs enjoy agility and flyball.

ISDs are not aggressive but are watchful and will bark when people approach their territory. Einarsdottir says, "Socialization at an early age is important, as these dogs can show aggression to dogs of the same sex." The breed is bright, has strong working instincts, and loves to learn. Training should be firm and structured so the dog learns household rules, but should also be fun.

The breed does best in a home where barking will not be a problem. Einarsdottir adds, "The breed does best in a working or training environment." She says that ISDs make wonderful therapy dogs. They are very good with children and can usually be trusted with smaller pets, although the dog may try to herd both the kids and the other pets. Health concerns include hip dysplasia and cataracts.

## Breed in Brief

**Registries:** AKC FSS, UKC, CKC

**Occupation:** Herder, watchdog

**Size:** 16.5 to 18 in tall; weight proportionate to height

**Longevity:** 14 to 16 years

**Exercise:** Moderate to active

**Training:** Moderate

**Grooming:** Moderate

# Irish Red and White Setter

The Irish Setter and the Irish Red and White Setter share the same ancestry and were both popular in Ireland in the 18th and 19th centuries. However, when the Irish Setter gained popularity, the Irish Red and White Setter became quite scarce and at one time almost disappeared. The breed was reestablished in the early 1900s and is now flourishing.

This setter stands between 22 and 26 inches tall and weighs 40 to 70 pounds. The head is broad, eyes dark and oval, and ears dropped. The body is strong and slightly longer than the dog is tall. The tail reaches to the hock. The coat is short and flat with feathering on the ears, backs of the legs, and tail. The coat is white with red patches and flecking.

This breed needs weekly brushing and combing to keep the coat neat and clean and to prevent matting. Most breed experts recommend that the coat be trimmed under the ears, under the tail, and around the feet.

Irish Red and White Setters are hunting dogs with strong instincts and great stamina. They need daily exercise and will run alongside a bicycle, go jogging, or enjoy a vigorous game of catch. All exercise should be on leash or inside a fenced-in yard. A young Red and White who does not get enough exercise will get into trouble.

These dogs are friendly and intelligent. Although they are easily trained as gun dogs, they do not always take well to rote obedience, so training should be firm, patient, and consistent, yet not harsh. The breed does enjoy active, fun canine sports, especially agility, flying disc, and flyball. Irish Red and White Setters have also been successful search-and-rescue dogs.

The Irish Red and White Setter does best with an owner who hunts or enjoys field trials; those instincts are strong in this breed. He is good with children when raised with them or well socialized to them. He is usually good with other dogs but may not be good with smaller pets. Health concerns include bloat and cataracts.

## Breed in Brief

**Registries:** AKC FSS, UKC, CKC
**Occupation:** Hunter
**Size:** 22 to 26 in tall; 40 to 70 lbs
**Longevity:** 10 to 12 years
**Exercise:** Daily exercise
**Training:** Moderate
**Grooming:** Easy to moderate

# Irish Setter

The early origins of the Irish Setter are unknown, although the many setter breeds from the British Isles may share some of the same ancestors. Today's Irish Setter came into being in the early 1800s and quickly became a favorite of both hunters and those looking for handsome companion dogs.

The Irish Setter stands 25 to 27 inches tall and weighs 60 to 70 pounds. The body is slightly longer than tall at the shoulders. The head is long and lean, the eyes are almond-shaped, and the ears are dropped and folded. The tail reaches the hocks. The crowning glory of this breed is the rich red coat. The coat is short on the head and forelegs but is of medium length elsewhere. There is feathering on the ears, backs of the legs, belly, and tail.

This breed requires regular grooming. The coat should be brushed daily to remove dirt and burrs and to prevent matting. The neck and feet are often trimmed, especially for show dogs, but many pet owners want the same clean look.

The Irish Setter is an active dog who needs vigorous daily exercise. He can run alongside a bicycle, go for a jog, or take long, brisk walks. This breed can be funny and silly and enjoys playtimes. All exercise should be inside a fenced-in yard or on leash; the breed's silliness can sometimes get him into trouble.

The Irish Setter Club of America recommends that all puppies go through training that is firm yet affectionate and not forceful. Although Irish Setters are silly dogs, they are also very bright, so training is good for keeping their minds busy. Puppies are slow to mature, so training should continue into adulthood. This breed also enjoys many dog sports, especially agility and flyball.

The Irish Setter needs a fun-loving owner who doesn't take life too seriously. He can be good with children, although puppies may be rowdy and rough. He is good with other dogs but should not be trusted with smaller pets. Health concerns include hip dysplasia, as well as thyroid and eye problems.

## Breed in Brief

**Registries:** AKC, UKC, CKC
**Occupation:** Hunter, companion
**Size:** 25 to 27 in tall; 60 to 70 lbs
**Longevity:** 10 to 12 years
**Exercise:** Vigorous daily exercise plus playtime
**Training:** Moderate
**Grooming:** Moderate

# rish Terrier

The Irish Terrier originated at least 300 years ago on the island from which it takes its name, but other than that, the breed's origins are unknown. The breed has been used to control vermin, hunt small game, protect the family farm and home, and retrieve both on land and in the water.

The Irish Terrier is about 18 inches tall and weighs between 25 and 27 pounds. His head is long, eyes are small and dark brown, and ears are dropped and set high on the head. His body is slightly longer than tall at the shoulder. The coat is double, with a soft, fine undercoat and a hard, wiry outer coat. Irish Terriers are red, with the shade of the red varying from wheaten through bright red.

The Irish's wiry coat needs special grooming. Ideally it should be hand-stripped, so potential owners should discuss coat care with a breeder to make sure they can do what is needed.

Lt. Col. Bill Harkins, USMC, says of his Irish Terrier, "Ruby is very active. She runs in our backyard and loves to go on long walks and runs." An Irish Terrier can be mischievous; however, with enough exercise many problems can be prevented.

Irish Terriers are intelligent and have historically been independent workers and hunters; they are very good at thinking for themselves. Early training should be fun and continue into adulthood. Lt. Col. Harkins says, "Irish Terriers like to learn, and although Ruby is strong-willed and likes to have her way, she does learn well for food rewards." This breed is also very protective, sometimes overly so. Early socialization can help the owner control overprotectiveness.

This breed does best with an experienced dog owner, preferably someone who understands the working terrier temperament. The Irish Terrier can be great with kids when well-socialized to them and when the kids treat him with respect. These terriers can be challenging to strange dogs and should not be trusted with smaller pets. The breed has few health concerns.

## Breed in Brief

**Registries:** AKC, UKC, CKC
**Occupation:** Farm dog, hunter, watchdog
**Size:** 18 in tall; 25 to 27 lbs
**Longevity:** 14 to 15 years
**Exercise:** Active
**Training:** Challenge
**Grooming:** Hand-stripping

# Irish Water Spaniel

Archeological finds in Ireland have verified experts' claims that these versatile dogs date back to the 7th century. At various times during its history, the breed (and direct ancestors of the breed) were known as Rat-Tail Spaniels, Whip-Tail Spaniels, and Shannon Spaniels. By the mid-1800s, the breed was being shown in dog shows, and several dogs—including Boatswain, his son Jack, and his great-grandson Doctor—were attracting attention to the breed.

The Irish Water Spaniel is the tallest of the spaniels, standing between 21 and 24 inches tall and weighing between 45 and 65 pounds. He gives the appearance of being strong, well-balanced, and slightly longer than tall. The head is large with a square, long muzzle. The eyes are medium, almond-shaped, and dark. The ears are long and set low on the head. The body is of medium length with a deep chest. The legs are strong, the feet are long and wide for swimming, and the tail is set low on the hips. The tail gets its "rat-tail" description because it is not covered by the curly coat. The coat is solid liver in color and is double. The undercoat is thick and the outer coat curly. The face has short coat, too, topped by a topknot of curls on the head.

This coat does not shed excessively but does need regular grooming. The ears need to be cleaned at least weekly. The curly coat should be brushed and combed thoroughly twice a week. The coat will need to be trimmed every six weeks to keep it neat and clean. Potential owners should talk with a breeder about the breed's grooming needs.

This dog was bred to be a hunting retriever able to find and retrieve downed birds in ice-cold water as well as on land. Today the breed is still an excellent hunting partner but is also being kept more and more as a family dog. When kept as a pet, an Irish Water Spaniel needs vigorous daily exercise. A natural retriever, he will play ball or flying disc and loves games of hide-and-seek. He is also a superb swimmer and will

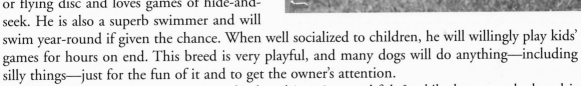

swim year-round if given the chance. When well socialized to children, he will willingly play kids' games for hours on end. This breed is very playful, and many dogs will do anything—including silly things—just for the fun of it and to get the owner's attention.

Early socialization is important, as this breed is quite watchful. Luckily, however, the breed is not prone to excessive barking. Training comes naturally to these dogs, and they thrive under fair, firm, yet fun training. The Irish Water Spaniel is very much a team player and will enjoy canine sports where dog and owner get to work together, such as agility and search and rescue. Training and socialization should continue into adulthood.

The Irish Water Spaniel can be a wonderful family dog but also needs a job to do, even if it is as simple as bringing in the morning newspaper. His owner should be actively involved with the dog; this breed does not do well when left alone for many hours each day. As a breed with strong hunting instincts, he should not be trusted with smaller pets. Health concerns include hip and elbow dysplasia, hypothyroidism, ear infections, and allergies. Some owners also report drug sensitivities.

## Breed in Brief

**Registries:** AKC, UKC
**Occupation:** Hunter, retriever
**Size:** 21 to 24 in tall; 45 to 65 lbs
**Longevity:** 11 to 13 years
**Exercise:** Daily exercise
**Training:** Moderate; socialization important
**Grooming:** Difficult

# rish Wolfhound

This breed has a history going back to the 4th century, although it may be even older. As with so many ancient breeds, history has been pieced together through depictions of the dogs in artwork or in the few known written records. The breed was treasured for its ability to hunt the wolves that preyed upon livestock, as well as the giant elk of Ireland.

This is a giant breed. The minimum size for a male is 32 inches at the shoulder and 120 pounds. The smallest a female should be is 30 inches and 105 pounds. The head is long, and the ears are small and dropped. The chest is very deep, and the tail is long. The legs are muscular and feet are large. The coat is hard, rough, and wiry; coat colors include brindle, gray, red, black, and white.

This coat needs weekly brushing and may need occasional plucking to stay neat. Prior to choosing a Wolfhound, potential owners should discuss coat care with a breeder.

Bred for running with great speed and stamina, these dogs still enjoy running. Since the instinct to hunt is strong, all off-leash exercise should be within a securely fenced-in yard. Although adult dogs are calm and dignified, Wolfhound puppies are very large, silly, clumsy clowns who love to play. A puppy who does not get enough exercise can get into a lot of trouble and be quite destructive.

Early training is very important so that the owner can assume a leadership role before the dog exceeds 100 pounds and becomes more powerful than his human. Training should be fair and fun, never harsh.

This breed does not do well when left alone for hours each day. Although large and imposing, Irish Wolfhounds are not watchdogs. Adult dogs are good with children, although puppies should be supervised. They are usually good with other dogs but have a strong chase instinct and should not be trusted with smaller running dogs or cats. Health concerns include hip and elbow dysplasia, bloat, heart and eye problems, and seizure disorders.

## Breed in Brief

**Registries:** AKC, UKC, CKC
**Occupation:** Hunter, sighthound
**Size:** 30 to 32+ in tall; 105 to 120+ lbs
**Longevity:** 6 to 8 years
**Exercise:** Loves to run!
**Training:** Moderate
**Grooming:** Weekly brushing; occasional plucking

# Italian Greyhound

The Italian Greyhound originated more than 2,000 years ago in the regions now known as Turkey and Greece. By the 1600s, the breed was a favorite in Italy, and as the breed's popularity spread, it became a favorite of many royal families in Europe, in countries including England, Prussia, Russia, and Denmark.

The Italian Greyhound is very much a sighthound but in miniature. Standing 13 to 15 inches tall, these delicate dogs weigh just 7 to 15 pounds. The head is long and tapered, the eyes are dark, and the ears are folded at half-mast. The back is curved, body is compact, and legs are those of a runner. The tail is slender and curved. The coat is short and fine and can be any color except brindle or black and tan.

The fine coat needs weekly brushing with a soft bristle brush or soft curry comb.

IG puppies can be quite active and need daily exercise to prevent destructive behavior. The exercise can also help strengthen fine bones and build muscles. IG puppies should be prevented from jumping from heights (even a sofa), as they can break fragile leg bones. Adults are not nearly as active, although they will always enjoy a good run. All exercise should be on leash or within a fenced yard.

Italian Greyhounds are affectionate and personable, but should meet a variety of people during puppyhood, as they can be aloof with strangers. Obedience training should be fun and fair. Housetraining can sometimes be a challenge. IG puppies need to eliminate often, and bowel and bladder control can take a few months to develop. Owners need to be patient and consistent in their training.

This breed does not do well when left alone for many hours each day. This is an inside breed; the fine coat offers no protection at all from inclement weather. IGs usually get along with children and other small dogs but are fragile and should be protected from rough play. Health concerns included broken bones, dental problems, and drug sensitivities.

## Breed in Brief

**Registries:** AKC, UKC, CKC
**Occupation:** Companion
**Size:** 13 to 15 in tall; 7 to 15 lbs
**Longevity:** 12 to 15 years
**Exercise:** Needs supervised exercise
**Training:** Challenge to housetrain
**Grooming:** Easy

# Jack Russell Terrier

The Jack Russell Terrier (or JRT) is a working terrier developed by Reverend John Russell of Devonshire, England, in the mid- to late 1800s. The Reverend Russell enjoyed fox hunting and wanted a breed of dog who could find, chase, and go-to-ground after the fox. He began with the Fox Terriers of the 1800s (who were quite different from today's Fox Terriers) and bred a small, sturdy, energetic, feisty little hunting dog.

The Jack Russell Terrier Club of America (JRTCA) is the parent club in the U.S. (with the Jack Russell Terrier Club of Great Britain) and is devoted to guiding the breed into the future as a healthy working terrier true to its heritage. The club opposed AKC and UKC recognition, although both registries went ahead and accepted the breed. It is now known as the Parson Russell Terrier in the AKC, but remains the Jack Russell Terrier with the UKC. (For more on this, see the Parson Russell Terrier profile on page 312.)

First and foremost, the JRT is a tough little terrier that stands between 10 and 15 inches tall. The eyes are dark, the ears dropped and V-shaped. The coat is either smooth, rough, or broken but not wooly. White is the predominant color, with tan, black, or brown markings. There are variations in body form and type, but in all cases, the dog should present a compact, balanced appearance and be strong and fit. The tail is docked. The Jack Russell Terrier Club of America says, "Jack Russell Terriers are a type, or strain, of working terrier; they are not a pure breed in the sense they have a broad genetic makeup, a broad standard, and do not breed true to type."

Grooming the JRT is not difficult. The smooth-coated dogs can be brushed with a soft bristle brush or curry comb twice weekly, while the rough or broken-coated dogs may need brushing with a pin or slicker brush a little more often. None of the coat types mats.

Vigorous daily exercise is needed to keep this breed happy. Although a long morning and evening walk will be enjoyed, that isn't enough. This little dog will also need a couple of long, vigorous games of fetch, a game of flying disc, or a training session on the agility course. The more exercise the better, because without it, these little dogs will amuse themselves, and that's rarely good.

Socialization and training are also important. JRTs are feisty and think for themselves; they need to be guided in the direction you wish them to go, and you need to make the training challenging and fun enough to keep them interested. JRTs have excelled in many canine sports, including agility and flyball.

Although this breed can be good with people of all ages, the JRT can sometimes be too pushy for small children or the elderly. This is a tough breed for a first-time dog owner; she will do better with someone who understands the terrier temperament. The JRT can be feisty with other dogs, and all interactions with small pets should be supervised. Remember, this is a hunting breed. The JRT gets along great with horses and is often used as a stable dog, keeping horses company and hunting mice and rats. Health concerns include eye and knee problems and obsessive-compulsive behavior problems.

## Breed in Brief

**Registries:** JRTCA, UKC
**Occupation:** Hunter, performance sports
**Size:** 10 to 15 in tall; 10 to 20 lbs
**Longevity:** 14 to 16 years
**Exercise:** Vigorous daily exercise
**Training:** Moderate; hard to keep challenged
**Grooming:** Easy

# Jagd Terrier

## (Smooth Coat and Rough Coat)

The Jagd Terrier, also known as the German Hunt Terrier, was created in Germany in the early 1900s. At the time, terriers were very popular in Great Britain and Europe, but Germany did not have an effective native hunting terrier. So the black and tan fell terriers (who were not good hunters) were crossed with Fox Terriers (excellent hunters), and the offspring were selectively bred to create a black and tan, versatile hunting terrier. In Germany, the breed hunts fox and boar; in the U.S., it hunts raccoons.

The American Jagd Terrier Registry says the breed should stand between 11 and 19 inches tall and weigh between 10 and 39 pounds. Her eyes are dark, the ears V-shaped, and the tail docked or natural. The body should be slightly longer than the dog is tall at the shoulder. The coat may be smooth and short, broken or rough. The most popular color is black and tan, but the dogs may also be chocolate or salt and pepper.

Twice weekly brushing is sufficient for these dogs, although many owners will trim Jagd Terriers with broken or rough coats just to keep them neat.

This is an active, athletic, bright breed with a strong hunting drive. If not allowed to hunt regularly, she needs another outlet for her energy and desire to work. Agility training, flying disc competitions, lure coursing, or other sports are a great idea for this breed. Training should begin early and continue into adulthood to keep the dog in control and focused. Positive training techniques are often not enough; this breed needs firm, structured training.

The Jagd Terrier needs an experienced dog owner who understands terriers and hunting dogs. She is affectionate and protective of her family and wary of strangers. She is good with children and can take rough kids' play. She gets along with other dogs but will never back down from a challenge; like many small terriers, she has no idea how small she is. She is a hunter and should not be trusted with other small pets. This is a healthy breed.

## Breed in Brief

**Registries:** American Jagd Terrier Registry
**Occupation:** Hunter
**Size:** 11 to 19 in tall; 10 to 39 lbs
**Longevity:** 13 to 15 years
**Exercise:** Very active; needs lots of exercise
**Training:** Challenge
**Grooming:** Easy

# Japanese Chin

The Japanese Chin, also known as the Japanese Spaniel, is an ancient toy breed with a much debated history. Some experts feel the breed originated in China, while others say Korea was the birthplace. In any event, at some point the breed was introduced to Japan, where it became a favorite of the nobility.

This is a small dog, standing 8 to 11 inches tall and weighing only 4 to 11 pounds. The head is large and rounded; the eyes are large, round, and dark; and the ears are hanging. The muzzle is short. The tail is set high and is carried up over the back. The coat is single (with no undercoat) and is straight and silky. She has feathering on her tail, the back of the legs, the ears, and around the neck down onto the front of the chest. The acceptable colors include black and white, red and white, and tricolored (black and white with rust markings).

This lovely silky coat needs brushing and combing at least every other day to prevent tangles and mats from forming.

The Japanese Chin loves to play and will demand a couple of play sessions every day. Those, along with a nice walk, will satisfy this breed's exercise needs.

This dog should attend a puppy socialization class where she can meet a variety of people, as the breed is a bit wary of strangers. She is not aggressive or protective, just aloof with people she doesn't know. Some owners say she's even catlike. The Japanese Chin is also very bright and enjoys learning new things. She will thrive in gentle, fun, yet structured training and will do well with trick training. Many Japanese Chins serve as wonderful therapy dogs.

The Chin is great for someone who wants a small, relatively calm companion. She is good with children who are gentle and treat her with respect, but is too small for rough play. She is usually very good with other small pets. The breed does have some health concerns, including cataracts, knee and back problems, and heart disorders.

## Breed in Brief

**Registries:** AKC, UKC, CKC
**Occupation:** Companion
**Size:** 8 to 11 in tall; 4 to 11 lbs
**Longevity:** 12 to 14 years
**Exercise:** Low activity level
**Training:** Easy
**Grooming:** Moderate

# Kai Ken

This is a very old hunting breed from the Japanese island of Honshu. Although not very large, these dogs hunted a variety of game, even wild boar. The Japanese people designated the Kai Ken as a national treasure in 1934 and, as such, all dogs are protected by law.

This breed stands from 17 to 22 inches tall and weighs 30 to 40 pounds. The head is wedge-shaped, with small, dark eyes and upright ears. The body is sturdy, and the tail curls up over the hips. The coat is double and does shed. All Kai Ken are brindle, although the colors can vary from red brindle to brown and even black brindle.

The coat needs brushing twice a week; make sure to get through the thick coat to the skin. During the worst shedding, usually in spring and fall, the coat may need to be brushed daily.

The Kai Ken needs daily exercise; however, since the breed retains its hunting instincts, all exercise should be within a fenced-in yard or on leash. The fence should be away from any overhanging trees, as this breed is known to climb trees capably.

Socialization should begin early in puppyhood and continue on into adulthood. Training, preferably in a group class, is helpful for socialization as well as behavior. Training should be structured yet fun. Breed expert Pam Peterson says, "The Kai Ken is intelligent, loyal to owners yet aloof with strangers, and very easy to housetrain."

This is not a city dog; he rarely does well in the hustle and bustle of an urban environment. The Kai Ken needs an owner who understands northern and spitz-type breeds. A Kai Ken is devoted and loyal to his family and watchful of strangers. He will thrive with attention and will do best when he can spend time with his owner. The breed is good with children who treat the dog with respect. Although Kai Ken may be good with smaller pets, owners should keep in mind that this breed was bred to hunt and retains those hunting instincts. This is a healthy breed.

## Breed in Brief

**Registries:** AKC FSS, UKC
**Occupation:** Hunter
**Size:** 17 to 22 in tall; 30 to 40 lbs
**Longevity:** 12 to 14 years
**Exercise:** Active
**Training:** Moderate; socialization is crucial
**Grooming:** Moderate; sheds

# Kangal Dog

The Kangal Dog is a native of Turkey, where it has been used to protect livestock for centuries. Of mastiff descent, the breed's isolation in the harsh Kangal District kept the Kangal Dog's development pure and free of cross-breeding. The native people of this region boast of the breed's ability to keep livestock safe from wolves, jackals, and other predators.

This is a large breed, standing 28 to 34 inches tall and weighing 90 to 140 pounds. The head is large and broad with dropped ears. The body is slightly longer than the dog is tall at the shoulders. The tail is curled and often carried high. The double coat is short and thick. Coat color can be fawn to gray with a black facial mask and ears.

The thick coat should be brushed twice a week, although when the undercoat is being shed, usually twice a year, daily brushing may be needed.

Kangal Dogs need daily exercise. When protecting livestock, they alternate between calm watchfulness and bursts of energy, and this can be reflected in their activity levels as pets. All exercise should be within a fenced-in yard or on leash, as this breed does enjoy running. As with many livestock protection dogs, this breed tends to be nocturnal.

Training is necessary and needs to be structured and firm, yet also fun, as Kangal Dogs who feel pushed will shut down and refuse to react. Breed expert Kathy Lambert says, "They need the boundaries for behavior that training can provide; a spoiled Kangal is a recipe for disaster." Socialization is also important, as these are, by nature, very watchful animals.

The Kangal Dog has been a livestock protection dog for centuries and needs a home where he can work. The owner must be willing to train him and be the dog's leader. Kangal Dogs are usually good with children who treat them with respect, although they will not tolerate rough handling. The primary health concern is hip dysplasia.

## Breed in Brief

**Registries:** UKC
**Occupation:** Livestock guardian
**Size:** 28 to 34 in tall; 90 to 140 lbs
**Longevity:** 10 to 12 years
**Exercise:** Moderate
**Training:** Hard to keep challenged
**Grooming:** Easy; sheds

# arelian Bear Dog

The Karelian Bear Dog (KBD) is an old breed that originated in the region of Karelia in northern Europe. These fearless dogs were used to hunt big game, including elk, bears, and wolves. Thousands of years ago, people and their dogs migrated from Karelia into what is now known as Finland, where the dog is still popular. Although this breed resembles the Russo-European Laika and shares a history, breed expert Gail Rasanen says that modern KBDs crossed with Laikas are considered mixed breeds.

These handsome dogs stand 19 to 23 inches tall and weigh between 44 and 50 pounds. The head is wedge-shaped, with small eyes and upright ears. The body is medium-sized and sturdy. The tail curls over the back. The coat is double with a thick, soft undercoat and a stiff, short to medium-length outer coat. The dogs are black with white markings.

The coat should be brushed thoroughly once a week, with the brush and comb going all the way through the undercoat. The undercoat does shed twice a year, and daily brushing is needed during the shedding seasons.

## Breed in Brief

**Registries:** AKC FSS, UKC, CKC

**Occupation:** Hunter

**Size:** 19 to 23 in tall; 44 to 50 lbs

**Longevity:** 10 to 12 years

**Exercise:** Vigorous daily exercise

**Training:** Moderate to challenging

**Grooming:** Easy; sheds

This active breed needs vigorous daily exercise. He can run alongside a bicycle, go jogging, or chase a tennis ball. Without enough exercise, he can be destructive. All exercise should be on leash or within a fenced-in yard, as this is a motivated hunting dog, and if an animal is scented, he will go after it.

Training the KBD can be a challenge. Rasanen says, "Training should be consistent and firm, but with love and consequence. It should be clear who the leader is." Training should begin early so that the puppy grows up understanding the household rules. Socialization should also begin early, as these dogs are wary of strangers.

This breed needs an experienced dog owner; it is too much for a first-time dog owner. This breed can also be dog-aggressive. When raised with children, KBDs can be very devoted. They should not be trusted with smaller pets. Some eye disorders have been noted recently.

# Keeshond

Keeshonden (the plural of Keeshond) became popular in Europe in the 17th century as watchdogs on barges and riverboats. Most likely descendants of spitz-type dogs in Germany or Russia, they became associated with a political party in Holland in the late 1700s. The breed was popular while that party was in power but lost that popularity when the political winds changed. Luckily, the breed retained many fans and quickly regained favor elsewhere in Europe.

The Keeshond stands 17 to 18 inches tall and weighs between 30 and 45 pounds. He has a foxlike face with upright ears and black markings around the eyes. The tail is plumed and curves over the back. The coat, one of the breed's distinctive features, is double, with a thick undercoat and a profuse outer coat that stands out from the body. The coat is gray and black with silver and cream touches.

The Keeshond's coat is not prone to matting unless the dog picks up burrs or foxtails, but it still requires twice weekly brushing with a pin brush. During shedding season, daily brushing may be needed.

This breed has moderate exercise needs and enjoys daily walks, brisk jogs, and training sessions on the agility course. Keeshonden have done well in agility competition.

The Keeshond Club of America recommends basic obedience training for all dogs. This breed is bright and easy to train and is not prone to trouble as long as training begins early and the lessons are structured but fun. Used as a watchdog in the past, the breed retains an alarm-dog quality, barking when trespassers approach. The breed is not aggressive and, when socialized as a puppy, is very friendly.

The Keeshond is a wonderful family dog, great with kids, other dogs, and small pets. Bred as companion dogs, they take this job seriously and are not happy when left alone for too long each day. The primary health concerns include hip dysplasia, heart disease, thyroid problems, and epilepsy.

## Breed in Brief

**Registries:** AKC, UKC, CKC
**Occupation:** Alarm dog, companion
**Size:** 17 to 18 in tall; 30 to 45 lbs
**Longevity:** 12 to 14 years
**Exercise:** Moderate
**Training:** Easy
**Grooming:** Moderate; sheds

# Kerry Blue Terrier

The Kerry Blue Terrier is an Irish breed that is supposed to have some Irish Wolfhound, some spaniel, perhaps some Poodle, and maybe even a little herding dog in its ancestry. This is all conjecture because the breed's actual ancestry is unknown. What is known, however, is the versatility of the breed. These dogs were (and still are) used as all-purpose dogs who hunt birds as well as vermin, herd livestock, and guard the farm and family.

The Kerry Blue Terrier is a long-legged terrier, standing 17 to 21 inches tall and weighing 30 to 45 pounds. He has a long head with a large nose, small dark eyes, and ears that are high on the head and fold forward. The body is sturdy, the chest is deep, and the tail is straight and erect. The coat is soft, dense, and wavy and varies from black on young puppies to blue-gray or even silver on adults.

The coat requires specific care. It must be brushed and combed twice weekly and after every romp in tall grass, as the soft coat will pick up dirt, burrs, and grass seeds. A monthly trim or haircut is also recommended. Potential owners should discuss grooming needs with a breeder prior to buying a Kerry.

## Breed in Brief

**Registries:** AKC, UKC, CKC
**Occupation:** Versatile farm dog
**Size:** 17 to 21 in tall; 30 to 45 lbs
**Longevity:** 10 to 12 years
**Exercise:** Active
**Training:** Hard to keep challenged
**Grooming:** Difficult

This breed is quite active and needs vigorous daily exercise. A daily run is great exercise, as are canine sports. Many Kerrys have been successful in agility, flyball, tracking, and herding.

Kerry Blue Terriers are bright and curious but can also be independent and stubborn. Early training can help teach them household rules, but do expect some challenges, especially during adolescence. Early socialization, especially to other dogs, is very important, as males can be dog-aggressive.

This breed needs an owner who is willing to be the dog's leader, as this breed is prone to take advantage of a soft owner. Kerrys are great family dogs and enjoy playing kids' games. The breed can be aggressive toward cats and other small pets. Health concerns include eye and ear problems, hip dysplasia, and immune system disorders.

# Komondor

The Komondor is an old breed from Hungary. Although written records are nonexistent, legends detail the breed's long use as a livestock protection dog. Today, the Komondor still protects flocks of sheep in the hills of Hungary but has also found a home protecting sheep in the western U.S.

The Komondor is large, standing no less than 25.5 inches tall for females and no less than 27.5 inches for males. Females weigh 75 to 85 pounds, and males usually weigh about 100 pounds. The dog has substantial bone and is muscular. The coat is white and, in mature dogs, corded. (The cords are tangles of fur that form hanging mats.)

Anyone who is thinking of sharing a home with a Komondor should discuss the coat's unique grooming needs with a breeder, as the cords require very specific care. If the dog gets wet, it can take two days for him to dry! The cords can also trap dirt.

Komondor puppies can be active and playful, but adults are calmer. A couple of brisk walks and a play session each day will keep this dog happy.

As a livestock protection dog, the Komondor is used to thinking for himself. He can be independent. However, with upbeat, fun, and structured training techniques, he is trainable and can learn to enjoy training. Many compete successfully in dog sports, including agility. Early socialization is vital, as this breed is wary of strangers and can be very protective.

This breed may be too much for a first-time dog owner. He will do best in a home with a knowledgeable owner who is not too meek and who understands his coat care needs. The Komondor is gentle and watchful of his family's children but may mistake rough play for something more sinister. The breed is protective and will bark at perceived threats; this can cause problems with neighbors. He is good with other dogs in the family but may be aggressive toward strange dogs. Health concerns include bloat, torsion, and hip dysplasia.

## Breed in Brief

**Registries:** AKC, UKC, CKC
**Occupation:** Livestock guardian
**Size:** Females: 25.5+ in; 75 to 85 lbs
Males: 27.5+ in; 100 lbs
**Longevity:** 10 to 12 years
**Exercise:** Moderate
**Training:** Moderate
**Grooming:** Corded coat; difficult

# uvasz

The history of this breed is shrouded in mystery. Some experts believe that the breed originated in Asia more than 5,000 years ago, while others think the breed is descended from Tibetan Mastiffs imported into Hungary. In any case, the Kuvasz has been treasured in Hungary as a livestock guardian and protective companion since the 1400s.

Kuvaszok (the plural of Kuvasz) stand 24 to 30 inches tall and weigh between 70 and 110 pounds. The head is long, the eyes are slanted, and the ears are small, triangular, and dropped. The tail is long. The white coat has a wooly undercoat and a long outer coat that is shorter on the face, lower legs, and feet.

The coat should be brushed or combed twice weekly. When the dog is shedding, the thick undercoat should be thoroughly brushed every other day.

This breed is active, bright, and curious. Walks are great, as they provide opportunities for socialization. But these dogs also need more vigorous exercise in the form of a jog, game of catch, or training session on the agility course. A young Kuvasz who does not get enough exercise will get into trouble.

The Kuvasz Club of America recommends early training and socialization in a puppy kindergarten class. Training can be a challenge, as Kuvaszok are intelligent but can also be independent and stubborn. Training should be structured and firm to help establish the owner as a leader, yet also fun enough to keep the dog interested. Early socialization is needed to balance the breed's natural protective instincts. An undersocialized dog may be shy and fearful.

This breed needs an experienced dog owner—a person who can be a leader. He also needs someone who enjoys a canine shadow and who will spend time with him. Kuvaszok are not happy spending hours alone. A Kuvasz is great with the family's children but will not tolerate rough play from visitors. Health concerns include hip dysplasia, eye disorders, and thyroid disease.

## Breed in Brief

**Registries:** AKC, UKC, CKC
**Occupation:** Livestock guardian
**Size:** 24 to 30 in tall; 70 to 110 lbs
**Longevity:** 9 to 11 years
**Exercise:** Moderate to active
**Training:** Challenge
**Grooming:** Moderate

# Labradoodle

## (Miniature, Medium, and Standard; Fleece Coat and Wool Coat)

## Breed in Brief

**Registries:** Australian Labradoodle Association, Australian Labradoodle Club of America

**Occupation:** Companion, service dog

**Size:** Mini:14 to 16 in tall; 15 to 25 lbs
Medium: 17 to 20 in tall; 30 to 45 lbs
Standard: 21 to 24 in tall; 50 to 65 lbs

**Longevity:** 12 to 14 years

**Exercise:** Most are active, but exercise needs vary

**Training:** Needs vary

**Grooming:** Moderate

The Labradoodle originated in Australia when a school for training dogs for the vision-impaired received a request for a dog from a woman whose husband was allergic to dogs. To try to suit her needs, a Labrador Retriever was crossed with a white Standard Poodle, and the offspring were called Labradoodles. After that beginning, a number of breeders became involved, but the crosses were not limited to the original two breeds. Poodles of all three sizes were used, along with Irish Water Spaniels and Curly Coated Retrievers, as well as American and English Cocker Spaniels. In the United States (and other countries), Labradoodles are still primarily crosses between Labrador Retrievers and Poodles, usually Standard Poodles.

The Australian Labradoodle Association and Australian Labradoodle Club of America are trying to establish a breed standard with the goal of getting the breed recognized as a pure breed. Their goal is to produce a dog in three sizes (Standard, Medium, and Miniature) with two coat types (fleece and wool). Until they gain the cooperation of the majority of breeders, conformation (such as height, head shape, ear size and position, and coat type) can vary depending upon the crosses used to produce each individual dog.

Although many Labradoodles are advertised as nonshedding and hypoallergenic, there is still too much variety among these dogs to make that statement accurately. Most dogs do have a lush coat that needs brushing and combing two or three times a week.

Many Labradoodles have served successfully as service dogs, but most are family pets. Since the breed is still in its formative stages, it is impossible to predict the dogs' needs regarding grooming, training, exercise, or health concerns, and every dog should be regarded as an individual. Happily, the majority of Labradoodles are bright, intelligent, attractive dogs who have the potential to be wonderful family pets.

# abrador Retriever

The Labrador Retriever originated in Newfoundland, Canada. Small water dogs were used to retrieve birds and fish; they even pulled small boats through the water. Their strong desire to work, versatility, and waterproof coats impressed fishermen, one of whom brought a dog back to England with him. Lord Malmsbury saw this dog, then called a St. John's Dog, and imported several from Newfoundland. Lord Malmsbury is credited with having started to call the dogs Labradors, although the reason is lost to history. Eventually, the English quarantine stopped additional imports from coming into the country, and the Labradors already in England were cross-bred to other retrievers. However, breed fanciers soon put a stop to that, and the breed as we know it today was born.

The Lab is a medium-sized, strongly built dog that retains its hunting and working instincts. Standing between 21.5 and 24.5 inches tall and weighing between 55 and 80 pounds, with females smaller than males, the breed is compact and well-balanced. Labs have short, weather-resistant coats that can be yellow, black, or chocolate. The head is broad, the eyes are friendly, and the tail is otterlike.

Grooming a Lab is not difficult, although it is amazing how much the coat can shed at times. Shedding is worst in spring and fall when the short, dense undercoat and coarser outer coat lose all the dead hair. Brushing daily during these times will lessen the amount of hair in the house.

Labs do everything with vigor. When it's time to play, they play hard. When it's time to take a nap, they do that with enthusiasm, too. But this desire to play and instinct to work means that Labs need vigorous exercise every day and a job to do. They need to bring in the newspaper every

morning, learn to pick up their toys, and train in obedience. Labs do very well in many canine activities, including agility, flyball, field tests and trials, tracking, search-and-rescue work, and therapy dog work. Labs still enjoy swimming, and if water is available, a swim is a great way to burn off excess energy.

Early socialization and training can teach a Lab puppy household rules and social manners. Training should continue throughout puppyhood and into adulthood so that the Lab's mind is kept busy. She can learn advanced obedience, tricks, or anything else her owner wishes to teach her.

Labrador Retrievers are great family dogs. They will bark when people approach the house but are not watchdogs or protective. Puppies are boisterous and rambunctious and need to be taught to be gentle with young children. Older kids will enjoy the Lab's willingness to play. Most Labs are also good with other dogs and can learn to live with small pets, although interactions should be supervised. Health concerns include hip and elbow dysplasia, knee problems, eye problems, and allergies.

## Breed in Brief

**Registries:** AKC, UKC, CKC
**Occupation:** Hunter, companion, performance sports
**Size:** 21.5 to 24.5 in tall; 55 to 80 lbs
**Longevity:** 11 to 13 years
**Exercise:** Moderate
**Training:** Easy; a challenge to keep motivated
**Grooming:** Easy

# akeland Terrier

This English breed originated in the Cumberland region in the 1800s. Her ancestors probably include the Border Terrier and the Bedlington Terrier, although experts believe that other terriers may also have been used. Her primary occupation was to hunt the foxes that would prey on the farmer's sheep during lambing season.

The Lakeland Terrier stands 14 to 15 inches tall and weighs between 15 and 17 pounds. Her head is broad and muzzle is strong. The eyes are small, and the ears are folded forward. The body is as long as the dog is tall at the shoulders. The tail is docked and carried erect. The coat is double, with a soft undercoat and a wiry outer coat. Acceptable colors include wheaten, red, liver, and black.

This coat requires twice weekly brushing and combing to remove dirt and dead hair and to prevent matting. The coat needs trimming once a month. Potential owners should discuss coat care and grooming needs with a breeder prior to purchasing a Lakeland Terrier.

This active breed needs daily exercise. Although a Lakeland will have fun on walks, she will also enjoy jogging, playing flyball, and training on the agility course. These dogs are busy and, if left alone too long, will find ways to amuse themselves. All exercise should be on leash or inside a fenced yard, as these dogs are instinctive hunters and love a good chase.

The Lakeland is bright and intelligent but is also independent and can be stubborn. Early training and socialization are important, but the training process can be challenging. Training should be structured yet fun, and the owner consistent and patient.

This breed needs an active, involved owner who understands the terrier temperament. Although usually good with children, this dog tends to bond more strongly with one owner than with the entire family. Lakelands are normally good with other pets in the family. This is a healthy breed but can suffer from Legg-Perthe's disease.

## Breed in Brief

**Registries:** AKC, UKC, CKC
**Occupation:** Hunter
**Size:** 14 to 15 in tall; 15 to 17 lbs
**Longevity:** 12 to 14 years
**Exercise:** Active
**Training:** Challenge
**Grooming:** Breed-specific needs

# Large Munsterlander

The Large Munsterlander is a hunting dog that originated in Germany from a variety of other breeds, including pointers and other bird dogs. It used to be known as a color variety of the German Longhair Pointer; however, in the early 1900s, the Large Munsterlander was recognized as an individual breed in Germany.

The Large Munsterlander stands between 23 and 26 inches tall and weighs 53 to 76 pounds. The head is long, with medium-sized eyes and broad, dropped ears. The body is as long as the dog is tall at the shoulders. The tail is long. The coat was developed as protection against briars and brambles in the field and is medium in length, black and white, with feathering on the legs, belly, tail, and ears. There can be differences in height, weight, and other characteristics, as this breed was bred specifically for its hunting abilities rather than as a show dog.

This breed needs twice weekly brushing and combing. Although the coat is relatively easy to care for, it can tangle, especially if the dog has been hunting or swimming.

These dogs are quite active and need daily exercise. They also need something to do; if not used for hunting, they need a chance to train in agility, learn tracking, or play flyball. A Large Munsterlander who does not get enough exercise can easily get into trouble. All exercise should be on leash or within a fenced-in yard.

This breed is not difficult to train, although she can be easily distracted by the scent or sight of birds. Training should be structured but fun. The breed can be quite vocal, which can cause neighborhood problems. Although these dogs are by nature friendly with other people and dogs, early socialization is nevertheless important.

The Large Munsterlander is still very much a hunting dog and does best in a home where she is used for that purpose. She is great with children, other dogs, and other small pets. The primary health concern is hip dysplasia.

## Breed in Brief

**Registries:** UKC
**Occupation:** Hunter
**Size:** 23 to 26 in tall; 53 to 76 lbs
**Longevity:** 10 to 12 years
**Exercise:** Vigorous daily exercise
**Training:** Needs a job or purpose
**Grooming:** Easy to moderate

# eonberger

The history of this German breed is full of mystery, as various historians have published conflicting versions of the breed's beginnings. Most agree that Landseer (black and white) Newfoundlands and Saint Bernards were foundation breeds, but the other breeds (including the Great Pyrenees, Pyrenean Mountain Dog, and others) are uncertain. One interesting fact is that this giant breed was bred primarily as a companion; most German dogs were bred to work.

These dogs stand 25.5 to 31.5 inches tall and weigh between 100 and 135 pounds. This is a strong, well-balanced breed with a big head that is longer than it is wide. The eyes are brown, the ears are dropped, and the muzzle is black. The tail is long and plumed. The breed has a double coat. The outer coat is medium to long in colors including gold, red, reddish-brown, and brown, all with or without black tips.

The Leonberger Club of America says, "Leos can cover your house with a lot more fur than a smaller dog can. Their fur can jam your vacuum cleaner many times over!" These dogs should be brushed two or three times per week, or more when shedding heavily.

This very intelligent, active, playful breed needs companionship, daily exercise, and something to keep the mind busy. Many do well as therapy, search-and-rescue, and water rescue dogs. When left alone too long, young Leos can be destructive. The Leonberger Club of America recommends using interactive toys (such as those that dispense treats) to keep puppies amused when left alone.

This breed thrives with gentle, patient, and firm yet fun training. Early socialization is also important, as Leos are wary of strangers.

Leos do best with owners who enjoy spending time with affectionate dogs and who want to do things with them. Leos are very good with children and are usually good with other pets, too. The breed has some drug sensitivities and can have problems with hip and elbow dysplasia, bloat, and Addison's disease.

## Breed in Brief

**Registries:** AKC FSS, UKC, CKC
**Occupation:** Companion
**Size:** 25.5 to 31.5 in tall; 100 to 135 lbs
**Longevity:** 10 to 12 years
**Exercise:** Busy and active
**Training:** Fun yet firm
**Grooming:** Sheds!

# Lhasa Apso

*I*n its native Tibet, the Lhasa Apso is known as Apso Seng Kyi, or Bearded Lion Dog. Lhasas were bred for hundred of years as companions and watchdogs for Buddist monasteries and Tibetan nobility.

The Lhasa Apso stands 10 to 11 inches tall and weighs between 14 and 15 pounds. The eyes are dark, the ears are hanging, and the body is slightly longer than it is tall. The tail is carried over the back. The coat is the breed's glory—thick, heavy, and straight. The coat is long and is parted in the middle of the skull, with the part continuing down the dog's back to the tail. In show dogs, the coat may drag on the floor. All colors are acceptable.

The coat requires considerable care and should be brushed and combed daily, especially if kept long. Many pet owners keep the coat trimmed to a shorter, more manageable length, but even when short, the coat must be combed daily to keep it clean and to prevent mats from forming. Particular care is needed to keep the eyes, ears, and mouth clean, as well as the feet and genitals.

Although Lhasa Apso puppies are quite playful, adults are calm. A daily walk and a play session will satisfy most dogs.

Training should begin early. Although bred to be companion dogs, Lhasa Apsos can have an independent and slightly stubborn nature. Training needs to be structured but fun and playful. Housetraining can take time; owners must be consistent and patient. Wary of strangers, these dogs require early socialization.

Lhasa Apsos are first and foremost companion dogs and are not happy when left alone too much. They are excellent with single adults who live by themselves. Lhasas can be good with children who treat them with respect, but they will not tolerate rough play or handling. They are watchdogs but are not overly yappy. Health concerns include eye problems, kidney disease, and allergies.

## Breed in Brief

**Registries:** AKC, UKC, CKC
**Occupation:** Watchdog, companion
**Size:** 10 to 11 in tall; 14 to 15 lbs
**Longevity:** 12 to 14 years
**Exercise:** Low activity level
**Training:** Challenge to housetrain
**Grooming:** Difficult

# Louisiana Catahoula Leopard Dog

This American breed is the Louisiana State Dog and is just as unique as that state. The breed's ancestry is not known for certain, but experts think that Native American dogs, red wolves, Spanish explorers' mastiffs, and probably even the French Beauceron all contributed genetics to the breed. This versatile breed is used for guarding the home and farm, herding livestock, and hunting.

Breed experts stress that the Catahoula is first and foremost a working dog, and her body conformation should reflect this focus. Most Catahoulas stand between 20 and 26 inches tall and weigh between 50 and 85 pounds. The head is strong, and the eyes are medium in size and may be any color or combination of colors. The body is slightly longer than tall and is strong without being bulky. The tail extends to the hock. The single short coat may be leopard-colored, brindle, or solid.

The coat is easy to care for and needs only weekly brushing.

This is an active breed with strong working instincts. The Catahoula needs daily exercise and will run alongside a bicycle, play on the agility course, or enjoy herding. She is calm in the house but is not a couch potato.

Early training and socialization are very important. Structured, firm, yet fair and fun training can help establish the owner as the dog's leader, and socialization can help the dog adjust to a variety of people. Although affectionate with their owners, Catahoulas are aloof, wary, and sometimes even intolerant of strangers. Catahoulas need a job to do, whether it's herding cattle, keeping rats out of the barn, or doing search-and-rescue work.

This breed needs an experienced dog owner who has a plan for the dog. When kept as pets with no occupation, Catahoulas can become frustrated and will get into trouble. They are good with the family's children but will not like rough play from visitors. The primary health concerns include deafness, eye disorders, and hip dysplasia.

## Breed in Brief

**Registries:** AKC FSS, UKC
**Occupation:** Versatile working dog
**Size:** 20 to 26 in tall; 50 to 85 lbs
**Longevity:** 11 to 13 years
**Exercise:** Active
**Training:** Needs training and socialization
**Grooming:** Easy

# Maltese

This breed has a distinguished history going back more than twenty-eight centuries in Malta. The tiny white dogs were so celebrated that poems were written about them, paintings were made, and stories told. The early Greeks built tombs for their Maltese, and numerous pieces of ceramic art depict dogs that look much like today's Maltese.

These toy dogs stand between 5 and 8 inches tall and weigh 4 to 7 pounds. The head is slightly rounded on top, the eyes are round and dark, and the ears are hanging and covered with long hair. The tail is a long plume that is carried over the back. The coat is long, flat, and silky. It hangs to the ground and is pure white. There is no undercoat.

The Maltese's wonderful coat must be brushed daily with a pin brush; make sure to go through the coat to the skin and not just brush over the top hairs. Particular care must be taken with the coat's cleanliness around the eyes, ears, mouth, feet, and genitals. Although the long, white coat is beautiful, many pet owners have their dogs trimmed shorter for ease of care.

This breed is quite playful, even as an adult, but is not overly active. Maltese are companion dogs and are happy to snuggle and cuddle. Daily walks and a play session or two will satisfy this breed's exercise requirements.

## Breed in Brief

**Registries:** AKC, UKC, CKC
**Occupation:** Companion
**Size:** 5 to 8 in tall; 4 to 7 lbs
**Longevity:** 13 to 15 years
**Exercise:** Low activity level
**Training:** Challenge to housetrain
**Grooming:** Difficult

Training should begin early, as the Maltese can be a challenge to housetrain. The American Maltese Association recommends crate training for housetraining and for keeping the tiny puppy safe. It also prevents other problem behaviors, including chewing. Potential owners should understand that housetraining a tiny dog requires consistency and patience.

The Maltese is a companion dog and is happiest when able to spend time with his owner. Although he can be good with children who handle him gently, most breeders will not sell a puppy to a family with young children, as the puppies are fragile. Health concerns include liver and trachea problems, hypoglycemia, and allergies.

# Manchester Terrier
## (Standard and Toy)

The Manchester Terrier is a ratter, bred to hunt and dispatch rats. A cross between a Whippet and an unknown terrier, the breed quickly became the favorite of anyone in need of vermin control, and in the early 1800s in England, that was just about every business owner who handled or served food. Until 1959, the Manchester Terrier and Toy Manchester Terrier were registered as two separate breeds, although interbreeding was permissible; however, today they are registered as one breed with two sizes.

The Manchester Terrier is sleek and elegant, yet sturdy. The two varieties are divided by weight, with toys weighing no more than 12 pounds. The standards weigh between 12 and 22 pounds. The head is long and narrow, and the eyes are small. The toys have naturally erect ears, while the standards may have naturally erect or cropped ears. The tail tapers to the hock. The coat is short and smooth. The only acceptable color is black with rich mahogany markings.

Grooming this breed consists of a weekly brushing with a soft bristle brush.

Manchester Terriers are active and playful and enjoy brisk walks, a game of catch, and a session of flyball, but they also like to cuddle and are happy to snuggle up with their owner on the sofa. Many enjoy canine sports.

These dogs are not as tenacious as some other terrier breeds, but they can still be a touch independent and stubborn when they wish to be. Training should be structured and firm, but with fun mixed in so that the dog wants to cooperate. This breed can be wary of strangers, so early socialization is a good idea.

Manchesters do best with owners who understand the terrier temperament. These dogs can be great with kids, as Manchesters love to play; however, they will not tolerate rough handling. This breed is usually good with other dogs but should not be trusted with smaller pets. Health concerns include a sensitivity to anesthetics, von Willebrand disease, and thyroid disease.

## Breed in Brief

**Registries:** AKC, UKC, CKC
**Occupation:** Vermin hunter
**Size:** Toy: no height standard; up to 12 lbs
Standard: no height standard; 12 to 22 lbs
**Longevity:** 12 to 14 years
**Exercise:** Moderate
**Training:** Moderate
**Grooming:** Easy

# Mastiff

The Mastiff, also called the Old English Mastiff, is a giant breed that has been claimed by the English as a native breed. The Romans, when invading England, were amazed by the ability and courage of these dogs as the British fought the invaders. The dogs stood by their owners' sides even during the worst of the fighting. Mastiffs were also used to protect land against trespassers and poachers and to control wolves.

Giant dogs, Mastiffs stand 27.5 to 30 inches or taller, with weight in proportion to height. The head is large and broad, with medium-sized eyes, a short, broad muzzle, and dropped ears. The body is longer than the dog is tall and is massive, with heavy bone. The tail reaches the hocks. The outer coat is short and coarse, while the undercoat is dense. The coat is fawn, apricot, or brindle, and the muzzle, ears, and nose are black.

This breed's short coat needs weekly brushing with a soft bristle brush.

Mastiff puppies can be clumsy, silly, and playful. Adults are dignified but can retain a sense of playfulness. Jo Ann Horne-Peller says of her Mastiff, "Margaret doesn't demand exercise, but she does love to play for about an hour each day."

Training is very important, as this breed is powerful enough to take advantage of an unwary owner. The training should emphasize self-control for the dog and the owner's leadership skills. Horne-Peller says that her dog loves training but cautions, "Mastiffs are very slow to mature and can be puppylike for a long time." Since the breed was bred to be a watchdog, socialization is critical.

This breed needs an owner who is able to assume a leadership role for the dog. In addition, Horne-Peller says, "Potential owners should know that giant breeds have a shorter life span than other dogs. Mastiffs also slobber and drool, snore, and have no idea they aren't lap dogs!" The breed has some health concerns, including hip and elbow dysplasia, eye problems, cancer, bloat, and torsion.

## Breed in Brief

**Registries:** AKC, UKC, CKC
**Occupation:** Watchdog
**Size:** 27.5 to 30+ in tall; weight proportionate to height
**Longevity:** 8 to 10 years
**Exercise:** Low activity level
**Training:** Essential because of breed's size
**Grooming:** Easy

# i-Ki

## (Erect Ears and Dropped Ears)

The Mi-Ki can trace his roots to the Papillon, Japanese Chin, and Maltese, although there may also be some other small companion breeds in this breed. Bred strictly for companionship, the Mi-Ki is not yet recognized, but the International Mi-Ki Registry says, "Through a strict breeding program, including DNA profiling (through the United Kennel Club, Inc.), we are developing and refining the Mi-Ki into a new 'Made in the USA' pure breed."

The International Mi-Ki Registry's official breed standard says that the Mi-Ki should never exceed 10 inches in height or 10 pounds in weight. The head is rounded, the eyes are large and dark, and the erect or dropped ears should wing out from the head. Heavily fringed ears are preferred. The body is slightly longer than tall. The tail is plumed and carried over the back. The coat is silky, single (with no undercoat), and may be any color.

The coat should be brushed and combed every other day to keep it clean and to prevent matting. Dogs being shown do need a specific trim; potential owners should discuss this with a breeder prior to getting a Mi-Ki. The coat is supposed to be non-shedding, but breed experts say that this characteristic is not yet firmly established throughout the breed.

The Mi-Ki is a very small companion dog who enjoys walks and playtimes outside but should always be kept in the house. These dogs like to play and will often amuse themselves with their toys.

This breed enjoys training that is fun and positive. A very social breed naturally, socialization is needed to prevent possible shyness to strangers later. Many Mi-Ki serve as therapy dogs. As with so many very small dogs, housetraining can take some time.

The Mi-Ki does not do well when left alone for many hours each day; he does best with an owner who is home a lot and wants a tiny canine shadow. Although normally good with children, the Mi-Ki is too small for rough play. Health concerns include luxated patellas, eye problems, and allergies.

## Breed in Brief

**Registries:** International Mi-Ki Registry
**Occupation:** Companion
**Size:** 8 to 10 in tall; 10 lbs or less
**Longevity:** 12 to 14 years
**Exercise:** Low activity level
**Training:** Challenge to housetrain
**Grooming:** Moderate

# Miniature Australian Shepherd

The Miniature Australian Shepherd is a smaller version of the standard Australian Shepherd. Through the standard-sized breed, the smaller one shares the same history and development. However, in the 1960s and '70s, several people began breeding smaller Aussies that stood 14 to 18 inches tall instead of the 18 to 23 inches of the original breed. At one time there was a movement to call these dogs North American Shepherds.

The Miniature Australian Shepherd is an Australian Shepherd in miniature; he is still an intelligent, hard-working, herding dog and is neither a toy nor a lap dog. The eyes are almond-shaped and brown, blue, amber, or marbled. The ears are folded. The body is slightly longer than tall, and the chest is deep. The tail is no longer than 3 inches and is a natural bobtail or docked. The coat is double, with an undercoat that varies according to climate and a medium outer coat. There is feathering on the backs of the legs, the belly, and the neck. Colors include black, red, blue merle, and red merle, with or without white and rust markings.

The coat requires twice weekly brushing, more when the dog is shedding.

This active dog needs daily exercise. Although walks are great socialization, they are nowhere near enough exercise. This breed needs to run and play hard.

This is a bright, intelligent breed, and training can help channel those traits. Early and continued socialization is important, as Mini Aussies are naturally reserved and wary with strangers. These dogs enjoy a variety of canine sports, including agility, flyball, herding, tracking, and search and rescue.

The Mini Aussie needs an involved owner who wants to do things with the dog. An Aussie home alone for too many hours will get into trouble. Although good with children, Aussies do often try to herd them and may nip legs. They are good with smaller pets, although the family cat may not wish to be herded. Health concerns include eye defects and hip dysplasia.

## Breed in Brief

**Registries:** Miniature Australian Shepherd Club of America
**Occupation:** Herder
**Size:** 14 to 18 in tall; weight proportionate to height
**Longevity:** 13 to 15 years
**Exercise:** Vigorous daily exercise
**Training:** Hard to keep challenged
**Grooming:** Sheds

# Miniature Bull Terrier

The development of the Bull Terrier began about 200 years ago in England when the Bulldog and White English Terrier were crossed to create a breed then known as the Bull and Terrier. Some breed experts believe that the Black and Tan Terrier was also an ancestor, as was the Spanish Pointer. Although never one to back down from a challenge, the Bull Terrier was called the White Cavalier for his wonderful temperament. The medium-sized dogs, then ranging from 15 to 17 pounds, became known as Miniature Bull Terriers, while the larger dogs were simply called Bull Terriers.

The Mini Bull is small but is still all Bull Terrier. He stands between 10 and 15 inches tall, and his weight should be in proportion to his height. His head should be long and deep, with a full oval face just like that of his larger cousin. The eyes are small and dark, and the ears are small and erect. The chest is deep and the body muscular. The tail tapers to a fine point. The coat is short and flat. White Mini Bulls should be pure white, while colored Mini Bulls may be of any color.

Grooming consists of a weekly brushing with a soft bristle brush.

The Mini Bull is a moderately active breed. He enjoys brisk walks, a chance to train in agility, and a good romp in the backyard. The breed can be busy and, if left alone for too many hours, also destructive.

Mini Bulls need early training and socialization. Training should be structured and firm, and the owner must establish leadership. The Miniature Bull Terrier Club of America says, "The dogs are active, stubborn (not stupid), and demanding of interaction. They need a firm, intelligent, consistent disciplinarian."

For an owner who understands the breed, a Mini Bull can be a fun, challenging, and sometimes chaotic companion. Mini Bulls can be great with kids but do not understand children's roughhousing. They can be dog-aggressive. Health concerns include eye problems, heart and kidney disease, and deafness.

## Breed in Brief

**Registries:** AKC, UKC, CKC
**Occupation:** Vermin hunter, companion
**Size:** 10 to 15 in tall; weight proportionate to height
**Longevity:** 10 to 13 years
**Exercise:** Moderate
**Training:** Challenge
**Grooming:** Easy

# Miniature Pinscher

This German breed is several hundred years old, and although it resembles the much younger Doberman Pinscher, they are not related. Breed experts say these small dogs, developed as ratters, have German Pinschers, Dachshunds, and Italian Greyhounds in their ancestry.

Miniature Pinschers stand between 10 and 12.5 inches tall and weigh between 8 and 11 pounds. The head is tapered, eyes are oval and dark, and ears are cropped upright or left natural. The body is as long as the dog is tall and is muscular. The tail is docked and erect, and the short coat is red, black, or chocolate. A signature characteristic of the breed is a hackneylike stepping action, with the front legs lifting high and forward with each step.

The coat needs weekly brushing with a soft bristle brush.

The Miniature Pinscher is a high-energy dog with a fearless attitude and a curious intelligence. Without close supervision and vigorous daily exercise, these little dogs will get into trouble. All exercise should be on leash or within a fenced-in yard, as these small dogs like to chase small animals.

Training is very important. Min Pins were bred to work, and training can help channel this work ethic. The training should be structured and firm yet fun. They love to play games and learn tricks. Min Pins also enjoy agility training. Socialization should begin early, too, as the breed is cautious with strangers. They can be very alert watchdogs.

Min Pins today are companion dogs and need to spend time with people. They can, however, take advantage of a soft owner. Although most Min Pins like to play with children (the dogs enjoy the playfulness and busyness of kids), these dogs are very small and fragile. Play with children, especially small children, should be limited and closely supervised. Many breeders will not sell puppies to homes with small children. This breed can be aggressive with other dogs. Health concerns include luxated patellas, Legg-Perthe's disease, and thyroid problems.

## Breed in Brief

**Registries:** AKC, UKC, CKC
**Occupation:** Vermin hunter, companion
**Size:** 10 to 12.5 in tall; 8 to 11 lbs
**Longevity:** 12 to 14 years
**Exercise:** Active
**Training:** Moderate
**Grooming:** Easy

# Miniature Schnauzer

All three of the Schnauzer breeds were developed in the agricultural areas of Wurttemberg and Bavaria in Germany. The Standard Schnauzer was the original breed, and the Miniatures are said to be derived from breeding the Standard with Poodles and Affenpinschers in the late 19th century. History doesn't say why the Miniature was developed or what his original occupation was, although some experts think he was a ratter and mouser. Today, he is a companion dog.

The Miniature should look as much as possible like a smaller version of the Standard Schnauzer. He is sturdy and active, should be between 12 and 14 inches tall at the shoulder, and should weigh between 12 and 16 pounds. He should never appear frail, fragile, or toylike. The eyes are oval and dark, with an alert expression that conveys a willingness to try anything. The ears can be cropped or fold normally in a V-shape. The breed has a double coat, with the undercoat close and soft. The outer coat is hard and wiry. Allowable colors are salt and pepper, black and silver, and solid black.

Grooming the Miniature Schnauzer can be a challenge. Those dogs who compete in the conformation show ring must be hand-stripped. If you wish to do this yourself, ask your dog's breeder for guidance. Most pet dogs are groomed every four to six weeks by professional groomers who use clippers and scissors. Although the Miniature Schnauzer doesn't shed, the dog will need twice weekly combing and brushing to keep the leg feathers from tangling. You may also want to wash and comb the beard regularly, as it can get wet, pick up dirt and debris, and trap bits of food.

Although Miniature Schnauzers are small dogs, they do need regular exercise. A long walk morning and evening will help satisfy those needs, but most young dogs will also need a couple of play sessions during the day. Many Miniature Schnauzers today enjoy participating in a variety of canine sports, especially agility.

Early socialization and training are important for all Miniature Schnauzers. They are by nature loyal and affectionate but can also be standoffish to strangers. Socialization can help the dog learn to accept a variety of people. Getting along with other puppies of the same age is also an important lesson for these sturdy little dogs who don't always understand how small they are. Training will help establish household rules. In addition, Miniature Schnauzers are excellent watchdogs who can sometimes take their job too seriously, barking more than their owners and neighbors might want. Training can help temper those impulses.

Miniature Schnauzers can be wonderful family dogs and are usually quite tolerant of children's antics. Rough play should be discouraged, as the dog may protest being handled disrespectfully. These dogs are loyal and attentive to the entire family and will greet friends with enthusiasm. They do, however, have the tendency to bond tightly with just one person. With early socialization, they can be quite social with other dogs but should not be trusted with small pets. Major health concerns include eye disorders, von Willebrand disease, and allergies.

## Breed in Brief

**Registries:** AKC, UKC, CKC
**Occupation:** Vermin hunter, companion, performance sports
**Size:** 12 to 14 in tall; 12 to 16 lbs
**Longevity:** 14 to 16 years
**Exercise:** Daily walks and playtime
**Training:** Challenge
**Grooming:** Difficult

# ixed-Breed Dog

$\mathcal{M}$ixed-breed dogs have been with people for as long as there have been dogs. The vast majority of breeds today were created from a mixture of older breeds, usually a purposely bred mixture of breeds. This selective breeding was done with a specific purpose in mind—for example, to create a better herding dog or a coonhound with a more sensitive nose.

Today, however, the term "mixed-breed" usually refers to breeding that was an accident. Often called random bred dogs (to differentiate from purposely bred ones), they can be amazing mixes. They may be the result of two purebred dogs of different breeds and therefore show traits of both breeds, or they can be the result of two mixed-breed parents, with no discernable purebred traits.

A purebred puppy is much more of a known entity than a mixed-breed puppy. With a purebred, you know what kind of coat the dog will have and how much grooming you will need to do. You know how big the dog will be when grown and how much exercise he will need. You'll even have a pretty good idea of how easy or difficult it will be to train him. A mixed-breed dog who is the result of two purebred parents will have traits of both breeds. However, if the breeds are dissimilar, traits will be difficult to predict. Now, if the puppy is a result of two mixed-breed parents, well, then, everything is going to be a surprise!

Many people enjoy the surprise of a mixed-breed dog. Watching a puppy grow up, they often try to pinpoint certain traits or physical characteristics, but most of the time they simply enjoy their unique dog. Because that's the other fun part of a mixed-breed—every single one is different. Even puppies in the same litter can be different because each one has its own set of genetics inherited from mom and dad.

Mixed-breed dogs are also reputed to be healthier than purebred dogs; however, that can be both true and false. Any dog, purebred or mixed-breed, is the result of his individual genetics. If the dog's parents, grandparents, and great-grandparents are genetically healthy, then chances are the puppy will be, too. But ultimately, all dogs are also healthy or not because of their care. The quality of the food they eat, the nurturing they receive from their owner, and regular veterinary care will also contribute to how healthy the dog is. That applies to all dogs, no matter what the breed or mixture of breeds.

# Neapolitan Mastiff

The Neapolitan Mastiff claims as her ancestors the war dogs that traversed Europe with the Roman Army. Since that time, Neapolitan Mastiffs have been used as guardians of large estates in Italy.

A male Mastino (a fancier's term for a dog of the breed) stands 26 to 29 inches tall and weighs 140 to 170 pounds. Females are slightly smaller. The body is longer than tall, and the breed is massively built. The head is very large, with deep-set eyes and ears that are usually cropped upright. The tail is normally docked by one-third its length. A characteristic of the breed is the loose skin all over the dog, including the head. The coat is short and dense. Primary colors are gray, black, and mahogany.

Grooming is not difficult; the short coat should be brushed weekly. The wrinkles sometimes need care and cleaning, especially the ones on the face. These dogs do drool, though, and can be messy. Most owners keep a towel at hand to mop up the drool.

Puppies can be quite active and playful. They should not be encouraged to run hard or jump for a ball; doing so could damage their growing bones and joints. Walks and playtimes are sufficient. Adults are generally calm.

## Breed in Brief

**Registries:** AKC, UKC, CKC
**Occupation:** Guardian
**Size:** 26 to 29 in tall; 140 to 170 lbs
**Longevity:** 8 to 10 years
**Exercise:** Low activity level
**Training:** Challenge; needs socialization
**Grooming:** Easy

Since this breed was bred to be watchful and protective, early socialization to a variety of people, dogs, and other animals is vital. Without it, the Mastino can be shy, and that is potentially dangerous. Early training is also important, as this very large, powerful breed could easily overpower an owner. Owners need to assume the role of the dog's leader.

This breed needs an owner who understands what a mastiff is and can handle the breed's natural protectiveness. Interactions with children must be supervised, as children could be inadvertently knocked down or hurt. These dogs are often dog-aggressive, especially with dogs of the same sex. Health concerns include sensitivity to heat, eye defects, heart and thyroid problems, and hip dysplasia.

# Newfoundland

The Newfoundland was developed on the island of Newfoundland on the east coast of Canada. The ancestors of the breed are uncertain. Some breed experts feel that the Great Pyrenees is the primary ancestor breed, while others believe that the Tibetan Mastiff was also an ancestor. In any case, the dogs were bred to the small black water dogs (most likely the same breed that produced Labrador Retrievers), producing a giant dog who was a hard worker on land and an excellent swimmer.

A Newfoundland stands between 26 and 28 inches tall at the shoulder and weighs between 100 and 150 pounds. She is heavily boned, muscular, and strong. Her body is slightly longer than she is tall, her head is large and broad, and the eyes are dark brown. The ears are triangular and folded. The tail is plumed and carried low. The Newfie has a double coat, with the undercoat soft and dense. The outer coat is coarse and moderately long. The backs of the legs are feathered. Coat colors include black, brown (bronze), gray (blue), and black and white.

The coat needs thorough brushing two or three times per week, more during the spring and fall when shedding is at its worst. If the dog spends any time in the water, the coat should be thoroughly dried afterward to help prevent tangles and mats. Most Newfies drool, especially around dinnertime and after drinking.

## Breed in Brief

**Registries:** AKC, UKC, CKC
**Occupation:** Water rescue, draft dog, companion
**Size:** 26 to 28 in tall; 100 to 150 lbs
**Longevity:** 9 to 11 years
**Exercise:** Moderate
**Training:** Bright and intelligent; moderately hard to motivate
**Grooming:** Moderate

The Newfie needs exercise each day, but her requirements are not excessive. A good long walk morning and evening will suffice, as will a chance to go swimming. Young Newfies with excess energy can be creative about getting into trouble and can be destructive chewers.

Training should begin early; a Newfie could easily overpower her owner. Newfie puppies enjoy the socialization of a puppy class and will join in with the play of other puppies. Training and socialization should continue after puppy class; this is a working dog who needs a job to do.

Newfoundlands can be wonderful family dogs. The puppies are big and clumsy and need to be taught to be gentle with small children. They are usually good with other dogs and can be good with small pets, although interactions should be supervised. Health concerns include hip and elbow dysplasia, bloat, torsion, and eye disorders.

# Norrbottenspets

This Swedish spitz-type dog is known in its homeland as an excellent hunting dog, able to handle the long winters and deep snows to hunt birds, moose, and even bears. There are many legends of these dogs chasing away bears who have attacked their owners.

Norrbottenspets are 16.5 to 17.5 inches tall and weigh 25 to 30 pounds. The head is wedge-shaped, with moderately large, almond-shaped eyes and erect ears. The body is as long as the dog is tall at the shoulder. The chest is deep and the body strong. The tail reaches the hocks but is carried high and curls over the back. The undercoat is fine and dense, while the outer coat is hard, short, and straight. All colors are permitted, although white with red patches is the most common.

This coat is easy to care for and requires twice weekly brushing. When the dog is shedding, additional brushing is advisable.

This is an active breed who will run alongside a bicycle or enjoy training on the agility course. A daily run or vigorous game of catch is necessary. A Norrbottenspets who does not get enough exercise will get into trouble. All exercise should be within a fenced yard, as these dogs still love to hunt and have a tendency to wander.

## Breed in Brief

**Registries:** UKC, CKC
**Occupation:** Hunter
**Size:** 16.5 to 17.5 in tall; 25 to 30 lbs
**Longevity:** 16 to 18 years
**Exercise:** Active
**Training:** Moderate
**Grooming:** Easy

Although this breed can be quite independent, Norrbottenspets are intelligent, curious, and can be trained as long as the training is fun yet firm. Many of these dogs are serving admirably as search-and-rescue dogs. When hunting or searching, they have great stamina and work tirelessly. They are not watchdogs, although they can sometimes bark too much during play, which could cause problems with neighbors.

The Norrbottenspets needs an active owner who enjoys working with the dog. Although small to medium in size, this dog is not a lap dog; she needs a job to do. Affectionate and gentle, the breed is great with kids. She may not be trustworthy with smaller pets, though she is usually great with other dogs. This is a healthy, long-lived breed.

# Norwegian Elkhound

This ancient breed has a documented history going back to 4000 B.C. A Scandinavian breed, she was a companion of the Vikings and was used as both a guard dog and a hunting dog. When hunting, the Elkhound does not kill the bear or other large game but instead finds and tracks it, then holds it until the hunter arrives.

This medium-sized dog stands 19.5 to 20.5 inches tall and weighs 48 to 55 pounds. She is square in profile, with her body being the same length as she is tall at the shoulder. Her head is broad and wedge-shaped, her eyes are dark and medium-sized, and her ears are erect. The chest is deep and the body compact. The tail is tightly curled and carried over the back. The gray coat has a dense undercoat and a coarse, straight outer coat.

This coat requires at least twice weekly brushing during most of the year. However, when the dog sheds (twice a year), daily brushing is needed to get out all of the dead coat.

This breed is moderately active. She will enjoy daily walks, a jog, and a chance to romp in the backyard and hunt for small animals in the woodpile, but she is also willing to relax with you in the house. All exercise should be on leash or within a fenced-in yard, as the breed retains those ancient hunting instincts.

The Norwegian Elkhound Association of America says, "Basic obedience training is the key to a well-adjusted dog." Elkhounds are wonderful companion dogs, but they do need to learn that their owner is their leader. Without leadership, an Elkhound can be inventive about getting into trouble. When dog and owner are in tune with their training, this breed can be great fun.

This breed needs an owner who is willing to follow through with training and who can be a leader. A breed who does best when allowed to be a companion, the Elkhound is not a backyard dog. She can be good with children when raised with them. Health concerns include hip dysplasia, eye problems, and kidney defects.

## Breed in Brief

**Registries:** AKC, UKC, CKC
**Occupation:** Hunter, guardian
**Size:** 19.5 to 20.5 in tall; 48 to 55 lbs
**Longevity:** 11 to 13 years
**Exercise:** Moderate
**Training:** Moderate
**Grooming:** Sheds heavily twice a year

# Norwegian Lundehund

The Norwegian Lundehund is a very old breed that originated in the Lofoten Islands. The breed has extra functional toes on the feet, which aids in the dog's ability to climb rocks to retrieve puffins from their nests. When puffins were hunted with nets (instead of with dogs) and then later became protected, the need for the dogs diminished. A distemper outbreak (and lack of vaccine) during World War II almost caused the breed to disappear.

This is a small to medium-sized breed, standing 12.5 to 15 inches tall and weighing 13 to 15.5 pounds. The head is wedge-shaped, the eyes are dark and medium-large, and the ears are upright. There are six toes on each foot, with at least five toes functional on each front paw. The breed has a double coat, and the outer coat is straight and lies flat. The coat is usually reddish brown with black tips.

This coat requires weekly brushing—more during the twice yearly shedding seasons.

This breed is alert, energetic, and needs daily exercise. These dogs like to run and play, and since they love to climb, they do well on the agility course. A bored Lundehund who doesn't get daily exercise will find something to amuse herself, and that can be destructive in nature.

## Breed in Brief

**Registries:** AKC FSS, UKC, CKC

**Occupation:** Puffin hunter, companion

**Size:** 12.5 to 15 in tall; 13 to 15.5 lbs

**Longevity:** 12 to 14 years

**Exercise:** Moderate to active

**Training:** Challenge

**Grooming:** Easy; sheds

Training this breed can be a challenge. The Norwegian Lundehund Club of America says, "Lundehunds are intelligent, cheerful, inquisitive, and stubborn." Training sessions should be short and fun. Incorporate games into the training to keep the dog interested. Housetraining can be tough, and male dogs are prone to marking their territory. Socialization is very important, as undersocialized dogs can be quite shy.

Potential owners should talk with breeders prior to committing themselves to a dog because of the breed's challenging nature. Lundehunds make excellent companion dogs and are fun to be around, but they can be barkers, which can cause difficulties with neighbors. They are also excellent climbers and can be escape artists. Health concerns include gastrointestinal problems.

# Norwich and Norfolk Terriers

Many different terriers originated in England prior to and during the 1800s. Vermin, including rats and small predators, were the prey for most of these working terriers. Frank "Roughrider" Jones, a charismatic dog breeder, developed the breed that became known as the Norwich Terrier. When the first breed standard was written, the erect ear and dropped ear varieties remained one breed, the Norwich. In 1964, the English Kennel Club made them two breeds: the Norwich with erect ears (pictured here) and the Norfolk with dropped ears.

These two terrier breeds are now separate but are still very similar. They stand 9 to 10 inches tall and weigh between 11 and 12 pounds. The head is wide and the eyes small and dark. The body is compact, with wide and rounded ribs. The tail is docked. The coat is hard and straight, with an undercoat. Acceptable colors include red, wheaten, black and tan, and gray.

The coat requires weekly brushing, except during the spring and fall shedding seasons, when the undercoat may need more frequent brushing. The outer coat needs hand-stripping a few times a year; potential owners should discuss this requirement with a breeder prior to buying a puppy.

## Breed in Brief

**Registries:** AKC, UKC, CKC
**Occupation:** Vermin hunter
**Size:** 9 to 10 in tall; 11 to 12 lbs
**Longevity:** 12 to 14 years
**Exercise:** Moderate
**Training:** Moderate
**Grooming:** Moderate to difficult

The Norwich and Norfolk Terrier Club says, "A long walk or vigorous play within the yard for twenty to thirty minutes a day will keep your Norwich or Norfolk happy and fit." Both of these breeds have participated successfully in terrier go-to-ground trials as well as agility and tracking.

Both breeds are receptive to training; however, as terriers, they can be quite independent. Luckily, they are usually food-motivated, which can make training easier. Although watchful and wary of strangers, they are not normally barkers.

A dog of either breed needs an owner who understands the terrier temperament. Both breeds are good with gentle children, although young dogs can be rowdy. These dogs should not be trusted with smaller pets. Health concerns include eye disorders and hip dysplasia.

# Nova Scotia Duck Tolling Retriever

The Nova Scotia Duck Tolling Retriever (or Toller) originated in Nova Scotia in the early 1800s. The breed tolls (or lures) ducks within shooting range of the hunter by playing along the shore. Once the ducks have been shot, the dog then retrieves the birds.

Tollers stand between 17 and 21 inches tall and weigh 40 to 55 pounds. The head is wedge-shaped, the eyes are almond-shaped, and the eye color either blends in with the coat or is dark. The ears are dropped and frame the face. The body is slightly longer than tall, and the chest is deep. The tail reaches the hock. The coat is double, with a water-resistant outer coat and a soft, dense undercoat. The color of the coat is any shade of red.

The coat needs twice weekly brushing for most of the year, but during the spring and fall shedding seasons, daily brushing is needed.

The Toller is a very active, energetic dog who needs vigorous daily exercise. This dog should go for a long run, play fetch, train on the agility course, go swimming, or play flyball. A bored Toller who does not get enough exercise will get into trouble. Although often mistakenly identified as a small Golden Retriever, the Toller is mentally and physically more active than a Golden.

This is a very intelligent breed that needs to learn household rules early; without the guidance of training and an owner who is willing to be a leader, a Toller will take over the household. Training should be fun yet firm, continue into adulthood, and challenge the dog. Tollers need a job to do, such as obedience training, learning tricks, or bringing in the newspaper each morning.

The Toller needs an actively involved, experienced owner who enjoys training and will keep this intelligent dog busy. Tollers are great with children, although puppies can be rowdy. They are normally good with smaller pets. Health concerns include hip dysplasia, eye defects, and thyroid disease.

## Breed in Brief

**Registries:** AKC, UKC
**Occupation:** Hunter
**Size:** 17 to 21 in tall; 40 to 55 lbs
**Longevity:** 11 to 13 years
**Exercise:** Vigorous daily exercise
**Training:** Easy; hard to keep challenged
**Grooming:** Sheds

# Old English Sheepdog

As with so many old utilitarian breeds, the ancestry of the Old English Sheepdog is unknown. Although the breed was developed in the south of England, some experts think the Russian Ovtcharka might have been an ancestor, while others feel the Scottish Bearded Collie was.

This is a large breed, standing 21 to 22 inches tall and weighing 80 to 100 pounds. The dog is strong, square, and well-balanced. His eyes are brown or blue, and his ears are medium-sized and dropped. His body is short and compact. His tail is either a natural bobtail or docked close to the body. His coat is his crowning glory. The undercoat is very thick, and the outer coat is profuse. The coat can be any shade of gray or blue merle with or without white markings.

This breed requires three to four hours of grooming every week. The coat does shed and can easily mat if not cared for correctly. Potential owners should discuss these aspects of ownership with a breeder prior to making a commitment to buy a dog.

Breed expert Diane Buckland of Tarawood Kennels says, "This is not an overly active dog, but it must have daily exercise for proper health. A couple of good walks daily and a run in the backyard are fine." She adds, "The breed is very affectionate; they would prefer to follow you around the house or curl up with you in front of the television."

Since this breed quickly grows to be a large dog, training is very important. Buckland says, "The OES is a very happy-go-lucky type of dog, not too serious about anything. They take to training pretty well, but like children, they like to test us to see what they can get away with."

The OES needs an owner who desires to have a canine shadow; this is not a backyard dog or a dog to be ignored. The breed is good with kids, although puppies can be rough. Old English Sheepdogs are also good with other pets, although they will try to herd cats. Health concerns include hip dysplasia, eye problems, and epilepsy.

## Breed in Brief

**Registries:** AKC, UKC, CKC
**Occupation:** Herder
**Size:** 21 to 22 in tall; 80 to 100 lbs
**Longevity:** 9 to 12 years
**Exercise:** Moderate
**Training:** Moderate
**Grooming:** Difficult, time-consuming

# tterhound

The Otterhound originated in England, and references to the breed have been found dating back to the 1100s, although that early dog was much different from today's Otterhound. The Bloodhound is one of the breed's ancestors.

The breed stands 24 to 27 inches tall and weighs between 70 and 130 pounds. The head is large and narrow, eyes are dark, and ears are long, pendulous, and folded. The chest is deep, and the tail reaches the hock. The undercoat is water-resistant and wooly. The outer coat is dense, rough, and coarse. Any color is acceptable.

The coat should be brushed weekly; it can mat if ignored. Most pet owners trim the hair on the feet, face, genitals, and under the tail for cleanliness. The breed has an oily coat but does not normally have a doggy smell.

This is not an overly busy dog, but he does need daily exercise. He can go for a long walk, swim, and play on the agility course. Otterhounds are not natural retrievers, but many are excellent tracking dogs. All exercise should be on leash or within a fenced-in yard; this breed has a tendency to roam.

Training should begin early, as these are big dogs who could inadvertently overpower an owner. Although Otterhounds are quite bright, silly, and fun, they are not necessarily compliant dogs. They do best when training involves some motivation to get the dog's compliance; most are motivated by food. These large, powerful dogs should meet a variety of people while puppies. The Otterhound Club of America says, "Socialization is just as important as basic obedience training for an Otterhound."

The Otterhound needs an owner who understands how hounds think; they love their owners but are not canine shadows as so many other dogs are. The Otterhound can also be quite loud, which can cause problems with the neighbors. The breed is great with kids, although puppies can be clumsy and rowdy. Health concerns include hip dysplasia, bloat, and bleeding disorders.

## Breed in Brief

**Registries:** AKC, UKC, CKC
**Occupation:** Hunter
**Size:** 24 to 27 in tall; 70 to 130 lbs
**Longevity:** 8 to 10 years
**Exercise:** Active
**Training:** Challenge
**Grooming:** Moderate

# Papillon
## (Erect Ears and Phalene Ears)

The origins of the Papillon (French for *butterfly*) go back centuries in Europe. Papillons were the darlings of royalty in France, Italy, Spain, and even Poland as early as the 1500s. Marie Antoinette was a Papillon owner, as were Madame Pompadour, Louis XIV, and numerous other notables. Dogs looking very similar to today's Papillons are in works of the old Masters, including Boucher, Fragonard, Watteau, Rubens, and other artists. Henry III was so infatuated with his dogs that he named the breed the official dog of the Royal Court. Papillons were first known as Epagneul Nain or Dwarf Spaniel.

The Papillon today is a fine-boned, elegant toy dog, with a happy, alert, and friendly disposition. The height is between 8 and 11 inches, and the weight is between 5 and 10 pounds. The body is slightly longer than the dog's height at the shoulders. The head is carried high and attentively, with dark, round, but not bulging, eyes. The ears are the breed's crowning glory and are large, erect, and feathered with long coat. The ears should look like butterflies. There is a drop-eared version called Phalene, and the ears are the same size and proportion as the erect ear. The Papillon's coat is long, fine, and silky, and there is no undercoat. The base color is always white, with patches of color. The ears and around the eyes must be a color other than white.

The Papillon's lovely silky coat can become matted if it is not brushed and combed every other day. If the dog gets wet (which most Papillons detest), she should be blow-dried and combed to prevent matting.

Papillons are active little dogs and need daily exercise. This can consist of a walk morning and evening, with a playtime in between. Luckily, the breed's small size makes playtime easy. A ball tossed across the room for the dog to retrieve can become an exciting game. But don't let the breed's small size fool you; these little dogs also make great agility dogs and flyball competitors. Papillons love to play games of any kind.

Socialization and training should begin when the dog is young. Papillons are alert little watchdogs, and barking can become a problem. With socialization, they can learn who to bark at and who not to, and training can control the tendency to bark too much. Intelligent dogs, Papillons also need training to challenge their minds. They have excelled in obedience competition, tracking, and many other canine sports.

Papillons are good with the elderly, as they are easy to exercise, are friendly, and, after a game, are willing to cuddle. Although they are usually also friendly with children, they are too fragile for kids who play rough. Most breeders will not sell a Papillon puppy to a family with children under the age of 8 to 10 years. Papillons are also good with other dogs, although interactions should be supervised so that the Papillon isn't injured by rough play. They are good with cats, but interactions with small pets should be supervised, as some Papillons are natural mousers and ratters. Health concerns include knee problems, dental problems, and eye disorders.

## Breed in Brief

**Registries:** AKC, UKC, CKC
**Occupation:** Companion, performance sports
**Size:** 8 to 11 in tall; 5 to 10 lbs
**Longevity:** 14 to 16 years
**Exercise:** Moderate
**Training:** Challenge to housetrain
**Grooming:** Moderate

# Parson Russell Terrier

The Parson Russell Terrier, Jack Russell Terrier, and Russell Terrier have a complicated relationship. The original breed, now referred to as the Jack Russell Terrier, was developed by Reverend John Russell as a fox hunting dog in the mid-1800s in England. He wanted a small, feisty dog able to go down holes after foxes. After the establishment of the breed and its introduction to the U.S., the Jack Russell Terrier Club of America and the Jack Russell Club of Great Britain have been the parent clubs for the breed. When the American Kennel Club and United Kennel Club recognized the breed, the JRTCA opposed the recognition. In 2003, the AKC and the Parson Russell Terrier Association of America (the parent club with the AKC) changed the breed's name to Parson Russell Terrier. The UKC now recognizes both the JRT and the Russell Terrier, a shorter-legged, stockier version of the breed. The Canadian Kennel Club recognizes the Parson Russell Terrier. (For more on the breed's history, see the Jack Russell Terrier profile on pages 272–273.)

Parson Russell Terriers are relatively square in outline, with a body just about as long as the dog is tall. Two hands should be able to fit around the dog's chest behind the elbows with the thumbs at the withers (point of the shoulders) and the fingers touching under the chest. The legs are long and made for running. The dog is predominantly white with black, tan, or tricolor markings. The coat is smooth or broken. The tail is docked.

Grooming the Parson is not difficult; the smooth coat can be brushed twice weekly with a soft bristle brush or curry comb. The broken, wiry coat can be brushed twice weekly with a pin or slicker brush. Neither type of coat mats.

This is an energetic breed designed to run hard and play rough. Vigorous daily exercise is needed. The Parson needs a long walk morning and evening, a fast game of tennis ball catch, and a training session on the agility course. It would be very difficult to give this breed too much exercise! Too little exercise, though, will lead to a bored terrier who will find something to do, most likely to your dismay!

Socialization and training are important for this feisty little terrier. She needs guidance to behave in a manner you can live with; however, the training needs to be challenging (rather than repetitive) and fun or she will get bored very quickly. Parson Russell Terriers excel in many canine sports, including agility and flyball.

Parson Russell Terriers can be very demanding pets; they thrive on attention and are very single-minded. They are not the best dogs for first-time dog owners and do best with someone who understands the terrier temperament. Although they can be good with kids, they can be very pushy and will not tolerate rough handling. They can be feisty with other dogs, and all interactions with other pets should be supervised; remember, these are hunting terriers! The Parson does get along great with horses. Health concerns include eye and knee disorders and obsessive-compulsive behaviors.

## Breed in Brief

**Registries:** AKC, CKC
**Occupation:** Hunter, performance sports
**Size:** 13 to 14 in tall; 13 to 17 lbs
**Longevity:** 14 to 16 years
**Exercise:** Vigorous daily exercise
**Training:** Moderate; hard to keep challenged
**Grooming:** Easy

# Patterdale Terrier

## (Smooth Coat and Rough Coat)

Many tough little terriers originated in northern England, a reflection of the inhospitable land and climate. The Patterdale Terrier (or Black Fell Terrier) was developed to hunt ground-dwelling vermin—foxes in England but often raccoons and badgers in the U.S.—and is a tough, courageous little dog.

This compact, well-balanced terrier stands 10 to 13 inches tall and weighs 10 to 11 pounds. Her head is strong, her ears are button and tight, and two hands should be able to span her chest. The tail is carried high, and, if docked, no more than one-fourth of the tail should be removed. The coat may be smooth or rough, but either coat should be dense and coarse. Acceptable colors include red, chocolate, black, and black and tan.

The coat needs weekly brushing. The rough terrier coat may need hand-stripping. Potential owners should discuss this with a breeder prior to buying a dog.

Breed expert Robert Burns says, "The Patterdale Terrier is not a black Jack Russell Terrier and should not be confused with one. This breed is laid back in the house and not yappish. However, it has a tendency to hunt on its own and is absolutely fearless." The breed needs daily exercise, including long walks, and this exercise should be on leash or within a fenced yard.

Burns says that the breed is receptive to training and is very social with people. These dogs have a desire to work and, when they are motivated to train, will enjoy it. They have participated in terrier go-to-ground trials, enjoy agility training, and do well in tracking. A Patterdale who doesn't get enough exercise and who doesn't have a job to do (or regular training sessions) will get into trouble.

This breed needs an owner who understands terriers, especially a terrier with strong hunting instincts. Burns says the breed is fine with children over about 7 years of age but does not recommend the breed for younger kids. Patterdales are usually good with other dogs. This is generally a healthy breed.

## Breed in Brief

**Registries:** UKC
**Occupation:** Vermin hunter
**Size:** 10 to 13 in tall; 10 to 11 lbs
**Longevity:** 13 to 15 years
**Exercise:** Moderate
**Training:** Moderate
**Grooming:** Easy to moderate

# Pekingese

This is a very old breed known to have been in existence during the Tang Dynasty in China in the 8th century. These small dogs (also called lion dogs or sun dogs) were sacred, and were kept and bred only by the imperial family. When the British looted the Imperial Palace in 1860, several dogs were stolen and taken back to England.

These toy-breed dogs stand 8 to 9 inches tall and weigh 8 to 14 pounds. The head is broad and flat, with wide-set eyes, a broad, short muzzle, and dropped ears. The body is heavier in the forequarters and lighter in the rear. The tail is carried over the back. There is a soft, thick undercoat and a profuse outer coat that stands out from the body. All colors are acceptable.

The coat requires considerable grooming, at least twice a week, but additional grooming is needed when the dog is shedding. The coat will tangle and mat if not brushed thoroughly. Pet owners often have the coat trimmed short for cleanliness and ease of care.

Although puppies are playful, the adult Pekingese is a calm dog. She enjoys walks but has not been bred to be an athlete and will prefer casual walks to brisk ones.

The Pekingese was never a working dog; she was a watchful companion. As a result, training this breed can be a challenge. She is dignified, independent, and amazingly stubborn. When training her, owners must be consistent and very patient. The Peke is aloof with strangers, so early socialization is important. Housetraining can sometimes be a problem.

Potential owners should understand that a Pekingese does not worship her owners as so many breeds do; in fact, the Peke thinks she should be worshipped. She does not always get along with children and will not tolerate rough play. She is not necessarily good with other dogs, either, although she is usually fine with cats. Health concerns include a sensitivity to anesthesia, breathing problems in hot, humid weather, disc disease, and eye problems.

## Breed in Brief

**Registries:** AKC, UKC, CKC
**Occupation:** Companion
**Size:** 8 to 9 in tall; 8 to 14 lbs
**Longevity:** 10 to 12 years
**Exercise:** Low activity level
**Training:** Difficult
**Grooming:** Difficult

# Pembroke Welsh Corgi

This very old breed has been used by the Welsh as a herding dog, guardian of the home and farm, and companion. Experts debate the origins of the breed; some say it is descended from the Swedish Vallhund, while others say the Schipperke is an ancestor.

The Pembroke stands between 10 and 12 inches tall and should weigh no more than 28 to 30 pounds. Her head is foxlike in shape, with oval brown eyes and upright ears. Her body is low-slung and sturdy without being heavy or coarse. Her tail either is a natural bobtail or is docked short. Her coat is of medium length with a thick undercoat. Acceptable colors include red, sable, fawn, and black and tan, all with or without white markings.

Pembroke Welsh Corgis do shed, and twice a year they shed a lot. Although a twice weekly brushing will suffice for most of the year, during shedding seasons, a daily brushing will be needed.

This active breed can go for a long, brisk walk and then play ball with you, or can train on the agility course. This breed also enjoys canine sports, including flyball, herding, and tracking. The Pembroke Welsh Corgi Club of America says, "The Pembroke is an energetic dog, and too much inactivity just might cause him to think up unacceptable activities for himself!"

The Pembroke is by nature a guardian breed and needs early socialization. These dogs should meet a variety of people during puppyhood as well as encounter many different sights and sounds. Early training is also recommended by the national club: "The time you spend in training, especially during the first year of your dog's life, will be repaid many times over by giving you a well-behaved companion."

This breed needs an owner who is willing to socialize and train the dog, and then is eager to do things with her. This breed is usually good with children but sometimes tries to treat the kids (and other pets) like sheep. Health concerns include eye defects, hip dysplasia, disc problems, and bladder stones.

## Breed in Brief

**Registries:** AKC, UKC, CKC
**Occupation:** Herder, guardian
**Size:** 10 to 12 in tall; 28 to 30 lbs
**Longevity:** 12 to 14 years
**Exercise:** Active; good in canine sports
**Training:** Easy to moderate
**Grooming:** Sheds

# Peruvian Inca Orchid

## (Hairless and Coated)

This breed has been known in Peru since 750 A.D. The Inca Indians valued the dogs, with the nobility keeping the hairless dogs as pets and bed warmers, while the coated dogs were used for hunting. The Spanish conquerors named the dog Perros Flora, or flower dog.

These dogs stand 17 to 24 inches tall and usually weigh between 24 and 40 pounds. This breed is an elegant sighthound, with a tapered head and medium-sized eyes. The hairless dogs have upright ears, while the coated dogs have folded ears. Hairless dogs may be missing some teeth, but coated dogs should have all their teeth. The body is strong but light with a runner's deep but narrow chest. The tail is long. The hairless dogs may have some fuzz on the forehead, lower tail, and feet. The coated dogs may have a short to medium-length single coat with feathering on the ears and tail. Colors include rose, gold, tan, black, and blue with or without white or pink markings.

The hairless variety may need sunscreen when outside; discuss this requirement with the dog's breeder. The coated dogs need weekly brushing.

These are playful dogs who enjoy interacting with their owners. Although not overly active, they do like walks, a chance to play, and time outside in good weather. They must be protected in cold climates.

Peruvian Inca Orchids are easily trained as long as the training is not overly harsh. They are bright and enjoy a challenge; training should continue into adulthood to keep the mind busy. They do well in trick training, and many serve as wonderful therapy dogs. This breed can be quite reserved with strangers, so early socialization is very important.

This is a very clean dog who hates to be dirty or wet; many clean themselves like cats. Although wary of strangers, these dogs are usually quiet and rarely aggressive. They will tolerate children but do not like rough handling. The primary health concerns include a sensitivity to sun and missing teeth, both in the hairless variety.

## Breed in Brief

**Registries:** AKC FSS, UKC
**Occupation:** Hunter, companion
**Size:** 17 to 24 in tall; 24 to 40 lbs
**Longevity:** 12 to 14 years
**Exercise:** Moderate
**Training:** Easy to moderate
**Grooming:** Easy

# Petit Basset Griffon Vendéen

What a name! *Petit* means small, *Basset* means low to the ground, *Griffon* means wire-coated, and *Vendeen* refers to the region in France where the breed originated. This is an old breed that was (and still is) used in the rough terrain of Vendée, France, to hunt small game.

This breed (called the PBGV) stands 13 to 15 inches tall and weighs between 25 and 40 pounds. The head is long, the eyes are large and dark, and the ears are dropped, narrow, fine, and folded. The muscular body is longer than the dog is tall. The tail is medium in length, tapered, and carried high. The coat is harsh and rough. The face has a beard and mustache, and the tail is well-covered. There is a thick undercoat. Coat colors include white with lemon, orange, sable, black, and tricolor.

The PBGV's coat should be brushed weekly, although it may need more frequent brushing when the undercoat is shedding. Potential owners should discuss specific coat care needs with a breeder.

Most PBGVs are playful, happy extroverts. They enjoy long brisk walks, a play session with the kids, and a training session on the agility course. Although not normally destructive, a bored PBGV who doesn't get enough exercise can get into trouble.

## Breed in Brief

**Registries:** AKC, UKC, CKC
**Occupation:** Hunter
**Size:** 13 to 15 in tall; 25 to 40 lbs
**Longevity:** 12 to 14 years
**Exercise:** Active
**Training:** Moderate
**Grooming:** Easy

Training this breed is not difficult as long as the owner can keep the dog motivated. Scenthounds by nature, PBGVs are easily distracted by interesting smells and love to follow their noses. Socialization is recommended, not because the breed's temperament warrants it, but because these dogs enjoy socializing!

This breed does best in a home where the owner understands hound characteristics. PBGVs vocalize and can do so often and with volume; this can cause problems when neighbors live close by. The breed is great with kids and other dogs, and usually with cats, too. Interactions with smaller pets should be closely supervised. Health concerns include eye problems, thyroid and heart disorders, and luxated patellas.

# Pharaoh Hound

Ancient Egyptian hieroglyphics and paintings dating back to 3000 B.C. show Pharaoh Hounds as hunting partners and companions, making them one of the oldest breeds known today. King Tutankhamen had a Pharaoh Hound named Abuwitiyuw that he treasured. When his dog died, he had him embalmed as a nobleman of that time would be.

These dogs are 21 to 25 inches tall with weight in proportion to height. These sighthounds are elegant, graceful, and made for speed. The head is wedge-shaped, the eyes are amber, and the ears are upright. The body is slightly longer than tall, with a deep chest and moderate tuck-up. The tail is tapered and usually has a white tip. The coat is short and is tan to chestnut, with white on the chest. The breed has an interesting characteristic: When excited, the insides of the ears and the nose blush to a rosy pink color.

The short coat should be brushed weekly.

As with most sighthounds, this breed loves to run and is incredibly fast. All exercise should take place in a fenced-in area, however, as this breed has a high prey drive; if a small animal is flushed, the dog could be gone in a flash. In the house, the Pharaoh Hound enjoys being a couch potato, curling up in a warm, comfy spot.

Pharaoh Hounds are bright and intelligent and want nothing more than to make their owners smile. Their training should be firm yet fun, and should begin early. Since the breed is often wary of strangers, socialization should begin early, too. Pharaoh Hounds have been successful in obedience competition, agility, and lure coursing.

Although bred for thousands of years to be a hunting sighthound, this breed can make a wonderful family pet. When raised with children, she can be a great friend but will not tolerate rough handling. She is also good with other dogs and with cats when raised with them. She does have a strong prey drive, so care should be taken with other smaller pets. Health concerns include hip dysplasia and allergies.

## Breed in Brief

**Registries:** AKC, UKC, CKC
**Occupation:** Hunter, companion
**Size:** 21 to 25 in tall; weight proportionate to height
**Longevity:** 12 to 14 years
**Exercise:** Moderate to vigorous
**Training:** Fun to train
**Grooming:** Easy

# Pointer

The Pointer, also known as the English Pointer, originated in Great Britain in the 1600s. The Pointer would find and point game, and then Greyhounds would be turned loose to run down the prey. When guns came into use, the Pointer was still valued for her ability to pinpoint prey.

Today's Pointer stands 23 to 28 inches tall and weighs 45 to 75 pounds. She is very much an athlete. Her head is medium width, and her muzzle has good length. Her eyes are round and dark and ears are dropped. Her back is strong, and her tail tapers to a fine point. Her coat is short and dense and is liver, lemon, orange, or black, with or without white.

The coat should be brushed weekly with a soft bristle brush.

The Pointer is a breed driven to hunt; she has a strong prey drive and the body of a superb athlete. She needs vigorous daily exercise; without it, she will find potentially destructive ways to amuse herself. She can run alongside a bicycle, go jogging with her owner, train on the agility course, or play flyball. Many Pointers have done well in canine sports, while others compete in field trials.

Pointers also need obedience training. Without training, this energetic breed can be hard to control and quite mischievous. Until taught the household rules, she can easily entertain herself—much to her owner's dismay. The American Pointer Club says, "This training will help to develop your Pointer's manners for the enjoyable years ahead as a true member of the family." Socialization is also important; Pointers can be protective of their homes. Their vocal abilities may be too loud for close neighbors.

The Pointer is not the right dog for a sedentary owner; she needs an owner who can keep her busy. The breed retains its hunting instincts and is still widely used as a superb hunting companion. She is usually great with children, although puppies can be rough and rowdy. Care should be taken with smaller pets. Health concerns include eye disorders and deafness.

## Breed in Brief

**Registries:** AKC, UKC, CKC
**Occupation:** Hunter
**Size:** 23 to 28 in tall; 45 to 75 lbs
**Longevity:** 11 to 13 years
**Exercise:** Vigorous daily exercise
**Training:** Moderate; can get into trouble
**Grooming:** Easy

# Polish Tatra Sheepdog

The Polish Tatra Sheepdog, or Polski Owczarek Podhalanski, is a very old livestock guardian dog from the Tatra Mountains of Poland. The breed probably shares some ancestry with mastiff breeds that came to Europe from Asia. The breed almost disappeared during World War II.

These big white mountain dogs stand between 23 and 27 inches tall and weigh 110 to 150 pounds. The head is broad with a long muzzle, the eyes are dark, and the ears are dropped. The body is slightly longer than tall, and the tail is long and profusely feathered. The white coat is thick and either straight or slightly wavy. There is a thick undercoat.

The coat should be brushed at least twice weekly for most of the year. When the undercoat is being shed, usually in the spring and fall, the coat needs a thorough brushing, making sure to get through the undercoat to the skin, every other day.

Although puppies can be rowdy and playful, for the most part this is a calm breed. Daily walks and a chance to run and play will satisfy the exercise needs of most dogs.

As with most livestock guardian dogs, the Polish Tatra Sheepdog was bred to think for herself and to solve the problems she faced on a daily basis. When training this breed, the owner must be the dog's leader and then must convince the dog that what she is doing is important. When properly motivated, these dogs are quick, eager learners. Socialization is very important, as these dogs are natural guardians and can be quite territorial.

The Polish Tatra Sheepdog is not for the first-time dog owner; this breed needs someone who understands the nature of livestock guardian dogs. This is also not a city dog; she will bark loudly at any perceived threat. She is wonderful with children, although she will not be happy about rough play with your kids' friends. She is good with other pets (although she may try to herd them) and is not as dog-aggressive as some other livestock guardian breeds. The primary health concern is hip dysplasia.

## Breed in Brief

**Registries:** Polish Tatra Sheepdog Club of America, Polish Tatra Sheepdog Club of Canada

**Occupation:** Livestock guardian

**Size:** 23 to 27 in tall; 110 to 150 lbs

**Longevity:** 9 to 11 years

**Exercise:** Moderate

**Training:** Challenge

**Grooming:** Sheds

# Pomeranian

This adorable toy breed traces its family tree back to sled dogs in Iceland and Lapland. At that point, the dogs probably weighed between 20 and 30 pounds and were used to herd sheep. In the mid-1800s, the breed was introduced to England, and Queen Victoria fell in love with the breed. The breed was gaining popularity in the U.S. by the late 1800s, although the dogs were bigger and heavier boned and had larger ears than the Poms we know today.

Pomeranians today are very small dogs, most weighing between 3 and 7 pounds (show dogs weigh between 4 and 6 pounds). Height is between 8 and 11 inches. The Pom's body is slightly shorter than it is tall at the shoulder and, although small, should feel sturdy. The head is rounded, with a short, fine muzzle, dark, bright, almond-shaped eyes, and small, erect ears. The tail is plumed and lies flat on the back. The Pom has a double coat, with a soft, dense undercoat and a long, straight outer coat. The outer coat stands out rather than lying close to the body. Colors include red, orange, cream, black, brown, brindle, and parti-color.

Show Poms have a lovely coat that makes the entire dog look like a powder puff. The majority of pet Poms, however, do not have this coat; instead, they have a lush coat that tends to lie down. In either case, the coat needs to be brushed two or three times a week to prevent tangles and mats from forming. Poms are very clean dogs. Cayla Horn's Pomeranian, Keely, will lick her paws after

eating and then wipe her face with her damp paws.

Although very small, Poms still need daily exercise, but their diminutive size makes this easy. A short walk will do, as will a game of ball thrown across the living room or down the hallway. They are happiest when active and love to train on the agility course or chase a small flying disc.

Housetraining Pomeranians can be a challenge, but with close supervision, perseverance, and patience, it can be accomplished. Poms are also protective little watchdogs, and barking, if uncontrolled, can become a problem. Training should continue past puppyhood to keep the breed's bright mind active and learning. Poms excel in trick training and love to be the center of attention. These dogs have participated very successfully in several dog activities, including obedience competition, agility, and therapy dog work.

Poms are happy, affectionate little extroverts who make great pets for the elderly. They are too fragile for very small children but can be wonderful companions for gentle older children. Interactions with other dogs must be carefully supervised, both because Poms are so tiny and because Poms have no idea how small they are and often try to control the situation with other dogs. Poms are usually good with other pets, although they may try to chase the family cat. Health concerns include knee problems, hypoglycemia, eye problems, and tracheal collapse.

## Breed in Brief

**Registries:** AKC, UKC, CKC
**Occupation:** Companion, performance sports
**Size:** 8 to 11 in tall; 3 to 7 lbs
**Longevity:** 14 to 16 years
**Exercise:** Moderate
**Training:** Challenge to housetrain
**Grooming:** Moderate

# Poodle (Toy)

It is generally accepted that all Poodles (toys, miniatures, and standards) are the same breed of dog. The standard variety is the oldest; you can read about the breed's shared history on page 326. But Toy Poodles are not new; Louis XVI of France had toys, and many paintings from the 15th and 16th centuries show tiny dogs that look much like today's Toy Poodles.

Toy Poodles stand 10 inches tall or less at the shoulder and weigh 5 to 7 pounds. There is no official size other than this; the Poodle Club of America does not recognize teacup toys or tiny toys. The head is moderately rounded, with a long muzzle. The eyes are dark and oval, and the ears are dropped. The tail is docked. The coat is curly and dense. Coat color should be one solid color and may be apricot, silver, cream, black, blue, or one of many other colors.

Grooming the Toy Poodle is a complicated process. Show dogs must be groomed in a specific cut that requires some knowledge, so potential owners who wish to show their dogs should discuss this with a breeder prior to buying a dog. Pet owners often take their dogs to a professional groomer on a monthly basis; potential owners should be aware of the cost. Between grooming sessions, the dog should be brushed every other day to prevent matting.

The Toy Poodle is an active dog but is small enough that her exercise needs are easily met. She will enjoy daily walks but can also play in the house.

Toy Poodles are bright and intelligent but are easily spoiled and, when spoiled, can be very demanding. Fun training, including housetraining, should begin early so the dog grows up understanding household rules. Toys also need early socialization, as they can be wary of strangers.

Toys are great companions for people who spend time at home. Most breeders will not sell Toys to families with young children, as the dogs can be fragile. Health concerns include Addison's disease, Cushing's disease, eye defects, luxated patellas, and epilepsy.

## Breed in Brief

**Registries:** AKC, UKC, CKC
**Occupation:** Companion
**Size:** 10 in tall or less; 5 to 7 lbs
**Longevity:** 14 to 16 years
**Exercise:** Moderate
**Training:** Moderate; easily spoiled
**Grooming:** Difficult

# Poodle (Miniature)

All three sizes of Poodles share the same history (see the Standard Poodle profile on the next page), but each size also has some unique characteristics. It is said that at some point during its history, the Miniature Poodle gained fame in England, Spain, and Germany as a truffle dog. The breed's fine nose found the subterranean fungus, which was sold as a delicacy.

The Miniature Poodle stands between 10 and 15 inches tall at the shoulder and weighs 13 to 16 pounds. The head is moderately rounded, with a long muzzle. The eyes are dark and oval, and the ears are dropped. The tail is docked and carried high. The coat is curly and dense. Coat color should be one solid color and may be apricot, silver, cream, black, blue, or one of many other colors.

Grooming the Miniature Poodle takes time, effort, and knowledge. Pet owners usually take their dogs to a professional groomer every four weeks; potential owners should be aware of the cost. Between grooming sessions, the dog should be brushed every other day to prevent matting. Show dogs must be groomed in a specific cut, which can be difficult to do and requires effort to maintain, so potential owners who wish to show their dogs should discuss this with a breeder prior to buying a dog.

The Miniature Poodle is usually said to be the calmest of the three sizes. Although active and playful, she is also very willing to snuggle with her owner. She will enjoy walks, playtimes, and training on the agility course. Miniature Poodles have done very well in canine sports, including agility and obedience competitions, and in therapy dog work.

Early training and socialization are important for this variety of the breed, just as it is for the others. Housetraining requires patience.

The Miniature is an excellent family dog. The dogs who are a little larger are great with children who play gently with them. Health concerns include Addison's and Cushing's diseases, epilepsy, eye disorders, and luxated patellas.

## Breed in Brief

**Registries:** AKC, UKC, CKC
**Occupation:** Companion
**Size:** 10 to 15 in tall; 13 to 16 lbs
**Longevity:** 13 to 15 years
**Exercise:** Moderate
**Training:** Easy
**Grooming:** Difficult

# Poodle (Standard)

*N*o one knows for certain where Poodles originated. They were popular in many parts of Europe, including Germany and France, and everyone wanted to claim these versatile dogs as their own. Most experts agree that the Standard variety is the oldest and was a water retriever. In fact, the practice of trimming the coat was intended to aid the dog in swimming.

Standard Poodles stand taller than 15 inches at the shoulder; most are between 21 and 27 inches tall. They usually weigh between 50 and 75 pounds. The Poodle Club of America says, "There is no officially recognized Poodle variety such as Royal Standard." The head is moderately rounded with a long muzzle. The eyes are dark and oval, and the ears are long and dropped. The tail is docked. The coat is curly and dense. Coat color should be one solid color and may be white, apricot, cream, black, blue, or one of many other colors.

Grooming the Standard Poodle is a complicated process. Show dogs must be groomed in a specific cut that requires some knowledge and considerable upkeep, so potential owners who wish to show their dogs should discuss this with a breeder. Pet owners often take their dogs to a professional groomer on a monthly basis; potential owners should be aware of the cost. Between grooming sessions, the dog should be brushed every other day to prevent matting.

The Standard Poodle is an active dog who needs vigorous daily exercise. She should go for a run, go for long walks, train on the agility course, or play flyball.

The Standard Poodle also needs training. This is an intelligent dog who may be quite large; she needs to learn basic obedience but is capable of much more. Early socialization is also recommended, as this breed can be wary of strangers.

This breed needs an owner who enjoys grooming and who wishes to do things with the dog. Standards are good with children and other pets. Health concerns are many and include Addison's and Cushing's diseases, epilepsy, eye disorders, hip dysplasia, and thyroid disease.

## Breed in Brief

**Registries:** AKC, UKC, CKC
**Occupation:** Retriever, companion
**Size:** 15+ in tall; 50 to 75 lbs
**Longevity:** 12 to 14 years
**Exercise:** Vigorous daily exercise
**Training:** Needs to be challenged
**Grooming:** Difficult

# Portuguese Podengo

## (Pequeno, Medio, and Grande; Smooth and Wirehaired)

The Portuguese Podengo is a very old breed with a known history dating as far back as the 12th century. She was used as a hunting dog throughout most of her history, both to rid farms and homes of vermin and to put food on the table.

The Portuguese Podengo is found in three sizes. The Pequeno is the smallest, at 8 to 12 inches tall and 9 to 13 pounds. This dog is solid, small, and short-legged so that she can enter burrows and rabbit warrens. The Medio is in the middle, at 15 to 22 inches and 35 to 44 pounds. She is longer-legged than the Pequeno. The Grande is the largest variety and is very rare. All three sizes have upright prick ears, a tapered muzzle in balance with the head, expressive eyes, and a high, curved tail. There are two coat types: a smooth coat and a terrierlike wire coat. The coat colors vary but include fawn, red, and white, with or without patches of color.

The grooming needs of this breed vary. Both coat types need at least twice weekly brushing. The wire coat has a beard, which may need cleaning to remove dirt and food particles. Many pet owners trim the wire coat to keep the dog neat and clean.

All three sizes of this breed were used as hunting dogs and retain those hunting instincts. Their daily exercise should always be on leash or within a fenced-in area, because if a rabbit or squirrel is flushed, these dogs will chase it.

Because the Portuguese Podengo is a very good watchdog, early socialization is important so that she can become comfortable with people outside of her family. Early training is also needed; this is a bright breed who is very curious. Training can channel her mind in productive ways. The breed enjoys agility and flyball training.

This adaptable breed can live in the city or suburbs but does need an active owner who will do things with her. She is great with children who treat her well but is not always good with small pets. This is a healthy breed.

## Breed in Brief

**Registries:** AKC FSS, UKC, ARBA

**Occupation:** Hunter, watchdog

**Size:** Pequeno: 8 to 12 in tall; 9 to 13 lbs
Medio: 15 to 22 in tall; 35 to 44 lbs
Grande: 22+ in tall; 44+ lbs

**Longevity:** 12 to 14 years

**Exercise:** Moderate

**Training:** Moderate

**Grooming:** Moderate

 # Portuguese Pointer

The Portuguese Pointer (or Perdigueiro Portugues) is descended from old Spanish hunting dogs dating as far back as the 12th century. The breed was used for hunting upland game birds, waterfowl, and sometimes even rabbits. In the 1700s, dogs were taken from Portugal to England, where the breed had an influence on the development of the English Pointer.

This breed stands between 20 and 22 inches tall and weighs 35 to 59 pounds. The head is distinctively square, with an abrupt stop and a wide muzzle. The eyes are large and oval-shaped, and the ears are dropped. The body is as long as the dog is tall, creating a square when viewed from the side. The tail is docked to half its length. The coat is short and flat and can be any shade of yellow or brown, with or without white markings.

Groom this coat by brushing it weekly with a soft bristle brush.

Breed expert Temple DaSilva says, "The breed is rather active but not with nervous energy. They should have opportunities to run as this is a sporting breed." DaSilva adds that the breed is very playful, athletic, and clever. Although the breed retains its ancient hunting instincts, it's not necessary for the dog to be in a hunting home; however, the dog should have a chance to run every day.

Portuguese Pointers are very people-oriented and very affectionate. They are also quite trainable. The training should be structured yet fun. They typically bond more strongly with one family member and may respond to training better with that person than with other family members.

This breed needs an owner who will enjoy an affectionate dog. This is not a reserved or standoffish breed who will relish life in the backyard; these dogs want to be with their people most of the time. The breed is great with kids. DaSilva says, "The breed's compact size makes for a good family pet, and the dogs have lots of energy for kids." The breed is also good with other family pets. Health concerns include hip dysplasia.

## Breed in Brief

**Registries:** AKC FSS, UKC
**Occupation:** Hunter
**Size:** 20 to 22 in tall; 35 to 59 lbs
**Longevity:** 12 to 14 years
**Exercise:** Daily run
**Training:** Easy; very affectionate
**Grooming:** Easy

# Portuguese Water Dog

The ancestors of the Portuguese Water Dog may have come from the rugged lands near the border between China and Russia. Horses, cattle, sheep, and camels were raised in these harsh lands, and dogs were needed to herd and protect them.

In more recent times, the Portuguese Water Dog worked in the water. All along Portugal's coast, these dogs would herd fish into nets and retrieve fishing gear accidentally dropped into the water.

PWDs stand between 17 and 23 inches tall and weigh 35 to 60 pounds. The head is large and well-proportioned, the eyes are dark, and the ears are heart-shaped, dropped, and held close to the head. The chest is deep, the back well-muscled, and the topline level. The feet are webbed. The tail is not docked; it is tapered, and when the dog is alert, is held in a ring up and over the back. The waterproof coat is thick and profuse and can be either curly or wavy. There is no undercoat. The coat may be various shades of brown, black, white, brown and white, or black and white.

The coat should be brushed and combed thoroughly two or three times weekly. The coat also requires regular, breed-specific grooming and trimming. It is important that potential owners discuss the breed's grooming needs with a breeder prior to acquiring a puppy.

This is an active breed that needs daily exercise. PWDs love to swim and are amazingly skilled divers. They enjoy playing flying disc and do well in a variety of performance events, including agility. What is more important to this breed is that the owner is involved in the activities, too.

Training should be a part of every Portuguese Water Dog's puppyhood. Not only do the dogs need to learn household rules and social manners, training will also channel this breed's bright, active mind. PWDs excel in water rescue work, tracking, flying disc, obedience, and flyball.

This breed needs an actively involved owner who enjoys having an energetic canine companion. The owner should enjoy grooming the dog, training her, and doing things with her, either competitively or just for fun. The breed is a devoted family dog and can be very protective of her territory. Health concerns include Addison's disease, cancer, eye problems, allergies, kidney disease, and hip dysplasia.

## Breed in Brief

**Registries:** AKC, UKC, CKC
**Occupation:** Water rescue dog
**Size:** 17 to 23 in tall; 35 to 60 lbs
**Exercise:** Daily
**Training:** Easy
**Grooming:** Difficult

# Pudelpointer

Pudelpointers originated in Germany in the late 1800s, resulting from an effort to create a hunting breed that enjoyed water, loved to hunt and retrieve, was easily trained, and had a strong desire to please. The German Hunting Pudel (Standard Poodle) and English Pointer were used to create the new breed, hence its name. The parent clubs have worked hard to retain the breed's hunting characteristics and temperament.

These dogs stand 22 to 26 inches tall and usually weigh between 45 and 75 pounds. The head is of medium length, and the eyes are round and yellow-brown. The ears are dropped. The body is strong and slightly longer than tall. The tail is docked, leaving two-thirds of its length. The ideal coat is harsh and wiry. The face is coated with heavy eyebrows, mustache, and beard. Acceptable coat colors are primarily variations of liver and brown, but fawn and light brown are permitted.

This coat requires thorough brushing every other day, as it can tangle and mat. Many owners trim the coat around the eyes, feet, under the tail, and around the genitals to keep the dogs clean.

Pudelpointers were bred to be hunting dogs, and, when out in the field, these dogs are active hunters, although in the house, most are relatively calm. Without daily exercise, however, Pudelpointers, especially puppies, will find something to do to occupy their time, and owners often don't like their choices. Pudelpointers need a good run or swim every day. Most are natural retrievers and love to play fetch games.

Breed enthusiasts rave about this breed's ease of training. It is an intelligent breed and has a strong desire to please. Training should be structured yet fun and not too repetitive.

Although Pudelpointers are wonderful companion dogs, they do best in a hunting home, as that is where the breed's heart is. These dogs are good with children and with other dogs. They should not be trusted with smaller pets. Health concerns include hip dysplasia and allergies.

## Breed in Brief

**Registries:** UKC, CKC, Pudelpointer Club of North America, North American Pudelpointer Alliance

**Occupation:** Hunter

**Size:** 22 to 26 in tall; 45 to 75 lbs

**Longevity:** 11 to 13 years

**Exercise:** Daily

**Training:** Easy

**Grooming:** Difficult

# Pug

Ah, the Pug! These little clowns have a long and rich history in China going back at least 2,000 years, although some breed historians believe they're much older than that. Pugs were so admired that diplomats, ambassadors, explorers, and travelers used them as barter or gifts to gain favors. This practice spread the Pug throughout the world, going first to Japan and then to Europe. In 1572, a Pug warned William, Prince of Orange, of an approaching enemy, so when William was crowned King of England, Pugs were included in the royal procession. Legend has it that when Napoleon married Josephine, one of her Pugs bit him in their honeymoon bed! Pug fanciers say the motto of the breed is "multum in parvo," which means "a lot in a little." Pugs are definitely a lot of dog in a small package.

The Pug is the largest of the toy breeds. She stands 10 to 11 inches tall and weighs between 14 and 18 pounds, although some dogs are heavier. One of the key features of the Pug is her head. It is large and round, with a very short muzzle. The skin over the muzzle is wrinkled, as is the forehead. The eyes are dark and expressive, and the ears are carried high and folded. The body is compact and sturdy. The tail is curled tightly over the hips. The Pug's coat is short and smooth and can be silver, apricot-fawn, or black. The face and ears are black.

Grooming the Pug is not difficult. The short coat can be brushed with a soft bristle brush or curry comb twice weekly and she'll look wonderful. The wrinkles in the face should be cleaned daily, especially if the Pug gets food or dirt in them.

The Pug is a brachycephalic breed, meaning that the muzzle is extremely short. This can cause breathing difficulties, especially during hard exercise or in hot, humid weather. The breed does

need exercise to remain strong and healthy, but care must be taken to exercise the dog wisely. A long walk morning and evening is great, as is a good game of ball in between.

When well-socialized as puppies, Pugs are friendly, playful extroverts. Although small when puppies, they should not be overprotected, as this could cause them to become fearful. Training should begin young, as Pugs do have a mind of their own. The training should be firm yet fun and should include games to keep the dog interested and focused. Housetraining can be a challenge, but with consistency and patience, it can be accomplished. Because of their potential breathing problems and their small stature, Pugs are limited in the canine sports in which they participate, but they enjoy agility and trick training and make wonderful therapy dogs.

Pugs are great companions for people of all ages. Although they are sturdy and will take some rough handling, small children should be taught to be gentle. They usually get along with other dogs quite well, but interactions with larger dogs should be supervised so the smaller Pug is not hurt. Pugs and the family cat can become great friends. Health concerns include eye disorders, knee problems, allergies, hip dysplasia, and Pug dog encephalitis. Because Pugs enjoy eating, obesity is also a potential problem.

## Breed in Brief

**Registries:** AKC, UKC, CKC
**Occupation:** Companion
**Size:** 10 to 11 in tall; 14 to 18 lbs
**Longevity:** 13 to 16 years
**Exercise:** Moderate
**Training:** Challenge to housetrain
**Grooming:** Easy

# Puli

The Puli has been used as a herding dog for Hungarian shepherds for more than 1,000 years. Often a Puli would be teamed with a Komondor; the Puli would herd the sheep or cattle and the Komondor would guard against predators. The plural of Puli is Pulik.

Pulik stand between 15 and 17 inches tall, usually weighing 25 to 35 pounds. The body is the same length as the dog is tall at the shoulder. The eyes are almond-shaped and dark, while the ears are hanging and V-shaped. The tail is carried up over the dog's back. The undercoat is soft and dense. The outer coat is wavy or curly and can either be brushed out or corded. In adults, the cords can eventually reach the ground. The coat may be black, gray, or white.

The cords on a Puli are much like controlled mats or hair tangles. Caring for this coat requires some expertise; it cannot be ignored. Longtime owner and photographer Melinda Peters says, "Unless the coat is clipped short, this is a high-maintenance breed." Potential owners should discuss coat care with a breeder.

The Puli is an active dog who needs daily exercise. She will enjoy daily walks and a chance to run. Pulik have done extremely well in many canine sports, including herding, obedience, therapy dog work, agility, and flyball.

## Breed in Brief

**Registries:** AKC, UKC, CKC
**Occupation:** Herder
**Size:** 15 to 17 in tall; 25 to 35 lbs
**Longevity:** 14 to 16 years
**Exercise:** Daily
**Training:** Easy; hard to keep challenged
**Grooming:** Difficult

The Puli retains her herding instincts and strong desire to work, and training can fulfill that need. Training should begin early and be fun yet firm and structured. Peters says, "The breed is receptive to training, although a passive trainer might experience difficulty." Pulik can also get bored with training that is too repetitive; this breed needs a challenge.

A Puli is versatile and can live in the city or on a ranch. She needs an owner who is going to be involved with grooming, training, exercise, and playtimes. The breed can be good with children, but some can be jealous or possessive. They should be supervised with other pets. Health concerns include hip dysplasia, ear infections, and cancer.

# umi

The Pumi, or Hungarian Pumi, is descended from the Puli, which was crossed with other European herding breeds imported into Hungary in the 16th and 17th centuries. Although the specific herding breeds used are unknown, some breed experts believe that at least one of the breeds had upright, pricked ears and may have been an early ancestor of the Belgian sheepdog breeds.

Pumik (plural of Pumi) stand between 15 and 18.5 inches tall and weigh between 17 and 33 pounds. The head is long and narrow, with a broad skull. The eyes are medium-sized, and the ears are upright and mobile. The body is as long as it is tall at the shoulder and is well-muscled. The tail forms a circle above the rump. The coat is double, with a soft undercoat and a wiry, wavy outer coat. The most common colors include gray, black, and fawn.

This coat is more like a terrier's coat than most other herding breeds and requires some specific hand-grooming. A breeder can demonstrate the correct technique. Between grooming sessions, these dogs should be brushed and combed twice weekly to prevent matting.

The Hungarian Pumi Club of America says of the breed, "Her appearance embodies a thirst for action. She is always active and ready for duty." This breed needs vigorous daily exercise, but more importantly, she also needs a job to do. She can herd sheep or ducks, protect livestock from intruders, watch the family children, or hunt vermin. She can also train in agility, play flyball, catch a flying disc, or compete in obedience. She is definitely not a sedentary lap dog! Training and socialization should begin early and continue into adulthood.

The Pumi is also a noisy breed, so she is not suited to apartment or tract home life. The Pumi is bold and can be watchful and wary of strangers. She does best in a rural environment where she has an active owner and a job that will keep her busy. She can be good with children but can also try to herd them. This is a healthy breed.

## Breed in Brief

**Registries:** AKC FSS, UKC
**Occupation:** Herder, vermin hunter
**Size:** 15 to 18.5 in tall; 17 to 33 lbs
**Longevity:** 13 to 15 years
**Exercise:** Vigorous daily exercise
**Training:** Hard to keep challenged
**Grooming:** Difficult

# Pyrenean Mastiff

The Pyrenean Mastiff originated in the Pyrenees Mountains of Spain, where it protected livestock, primarily sheep, from wolves, bears, and poachers. The breed dates back to the Middle Ages.

This is a massive dog, standing 28 to 32 inches tall, although there is no established maximum height. These dogs weigh 120 to 155 pounds or more. The head is large and moderately long, the eyes are small and dark, and the ears are medium-sized and dropped but mobile. The body is longer than tall, with a wide chest. It has double dew claws. The tail is held in a saber shape and reaches the hocks. The coat is about 3 inches long and is always white with color around the eyes and ears. There may be patches of color on the body as well.

The coat requires thorough brushing at least twice a week. These dogs shed heavily twice a year, so additional brushing will be needed.

Breed expert Karin Graefe of De La Tierra Alta Kennels says, "A good daily walk or even a hike on a trail following an owner on horseback is all fun to this breed. It is not a high-energy breed, but if young dogs are left to their own devices without a good walk to use up energy, they may find their own mischief."

This breed is very receptive to training; Graefe says that consistency and gentle discipline are the keys to training these dogs. She adds, "This breed matures more slowly than many other breeds, so trainers must be patient." The Pyrenean Mastiff is also a very protective watchdog and guardian, so socialization should begin very young and continue into adulthood.

This breed may be too much for most first-time dog owners. The Pyrenean Mastiff needs her owner to be a leader, and the dog needs to spend time with her owner. Even though this is a livestock guardian, she also needs companionship. She is good with kids and other dogs but is very watchful of strange dogs and people. Most of these dogs drool. The primary health concern is hip dysplasia.

## Breed in Brief

**Registries:** Pyrenean Mastiff Club of America

**Occupation:** Livestock guardian

**Size:** 28 to 32+ in tall; 120 to 155+ lbs

**Longevity:** 8 to 10 years

**Exercise:** Moderate

**Training:** Patient training needed

**Grooming:** Moderate

# Rat Terrier

## (Miniature and Standard)

The Rat Terrier is an American breed developed in the 1800s from the old Fox Terriers, English White Terriers, Bull Terriers, and Manchester Terriers. Later, Smooth Fox Terriers and Toy Fox Terriers were used, and some experts say even Beagles and Whippets were a part of the mix. Primarily farm dogs and bred for working ability rather than looks, the Rat Terrier was—as his name implies—a vermin hunter.

Because of their varied ancestry, Rat Terriers are not cookie-cutter dogs all fitting into the same mold. The Rat Terrier Club of America states that a Miniature is between 10 and 13 inches tall and the Standard is between 13 and 19 inches tall at the shoulder. Both sizes are sturdy, with a wedge-shaped head, rounded dark eyes, and an alert expression. The ears are upright and large but also may be semi-pricked or slightly folded. The tail is docked or is a natural bobtail. The coat is short and smooth and may be a variety of colors but is predominantly hound colors—white with patches of color, from apricot, tan, and blue fawn through black.

Grooming the Rat Terrier is easy. The short coat can be brushed with a soft bristle brush or curry comb twice weekly.

This is an active breed that needs vigorous daily exercise. A brisk walk morning and evening plus a game of catch in the backyard will keep most Rat Terriers happy.

Rat Terriers tend to be wary and cautious of strangers, so early socialization is very important. Early training can teach the Rat Terrier household rules and social manners. Although they are bright and inquisitive, these dogs can also be stubborn and tenacious, so training needs to be firm yet fun, with games and toys included so that the dog's motivation level stays high.

Rat Terriers are loyal and devoted to their owners and can easily become one-person dogs. They can be good with older children but will not tolerate rough handling. Rat Terriers are usually good with other dogs, although play with larger dogs should be supervised so that the smaller dog is not injured. Interactions with other small pets should be closely monitored; remember, these are hunting dogs. Health concerns include knee problems, hip and elbow dysplasia, and allergies.

## Breed in Brief

**Registries:** AKC FSS, UKC, Rat Terrier Club of America, National Rat Terrier Association

**Occupation:** Vermin hunter, companion

**Size:** Mini: 10 to 13 in tall
Standard: 13 to 19 in tall

**Longevity:** 14 to 16 years

**Exercise:** Vigorous daily exercise

**Training:** Challenge

**Grooming:** Easy

# Rhodesian Ridgeback

The Rhodesian Ridgeback is descended from native African dogs, notably the Khoi cattle dogs, crossed with European breeds brought in by settlers. Those breeds included English Greyhounds, mastiffs, and pointers, as well as Irish Wolfhounds. African farm dogs were also a part of the breed's development. The big game hunter Cornelius Van Rooyen of Southern Rhodesia is credited with the development of the breed, known today as a fearless, versatile hunter and a protective guardian.

These dogs stand 24 to 27 inches tall and weigh between 70 and 85 pounds. The head is broad and flat, the muzzle is long and powerful, the eyes are round, and the ears are dropped. The body is slightly longer than tall, and the tail is tapered and long. The coat is short and wheaten in color. The ridge on the back is characteristic of the breed, starting behind the shoulders and continuing to the hips. It is created by hairs growing in whorls (curled or spiral shapes) and in opposite directions of the coat.

The coat is easy to care for and needs only a weekly brushing.

The Rhodesian Ridgeback enjoys being lazy and is great at finding comfortable spots for sunbathing or sleeping. However, this watchful breed can come alert in a second and is never lacking in energy when it's needed. Dogs of this breed enjoy daily walks, a run alongside a bicycle, or a chance to hunt for small critters in the woodpile.

The Rhodesian Ridgeback Club of America says of the breed, "Basic obedience training is a must, or he will not be the pleasurable companion you seek." Training must be fair and consistent, and owners should understand that it takes many big dogs quite a while to mature.

Most breed experts agree this is not the breed for first-time dog owners, primarily because the breed is very intelligent and can be a threatening watchdog. He is great with children and good with other dogs but should be supervised with smaller pets. Health concerns include problems with the dermoid sinus and hip dysplasia.

## Breed in Brief

**Registries:** AKC, UKC, CKC
**Occupation:** Hunter, guardian
**Size:** 24 to 27 in tall; 70 to 85 lbs
**Longevity:** 10 to 12 years
**Exercise:** Moderate
**Training:** Easy to moderate
**Grooming:** Easy

# Rottweiler

When the Romans invaded Europe 2,000 years ago, they moved huge armies in waves across Europe. Feeding an army this large was a massive undertaking, so they drove herds of cattle along with them. The Romans used Rottweilers to move the herds. In their new lands, the dogs continued to ply their trade until the mid-1800s, when the driving of cattle was made illegal.

The Rottweiler stands 22 to 27 inches tall and weighs 85 to 140 pounds. The Rottie is strong, muscular, and powerful. The head is broad, eyes are almond-shaped and dark, and ears are folded and triangular. The body is slightly longer than it is tall at the shoulder. The coat is straight and coarse and is always black with rust-colored markings. The tail is docked.

The breed's temperament is dignified, calm, and confident. They are naturally reserved with strangers but should not be aggressive unless there is danger facing the dog or his people. Katy Silva is the owner of Sasha, her second certified therapy dog Rottweiler. She says, "Sasha will bark and simply place herself between me and the person she senses is a danger."

Grooming a Rottie is not difficult. The medium-length coat can be brushed twice weekly with a pin brush or slicker brush.

The Rottweiler was developed for strength, not speed, so long-distance running is not the breed's favorite exercise. A long walk, a game of fetch, and some carting training will use up that excess energy. Silva says that Rotties are not always as play-oriented as other breeds are: "They are more serious minded."

All Rottie puppies should attend a puppy training class that emphasizes socialization. Because the breed is naturally reserved with strangers, the puppies should meet many different people. Puppies should also meet and play with puppies of other breeds and sizes. Training can begin at an early age, too, to teach obedience commands and household rules.

Rottweilers are devoted and loyal to their families, and friends will be remembered forever and greeted with a wiggling stump of a tail. The breed is not particularly friendly to strange dogs; this is not a dog park breed. Rotties can be good with children as long as the kids treat the dog with respect. They can also be good with other pets. Health concerns include hip and elbow dysplasia, osteosarcoma, bloat, torsion, and allergies.

## Breed in Brief

**Registries:** AKC, UKC, CKC
**Occupation:** Drover, police dog, guardian, companion
**Size:** 22 to 27 in tall; 85 to 140 lbs
**Longevity:** 8 to 10 years
**Exercise:** Moderate
**Training:** Moderate; retains training well
**Grooming:** Easy

# Saint Bernard

## (Short Coat and Long Coat)

Although these dogs gained fame as rescue dogs for the hospice in the Alps between Switzerland and Italy, and have been doing that work since the 1600s, this breed was a popular farm dog for hundreds of years prior to their rescue work. Saint Bernards are most likely descendants of Mastiffs accompanying the Roman Legion and native Swiss dogs. In the 1800s, Newfoundlands were crossed with the Saint Bernard.

This is a powerful breed, standing at least 25.5 to 30 inches tall (or taller) and weighing 120 to 180 pounds. The head is large and wide, the muzzle is short, the eyes are medium-sized and dark brown, and the ears are dropped. The breed is strong and well-proportioned with heavy bones. The tail is long and heavy. The undercoat is thick and dense, while the outer coat can be short or long. The coat is white with red or brindle markings.

Both the short and long coats need twice weekly brushing to keep them clean and free of mats. When the dog is shedding heavily, usually twice a year, additional brushing is needed.

Puppies are active, alternating nap times with playtimes. Adults enjoy a long brisk walk and a chance to play but are usually calm in the house. The national breed club recommends that all exercise be either on leash or in a fenced-in yard.

Training is a necessity for this breed. Puppies grow rapidly and become strong and heavy very quickly. They need to learn household rules and social manners early so that they do not take advantage of their size and overpower family members or guests.

The Saint Bernard needs an owner who doesn't mind grooming the dog, is willing to do the training needed to create a good companion, and doesn't mind that these dogs drool. Although puppies can be rowdy, most Saints are excellent with children. They are usually good with other pets, too. Health concerns include hip dysplasia, allergies, epilepsy, and a sensitivity to heat.

## Breed in Brief

**Registries:** AKC, UKC, CKC
**Occupation:** Farm dog, rescue dog
**Size:** 25.5 to 30+ in tall; 120 to 180+ lbs
**Longevity:** 8 to 10 years
**Exercise:** Moderate
**Training:** Moderate
**Grooming:** Moderate; sheds

# aluki

## (Smooth Coat and Feathered Coat)

The Saluki may be one of the oldest breeds of dogs still in existence. Excavations of the Sumerian empire, dating back to 7000 B.C., found carvings of dogs looking much like today's Salukis, with both smooth and feathered coats.

Salukis are hunting sighthounds and have bodies built for speed and agility. Males stand 23 to 28 inches and weigh 40 to 60 pounds. Females are smaller. Salukis have a long narrow head, large eyes, and dropped ears. The tail is long and carried in a curve. The feathered coat

has long silky hair on the ears, back of legs, thighs, and tail, while the rest of the body has a smooth, soft coat. The smooth coat dogs have a soft, short coat with no feathering. Colors include white, cream, gold, red, and black and tan.

Grooming this breed requires weekly brushing with a soft bristle brush for the coat and twice weekly combing of the feathers.

Although Salukis are calm in the house, they were bred to run and still enjoy a chance to run at full steam. Watching Salukis run is like watching birds fly; they are graceful, powerful, and awesome! However, all exercise should be within a fenced-in yard or on leash. This breed retains its natural hunting instincts, and if a rabbit or squirrel is spotted, these dogs will be off in a flash. Young Salukis can be destructive if they don't get enough exercise.

Salukis were not bred to take orders; they have been hunters for thousands of years. Training, therefore, can be a challenge. Training should be upbeat, fun, and varied—not repetitive—and the owner must be patient. This breed will never be as obedient as most of the herding and working breeds are.

Salukis may not be the stars of the obedience world, but they are very loving and affectionate. Many owners consider them addictive! They can be wonderful family dogs but should be supervised with smaller pets. Health concerns include a sensitivity to anesthesia, thyroid problems, heart problems, and cancer.

## Breed in Brief

**Registries:** AKC, UKC, CKC
**Occupation:** Hunter
**Size:** Males 23 to 28 in tall; 40 to 60 lbs (females smaller)
**Longevity:** 13 to 15 years
**Exercise:** Loves to run!
**Training:** Challenge
**Grooming:** Easy

# amoyed

This is an ancient breed who has lived with the Samoyede people of Siberia for more years than can be counted. To these people, the Samoyed is much more than just a dog; she is in reality a partner, for they could not survive without their dogs' assistance. The beautiful white dogs herd the reindeer, hunt, and pull sleds. In addition, they sleep in the reindeer hide tents with their owners, providing extra warmth during the long Siberian winters. The breed has also been used as a reliable sled dog outside of Siberia. Samoyeds were on sled dog teams exploring both the north and south poles, and were treasured for their strength, reliability, and willingness to work.

The Samoyed today is still a working dog and should present a picture of both beauty and strength. This breed stands 19 to 23.5 inches tall and weighs 40 to 70 pounds, with the females smaller than the males. The Samoyed's smiling face is a treasure, with dark, intelligent eyes and upright ears; the dogs always look happy. The Samoyed is well-balanced with a body long enough to do draft work and legs long enough to run. The coat has a thick undercoat of soft, dense wool and a longer outer coat of harsh hair that stands out from the body, creating a fluffy look. The coat can be white, cream, or biscuit.

Grooming the Samoyed takes some time and effort. The coat can mat and must be brushed at least twice a week during most of the year. However, when the dog is shedding (usually spring and fall), she should be brushed daily.

These dogs need daily aerobic exercise. Bred to be multipurpose working dogs, they can be mischievous without enough exercise. In addition, obesity can be a problem. Samoyeds like to jog, run alongside a bicycle, and participate in dog sports. Pulling a sled or wagon is a natural job for them, of course, but they also enjoy weight pulling, skijoring, and pack hiking. The breed also loves games, and many owners swear their dog has a sense of humor.

The Samoyed Club of America, Inc., recommends training for all Samoyeds, "Elementary obedience training will make your dog a good citizen and the best possible companion. Additionally, the time you spend with your dog will create a close bond between the two of you." Although training the Samoyed is not usually difficult—they are bright dogs who usually want to please you—they can also be independent thinkers. The owner must keep the training structured yet fun.

Samoyeds are great family dogs for those who understand the care that the beautiful coat needs and those who want a white canine shadow. Samoyeds who are isolated too much will get into trouble. They can be barkers, much to the dismay of neighbors, so this should be addressed early before it becomes a problem. The breed is good with people of all ages. Although friendly and affectionate with everyone in the family, they often single out one family member and bond more strongly to that person. Samoyeds are usually very good with other dogs and other pets. Health concerns include hip dysplasia, bloat, torsion, hypothyroidism, and eye disorders.

## Breed in Brief

**Registries:** AKC, UKC, CKC
**Occupation:** Herder, hunter, sled dog, companion
**Size:** 19 to 23.5 in tall; 40 to 70 lbs
**Longevity:** 11 to 13 years
**Exercise:** Daily aerobic exercise
**Training:** Easy to moderate
**Grooming:** Moderate; lots of brushing

# Schapendoes

The Schapendoes is a Dutch sheepdog but should not be confused with the Dutch Shepherd, a very different breed. The Schapendoes is a drover and was used to move the sheep from the farm to pasture and back again. Breed experts say the breed is related to the Puli, the Briard, and perhaps the Bearded Collie.

These dogs stand between 15 and 19.5 inches tall and weigh 30 to 40 pounds. They are lightly built and should never be heavy and cumbersome. The skull is broad, the muzzle is short, the eyes are large and brown, and the ears are dropped. The body is slightly longer than the dog is tall at the shoulder. The tail is long. The undercoat is thick and the outer coat is long and wavy. The face is coated and has a topknot, mustache, and beard. All colors are permitted.

The coat requires twice weekly brushing to prevent matting. These dogs love to play, and additional grooming is needed when they get wet or pick up dirt, debris, or grass seeds in their coats.

Breed expert Lorie Godin says, "These dogs are calm in the house and will adapt to a wide variety of lifestyles. However, they require a good walk and time for play each day." She adds that the breed is not hyper or high-strung although they are active dogs. They love to play and have a delightful sense of humor.

Training can help challenge this breed's clever mind, and during the training the breed is easily motivated by food. Godin adds, however, "The breed can be stubborn at times or can be distracted by more interesting alternatives to the training." The training needs to be varied and fun. Although socialization is always important, this is not a guardian breed. They will announce arrivals to their home but are not aggressive.

Schapendoes need an owner who enjoys having a canine shadow; these are companion dogs. The owner should also enjoy grooming the dog. The breed is great with children, is not at all dog-aggressive, and is also good with other pets. The primary health concern is hip dysplasia.

## Breed in Brief

**Registries:** UKC, CKC
**Occupation:** Herder, companion
**Size:** 15 to 19.5 in tall; 30 to 40 lbs
**Longevity:** 12 to 14 years
**Exercise:** Moderate
**Training:** Moderate
**Grooming:** Moderate to difficult

# Schipperke

Although many people assume that this is a Dutch breed, it is really a descendant of a Belgian black sheepdog, the Leauvenaar. The Schipperke was bred to be a smaller dog than the sheepdog, and although it has been a distinct breed for several hundred years, it wasn't known as the Schipperke until the late 1800s.

These small dogs stand between 10 and 13 inches tall and usually weigh 8 to 14 pounds. The head is foxlike, the eyes are oval and dark, and the ears are upright. The body is square in profile, with a broad, deep chest and no tail. The undercoat is soft and dense. The outer coat is short on the face and the front of the legs, medium length on the body, and longer on the ruff and the back of the legs. The coat is always black.

The coat is easy to care for and needs only weekly brushing. When the dog sheds heavily, usually in the spring and fall, more brushing may be needed.

This is an active dog who enjoys brisk walks, daily playtimes, a run on the agility course, and a chance to play ball. Many Schipperkes have done very well in agility, flyball, and obedience competitions.

## Breed in Brief

**Registries:** AKC, UKC, CKC
**Occupation:** Herder, hunter, companion
**Size:** 10 to 13 in tall; 8 to 14 lbs
**Longevity:** 14 to 16 years
**Exercise:** Moderate to active
**Training:** Moderate; hard to keep challenged
**Grooming:** Easy; sheds

Early socialization is important, as this is a very watchful breed. The Schipperke is wary of strangers and doesn't realize she is small; she's ready to protect her family if the need arises. Under-socialized dogs can be overly cautious and fearful. Training can help occupy this very intelligent breed's mind. The training should be structured and firm, yet fun and positive, and should continue into adulthood.

Although this breed is small, it is not a toy breed. Schipperkes retain much of their herding dog heritage and are intelligent, watchful, trainable, and at times, challenging. They need an owner who is willing to be a leader and will not spoil the dog; a spoiled Schipperke can be a tyrant. The breed is great with children who treat the dog with respect. The primary health concerns are Legg-Perthe's disease and thyroid problems.

# Scottish Deerhound

The Scottish Deerhound is an ancient breed, although its origins are lost in history. However, the breed has been known as Deerhound since the 16th century. During their history, these dogs were prized for their hunting abilities as well as their character. In the age of chivalry, only those people holding a rank of earl or higher could own Deerhounds.

These are tall dogs, standing 28 to 32 inches tall and weighing 80 to 100 pounds. They are powerful dogs with narrow heads, dark eyes, and small ears. The chest is deep and the tail is long. The medium-length coat is wiry, and they have mustaches and beards. The coat is usually dark blue–gray but may also be fawn or red.

The coat needs to be brushed and combed at least twice a week. Most owners like to trim the hair on the face to keep the dog neat. Dogs being shown will need hand-stripping on the face rather than scissoring.

Two walks a day is great for these dogs, but Deerhounds also need a chance to run. Young dogs will need a daily run; adults will settle for several runs a week. Make sure the dog runs in a securely fenced-in yard, as this breed was bred to hunt; if a critter is flushed during a run, the dog will take off.

The Deerhound has a wonderful temperament. Although she loves a good run, she is usually calm and amiable in the house. She loves a soft place to snooze. Training should be light and fun without too much repetition. Don't expect her to be as responsive to training as many other breeds; she may not bring back thrown toys and she will respond to commands when it pleases her.

This breed is reserved with strangers but cannot be considered a watchdog. She is great with children and other dogs in the family. She may chase strange dogs, and she should not be trusted with small pets who may run from her. She has a short life span, living only 8 to 10 years. Health concerns include bloat, torsion, heart problems, dwarfism, and anesthesia sensitivities.

## Breed in Brief

**Registries:** AKC, UKC
**Occupation:** Hunter
**Size:** 28 to 32 in tall; 80 to 100 lbs
**Longevity:** 8 to 10 years
**Exercise:** Daily run
**Training:** Challenge
**Grooming:** Easy

# Scottish Terrier

The Scottish Terrier originated in the Highlands of Great Britain, where she was valued as a very effective fox and vermin hunter. Many breed experts feel the Scottie was a parent breed to many terrier breeds developed later.

The Scottie stands 10 inches tall and weighs 18 to 22 pounds. The breed is compact and sturdy. Their heads are long, eyes are small and almond-shaped, and ears are small and upright, never cropped. The body is slightly longer than tall. The tail is about 7 inches long and not docked. The coat is hard and wiry. There is longer coat above the eyes and on the beard, legs, chest, and belly. Coat colors include black, brindle, and wheaten.

The coat should be brushed several times a week to keep it clean and to prevent tangles and mats. The Scottie's coat needs grooming every six to eight weeks. Show dogs need to have their coat hand-stripped, while pet dogs are often clipped. Potential owners should discuss the breed's grooming requirements with a breeder.

Scottie puppies are full of fun and will play whenever they are not napping or eating. Adults are calmer and more dignified but never lose their sense of fun. A daily walk and a chance to play in the backyard will satisfy this breed's exercise needs.

## Breed in Brief

**Registries:** AKC, UKC, CKC
**Occupation:** Vermin hunter, companion
**Size:** 10 in tall; 18 to 22 lbs
**Longevity:** 12 to 14 years
**Exercise:** Moderate
**Training:** Moderate
**Grooming:** Difficult

Scotties are intelligent but can also be independent and stubborn. Training an independent spirit requires patience and consistency. The training should also be firm but fun. Training should never be harsh; this breed will either turn off or fight back when faced with harsh training.

This breed needs an owner who understands terriers. Scotties are companion dogs and although they like to play outside, they prefer to spend most of their time inside with their owners. They are good with children but will not tolerate rough play. They can be dog-aggressive. They are usually fine with cats. Health concerns include von Willebrand disease, Scottie Cramp, allergies, thyroid problems, cancer, and liver shunt.

# Sealyham Terrier

The Sealyham Terrier was the creation of retired Army officer John Edwards of Sealy Ham, Haverfordwest, Wales, in the mid- to late 1800s. Edwards wanted a bold, game little terrier who could dispatch the badgers and otters found in the region. Unfortunately, records were not kept as to the breed's ancestry; Edwards was more concerned with the dogs' abilities to hunt.

These small terriers stand about 10.5 inches tall and weigh 20 to 24 pounds. The head is long and broad, the eyes are medium-sized and very dark, and the ears are folded.

The body is strong, the chest deep, and the tail docked. The undercoat is dense and the outer coat is hard and wiry. The dogs are white but may have lemon, tan, or badger markings on the head.

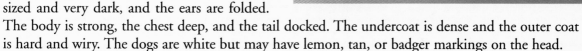

The coat needs twice weekly brushing to keep it clean and to prevent tangles and mats. The hair needs trimming every six to eight weeks. Show dogs must be hand-stripped, while most pet owners have their dogs clipped. Potential owners should discuss the breed's grooming needs with a breeder.

The Sealyham Terrier is a moderately active terrier. When she plays, she puts her all into it but when not playing, she's willing to relax and be quiet. This breed enjoys long, brisk walks and a chance to hunt for small animals in the wood pile. Sealyhams also have a sense of humor, and making their owners laugh is one of their joys.

This dog is a very good watchdog, with protective instincts and a bark that sounds like it comes from a much larger dog. Because they are so watchful, socialization is very important for Sealyham puppies. Training this breed can be a challenge. They are bright but can also be stubborn. Owners need to find out what motivates their dog and then use that to build compliance.

This breed needs an owner with a sense of humor who can laugh at terrier antics. They are patient with children who treat them with respect and do not play too rough. Health concerns include eye problems and allergies.

## Breed in Brief

**Registries:** AKC, UKC, CKC
**Occupation:** Hunter, companion
**Size:** 10.5 in tall; 20 to 24 lbs
**Longevity:** 14 to 16 years
**Exercise:** Moderate
**Training:** Challenge
**Grooming:** Difficult

# hetland Sheepdog

The Shetland Sheepdog (or Sheltie) is an old breed, probably derived from the ancestors of the rough Collie. These dogs were brought to the Shetland Islands of Great Britain, where the tough conditions favored smaller livestock (smaller sheep and ponies instead of horses). Smaller herding dogs just made sense, too, both to work the smaller livestock and because smaller dogs required less food. Because the dogs on the islands were isolated, they were able to breed true quickly, and the breed came to be.

Shelties today are very much a smaller version of the rough Collie. They stand between 13 and 16 inches tall and weigh 18 to 25 pounds (many pets are larger). The Sheltie's head is wedge-shaped,

with dark almond-shaped eyes and small ears that are three-quarters erect, with just the tips folded over. The body is longer than tall, the chest deep, and the legs strong. The undercoat is short and dense, while the outer coat is long and straight, standing out from the body. The mane is full, the legs are feathered, and the tail is plumed. Colors include sable in all its shades, blue merle, and black. White and tan markings are acceptable.

The Sheltie's profuse coat can shed, and shed quite impressively. Although the worst of shedding is usually in the spring and fall, there is some hair loss year-round. The coat should be brushed at least twice a week normally and daily during the shedding seasons.

Nancy Mueller, a lifelong Sheltie owner, says of the breed's exercise needs, "Shelties can get along with limited exercise, but do best when walked and played with daily. If they get the exercise they need, they seem less likely to develop habits you won't like." Shelties thrive in many canine sports, including agility, obedience competitions, herding trials, and flying disc competitions.

Socialization is very important for all Shelties. They are naturally wary of strangers and quite reserved to everyone except their families. Early socialization can help them recognize that not everyone is a danger. Training is also very important, not just to teach household rules but because the breed is very intelligent and thrives with training. Mueller says, "Shelties love training, are quick to catch on, and are quite proud of themselves when they learn something." Of course, Shelties are also smart enough to figure out when they can get away with bad behavior, too!

Shelties are very much people dogs. They thrive when allowed to live with people, underfoot, and are able to shadow their people. They can be quite good with children, although the kids need to be taught to respect the dog and be gentle. Many children get frustrated when the dog tries to herd (circle) them. Shelties are also good with other pets, but again, many cats detest being herded! Shelties are prone to one behavior that can cause problems with neighbors: Mueller says, "Breeders say Shelties talk a lot. That's a euphemism for they bark a lot! Big trucks, joggers, brooms, hummingbirds at the feeder—everything deserves comment in the Sheltie's mind. Don't get one if you have neighbors who detest barking dogs." Health concerns include autoimmune disorders, allergies, and knee, skin, and eye problems. Many are sensitive to ivermectin, a heartworm preventative.

## Breed in Brief

**Registries**: AKC, UKC, CKC
**Occupation**: Herder, companion, performance sports
**Size**: 13 to 16 in tall; 18 to 25 lbs
**Longevity:** 14 to 16 years
**Exercise:** Active; more is better
**Training:** Easy; hard to keep challenged
**Grooming:** Lots of brushing

# Shiba Inu

The Shiba Inu is the smallest of Japan's native dogs and for centuries was a hardy, capable hunter in the mountainous terrain of that island. Although World War II almost caused the breed to become extinct, dogs from many remote communities were added to a breeding program, which eventually created the breed as it is known today.

The Shiba Inu stands 13.5 to 16.5 inches tall and weighs 15 to 28 pounds. The breed is spitz-like in appearance, with a foxy face, dark eyes, and upright ears. The body is slightly longer than tall, and the tail is long and carried over the back. The dog has a soft, dense undercoat. The outer coat is fine and can be fawn, brindle, or brindle and white.

This breed needs twice weekly brushing for most of the year. However, in the spring and fall when shedding is at its worst, daily brushing might be needed.

Although Shibas are not a high-activity breed, they do enjoy long, brisk, daily walks. The walks are also great socialization opportunities, which Shibas need, as they can be watchful and wary of strangers. This breed is also playful, and if you don't play with them, they will find ways to amuse themselves. Puppies can be destructive.

## Breed in Brief

**Registries:** AKC, UKC, CKC
**Occupation:** Hunting, companion
**Size:** 13.5 to 16.5 in tall; 15 to 28 lbs
**Longevity:** 14 to 16 years
**Exercise:** Moderate
**Training:** Challenge
**Grooming:** Easy; sheds

Training, to a Shiba, means the dog's ability to train her owner, something this breed is very good at. However, it is important that Shiba owners establish some control, so training should begin when the dog is young and continue through young adulthood. Training should be structured yet fun. Training a Shiba has been compared to training a cat; patience and good motivators are the keys to success.

The Shiba Inu may be too much for a first-time pet owner, although many cat owners think a Shiba is an excellent choice for their first dog. The Shiba is great with children who treat her gently and with respect; she will not tolerate rough handling. She may also be dog-aggressive. Health concerns include eye defects, luxating patellas, and allergies.

# Shih Tzu

As with so many old breeds, the Shih Tzu's history has been highly debated. What is known is that the breed was revered during the Tang and Ming dynasties in China, and breedings were carefully planned. The breed was solely a companion dog; it was never a hunter or a guardian.

This toy breed stands between 8 and 11 inches tall and weighs 9 to 16 pounds. The head is round and broad, the eyes are large and very dark, and the ears are large and dropped. The body is compact and sturdy, with a tail carried in a curve over the back. The undercoat is soft, and the outer coat is long and flowing. All colors are permitted. The American Shih Tzu Club says there is only one size and no such thing as an imperial or tea cup; those are simply ploys to sell dogs.

This breed's coat requires time and effort to keep it looking good. Show dogs may have hair that reaches and drags on the ground, but most pet owners keep the hair trimmed. Daily brushing and combing is needed, even if the hair is trimmed, because the coat can easily tangle and mat.

The Shih Tzu is a happy, playful breed. They will enjoy daily walks and a play session or two during the day but are not high-energy dogs. Although not demanding of exercise, daily exercise is important, as this breed can become fat with too many snacks and not enough exercise.

## Breed in Brief

**Registries:** AKC, UKC, CKC
**Occupation:** Companion
**Size:** 8 to 11 in tall; 9 to 16 lbs
**Longevity:** 14 to 16 years
**Exercise:** Low activity level
**Training:** Challenge to housetrain
**Grooming:** Difficult

Housetraining Shih Tzu can sometimes be a challenge. Owners should be patient, follow a schedule, and supervise the puppy. Although training is not as important with this breed as with so many others, Shih Tzu do thrive in a training program that is fun. Shih Tzu are also easily spoiled, so training can help prevent bad behaviors.

This breed was bred to be a companion, plain and simple. These dogs love people and are friendly and affectionate. The breed is also great with children, as long as the kids are not too rough. They are fine with other dogs and with smaller pets. Health concerns include allergies and eye and kidney problems.

# Shiloh Shepherd

## (Smooth Coat and Plush Coat)

The Shiloh Shepherd breed was founded by Tina Barber as a means of preserving the old type German Shepherd Dog. Barber is the President of the Shiloh Shepherd Dog Club of America and, through this group, attempts to guide the breed's continuing development. However, there has been considerable controversy within the breed, and other organizations were founded in competition with hers.

With multiple organizations representing the breed, the standards vary. Under the American Rare Breed Association, the breed is a large, powerful dog, with adult males standing no less than 28 inches tall (with 30 inches preferred) and females no less than 26 inches (28 inches preferred). Weight is proportionate to height and is generally 100 to 160 pounds. The breed has a German Shepherd Dog appearance, with erect ears, brown eyes, a body that is longer than tall at the shoulder, and a long, full tail. Two coat types are acceptable, both with a double coat. The smooth coat is of medium length, and the plush coat is longer, with more profuse feathering. Both coats shed and should be brushed at least twice weekly, especially during spring and fall, when shedding is heaviest.

Shiloh Shepherds need vigorous daily exercise. Although walks are great for socialization and training, they are not enough. This breed needs a chance to run, as well as daily playtimes.

These dogs need early socialization, as they are watchful and reserved with strangers. Training should also begin early to teach household and social manners and should continue into adulthood; these dogs need a mental challenge and training can help with that.

A well-trained Shiloh Shepherd can be a wonderful family dog. She can be great with children, although puppies can be rambunctious. She can also be good with other family pets when raised with them. Health concerns include hip and elbow dysplasia, bloat, torsion, and allergies.

## Breed in Brief

**Registries:** ARBA
**Occupation:** Herder, guardian
**Size:** Males: 28+ in tall, females 26+ in tall; 100 to 160 lbs
**Longevity:** 10 to 12 years
**Exercise:** Vigorous daily exercise
**Training:** Easy; hard to keep challenged
**Grooming:** Easy to moderate

# Siberian Husky

The Siberian Husky is first and foremost a sled dog. Bred originally by the Chukchi people of Siberia, the breed became well-known after its introduction to Alaska and participation in the lifesaving run to Nome with diphtheria serum.

This athletic breed stands between 20 and 23.5 inches tall and weighs 35 to 60 pounds. Bred to run long distances very quickly while pulling light loads, the breed is never to be heavy or cumbersome. The eyes are almond-shaped and either brown, blue, or parti-colored. The ears are erect and well-furred. The body is slightly longer than the dog is tall, and the tail is well-furred. The undercoat is soft and dense, while the outer coat is straight and of medium length. The coat may be all colors, from white to black.

This coat needs weekly brushing for most of the year, but during shedding seasons, usually spring and fall, daily brushing is typically needed.

Siberian Huskies were bred to run and still have that need. These dogs can go jogging with their owners, run alongside a bicycle, or run in the yard. All exercise should be either on leash or within a securely fenced area, as they have a tendency to be escape artists and to wander.

Training is also important to help keep these dogs safe and should begin in early puppyhood. However, even a well-trained Siberian may not be trustworthy off leash outside of a fenced yard. Siberians have a funny sense of humor, and this can interfere with training sessions. Siberians are extroverts, friendly with just about everyone; they are not watchdogs.

This breed needs an owner who doesn't mind dog hair in the house, who is active, and who understands the breed's need to run. Siberians also do better with company, either with someone home all day or the company of another dog. The breed is usually great with kids. These dogs should not be trusted with smaller pets; they have a strong prey drive. Health concerns include eye problems and hip dysplasia.

## Breed in Brief

**Registries:** AKC, UKC, CKC
**Occupation:** Sled dog
**Size:** 20 to 23.5 in tall; 35 to 60 lbs
**Longevity:** 11 to 13 years
**Exercise:** Daily run
**Training:** Moderate to difficult
**Grooming:** Sheds

# Silken Windhound

Francie Stull and her husband, Chuck, had bred champion Borzoi under the kennel name Kristull for many years when they decided they wanted a second breed. After thinking about many existing breeds, they realized what they actually wanted didn't exist. In 1984, Francie began the development of what would eventually become the Silken Windhound, a small, elegant sighthound with a silky coat.

This breed stands 18 to 23.5 inches tall and weighs between 22 and 55 pounds, with females smaller than males. The Silken Windhound is very much a sighthound, with a long narrow head, long neck, deep chest, and high tuck up. The tail is long and low. The coat varies from moderately long to long and can be straight or wavy.

Most dogs need twice weekly brushing and combing to keep the coat clean and free of tangles. Grooming this breed can be very easy to moderately difficult, depending upon the length of the coat and how much the coat sheds. There is still quite a bit of variety in the breed.

Silken Windhounds love to run, and although they can do fine in an apartment or small house, they need a chance to run several times a week. A daily run is even better. They should never be allowed to run free outside of a fenced-in yard, however, as they will chase a rabbit or squirrel if they get the chance. No amount of calling will bring the dog back in mid-chase. Once they have had a chance to run, these dogs are happiest curled up on the sofa.

Joyce Chin, chairperson of the national rescue group for the breed, says, "The Silken Windhound trains easily and most effectively using reward- and affection-based training. With these methods, Silkens will work eagerly and form strong relationships with their owners." She adds, "This is not a breed that will work all day, and they will not tolerate endless repetition." However, with the correct training approach, many have enjoyed agility and therapy dog work, and a few are even serving as assistance dogs. Chin also says that the collar most often used is a martingale collar (the breed can slip out of most other types of collars). Anyone who has researched and understands sighthounds will enjoy this breed; however, people who have previously had herding or working dog breeds might be a little frustrated, as sighthounds are different.

## Breed in Brief

**Registries:** International Silken Windhound Society
**Occupation:** Sighthound, companion
**Size:** 18 to 23.5 in tall; 22 to 55 lbs
**Longevity:** 16 to 18 years
**Exercise:** Needs to run!
**Training:** Moderate
**Grooming:** Easy to moderate

Silkens are quite social and affectionate with their families, although some do appear to love all mankind. The breed is not protective, and many will not even bark when someone approaches the house. Chin says, "This is a wonderful family-friendly breed for gentle, considerate children. They do not have the pain tolerance of some other breeds and will not be able to cope with rough and rowdy children." As with many sighthound breeds, the Silken prefers to play with other sighthounds who like to chase rather than playing wrestling games with dogs of other breeds. Some Silkens can be trusted with smaller pets, especially when raised with them, but many will chase cats who run. The breed is, for the most part, quite healthy, with many dogs living to their upper teens, but the breed does have some sensitivities to ivermectin (a heartworm preventative), so that drug should be avoided.

# Silky Terrier

The Silky Terrier (or Silky) is a true Australian; she was derived from the crossing of imported Yorkshire Terriers with native Australian Terriers. Although the first breedings were done to improve the coat and color of the Australian Terriers, the offspring of these mixes soon became popular and known as Sydney Silky Terriers. The Silky Terriers were bred together until they bred true to type and the breed was established. The first regional breed standards were created in the early 1900s, with a national breed standard adopted in 1926.

The Silky is a toy terrier, standing only 9 to 10 inches tall and weighing 8 to 12 pounds. The body is longer than it is tall at the shoulder and is refined as benefits a toy breed, yet sturdy enough to hunt rodents. The head is wedge-shaped, with dark almond-shaped eyes and upright, V-shaped ears. The tail is docked. The coat is silky, straight, shiny, and long, yet does not fall to floor length as the Yorkshire Terrier's coat does. The coat is parted down the backbone from head to tail and is blue and tan.

Grooming the Silky takes a little effort, as the coat can tangle, especially if the dog is active. Brushing and combing the coat once a day will keep it looking wonderful. Many pet owners trim the dog's feet and the area under the tail to help keep the dog clean.

Although the Silky is an alert, active little dog—very much a terrier—she is not as busy as many of the other terrier breeds. Daily aerobic exercise is still important, though. The Silky Terrier Club of America says, "A Silky isn't hyper, but they do have tons of energy and love to play fetch, go for long walks, and in general, be involved in whatever the family is doing!" Silkys should be exercised on leash or in a fenced-in area. If a squirrel or rabbit is spotted and the dog is off leash, she will be after it in a flash, and no amount of calling will bring her back.

Training should begin early. Silkys are intelligent dogs (with just a touch of a stubborn streak) and need guidance. Teach basic obedience as well as household rules, and then continue training. Silkys thrive in many dogs sports, including agility, flyball, go-to-ground competitions, and obedience competition. The breed is a favorite for many serious canine sports competitors because of its intelligence, terrier tenacity, and natural athleticism. At home, without regular training and an activity to keep her busy, a Silky will find something else to do and her owner may not appreciate it!

Silkys are great companions for active people who understand the breed's nature and who want a dog to do things with. The breed does not do well when isolated for long hours. These dogs can be barkers and when left alone can be problem barkers. They can also be mischievous. They are good with children who treat them with respect but are not always good with other dogs. Silkys should not be trusted with small pets; remember, these dogs are vermin hunters. The breed does have some health concerns, including knee problems, Cushing's disease, hypothyroidism, Legg-Perthe's disease, and epilepsy.

## Breed in Brief

**Registries:** AKC, UKC, CKC
**Occupation:** Vermin hunter, companion, performance sports
**Size:** 9 to 10 in tall; 8 to 12 lbs
**Longevity:** 14 to 16 years
**Exercise:** Active; long walks, lots of games
**Training:** Easy to moderate; hard to keep focused
**Grooming:** Moderate

# Small Munsterlander Pointer

*I*n Germany, where the Small Munsterlander Pointer originated, the breed is known as the Kleiner Munsterlander. This breed has been known as a versatile hunting dog for more than 500 years. These dogs were owned by the common people who used them to point, track, and retrieve game for the dinner table.

Small Munsterlanders stand 19 to 22 inches tall and weigh 35 to 55 pounds. They have brown eyes and dropped ears. The body is longer than it is tall, and the tail is of medium length. The undercoat is soft, while the outer coat is straight to slightly wavy with feathering on the ears, legs, and tail. The coat is brown and white. For much of its history, this breed was bred for performance rather than appearance.

The coat needs twice weekly brushing to keep it free of tangles. If the dog has been working in the field, the coat will need additional brushing to remove burrs and grass seeds.

This is an active breed that needs daily exercise. If not used for hunting on a regular basis, these dogs need a chance to go for a long run or even for a swim (the breed loves water). They also enjoy retrieving, which can be great exercise. All exercise should be on leash or within a fenced-in yard.

Although generally easy to train, the breed was bred to be a persistent hunter and can be stubborn. Training should not be harsh or forceful; this will cause the dog to fight back. Instead, this breed is generally eager to please and will do much better with a varied, fair, and fun training method. A bored Small Munsterlander will invent ways to amuse herself.

The Small Munsterlander is still a popular hunting dog, especially in Europe, but is also a wonderful family pet. These dogs are very affectionate and good with children and other dogs. They do have a strong prey drive and should not be trusted with smaller pets. The primary health concern is hip dysplasia.

## Breed in Brief

**Registries:** AKC FSS, UKC
**Occupation:** Hunter
**Size:** 19 to 22 in tall; 35 to 55 lbs
**Longevity:** 11 to 13 years
**Exercise:** Active
**Training:** Moderate
**Grooming:** Easy to moderate

# Soft Coated Wheaten Terrier

$\mathcal{M}$any of the breeds in this book have been cultivated and favored by nobility and royalty in the past, but not these dogs. Known for more than 200 years in Ireland, this breed was known as the poor man's terrier. Throughout her history, the Soft Coated Wheaten was a versatile, hardy, hard-working dog who could do everything from hunt vermin to turn the spits in the kitchen.

Today, the Wheaten is a medium-sized terrier, standing 17 to 19 inches tall and weighing 30 to 40 pounds. The head is well-balanced, the eyes are dark brown, and the ears drop forward. The body is compact and as long as the dog is tall at the shoulders. The tail is docked. There is no undercoat, and the outer coat is soft and silky. The coat may be any shade of wheaten.

This coat requires some regular care. The soft coat can tangle and mat if not brushed and combed several times a week. Show dogs must be groomed in a specific manner; most pet owners keep the dog's coat short.

This breed needs a chance to run and play every day; these are active dogs who can easily get into trouble if bored. All exercise needs to be on leash or within a fenced-in yard; Wheatens do have a strong prey drive and will chase small animals. Socialization is important, as these dogs are wary of strangers.

Training the Wheaten can be a challenge. Although intelligent and cheerful, they can be stubborn. Training should be structured and establish the owner as the leader, while at the same time remaining fun and motivating. Wheatens love games, so trick training, agility, or other games should be incorporated into their training regimen. Many Wheatens do well in canine sports.

This breed needs an owner who can establish leadership without being rough or harsh. Although adult Wheatens are usually good with children, puppies can be rowdy. Most Wheatens are good with other dogs but some can be scrappy. Health concerns include eye problems, kidney disorders, Addison's disease, and allergies.

## Breed in Brief

**Registries:** AKC, UKC, CKC
**Occupation:** Versatile farm dog, companion
**Size:** 17 to 19 in tall; 30 to 40 lbs
**Longevity:** 12 to 14 years
**Exercise:** Daily
**Training:** Moderate to difficult
**Grooming:** Difficult

# South African Boerboel

The South African Boerboel is a versatile breed with a long history as a hunter and guardian, with ancient roots going back to dogs that came with immigrants to South Africa, primarily in the 1600s and 1700s. They definitely have some Mastiff ancestry, but a variety of other breeds were also used.

This is a large breed that stands between 22 and 30 inches tall with a heavy boned muscular body in proportion to her height. The head is broad and muzzle wide, and the ears are dropped. The back is strong and broad, the chest is deep, and the tail is docked. The coat is short and smooth. Acceptable colors include brindle, tawny, brown, and red brown, all with or without white markings; a dark muzzle is preferred.

The coat should be brushed weekly.

The Boerboel is not an active dog, nor is she a couch potato. This breed was bred to be watchful and protective and can spring into motion at the slightest sign of a threat. At other times, she is calm. Puppies can be quite playful. Daily exercise is recommended to keep the dog fit and strong and to prevent obesity.

This intelligent working dog is confident and self-assured. Training should begin early to make sure the growing dog understands that the owner is her leader and to build compliance. Training should be firm and structured, yet not harsh. Boerboels like to work and need a job to do; without a sense of purpose, they will find something to do.

These dogs do best with an owner who has owned Mastiffs in the past or who understands the working dog temperament. These strong, confident, protective dogs can be too much for a first-time dog owner. With an owner who understands them, this breed is extremely devoted and fiercely loyal; they will give their lives in protection of their owners. Although puppies are rowdy, the breed is wonderful with children. Health concerns include bloat, torsion, eye problems, wobbler's sydrome, and hip and elbow dysplasia.

## Breed in Brief

**Registries:** United States Boerboel Association
**Occupation:** Working dog, guard dog
**Size:** 22 to 30 in tall; weight proportionate to height
**Longevity:** 9 to 10 years
**Exercise:** Low to moderate
**Training:** Hard to keep challenged
**Grooming:** Easy

# Spanish Greyhound

## (Smooth Coat and Wirehaired Coat)

The Spanish Greyhound, or Galgo Espanol, is probably descended from several different sighthound breeds, including the Saluki, Ibizan Hound, and English Greyhound. The breed has been used for centuries in Spain as a hunting dog capable of running quickly over rough terrain. It was primarily used for hunting hare.

This dog is a sighthound, with a long head, long neck, long flexible body, and strong legs. The Spanish Greyhound has a deep chest but not as deep as the English Greyhound. The tail is very long. She is tall, between 23.5 and 27.5 inches at the shoulder. Her coat may be short and smooth or wirehaired. The colors are primarily brindle, black, cream, and red, often with white markings.

Grooming these dogs is easy. Both coat types should be brushed twice weekly.

Spanish Greyhounds need a chance to run in a safe, fenced-in area. They are strong hunters. If allowed to run off leash outside of a fenced-in area, they may flush a rabbit and will be gone in a flash; calling will not bring them back. When she has had her run, the Spanish Greyhound will be a happy to curl up on a comfortable cushion.

This breed can be reserved with strangers, so early socialization is important. Training should be fun yet structured. The ideal owner for this breed is someone who understands sighthounds. A dog owner who has previously owned herding or working dogs may be puzzled by the Spanish Greyhound's temperament, especially her refusal to participate in repetitive or forceful training. When in a pet home where they do not hunt, these dogs will enjoy the sport of lure coursing.

Spanish Greyhounds are affectionate to their family and calm in the house. Although wary of strangers, they should not be considered watchdogs. They are great with children who are gentle and treat them with respect. They are good with other dogs but should not be trusted with other small pets. This is a healthy breed.

## Breed in Brief

**Registries:** UKC, Galgo Espanol Club of America
**Occupation:** Sighthound
**Size:** 23.5 to 27.5 in tall; weight proportionate to height
**Longevity:** 11 to 13 years
**Exercise:** Daily run
**Training:** Moderate challenge
**Grooming:** Easy

# Spanish Mastiff

These livestock guardian dogs have been protecting sheep and cattle in the Estremadura region of Spain for thousands of years. The Spanish Mastiff, or Mastin Espanol, is thought to have been brought to the Iberian Peninsula by Phoenician traders.

This is a massive breed, standing 28 to 32 inches tall and weighing 150 to 200 pounds or more. The head is well-proportioned, with small eyes, dropped ears, and full lips. There is a dewlap on the lower neck. The body is rectangular, with a deep chest. The rear feet have double dewclaws. The skin is loose, the undercoat is dense, and the outer coat is short and straight. The colors include brown, red-brown, wolf-gray, and yellow.

The coat should be brushed weekly except during shedding seasons, generally the spring and fall, when more brushing is needed. These dogs also drool.

Breed expert Karin Graefe of De La Tierra Alta Kennels says, "The Spanish Mastiff does not require a great deal of exercise. However, a good sized yard where the dog can bound around is preferred." They can be playful and are very curious; they will notice anything new in the house or yard right away.

This breed was bred to be watchful and protective, even to the point of aggressiveness when needed. They are suspicious of strangers, so early socialization is needed. Graefe says, "Spanish Mastiffs are calm and steady in temperament and are easy to train." Training should continue into adulthood, as these dogs are slow to mature.

The Spanish Mastiff needs an owner who understands livestock guardian dogs and their characteristics, especially their desire to protect the home and family. The owner must also be willing to do the training needed to control a large, powerful dog. The breed is good with children, although puppies may be rough and rowdy. The breed is good with dogs it is raised with but will not tolerate strange dogs. Health concerns include heart problems, eye problems, bloat, torsion, and hip dysplasia.

## Breed in Brief

**Registries:** UKC, CKC
**Occupation:** Livestock guardian
**Size:** 28 to 32 in tall; 150 to 200+ lbs
**Longevity:** 10 to 12 years; some to 14 years
**Exercise:** Low to moderate
**Training:** Easy; socialization required
**Grooming:** Sheds and drools

# Spanish Water Dog

The Spanish Water Dog, or Perro de Agua Espanol, is a versatile, ancient breed found on the Iberian Peninsula. For centuries, this breed was used to herd goats and sheep, but it is also a water retriever.

These dogs stand 17 to 19.5 inches tall and weigh between 30 and 50 pounds. The head is strong, with a slightly flat skull, hazel to chestnut colored eyes, and dropped ears. The body is slightly longer than tall, with a deep chest, and a docked or naturally bobbed tail. The coat is curly and wooly. When the coat grows in length, cords form. The coat can be white, chestnut, black, or tricolored.

The coat will grow and cord naturally, but the cords should be helped to grow without turning into mats, which can pull the skin or cause skin problems underneath. Special care must be taken when bathing the dog, too. The coat is usually shaved short once a year. Potential owners should discuss this breed's coat care with a breeder.

Breed expert Linda Kardonis says, "The SWD is an active breed. They do need their playtime; however, when one finds themselves wrapped up in the everyday chores, these dogs are naturally inclined to amuse themselves." She adds, "The SWD is always ready to entertain, to retrieve, to swim, hike, herd, or to entice you into playing a game of ball."

This is an intelligent breed. Kardonis says, "They are easy to train and have a high motivation to please." The training technique should be fun. She adds that early and continued socialization is important, as those who are not well-socialized may be overprotective or shy.

This breed needs an owner who can socialize and train the dog. The owner must be aware of the breed's grooming needs and be willing to take the time to groom the dog properly. Many breeders will not sell dogs to families with children under the age of 5, as the dogs often try to herd the kids. These dogs are also good with other dogs and smaller pets. Health concerns include eye defects, thyroid disease, and hip dysplasia.

## Breed in Brief

**Registries:** AKC FSS, UKC
**Occupation:** Herder, water retriever
**Size:** 17 to 19.5 in tall; 30 to 50 lbs
**Longevity:** 12 to 14 years
**Exercise:** Daily
**Training:** Easy
**Grooming:** Difficult

# Spinone Italiano

The Spinone Italiano, or Italian Griffon, is one of the oldest griffon (wire coated) breeds, with ancestors known to be in existence more than 2,500 years ago. The breed originated in the Piedmont region of Italy. These dogs are very capable gun dogs, pointers, and enthusiastic retrievers.

These dogs stand 22 to 27 inches tall and weigh between 65 and 90 pounds. The head is long, the eyes are large, and the ears are hanging. The dog has a square build with a deep chest and a docked tail. The coat is weather-resistant, wire-haired, dense, stiff, and flat or slightly wavy. The face has eyebrows, a beard, and a mustache. Some of the acceptable colors include white, orange and white, and brown and white.

The coat needs to be brushed weekly, and once in a while will need hand-stripping to remove dead coat. Potential owners should discuss coat care with a breeder. The beard can be messy and may need daily care.

This is an active breed. These dogs enjoy walks but should also have a chance to run. Many dogs of this breed have excelled in canine sports, including agility, flyball, tracking, search and rescue, and even carting. The Spinone Italiano is also an excellent swimmer.

Early socialization is very important for these dogs. Unsocialized dogs may be timid or fearful. A puppy class is a great idea, but socialization should continue into young adulthood. Happy, upbeat, and playful, these dogs thrive on training that is fun and not too repetitive. They can have a stubborn streak, though, and sometimes need additional motivation to perform a given task or exercise.

These dogs crave interaction with their people and need a situation where they are not alone for too many hours each day. When alone and bored, these dogs have been known to become escape artists, jumping fences or tunneling under them. They are great with children and are also good with other dogs. Primary health concerns include hip dysplasia and cerebellar ataxia.

## Breed in Brief

**Registries:** AKC, UKC, CKC
**Occupation:** Gun dog, retriever
**Size:** 22 to 27 in tall; 65 to 90 lbs
**Longevity:** 12 to 14 years
**Exercise:** Vigorous daily exercise
**Training:** Moderate
**Grooming:** Difficult

# Staffordshire Bull Terrier

The Staffordshire Bull Terrier originated in England when blood sports (bear and bull baiting and then later dog fighting) were still popular. Descended from Mastiffs, the old Bulldog, and a small terrier, the dogs were known in the mid-1800s as Old Pit Bull Terriers. The dogs that were brought to the U.S. in the mid-1800s developed into taller, heavier-bodied dogs than those that remained in England.

The Staffordshire Bull Terrier stands 14 to 16 inches tall and weighs 24 to 38 pounds. These dogs are muscular, yet agile. The head is broad with a short foreface, with half-pricked ears, and round, medium-sized eyes. The body is compact, with a wide chest. The tail is of medium length and is not docked. The coat is short and smooth. Coat colors include red, fawn, black, blue, or brindle, with or without white markings.

The coat is easy to maintain; it requires brushing once a week to keep it clean. The coat does shed, though, about once a year.

This is an active, athletic breed that needs vigorous daily exercise. They like to run, train in agility, or chase toys. Walks are great opportunities for socialization but are not enough exercise for a young, healthy Stafford. All off-leash exercise should be within a fenced-in yard, as Staffords have a strong prey drive and many adult Staffords are not good with strange dogs.

Training a Stafford requires a balance of firmness (so that the owner can establish control) and leadership yet a light hand, as these dogs can be surprisingly sensitive. At the same time, they can be stubborn. Socialization and training should both begin in early puppyhood.

The Stafford does better when she is not left alone for too many hours each day. When bored and lonely, a Stafford can be amazingly destructive when trying to amuse herself. The breed is good with children and will join in with the kids' games. They can be aggressive to other dogs. Health concerns include hip dysplasia, eye defects, and cleft palate.

## Breed in Brief

**Registries:** AKC, UKC, CKC
**Occupation:** Companion
**Size:** 14 to 16 in tall; 24 to 38 lbs
**Longevity:** 12 to 14 years
**Exercise:** Vigorous daily exercise
**Training:** Moderate
**Grooming:** Easy

# Standard Schnauzer

The Standard Schnauzer is the oldest of the three schnauzer breeds and an ancestor of the other two—the Giant Schnauzer and the Miniature Schnauzer. Paintings from the Middle Ages show dogs that look much like today's Standard Schnauzer. The dogs were multipurpose dogs—catching vermin, protecting the farm, livestock, and family, and driving livestock to market.

These dogs stand 17 to 20 inches tall and weigh 35 to 45 pounds. The head is strong and rectangular, the eyes are oval and dark brown, and the ears are either folded or cropped. The body is as long as the dog is tall and is strong and well-muscled. The undercoat is soft and dense. The outer coat is tight, hard, and wiry. The two acceptable colors are black and salt and pepper.

The coat can tangle and mat, especially the beard and feathers on the legs, so it must be brushed or combed at least twice a week. The undercoat does shed and needs brushing. The outer coat must be either hand-stripped or groomed with clippers. Potential owners should discuss coat care with a breeder.

Standard Schnauzers are active dogs who need daily walks and a chance to run and play. These dogs will enjoy a chance to train on the agility course, play flyball, or even go for a jog. This breed prefers to be a companion and will enjoy any activities the owner wishes to do with her.

These are intelligent dogs who have a tendency to be a touch stubborn. Training should begin young and continue on into adulthood, not just to establish the owner's control but also to keep the dog's mind busy. These versatile dogs were bred to work and still have a strong work ethic.

The Standard Schnauzer is a family dog who wants to be a part of daily life; she is not a backyard dog. She is watchful and wary of strangers. She is good with children and good with other dogs when well-socialized to them but should not be trusted with smaller pets. The primary health concern is hip dysplasia.

## Breed in Brief

**Registries:** AKC, UKC, CKC
**Occupation:** Versatile farm dog
**Size:** 17 to 20 in tall; 35 to 45 lbs
**Longevity:** 12 to 14 years
**Exercise:** Daily
**Training:** Moderate
**Grooming:** Difficult

# Stumpy Tail Cattle Dog

Stumpy Tail Cattle Dogs, also known as Australian Stumpy Tail Cattle Dogs, are usually simply referred to as Stumpies. This Australian breed originated in the 1800s from a cross between dingos and the Smithfield Collie. It is a close relation to the Australian Cattle Dog.

For most of this breed's history, performance, working instinct, and stamina were much more important than appearance. Most Stumpies stand between 17 and 20 inches tall and weigh between 35 and 50 pounds. The ears are erect, the muzzle is tapered, and the tail is naturally bobbed. The body is level, strong, and muscular. The coat is medium to short, dense, and harsh. Colors include red roan and blue roan.

Stumpies need twice weekly brushing, although more may be needed when shedding.

This is a very active breed who was bred to herd. Breed expert Grace Harper of Silver Park Kennel, says, "Their stamina is such that they can follow a horse all day working cattle and you still can't tire them out." This energy has attracted people who enjoy training their dogs in performance sports, and Stumpies are now competing in flyball, agility, and herding. This breed is not a couch potato!

Harper says, "Stumpies are extremely intelligent, sometimes downright scary in their ability to learn." This means training is very important. Training should begin early, continue into adulthood, and challenge the dog's abilities. Stumpies can learn tricks and should definitely have a job to do. Socialization should begin in puppyhood, as this breed is watchful and protective.

Stumpies need an actively involved owner who enjoys a canine shadow. This breed has a tendency to bond more closely with one owner than with multiple people. They are good with children when raised with them but, if not raised with them, will usually avoid them. They can be good with other dogs but often wish to be in charge. Health concerns include deafness, cleft palate, and back problems.

## Breed in Brief

**Registries:** CKC, UKC
**Occupation:** Herder
**Size:** 17 to 20 in tall; 35 to 50 lbs
**Longevity:** 12 to 14 years
**Exercise:** Vigorous daily exercise
**Training:** Hard to keep challenged
**Grooming:** Easy

# Swedish Vallhund

The Swedish Vallhund, often called the Viking dog, is a very old breed dating back as far as 1,000 years. Used as a cattle herding dog and as a versatile farm dog, these dogs retain their herding instincts today. The breed is believed to be related to the welsh corgis, although the exact relationship has yet to be determined.

These long, low-slung dogs stand between 11.5 and 13.5 inches tall and weigh 25 to 35 pounds. The head is wedge-shaped, with upright ears and dark brown eyes. The body is long, the legs are strong, and the tail is either long or a natural bobtail. The undercoat is soft and dense, while the outer coat is of medium length and harsh. Colors include gray, grayish brown, grayish yellow, or reddish brown, with a distinct harness pattern on the shoulders.

This coat needs twice weekly brushing. The coat does shed, and during the spring and fall, additional brushing may be needed.

These are active dogs of herding heritage who need a chance to run and play. Although walks are great opportunities for socialization, these dogs need more exercise than a walk can provide. They will enjoy a chance to train on the agility course or play flyball. Many have excelled in herding trials. A bored Vallhund will get into trouble!

## Breed in Brief

**Registries:** AKC FSS, UKC, CKC
**Occupation:** Herder
**Size:** 11.5 to 13.5 in tall; 25 to 35 lbs
**Longevity:** 12 to 14 years
**Exercise:** Active
**Training:** Hard to keep challenged
**Grooming:** Easy; sheds

This breed thrives on training, although the owner is often challenged to keep up. Training should not be repetitive and rote but instead should continue to add new things such as advanced obedience, trick training, and canine sports. The breed is also watchful and protective, so early socialization is important.

The Swedish Vallhund needs an owner who will train her and, ideally, will do activities with her, preferably canine sports or herding. The breed can be noisy and this can cause problems with neighbors, but training can control the barking. The breed is good with kids, other dogs, and smaller pets. Health problems include hip dysplasia, eye problems, luxated pattellas, and cleft palate.

# Thai Ridgeback

Thai Ridgebacks have been in existence in Thailand for more than 400 years and maybe even as long as 1,000 years, as early cave paintings portraying dogs with ridges have been found in Cambodia and Thailand. These sighthounds were used to hunt deer, tapir, and birds.

These dogs stand 21 to 24.5 inches tall and weigh 37 to 60 pounds. The head and muzzle are wedge-shaped, the eyes are almond-shaped and dark brown, and the ears are upright. The body is longer than the dog is tall. The coat is short and may be black, red, blue, or fawn. The ridge on the back consists of hairs growing in the opposite direction of the coat and may be found in eight different patterns. The ridge begins at the shoulders and runs down the back to the point of the hips.

The coat is easy to care for and needs only weekly brushing.

The Thai Ridgeback is a moderately active dog. He will appreciate a couple of walks each day and a chance to run. Exercise should be on leash or inside a fenced yard. Like most sighthounds, if a small animal is flushed while he's running, a Ridgeback will take off after it.

These dogs are natural watchdogs and protective of their homes and families. Early socialization to a variety of people is important to make sure the dogs are not shy, fearful, or overly aggressive. Breed expert Mary Ann Nemisz says, "The breed can be dog-aggressive and so requires lots of socialization with other dogs from an early age." She adds, "Thai Ridgebacks do well with training that is positive and fast paced; they bore easily and repetitive training is not for them."

Nemisz says, "This breed is not for everyone and is best for an experienced dog owner." Ridgebacks can be good with children when raised with them, but dogs not accustomed to kids may be aloof. The breed has a strong prey drive and loves to chase, so interactions with cats and other small animals should be carefully supervised. The primary health concern is problems with the dermoid sinus.

## Breed in Brief

**Registries:** AKC FSS, UKC
**Occupation:** Hunter, watchdog
**Size:** 21 to 24.5 in tall; 37 to 60 lbs
**Longevity:** 13 to 15 years
**Exercise:** Daily run
**Training:** Requires extensive socialization
**Grooming:** Easy

# Tibetan Mastiff

The Tibetan Mastiff, also known as the Do-Khyi, is an ancient breed who served as both a herding dog and a guardian dog for the nomads of Tibet and a watchdog at the Tibetan monasteries. There are many varieties of this breed (from the sheep-herding varieties to the heavier-boned Mastiff ones), as working performance and physical soundness were historically much more important than physical characteristics.

The large Mastiff variety of this breed (the better-known variety) stands from 24 to 30 inches tall and weighs 80 to 160 pounds. The head is broad and heavy, with a broad muzzle, medium-sized eyes, and pendant ears. The body is strong, with a deep chest and a medium-length tail that is carried high and curled over the back. The undercoat is wooly, while the outer coat is thick and dense. The coat may black, blue, or brown, with or without tan markings.

This breed's coat requires twice weekly brushing for most of the year. However, the coat does shed, and when it does, daily brushing will help keep the hair in the house under control.

## Breed in Brief

**Registries:** AKC FSS, UKC, CKC

**Occupation:** Livestock guardian

**Size:** 24 to 30 in tall; 80 to 160 lbs

**Longevity:** 10 to 12 years

**Exercise:** Moderate

**Training:** Challenge

**Grooming:** Moderate

This is not an overly active breed and will do well with daily walks and a chance to play in the yard. Puppies are more active than adults and, without exercise, can be destructive.

Socialization is very important, as this breed is quite watchful and protective. These dogs should meet a variety of people and other dogs, both in a puppy class and out on walks. Training can be challenging, as these dogs can be quite independent and sometimes stubborn. However, if the training is firm and structured, yet fun and upbeat, this breed can be trained.

Tibetan Mastiffs need experienced dog owners. They are protective, and the owners must have control. They can be good with children but may not understand rough play. They are good with other family dogs but will not tolerate strange dogs. Health concerns include hip and elbow dysplasia, eye problems, and thyroid disease.

# Tibetan Spaniel

Tibetan Spaniels were used as both companions and watchdogs in Tibetan villages and monasteries. Although not large enough to be effective guard dogs, their barking would alert their owners to visitors, trespassers, or predators. The breed's ancestors include the Pekingese and the Japanese Chin. Tibetan Buddhists placed ceramic statues of these dogs in tombs so that the departed would have the companionship of their dogs after death.

The Tibetan Spaniel stands from 9 to 11 inches tall and weighs 9 to 15 pounds. The head is small and slightly domed with oval-shaped dark brown eyes and pendant ears. The body is slightly longer than the dog is tall, and the tail is plumed and carried over the back. The undercoat is soft, and the outer coat is silky. The coat is smooth on the face and the front of the legs. The ears, backs of the legs, tail, and ruff are feathered.

This breed needs brushing and combing two to three times a week. The coat, especially the feathers, can tangle and mat. The coat also sheds.

Lynn Parazak says of her Tibetan Spaniel, "Aja needs a daily walk, but if I can't get out, she can get enough exercise playing ball in the house or backyard." She adds that Aja is very playful, even as an adult, and loves fetch games.

## Breed in Brief

**Registries:** AKC, UKC, CKC
**Occupation:** Watchdog, companion
**Size:** 9 to 11 in tall; 9 to 15 lbs
**Longevity:** 13 to 15 years
**Exercise:** Low activity level
**Training:** Easy to moderate
**Grooming:** Easy to moderate

Bred for centuries as a watchdog, this breed can be quite standoffish and wary of strangers. Early socialization, beginning in puppyhood, can prevent fearfulness or aggression. As watchdogs, they can also be barkers, but training can help control that. For the most part, training is easy, as these dogs are very eager to please. Many Tibetan Spaniels serve as therapy dogs.

This breed is very affectionate and loves to be with people. They are good with children who do not treat them roughly or with disrespect. Parazak says that Aja can get overwhelmed in situations with a lot of children. The primary health concern is eye problems, including PRA and cataracts.

# Tibetan Terrier

Tibetan Terriers are more than 2,000 years old, originating in Tibet as companions for the monks in the monasteries in the region that eventually became known as the Lost Valley. The Lost Valley in Tibet became "lost" when an earthquake in the 14th century destroyed the only path into the region. The monks called the dogs Holy Dogs.

The breed was also owned by villagers in that region, who considered the dogs lucky and called them Luck Bringers. The dogs were never sold, although a dog could be given away as a token of

friendship or goodwill. Owners who mistreated one of these dogs or allowed a dog to mate with a dog of another breed were in danger of losing their luck and could even be scorned or shunned by the other villagers.

Although called a terrier, this breed is not one. Because the names Holy Dog and Luck Bringer were deemed not suitable breed names once the dogs were introduced to people outside of Tibet, a new name was needed, and these dogs are the same size as many of the well-known terrier breeds. Tibetan Terriers do not have a terrier temperament, nor are they vermin hunters.

These dogs stand between 14 and 17 inches tall and usually weigh 18 to 30 pounds. The head is of medium size, with large, dark brown eyes and pendant ears. The body is slightly longer than tall at the shoulder, and the tail curls over the back. The undercoat is soft and wooly, while the outer coat is fine, profuse, and may be wavy or straight. The coat is long but does not reach the ground. It may be any color.

This coat needs to be brushed and combed at least every other day, as it will tangle and mat. Although show dogs are not to be shaved or trimmed, many pet owners do have the coat trimmed. Pet owners who enjoy the long coat may have only the feet, face, genitals, and under the tail areas trimmed slightly for cleanliness. Potential owners should discuss the breed's coat care needs with a breeder.

Since Tibetan Terriers were bred to be companion dogs, they are very adaptable. In a home where people are busy and active, the dog will be, too. In a more sedentary home, the dog tends to be calmer. However, these dogs should have at least one walk per day and a good play session to help keep them fit and to prevent obesity. Many dogs have done very well in agility and therapy dog work.

Training this breed is not difficult; Tibetan Terriers are bright and enjoy learning as long as the training is fair and fun. Socialization should begin early, as these dogs are standoffish with strangers. Although walks are great opportunities for socialization, a kindergarten puppy class is a wise idea, too. Training should continue into adulthood so that dog and owner can do something together.

The Tibetan Terrier needs an owner who enjoys grooming the dog, because even if the coat is trimmed, it still needs regular care. These dogs are excellent family dogs and are great with children as long as the kids are not too rough. They are usually good with other dogs, cats, and small animals. Health concerns include hip dysplasia and several different eye problems.

## Breed in Brief

**Registries:** AKC, UKC, CKC
**Occupation:** Companion
**Size:** 14 to 17 in tall; 18 to 30 lbs
**Longevity:** 13 to 15 years
**Exercise:** Low to moderate
**Training:** Easy
**Grooming:** Difficult

# Tosa Ken

In the mid- to late 1800s and early 1900s, Mastiffs, Saint Bernards, Great Danes, and Bulldogs were imported into Japan to be bred with native dogs in the hopes of creating the ultimate fighting dog. The Tosa Ken was (and still is) known to be quiet, courageous, and deadly. Developed in the old Tosa province, now known as the Kochi prefecture, the breed almost went extinct during World War II but was saved by fanciers. The Tosa Ken is revered in Japan; he is the Sumo wrestler of the canine world.

These dogs stand 21.75 to 23.5 inches or taller and usually weigh between 100 and 200 pounds, although some may be heavier. The head is large and blocky, the eyes are brown, the nose black, and the ears medium-sized and dropped. The body is strong, muscular, and slightly longer than the dog is tall. The tail hangs naturally to the hocks and is never carried over the back. The dog's skin is loose, with pendulous lips, a large flap of skin that hangs beneath the chin, and wrinkles on the forehead. The coat is short and dense. Dogs may be red, brindle, black, or brown.

The coat should be brushed weekly with a soft bristle brush or curry comb.

The Tosa Ken is an athletic, agile dog who needs daily exercise. He needs a couple of brisk, long walks and a chance to run and play.

## Breed in Brief

**Registries:** AKC FSS, UKC
**Occupation:** Fighter
**Size:** 21.75 to 23.5+ in; 100 to 200+ lbs
**Longevity:** 9 to 11 years
**Exercise:** Moderate
**Training:** Easy; socialization required
**Grooming:** Easy

Socialization is very important for this breed. Tosa Kens are very watchful of strangers and need a lot of socialization to other people as puppies and on into adulthood. These dogs are still used in Japan for ritualistic dog fights and retain those instincts. Training this breed is not difficult; Tosa Kens are eager to learn and very willing to please.

The Tosa Ken needs an experienced dog owner who can be the dog's leader. The owner must be willing to take the time to socialize and train the dog. The dog may live peacefully with other family dogs when raised with them but is usually aggressive toward unknown dogs. Health concerns include hip and elbow dysplasia, eye problems, bloat, and torsion.

# Vizsla

The Vizsla's history has been hotly debated. One theory is that the breed, also known as the Hungarian Vizsla, is relatively new and is descended from the Weimaraner. The most popular theory is that the breed goes back more than 1,000 years to the hunting dogs used by the Magyar people in central Europe. No matter where these dogs come from, they were and still are talented hunting dogs used primarily for birds but also for larger game.

This medium-sized dog stands between 21 and 24 inches tall and weighs 45 to 65 pounds. The head is narrow and the muzzle is deep. The eyes are a shade of brown blending in with the coat color. The ears are dropped. The body is strong, chest deep, and tail docked to one-third its natural length. The coat is short and dense and does not have a wooly undercoat. The coat color is distinctive golden rust.

The coat requires weekly brushing with a soft bristled brush.

The Vizsla is a high-energy dog who needs vigorous daily exercise. Although walks will be enjoyed and are great for training and socialization, these dogs need a chance to run hard or swim every day. Without enough exercise, Vizslas can and will get into trouble, especially when young. A tired Vizsla is a happy Vizsla!

Vizslas are bright and take well to training, although they can be surprisingly sensitive. Training should be fun yet firm and consistent. The breed has done well in many canine sports, including agility, hunt tests, tracking, and search and rescue.

This breed needs an active owner who wants to do things with the dog; this is not a good dog for the backyard. The ideal owner would be as athletic as the dog is. These dogs can be great with kids, although puppies can be rough and rowdy. The Vizsla is usually good with other dogs but may not be trustworthy with smaller pets. Health concerns include hip dysplasia, epilepsy, von Willebrand disease, and eye problems.

## Breed in Brief

**Registries:** AKC, UKC, CKC
**Occupation:** Hunter
**Size:** 21 to 24 in tall; 45 to 65 lbs
**Longevity:** 12 to 14 years
**Exercise:** Vigorous daily exercise
**Training:** Moderate
**Grooming:** Easy

# Weimaraner

Germany has produced many fine hunting dogs, and the Weimaraner is one of them. Related to the German Shorthaired Pointer, this breed was bred to be fast, have a good nose, and be a courageous problem solver. The Weimaraner has hunted large game as well as birds.

Weimaraners stand 23 to 27 inches tall and weigh between 60 and 90 pounds. The head is moderately wide between the ears and moderately long. The eyes are light amber or gray to blue-gray, and the ears are wide and dropped. The nose is gray. The body is athletic and the chest is deep. The tail is docked. The coat is short and smooth, with the breed's distinctive feature being silver-gray coloring. The short coat needs only weekly brushing.

This high-energy breed was designed to run and hunt all day. Weimaraners are not couch potatoes, and all the training in the world will not change what they are: energetic hunting dogs. These dogs need vigorous exercise—a run, training on the agility course, or a game of flyball—every single day.

Training should begin early so that the owner can establish control and the puppy can learn household rules and social manners. This breed is intelligent, and these dogs often try to get their own way in life. Weimaraners left alone for too many hours may become problem barkers or escape artists. Socialization is also important, beginning young and continuing on into adulthood. Housetraining can be a challenge; the owner must be patient and consistent.

The Weimaraner needs an owner who is dedicated to keeping this dog busy and who isn't away from the house for too many hours each day. The breed is usually very good with children, although puppies can be rowdy and rough. He is good with other dogs his size, but since the breed has a strong prey drive, he is not to be trusted with smaller pets. Health concerns include hip dysplasia, eye problems, bloat, torsion, and von Willebrand disease.

## Breed in Brief

**Registries:** AKC, UKC, CKC
**Occupation:** Hunter
**Size:** 23 to 27 in tall; 60 to 90 lbs
**Longevity:** 11 to 13 years
**Exercise:** Vigorous daily exercise
**Training:** Challenge
**Grooming:** Easy

# elsh Springer Spaniel

ed and white spaniels portrayed in paintings during the Renaissance look very much
like the Welsh Springer Spaniels of today. Although
this breed shares the name Springer Spaniel, the Welsh
is not directly related to the English Springer Spaniel.
The Welsh breed developed in the isolation of South
Wales and is a hardy, tireless gun dog.

These dogs stand from 17 to 19 inches tall and
weigh 30 to 50 pounds. The head is of medium
width and length, with medium brown, oval-shaped
eyes and dropped ears. The body is slightly longer
than the dog is tall at the shoulder. The tail is
docked. The coat is soft and flat. The ruff, ears, backs
of the legs, and belly are feathered. The coat should be weatherproof and thorn-proof without
being so heavy as to create a problem when the dog is hunting. The coat is red and white.

The coat should be brushed at least twice a week to keep it clean and free of dirt and grass seed.
If the dog works in the field or gets wet, it may need additional grooming.

The Welsh Springer Spaniel was bred to work tirelessly with a hunting partner, so he has a great
deal of energy. When not hunting, he needs a good run every day. These dogs also enjoy agility and
flyball; many are also enthusiastic swimmers. All exercise should be on leash or within a fenced-in
yard so the dog doesn't decide to go hunting on his own.

Socialization should begin early, as this breed can be aloof
toward strangers. Training the Welsh Springer Spaniel is not
hard; these dogs are bright, affectionate, and eager to please.
They can be a touch independent at times, though.

This breed needs an owner who wishes to have a canine
shadow. Although Welsh Springer Spaniels enjoy the company
of others of their breed, they much prefer to spend time with
their owners. They are great with children and other dogs and
are usually good with smaller pets. Health concerns include hip
dysplasia and eye problems.

## Breed in Brief

**Registries:** AKC, UKC, CKC
**Occupation:** Gun dog
**Size:** 17 to 19 in tall; 30 to
50 lbs
**Longevity:** 12 to 14 years
**Exercise:** Daily run
**Training:** Easy to moderate
**Grooming:** Moderate

# elsh Terrier

Although the lineages of these dogs were not documented until the mid-1800s, rough-coated red and black terriers were known in Wales as early as the 1400s. Used for hunting fox, badgers, and otters, these dogs were (and still are) sturdy and game.

This compact, long-legged terrier stands about 15 inches tall and weighs about 20 pounds. His head is rectangular, eyes are small and dark brown, and ears are folded. The body is as long as the dog is tall at the shoulder. The tail is short. The undercoat is short and soft, and the outer coat is hard and wiry. The back is black with color going up the back of the neck and down to the tail, while the rest of the dog is a reddish tan.

The coat needs regular brushing and combing to keep it clean and neat. The beard can be messy and drip water after the dog drinks. The coat needs either regular grooming or hand-stripping; potential owners need to discuss coat care with a breeder.

The Welsh Terrier is an active dog who has fun hunting for small critters in the woodpile but also enjoys long, brisk walks. Although not as active as some other terrier breeds, these dogs will get into trouble if they don't get enough exercise. Welsh Terriers also participate in many canine sports, including agility, flyball, and terrier go-to-ground trials.

These intelligent dogs will thrive with firm, structured, yet fun training. Training should include tricks and games to keep the dog from becoming bored. Although usually more social with other dogs than many other terrier breeds, Welsh Terriers still need early and continued socialization with friendly dogs.

This breed does best with an owner who understands terriers; they may be too much for a first-time dog owner. They are not always patient with children. Most Welsh Terriers are good with other dogs but should not be trusted with other types of pets. Health concerns include epilepsy, eye and thyroid problems, and allergies.

## Breed in Brief

**Registries:** AKC, UKC, CKC
**Occupation:** Vermin hunter
**Size:** 15 in tall; 20 lbs
**Longevity:** 13 to 15 years
**Exercise:** Moderate
**Training:** Moderate
**Grooming:** Moderate to
　difficult

# West Highland White Terrier

Scotland is the home of several terriers, including the Cairn Terrier, Dandie Dinmont Terrier, Scottish Terrier, and West Highland White Terrier. All of these breeds share ancestry at some point in history. A Westie fancier, Colonel Edward Malcolm, is said to have had a reddish-colored dog who was shot by hunters who mistook the dog for a fox. At that point, Colonel Malcolm decided to breed white dogs who would stand out in the field.

Westies stand between 10 and 11 inches tall and weigh 15 to 20 pounds. This is a compact dog, with medium-sized, dark brown eyes and small, erect ears. The body is slightly shorter than the dog is tall at the shoulders. The tail is short. The undercoat is soft, while the outer coat consists of hard, straight, white hairs. The face is framed by the coat to present a round appearance.

The coat should be brushed a couple of times each week to keep it neat and clean. Show dogs must be presented in a specific way, with the coat hand-stripped (or plucked). Pet owners usually have the dog clipped every four to six weeks. Potential owners should discuss coat care with a breeder.

Westies are active dogs who enjoy long, brisk walks and a chance to play in the yard. They can be great at amusing themselves with toys, but when bored can be destructive chewers or dig amazingly large holes. All exercise should be on leash or within a fenced-in yard.

Westies are easily trained when the owner has figured out what motivates the individual dog. Although not stubborn, Westies can be independent.

A Westie may be too much terrier for a first-time dog owner. They can be good with children but will not tolerate rough play and are too easily stimulated to be a part of a large group of kids playing. Male Westies can be aggressive toward other male dogs. Most Westies should not be trusted with other small pets. Health concerns include eye problems, deafness, copper toxicosis, and Legg-Perthe's disease.

## Breed in Brief

**Registries:** AKC, UKC, CKC
**Occupation:** Vermin hunter, companion
**Size:** 10 to 11 in tall; 15 to 20 lbs
**Longevity:** 13 to 15 years
**Exercise:** Moderate
**Training:** Moderate
**Grooming:** Difficult

# Whippet

The Whippet originated in England. Greyhounds were crossed with the Italian Greyhound and a long-legged terrier, as well as a few other now-unknown breeds. The Whippet was the working man's Greyhound, smaller and easier to feed, yet able to hunt and provide food for the table. When the working day was over, Whippets also provided entertainment and sport, as the dogs' owners would race them.

The Whippet may be smaller than the Greyhound but is a true sighthound, able to run thirty-five miles an hour. Whippets stand 18 to 22 inches tall and weigh 20 to 30 pounds. The head is long and lean, eyes are large and dark, and ears small, fine, and rose-shaped. The body is equally long or just slightly longer than the dog is tall. The chest is deep, the back is strong, and the tail is long. The coat is short and close, and any coat color is acceptable, including solid colors, patches of color, and brindle. The coat needs only weekly brushing.

In the house, adult Whippets are quiet and calm, but once outside—look out! Whippets love to run and are capable of great speed. They should get a chance to run safely in a fenced-in area at least once a day. Young Whippets who do not get enough exercise can be amazingly destructive. Whippets enjoy several canine sports, including lure coursing, flyball, and therapy dog work.

Whippets need gentle training, as the breed can be sensitive. Socialization is also a good idea, as undersocialized Whippets can be shy or fearful.

When Whippets love their people, they do so with all their hearts, so they need an owner who wishes to be worshipped. These are not backyard dogs because they need to be with their owners and may also suffer when left outside in cold weather. Whippets are good with children, but may inadvertently knock over toddlers. They are also good with other dogs. Whippets may, however, chase running cats (with drastic consequences), so care should be taken with smaller pets. The primary health concern is eye defects.

## Breed in Brief

**Registries:** AKC, UKC, CKC
**Occupation:** Hunter, sighthound
**Size:** 18 to 22 in tall; 20 to 30 lbs
**Longevity:** 12 to 15 years
**Exercise:** Daily run
**Training:** Socialization important
**Grooming:** Easy

# White German Shepherd Dog

The American Kennel Club does not allow white German Shepherd Dogs ("GSDs") to compete in conformation competition even though the color white was one of the original allowed colors. In fact, Max Von Stephanitz, the founder of the breed, was known to have had several white GSDs. Several organizations have been founded to promote the breed as a separate and equal breed (White German Shepherds or White Shepherds), while other groups would prefer that these dogs remain German Shepherds. They would rather see the existing breed standards changed to again allow white dogs to compete.

The various organizations promoting white GSDs do have individual breed standards, and while they have many similarities, there are also some differences. Most GSDs stand between 22 and 26 inches tall and weigh between 65 and 120 pounds, although some may be heavier. The head is wedge-shaped, the eyes are almond-shaped and dark, the nose is black, and the ears are large and erect. The body is longer than the dog is tall, and the tail is long. The undercoat is soft and thick, while the outer coat is coarse and dense.

The coat needs brushing twice a week, although when the dog is shedding, daily brushing may be needed.

This breed is very active and should run and play hard every day. Without adequate exercise, they can be destructive chewers and diggers.

GSDs were bred to work and need a job to do. Training should begin early and continue on into adulthood. Once past puppy and basic obedience training, these dogs can learn trick training, advanced obedience, hand signals, agility, tracking, and more. White GSDs serve capably on police and security forces, on search and rescue teams, and as therapy dogs.

These dogs need owners who are smarter than they are and who will train, socialize, and keep the dog's mind busy. Although puppies are rough and rowdy, the breed is good with children. The primary health concerns include hip dysplasia, bloat, and epilepsy.

## Breed in Brief

**Registries:** AKC (with restrictions), UKC, CKC
**Occupation:** Herder
**Size:** 22 to 26 in tall; 65 to 120 lbs
**Longevity:** 10 to 12 years
**Exercise:** Vigorous daily exercise
**Training:** Hard to keep challenged
**Grooming:** Sheds

# Wirehaired Pointing Griffon

*I*n 1873, a young Dutch man, Eduard Korthals, wanted a gun dog suited for hunters on foot (rather than on horseback). He wanted a dog who worked close to the hunter and in all types of terrain, especially the marshy lands of the Netherlands. The ancestors of today's Wirehaired Pointing Griffon include several wire coated dogs known to be good hunting dogs, the Otterhound, a French Barbet, and several other unknown dogs and breeds.

These dogs stand 20 to 24 inches tall and weigh 50 to 65 pounds. The head is of medium width, the nose is always brown, and the eyes are large and may be from yellow to brown. The ears are medium-sized and dropped. The body is slightly longer than the dog is tall, and the tail is docked. The undercoat is thick, and the outer coat is harsh, straight, and wiry. Coat colors include steel gray with brown markings, chestnut brown, white and brown, and orange and white.

The coat needs twice weekly brushing to keep it neat and clean. Show dogs need some hand-stripping.

The Wirehaired Pointing Griffon is a very active breed that needs a chance to run every day. He can run alongside a bicycle or go jogging with his owner. These dogs also like to retrieve, so fetch games are great fun.

Eager to please, these dogs are usually quite easy to train. Their good noses, however, can also make them easily distracted, especially while young. If the training is too repetitive, these dogs may get bored, so the training should be firm and structured, yet challenging enough to keep their interest.

The Wirehaired Pointing Griffon is a young breed, and the individual dogs have strong hunting instincts. As such, they do best in homes where they are used for hunting, competitive field trials, or hunt tests. The Griffon is a good family dog and very patient with children. He is good with other dogs but, as a hunting dog, should be supervised with smaller pets. The primary health concern is hip dysplasia.

## Breed in Brief

**Registries:** AKC, UKC, CKC
**Occupation:** Hunter
**Size:** 23 to 27 in tall; 60 to 90 lbs
**Longevity:** 11 to 13 years
**Exercise:** Vigorous daily exercise
**Training:** Challenge
**Grooming:** Easy

# Wirehaired Vizsla

The Wirehaired Vizsla was developed in the early 1900s by Vizsla breeders and fanciers who wanted a breed with all the attributes of the Hungarian Vizsla but with a coat that would help the dogs withstand rough field conditions and cold weather. Initially, the red, shorthaired Vizsla was crossed with a brown Wirehaired Pointer, but it is believed that throughout the years, as the breed developed, Wirehaired Pointing Griffons, Pudelpointers, and Irish Setters may have been added to the mix.

These dogs are medium-sized, more heavily boned than a Vizsla, and stand from 21 to 25 inches tall with weight in proportion to height. The head is moderately wide, eyes are oval, and eye color matches the coat. The ears are dropped. The body is slightly longer than the dog is tall and is well-muscled. The tail may be docked by one-quarter its length. The coat is wiry, dense, and can be any shade of russet red.

This coarse coat needs weekly brushing to keep it clean. Hand-stripping is needed occasionally to pull out dead coat.

## Breed in Brief

**Registries:** CKC, North American Versatile Hunting Dog Association
**Occupation:** Hunter
**Size:** 21 to 25 in tall; weight proportionate to height
**Longevity:** 12 to 14 years
**Exercise:** Vigorous daily exercise
**Training:** Moderate
**Grooming:** Easy to moderate

The Wirehaired Vizsla is an active dog bred to hunt in tough terrain and in all weather conditions. He needs vigorous daily exercise to keep him happy and to prevent potential problem behaviors that can arise out of boredom. He can run, swim, hunt, play ball, or train on the agility course.

As a hunting dog, this breed is persistent and stubborn; he simply does not give up. Although these traits are wonderful in hunters, they can make life tough for pet owners. Because of this, training these dogs is not always easy, even though they are affectionate and intelligent.

This breed does best in a home where he can hunt regularly or, if that isn't possible, where the owner wishes to train the dog in a canine sport. The Wirehaired Vizsla is too driven to be a good backyard pet. These dogs are good with children, although puppies may be rowdy. The primary health concern is hip dysplasia.

# Xoloitzcuintli

## (Miniature, Intermediate, and Standard; Hairless and Coated)

This Latin American breed is very old, with a documented existence going back 3,000 years. Xoloitzcuintli dogs ("Xolo") were treasured by the Toltec and Mayan people, while the Aztecs used them for medicinal purposes as well as companionship. The Aztec people believed that holding the dog could cure certain ills and eating the meat of the dog could cure others. The dogs were said to be the representatives of the god Xoloti.

The Xolo is found in three sizes: miniature (10 to 15 inches), intermediate (15 to 20 inches), and standard (20 to 25 inches). The skull is broad and strong, and the muzzle is wedge-shaped. The eyes are medium-sized and almond-shaped. The ears are uncropped and large. The body is slightly longer than the dog is tall. The tail is long. The hairless variety should have no hair, although a little fuzz on the top of the head, feet, and tail is common. The coated variety has short, smooth hair. Any color is acceptable.

Hairless Xolo need protection from the sun and are sensitive to cold weather. Some hairless dogs also get acne and may need specific care. The coated dogs need only weekly brushing.

Adult Xolos are calm and even tranquil. They have great bearing and look regal, but don't let that fool you; this breed loves a good run and a chance to play. Although not high-energy dogs, they should have exercise every day.

Xolos are wary of strangers. Socialization should begin early, and the puppies should meet a variety of people. Undersocialized dogs may be timid. The breed is bright and intelligent and enjoys training that is structured yet upbeat and fun.

The owner of a Xolo must be comfortable with being the center of attention. Every walk with the dog will bring the question, "What is that?" You cannot blend into a crowd with a Xolo! When raised with children, this breed is very good with them. The primary health concerns include skin problems and allergies. As with most hairless breeds, some teeth may not be present.

## Breed in Brief

**Registries:** AKC FSS, UKC, CKC

**Occupation:** Companion

**Size:** Mini:10 to 15 in tall
Intermediate:15 to 20 in tall
Standard: 20 to 25 in tall

**Longevity:** 13 to 15 years

**Exercise:** Moderate

**Training:** Moderate

**Grooming:** Easy

# Yorkshire Terrier

The Yorkshire Terrier (or Yorkie) originated in the late 1800s and is descended from several old English terrier breeds, including the Black and Tan English Terrier, Paisley Terrier, Clydesdale Terrier, and, most recently, Waterside Terrier. The breed originally was owned by working-class people and was used for vermin control as well as companionship, but it wasn't long before this tiny terrier was appreciated by the upper classes and royalty.

The Yorkie is very much a terrier even though he is small. He carries his head high and projects an aura of self-importance. Standing 8 to 9 inches tall and weighing less than 7 pounds, he is well-balanced and square. The eyes are dark and full of personality; the ears are small, V-shaped, and carried erect. The coat is silky and long and, in adults, falls to the floor. The hair is parted along the backbone from head to tail. The coat color is blue with tan on the head, under the tail, and on the legs. The tail is docked.

Grooming is a big part of a Yorkie's life, especially if you keep the coat long. The coat will tangle if not combed and brushed every day and again after outdoor play sessions. Many pet owners keep the coat trimmed to a shorter length simply for ease of care.

Yorkies are active little dogs. They enjoy walks, play sessions, and hunting for critters in the backyard. Bonnie Gray, the owner of Tootsie, a certified therapy dog, says, "Tootsie and I walk twice a day and play fetch games in between. She will also tease my other dog, a Papillon named Maddie, until Maddie finally plays with her."

Yorkies can have difficulty with housetraining, but with supervision, persistence, and patience, it can be accomplished. Early obedience training can help channel this breed's quick mind, giving the dog something constructive to do. Gray offers a caution, though: "Yorkies are bright and intelligent but can be a little stubborn. They do have a mind of their own." Many Yorkie owners teach their little dogs tricks, as the breed is a natural showoff and loves to be the center of attention. These dogs can also participate in canine sports. Many flyball teams want to include a small dog to keep the jump heights low, and ball-crazy Yorkies make great competitors.

This breed is very attached to the family but can also become more strongly bonded to one particular family member, especially if more time is spent with that one person. They can be reserved toward strangers, but friends are greeted with enthusiasm. They can be good with children who are gentle and treat them with respect. Gray says, "My grandchildren, who range from age 7 to 12, all help me with Tootsie's obedience training, and as a result, they are good with her and she loves them." Yorkies tend to bark at strange dogs and can put on an aggressive act, although they are too small to back up any threats. This behavior should be discouraged, as larger dogs could easily harm them. Health concerns include dental problems, hypoglycemia, and knee problems.

## Breed in Brief

**Registries:** AKC, UKC, CKC
**Occupation:** Companion
**Size:** 8 to 9 in tall; under 7 lbs
**Longevity:** 14 to 16 years
**Exercise:** Daily walks and games
**Training:** Challenge to housetrain
**Grooming:** Long coat requires daily upkeep; trimmed coat easier

# *Index*

# Photo Credits for Breed Profiles

Affenpinscher, page 114
Dog: Ch. She's Got Charisma
Owner: Mary K. Downey
Photographer: Sean Downey

Afghan Hounds, page 115
Dogs: Justice-Rocks SBIS Gazon the
Truth Be Told; Taza Kaimar Maybe
Frank
Owners: Beth Collins, Deb and Jim
Webb; Beth Collins, Kathryn Cair,
and Rosemary Zednick
Photographer: Tom Collins

Airedale Terrier, pages 116–117
Dog: Quimby
Owner: Maggie Moore
Photographer: Sheri Wachtstetter

Akbash Dog, page 118
Dog: Odessa Yazar Icine Konut
Owner: Orysia Dawydiak, Odessa
Farms Akbash Dogs
Photographer: David Sims

Akita, page 119
Photographer: Sheri Wachtstetter

Alapaha Blue Blood Bulldog, page
120
Dog: ImanJohn
Owners: Jesse and Channa Kelly,
Alapaha Connection Kennels
Photographer: Jessica Swartz

Alaskan Klee Kai, page 121
Dog: Taku
Owner: Terry Wright
Photographer: Photo courtesy of
owner

Alaskan Malamute, page 122
Photographer: Mary Fish Arango

American Bulldog, page 123
Dog: Multiple Best In Show UKC
Ch. Sunstar Devonshire, CGC,
HCT, TC, TDI
Owner: Jan Magnuson
Breeder: Browns Creek American
Bulldogs
Photographer: Creative Indulgence
Photography, with permission by
owner

American Eskimo Dog, page 124
Dog: Agility Ch. Coyote Cody
Photographer: Mary Fish Arango

American Eskimo Dog, page 125
Dog: Barkley's Epiphany
Owner: Kathy Workman
Photographer: Photo courtesy of
owner

American Foxhound, page 126
Dog: Harry
Photographer: Photo courtesy of
Claudia Bazinet, Foxhound
Relocation and Retirement

American Hairless Terrier, page 127
Dog: UWP GR Ch. 'PR' Wade's Red
Wine
Owners: Karyn and Ryan Pingel
Breeder: Patti Wade
Photographer: Photo courtesy of
owners

American Pit Bull Terrier, page 128
Dog: Judah
Owner: Terri McGee
Photographer: Sheri Wachtstetter

American Pit Bull Terrier, page 129
Dog: Jake, therapy dog
Owner: Nicole Rattay
Photographer: Sheri Wachtstetter

American Staffordshire Terrier, page
130
Dog: Katie
Photographer: Mary Fish Arango

American Water Spaniel, page 131
Dog: Callie
Owner: Linda Ford
Photographer: Joseph Carroll
Photography, with permission by
owner

Anatolian Shepherd Dogs, page 132
Photographer: Photo courtesy of
Jim and Genia Kyres, Aegean
Anatolians

Appenzeller Sennenhundes, page 133
Dogs: Cama vom Sennestarn;
Cresta vom Jurarosli; Evviva vom
Sennestarn and puppies
Breeder: Sandra Klein,
Ch-Rueggisberg Kennel
Photographer: Photo courtesy of
breeder

Australian Cattle Dog, page 134
Dog: Eddie
Owner: Tammy Tholl
Photographer: Sheri Wachtstetter

Australian Kelpie, page 135
Dog: Sadie
Owner: Ledge Rock Working Kelpies
Photographer: Linda Tesley Lehman

Australian Shepherds, page 136
Dogs: Left: Hatcreek's Logan; mid-
dle back: Asha; right: Rebel; front:
Hatcreek's Doctor Bashir
Owners: Logan: Petra Burke; Asha
and Rebel: David and Dawn
Sullivan; Bashir: Liz Palika
Breeder: Logan and Bashir: Karen
Russell
Photographer: Sheri Wachtstetter

Australian Shepherds, page 137
Dogs: Back: Hatcreek's Logan and
Hatcreek's Doctor Bashir; front:
Rebel and Asha
Owners: Logan: Petra Burke;
Bashir: Liz Palika; Asha and Rebel:
David and Dawn Sullivan
Breeder: Logan and Bashir: Karen
Russell
Photographer: Sheri Wachtstetter

Australian Terrier, page 138
Dog: Chelsey
Owner: Darlene Evans
Photographer: Photo courtesy of
owner

Azawakh, page 139
Dog: Multiple BISS Ch. Kel Simoon
Essari FCH
Owners: Deb Kidwell and Rhonda
Mann, Kel Simoon Azawakhs
Breeders: Deb Kidwell and Rhonda
Mann
Photographer: Tobias Joesch

Basenji, page 140
Owner: Karen Butler
Photographer: Photo courtesy of
owner

Basset Hound, page 141
Dog: Socrates
Owners: Dorothy and Meghan
Kennedy
Photographer: Sheri Wachtstetter

Beagle, page 142
Photographer: Sheri Wachtstetter

Beagle, page 143
Photographer: Mary Fish Arango

Bearded Collie, page 144
Photographer: Mary Fish Arango

Beauceron, page 145
Dog: Ch. Aleera de Nanrox
Owner: Linda Richard, Nanrox
Kennels
Photographer: Linda Richard

Bedlington Terrier, page 146
Dog: Ch. MACH3 Serendipity's
Heartbreaker MX, CGC
Owner: Melody Guiver
Photographer: Mary Fish Arango

Belgian Laekenois, page 147
Dog: Blade, CDX
Owner: Heidi Lund
Photographer: Heidi Lund

Belgian Malinois, page 148
Dog: MPACT Malinois
Owners: Chris and Tammy Domico
Breeder: Penny Winegartner
Photographer: Mary Fish Arango

Belgian Sheepdog, page 149
Dog: Blazer
Photographer: Mary Fish Arango

Belgian Tervuren, page 150
Dog: Ch. FCI-CACIB Crestar's
MakaiNespa d'Ember CD, RE, PT,
OA, AXJ Schutzhund BH
Photographer: Mary Fish Arango

Bergamasco Sheepdog, page 151
Dog: Lindoro
Owner: Donna De Falcis, Silver
Pastori Bergamascos
Photographer: Photo courtesy of
owner

Berger des Pyrenees, page 152
Dogs: Valdazun's Mischief Maker;
Chaparral's Eminence Rouge
Owners: Sue and Mike Bita; Susan
Buttivant
Breeders: Sue and Mike Bita; Susan
Buttivant
Photographer: Mike Bita

Berger Picard, page 153
Dog: Urricaine
Owner: Chris Rogers, Silver Glen
Kennel
Photographer: Gretchen Rogers

Bernese Mountain Dog, page 154
Dog: Kiba
Photographer: Mary Fish Arango

Bernese Mountain Dogs, page 155
Photographer: Mary Fish Arango

Bichon Frise, pages 156–157
Dog: Sophie
Owner: Shar Jorgenson
Photographer: Sheri Wachtstetter

Black Mouth Cur, page 158
Dog: Sharon's Brinda Sue
Owner: Sharon Inman, Seco Creek Kennel
Photographer: Elisabeth Phillips

Black Russian Terriers, page 159
Dogs: Shadow; Ellie
Owners: Steve and Linda Barkas
Photographer: Sheri Wachtstetter

Black and Tan Coonhound, pages 160–161
Dog: Miss Daisy Mae
Owner: Robert Jenkins
Photographer: Sheri Wachtstetter

Bloodhound, pages 162–163
Photographers: Buddy Wachtstetter (page 162); Sheri Wachtstetter (page 163)

Bolognese, page 164
Dog: Whisper
Owners: Mary and Ian Poulter, Tenderella Bolognese
Photographer: Ian Poulter

Border Collie, page 165
Dog: PC's Zip Drive MAD, TM, AX, AXJ, NGC, AKC CD, ASCA CD, RA, RL1, FDCh, CGC, TDI
Photographer: Mary Fish Arango

Border Terrier, page 166
Dog: Zetroc's Stanley Marsh MX, MXJ
Owner: Karen Shell
Photographer: Melinda Peters

Borzoi, page 167
Dog: WindnSatin Xactlyazuwish JC, CGC
Owners: Dale and Juliet Rigtrup
Breeders: Mary Childs and Karen Murry
Photographer: Terry Albert

Boston Terrier, page 168
Photographer: Sheri Wachtstetter

Boston Terrier, page 169
Dog: Kobe
Photographer: Mary Fish Arango

Bouvier des Flandres, page 170
Dog: Ch. Hirsch's Rhythm of the Rain RN, CD
Owner: Dominique O'Shia
Breeder: Hirsch Bouviers
Photographer: Lynette Hirsch

Boxer, page 171
Dog: Am Can Ch. Pawz IV Rusric's Duke of Earl, CGC
Owner: Judi Chouinard, Pawz IV Boxers
Photographer: Sheri Wachtstetter

Boykin Spaniel, page 172
Dog: UWPO UWPCH GRCH Hollow Creek's Gus, CGC
Owner: Patricia Watts, Hollow Creek Kennel
Breeder: Patricia Watts
Photographer: Patricia Watts

Bracco Italiano, pages 4 and 173
Dog: Edoardo's Romeo di Casa Bravo
Owner: Ericka Dennis
Photographer: Don Barthel

Briard, page 174
Dog: Matisse
Owner: Stacy Dawson
Photographer: Sheri Wachtstetter

Briard, page 175
Dog: Beaujolais
Owner: Stacy Dawson
Photographer: Sheri Wachtstetter

Brittany, page 176
Photographer: Mary Fish Arango

Brussels Griffon, page 177
Photographer: Sheri Wachtstetter

Bulldog, page 178
Dog: Buck
Owners: Daryl Trumbs and Casey Lydon
Photographer: Sheri Wachtstetter

Bullmastiff, page 179
Photographer: Mary Fish Arango

Bull Terrier, page 180
Photographer: Terry Albert

Bull Terrier, page 181
Dog: Ch. Ardry's Frightfully Fun, ThD
Photographer: Mary Fish Arango

Cairn Terrier, pages 182–183
Dog: Brigadoon's Castlekeep Flame CD, NR, AR, CGC, TDI
Owner: Nancy Miller
Breeder: Pauline Hardy
Photographers: Buddy Wachtstetter (page 182); Mary Fish Arango (page 183)

Canaan Dog, page 184
Photographer: Sheri Wachtstetter

Canadian Eskimo Dog, page 185
Dog: Rita
Owner: Nahman Korem, Crown Jewel Resort Ranch
Photographer: Photo courtesy of owner

Cane Corso, page 186
Dog: Multiple GRCH Val Derro Astro
Owner: Michael Ertaskiran
Photographer: Photo courtesy of owner

Cardigan Welsh Corgi, page 187
Photographer: Melinda Peters

Carolina Dog, page 188
Dog: Ch. Lady's Palace Carpe Diem ARBA CH
Owners: Rick and Jackie Lancaster
Breeders: Rick and Jackie Lancaster
Photographer: Patti Downing

Caucasian Ovtcharka, page 189
Dog: Ch. Klitchko Courageous
Owner: Jackie Renner, Courageous Caucasians
Photographer: Photo courtesy of owner

Cavalier King Charles Spaniel, page 190
Dog: Sandi's Claire's Lady Corie MX, MXJ, TDI
Photographer: Mary Fish Arango

Chart Polski, page 191
Dog: Bursztyn Chessmont Arja Gioconda AIBCA Champion
Owner: Lynda Mulczynski
Breeder: Lynda Mulczynski
Photographer: Lynda Mulczynski

Chesapeake Bay Retriever, page 192
Dog: Quail Run's Annie UDX
Owner: Edward Cohen
Photographer: Photo courtesy of owner

Chesapeake Bay Retriever, page 193
Dog: Sydney
Owners: Rick and Debbie Founds
Photographer: Sheri Wachtstetter

Chihuahua, page 194
Dog: Pistache
Owner: Edna St. Hilaire, President Chihuahua Club of Canada
Photographer: Photo courtesy of owner

Chihuahua, page 195
Dog: Peanut
Owner: Patty Carvajal
Photographer: Sheri Wachtstetter

Chinese Crested, page 196
Photographer: Sheri Wachtstetter

Chinese Crested, page 197
Dog: Puppy
Owner: Margaret George
Photographer: Sheri Wachtstetter

Chinese Foo Dog, page 198
Dog: Ch. Stockbury Chinese Magic Box
Owner: Brad Trom
Photographer: Photo courtesy of owner

Chinese Shar-Pei, page 199
Photographer: Buddy Wachtstetter

Chinook, page 200
Dog: Channahons Zoe
Owner: Amanda Bays
Photographer: Photo courtesy of owner

Chinook, page 201
Dog: Ch. Mountain Laurel Jade
Owner: Amanda Bays
Photographer: Photo courtesy of owner

Chow Chow, page 202
Dog: Shantara's Run for the Roses RN, NA, NAJ, OJP
Photographer: Mary Fish Arango

Clumber Spaniel, page 203
Photographer: Mary Fish Arango

Cockapoo, pages 204–205
Dog: Walter
Owner: Kate Abbott
Photographer: Sheri Wachtstetter

Cocker Spaniel, page 206
Dog: Penny
Owners: Ed and Barbara Upson
Photographer: Sheri Wachtstetter

Cocker Spaniel, page 207
Photographer: Melinda Peters

Collie, page 208
Photographer: Mary Fish Arango

Coonhounds, page 209
Photographer: Melinda Peters

Coton de Tulear, page 210
Dog: Sashi
Owner: Kim Kaufman
Photographer: Sheri Wachtstetter

Curly-Coated Retriever, page 211
Dog: SHR, U-ACHX, U-CD, SW Charmstar Enchanted Color CDX, JH, OAP, OAJP, SR, RAE
Owner: Ann Shinkle
Breeder: Doris Hodges, Summerwind Kennels
Photographer: Ray Shinkle

Dachshund, page 212
Dog: Ch. Schoolhouse Francis Rocks
Owners: Diane Jones and Clay Tedeschi
Photographer: Mary Fish Arango

Dachshund, page 213
Dog: JayKay's Mesquite
Owners: Jim and Karyn Davis, JayKay's Dachshunds
Photographer: Terry Albert

Dalmatian, pages 214–215
Photographer: Buddy Wachtstetter

Designer Dog (Weimerdoodle), page 216
Dog: Kona
Owner: Cindee Gratz
Photographer: Sheri Wachtstetter

Designer Dog (Goldendoodle), page 217
Dog: Paige
Owner: Ashley Scully
Photographer: Sheri Wachtstetter

Doberman Pinscher, pages 218–219
Dog: Rebel
Owner: Chris Downs
Photographer: Sheri Wachtstetter

Dogo Argentino, page 220
Dog: Multiple Ch. Maca de la Cocha
Owner: Carla Ghilardi, Debonair Dogos
Photographer: Photo courtesy of owner

Dogo Canario, page 221
Dog: Ch. King Size de Presa Awangarda
Owner: Ewa Ziemska, Kennel Rey Gladiador
Photographer: Photo courtesy of owner

Dogue de Bordeaux, pages 222–223
Photographer: Mary Fish Arango

Dutch Shepherd, page 224
Dog: Zander
Owner: Lars Vallen
Photographer: Samson Reed

English Cocker Spaniel, page 225
Photographer: Mary Fish Arango

English Foxhound, page 226
Dog: Ch. Mr. Stewart's Cheshire
Winslow
Owners: Emily Latimer and Suzy
Reingold
Breeder: Mr Stewart's Cheshire
Hunt
Photographer: John Ashbey

English Setters, page 227
Dogs: Torrey; Kramer
Owners: Paul and Claudia Riha
Photographer: Sheri Wachtstetter

English Shepherd, page 228
Dog: Wingler's Dillon AG AGII
Owner: Rebecca Wingler
Photographer: Photo courtesy of
owner

English Shepherd, page 229
Dog: Caleb
Owners: Gary and Deborah Bertolin
Photographer: Sheri Wachtstetter

English Springer Spaniel, page 230
Dog: Bailey
Owner: Kelly Rodrigues
Photographer: Sheri Wachtstetter

English Springer Spaniels, page 231
Photographer: Melinda Peters

English Toy Spaniel, page 232
Dog: Ch. Dreamridge Dear Robert
Owner: Janelle Smedley
Photographer: Tom Smedley

English Toy Spaniel, page 233
Dog: Ch. Royalist American Beauty
Owner: Christina Van Patten,
Royalist English Toy Spaniels Kennel
Photographer: The Winning Image,
with owner's permission

Entlebucher Sennenhund, page 234
Dog: Switters
Owner: Carol Clarke
Photographer: Sheri Wachtstetter

Eurasier, page 235
Dog: Ginger-Cooper vom
Maerchenwald
Owner: Josee Dessouroux
Photographer: Photo courtesy of
owner

Field Spaniel, page 236
Photographer: Melinda Peters

Field Spaniel, page 237
Dog: C.C.
Photographer: Mary Fish Arango

Fila Brasileiro, page 238
Dog: Baskervilles I Diva Zappa
Owner: Trisha Porter, Rising
Phoenix Kennels
Photographer: Photo courtesy of
owner

Finnish Spitz, page 239
Dog: Marshall's Best Buddy
Owner: Sue Marshall
Photographer: Photo courtesy of
owner

Flat-Coated Retriever, page 240
Photographer: Mary Fish Arango

Fox Terrier (Smooth), page 241
Photographer: Buddy Wachtstetter

Fox Terrier (Toy), page 242
Dog: Lily
Owner: Hella Heiserman
Photographer: Photo courtesy of
owner

Fox Terrier (Wire), page 243
Photographer: Sheri Wachtstetter

French Bulldog, page 244
Dog: Sparky
Photographer: Mary Fish Arango

German Pinscher, page 245
Dog: FireDragon Celestial Drm
Owner: A. Tansey, Melka Kennels
(NZ)
Breeders: Chris and Kate Graham,
FireDragon Kennels
Photographers: Kate and Chris
Graham

German Shepherd Dog, page 246
Dog: Enzo
Owner: Joel Towart, Bellington
GSDs
Photographer: Sheri Wachtstetter

German Shepherd Dog, page 247
Photographer: Mary Fish Arango

German Shorthaired Pointer, page
248
Dog: Sassy
Owner: Kris Hernandez
Photographer: Sheri Wachtstetter

German Wirehaired Pointer, page
249
Photographer: Mary Fish Arango

Giant Schnauzer, page 250
Dog: Cassie
Owner: Deirdre Bogan
Photographer: Sheri Wachtstetter

Giant Schnauzer, page 251
Dog: Cassie, with Anders Bogan
Owner: Deirdre Bogan
Photographer: Sheri Wachtstetter,
with mother's permission

Golden Retriever, page 252
Dog: Scooter
Owner: Linda Hughes
Photographer: Sheri Wachtstetter

Golden Retriever, page 253
Dog: Spirit
Owner: Paula Horning
Photographer: Sheri Wachtstetter

Gordon Setter, page 254
Dog: Amethyst Madison
Gordonstar
Owner: Brigette Grise, Gordonstar
Kennels
Photographer: Photo courtesy of
owner

Great Dane, page 255
Dog: Frank
Owner: Debbie Boston
Photographer: Sheri Wachtstetter

Great Pyrenees, page 256
Dog: Ben
Owner: Janine Staudt
Photographer: Sheri Wachtstetter

Greater Swiss Mountain Dog, page
257
Dog: Cisco
Owner: Catherine Knebel
Photographer: Sheri Wachtstetter

Greyhound, pages 258–259
Dog: Moose
Owner: Tammy Zybura
Photographer: Sheri Wachtstetter

Harrier, page 260
Photographer: Mary Fish Arango

Havanese, page 261
Dog: Rugby
Owner: Joan Swanson Hamilton
Photographer: Liz Palika

Hovawart, page 262
Dog: Aminah vom Sonnenschein
Owner: Susan Garka
Breeder: Christa Wendlandt
Photographer: Susan Garka

Ibizan Hound, page 263
Photographer: Mary Fish Arango

Icelandic Sheepdogs, page 264
Dogs: Sand Creek Maeja; Emerald
Isle Tibra
Owner: Cheryl Shelton
Photographer: Cheryl Shelton

Irish Red and White Setter, page
265
Photographer: Sheri Wachtstetter

Irish Setter, page 266
Photographer: Mary Fish Arango

Irish Terrier, page 267
Photographer: Sheri Wachtstetter

Irish Water Spaniel, pages 268–269
Dog: Realta's Star Gazer RN
Owner: Nancy Bogusch
Breeder: Rosemary Sexton
Photographer: Mary Fish Arango

Irish Wolfhound, page 270
Dog: Ivanhoe
Owner: Carol Gabriel
Photographer: Tom Bruni

Italian Greyhound, page 271
Dog: Moonglow June Allison
Owner: Marsha Pugh
Photographer: Photo courtesy of
owner

Jack Russell Terrier, pages 272–273
Dog: Lily
Owner: Katy Silva
Photographer: Sheri Wachtstetter

Jagd Terrier, page 274
Dog: Buddy
Owner: Carl Wood
Photographer: Photo courtesy of
owner

Japanese Chin, page 275
Dog: Blake's America's Finest NAJ
Owners: Linda McNamara and
Michele Blake
Photographer: Trista Hildago,
Dynamic Dog Photos, used with
permission

Kai Ken, page 276
Dog: Player
Owner: Pam Peterson, Royal
Kennels
Photographer: Photo courtesy of
Peterson Family

Kangal Dog, page 277
Dog: Turkmen Chicek's Zerrin
Owner: Kathy Lambert, Rancho
Borrego Kennel
Photographer: Sheri Wachtstetter

Karelian Bear Dog, page 278
Dog: Bjornehusets Lasse
Owner: Gail Rasanen
Breeder: Hanne Larsen,
Bjornehusets Kennel
Photographer: Photo courtesy of
owner

Keeshond, page 279
Photographer: Melinda Peters

Kerry Blue Terrier, page 280
Dog: Pot'O'Golds Night Shade
Photographer: Mary Fish Arango

Komondor, page 281
Dog: Company
Photographer: Photo courtesy of
Lyn Bingham

Kuvaszok, page 282
Dogs: Ghillie; Panta
Owners: Agi and Sandor Heijja,
Starhaven Kuvasz
Photographer: Photo courtesy of
owners

Labradoodle, page 283
Dog: Kashmere
Owner: Jaime Kallweit
Photographer: Sheri Wachtstetter

Labrador Retriever, page 284
Dog: Stonecreek's Gold Dust CGC,
TDIA
Photographer: Mary Fish Arango

Labrador Retriever, page 285
Dog: Kadi
Photographer: Mary Fish Arango

Salukis, page 343
Dogs: Am/Can Ch. Sandstorm
Overcast Skies CGC TDI;
Sandstorm November Rain JC, CGC
Owner: Kathy Morton
Breeder: Kathy Morton
Photographer: Kathy Morton

Samoyed, page 344
Photographer: Buddy Wachtstetter

Samoyed, page 345
Dog: Toby
Owners: Kathy and Matt Fielder
Photographer: Sheri Wachtstetter

Schapendoes, page 346
Dog: Tulip
Owner: Colette Peiffer
Photographer: Denis Lavoie

Schapendoes, page 347
Dog: Billy
Owner: Colette Peiffer
Photographer: Denis Lavoie

Schipperke, page 348
Dog: Raffinee Diamonds Are
Forever
Owner: B. J. Mulder
Photographer: Photo courtesy of
owner

Scottish Deerhounds, page 349
Dogs: Ch. Tannochbrae's Arden
House JC; Ch. Tannochbrae's Firiel
Owner: Lyn Robb
Breeder: Tannochbrae Scottish
Deerhound
Photographer: Photo courtesy of
Joan Garth

Scottish Terrier, page 350
Dog: Frosty CGC ThD
Owner: Lee Juslin
Photographer: Michael Siener

Sealyham Terrier, page 351
Photographer: Sheri Wachtstetter

Shetland Sheepdog, page 352
Dog: Nyssa
Owners: Bruce and Margaret
Reinbolt
Photographer: Sheri Wachtstetter

Shetland Sheepdogs, page 353
Dogs: Coriolis; Cobalt
Owners: Dan Townley and Nancy
Mueller
Photographer: Sheri Wachtstetter

Shiba Inu, page 354
Dog: Am/Can/UKC Ch. San Jo
Wild Wild West
Owner: Pam Peterson, Royal
Kennels
Breeders: Piper and Ariel Woodruff,
Leslie Engen
Photographer: Photo courtesy of
Pam Peterson

Shih Tzu, page 355
Dog: Sammi
Owner: Shari Betts
Photographer: Sheri Wachtstetter

Shiloh Shepherd, page 356
Dog: Abbey
Owners: Ken and Barb Taylor,
Shamrock Shilohs Kennel
Photographer: Ken Taylor

Siberian Husky, page 357
Dog: Kontoki's Rowdy Shaman MX,
MXJ, OF, JCh, AD, AG, AR, AS
Photographer: Mary Fish Arango

Silken Windhound, page 358
Dog: Talisman of Electra Sarafias
Owners: Salla Klemetti and Eero
Juhola
Breeder: Joyce Chin
Photographer: Joyce Chin

Silken Windhound, page 359
Dog: Ch. Talisman's Viking
Kumbaya
Owners: Kent Jones and Jay Cusker
Breeder: Joyce Chin
Photographer: Joyce Chin

Silky Terrier, pages 360–361
Photographers: Terry Albert
(page 360); Melinda Peters
(page 361)

Small Munsterlander Pointer, page
362
Dog: Thor
Owner: Mick Jensen, Thor Winds
Kennel
Photographer: Photo courtesy of
owner

Soft Coated Wheaten Terrier, page
363
Dog: Maddie RN, TD
Photographer: Mary Fish Arango

South African Boerboel, page 364
Dog: Kamy
Owner: Ryan Holt
Photographer: Photo courtesy of
owner

Spanish Greyhound, page 365
Photographer: Photo courtesy of
Joan Garth

Spanish Mastiff, page 366
Dog: Aleeda Tornado Erban
Owner: Karin Graefe, Tierra Alta
Kennel
Photographer: Karin Graefe

Spanish Water Dog, page 367
Dog: Dulcinea de LIJA
Owner: Thomas Berry
Breeders: Linda Kardonis and Dale
Huelin, LIJA Spanish Water Dogs
Kennel
Photographer: Thomas Berry

Spinone Italiano, page 368
Photographer: Melinda Peters, at
the World Dog Show, Poland, 2006

Staffordshire Bull Terrier, page 369
Dog: Caminos Popsicle Toes UD, RX
Owner: Susan Aguilar
Photographer: Mary Fish Arango

Standard Schnauzer, page 370
Dog: Ch. Stardust Heavenly Daze
CD, HT, RN, NA, NAJ
Owners: Ed and Carol Karas
Photographer: Mary Fish Arango

Stumpy Tail Cattle Dog, page 371
Photographer: Photo courtesy of
Grace Harper, Silver Park Kennel

Swedish Vallhund, page 372
Dog: Osafin Blaze to Glory; AKC
titles: NA, AOP, OJP, CGC. ARBA
titles: MChH. AHBA title: HCT.
ASCA titles: STDs, RS-E, JS-E, GS-O.
NADAC titles: N-vers, O-NAC,
OAC, NGC, TN-O, TG-O, WV-N.
Owners: Ivy and Dan Underdahl
Breeder: Cynthia Kingsley
Photographer: Mary Fish Arango

Thai Ridgeback, page 373
Dog: GR Ch. Si Dang's Kom-Kai
Owner: Mary Ann Nemisz, Urban
Legends Thai Ridgeback Dogs
Photographer: Mary Ann Nemisz

Tibetan Mastiff, page 374
Dog: Captain
Owner: Kathleen McDaniel, Citadel
Tibetan Mastiffs
Photographer: Kathleen McDaniel

Tibetan Spaniel, page 375
Dog: Aja
Owner: Lyn Parazak
Photographer: Sheri Wachtstetter

Tibetan Terriers, page 376
Dogs: Tasha; Nisha
Owner: Marilyn Moran
Photographer: Photo courtesy of
owner

Tibetan Terrier, page 377
Photographer: Melinda Peters

Tosa Ken, page 378
Dog: Kenshoryu-go
Owner: Bill Meunier, Pharsyd Tosas
Photographer: Photo courtesy of
owner

Vizsla, page 379
Dog: Ch. Everwhen Whirling
Dervish VCD1, TD, CD, MX, MXJ,
RN, NF
Owner: Carol Dostal
Photographer: Mary Fish Arango

Weimaraner, page 380
Photographer: Melinda Peters

Welsh Springer Spaniel, page 381
Photographer: Sheri Wachtstetter

Welsh Terrier, page 382
Dog: Caminos Cisseldale's Lookin
for Trouble CGC
Owner: Linda Brisbin
Photographer: Mary Fish Arango

West Highland White Terrier, page
383
Dog: Winston
Owner: Karen Rivas
Photographer: Sheri Wachtstetter

Whippet, pages 384–385
Photographer: Melinda Peters
(page 384); Mary Fish Arango
(page 385)

White German Shepherd Dog, page
386
Dog: Luna
Owner: Bethany Dickson
Photographer: Sheri Wachtstetter

Wirehaired Pointing Griffon, page
387
Photographer: Sheri Wachtstetter

Wirehaired Vizsla, page 388
Dog: Seamus
Photographer: Mary Fish Arango

Xoloitzcuintli, page 389
Dog: Mora
Owner: Drew McFadden
Photographer: Photo courtesy of
owner

Yorkshire Terrier, page 390
Dog: Tootsie
Owner: Bonnie Grey
Photographer: Sheri Wachtstetter

Yorkshire Terrier, page 391
Dog: MACh9 Desmond Aloysius
Shelby, CD
Owner: Pam Shelby
Photographer: Melinda Peters